M000216097

Gaiseric

Gaiseric

The Vandal Who Destroyed Rome

Ian Hughes

Pen & Sword
MILITARY

First published in Great Britain in 2017 by
Pen & Sword Military
an imprint of
Pen & Sword Books Ltd
47 Church Street
Barnsley
South Yorkshire
S70 2AS

Copyright © Ian Hughes, 2017

ISBN 978 1 78159 018 8

The right of Ian Hughes to be identified as Author of this work has been asserted
by him in accordance with the Copyright, Designs and Patents Act 1988.

A CIP catalogue record for this book is available from the British Library.

All rights reserved. No part of this book may be reproduced or transmitted in any
form or by any means, electronic or mechanical including photocopying, recording
or by any information storage and retrieval system, without permission from the
Publisher in writing.

Printed and bound in Malta by Gutenberg Press Ltd.

Pen & Sword Books Ltd incorporates the Imprints of Pen & Sword
Archaeology, Atlas, Aviation, Battleground, Discovery, Family History,
History, Maritime, Military, Naval, Politics, Railways, Select, Transport,
True Crime, Fiction, Frontline Books, Leo Cooper, Praetorian Press,
Seaforth Publishing, Wharncliffe and White Owl.

For a complete list of Pen & Sword titles please contact
PEN & SWORD BOOKS LIMITED
47 Church Street, Barnsley, South Yorkshire, S70 2AS, England
E-mail: enquiries@pen-and-sword.co.uk
Website: www.pen-and-sword.co.uk

Contents

List of Maps

Introduction

'What ruined everything ... was the action of the Vandals in crossing from Spain to Africa ... the Vandal chief Gaiseric ... was not only a man of genius but one of the most fateful figures in history, for it was he who really brought about the downfall of the Western Empire.'

Saunders, J.J., 'The Debate on the Fall of Rome'(1963), p.15

Ask a member of the general public to name the individuals or tribes involved in the fall of the (Western) Roman Empire, and the chances are that the questioner will receive blank stares in response. The more knowledgeable will answer with 'Attila the Hun', at which point even the most uninterested will acknowledge that they have, indeed, heard of Attila. Yet Attila's part in the downfall of the Western Empire was, in reality, minor. He led an invasion of Gaul in AD 451 and Italy in 452, before he died of a haemorrhage in 453. As this was almost a quarter of a century before the accepted date of 476 for the death of the last Roman emperor, it would seem that he actually played only a supporting role in the collapse of the West. Very few will know the name of Gaiseric.

Interestingly, the names of the three major tribes have been distorted over the intervening centuries: 'Hun' is a nickname given in Europe and North America to modern Germans, 'Gothic' is a style of architecture and 'Vandal' is the name given to any form of wanton destruction.

Yet, as demonstrated in the quote at the beginning of this Introduction, the actions of Gaiseric, King of the Vandals, is acknowledged by all students of the period as having a major impact upon the 'Fall'. There is little question that Gaiseric was the most important Vandal king and was 'among the most influential figures of the fifth-century Mediterranean world'.[1]

Yet strangely, his name has fallen out of use, and memory of his actions is limited to a small group of specialists who concern themselves with the question of why the Western Empire fell. The reason for his fall from grace is easy to understand. The main cause is that for many historians of the past centuries, the main focus has been on the actions of the Roman Empire rather than on their enemies. In addition, the sources for any of the barbarian kings are limited and hard to reconcile, so their histories remained largely unwritten.

A second factor is that Gaiseric did not have a 'demonic' label attached to him. Being pagan, the Huns did not acknowledge the sanctity of Christian churches. In addition, they are described by contemporary sources as being hardly human, and in Attila they had a leader who earned the epithet 'Scourge of God'. Of even more importance, when the Huns invaded Italy in 452, Christian tradition ascribed his sparing of Rome to Pope Leo I, aided by divine intervention. The 'miraculous' saving of Rome resulted in the name of Attila being preserved in Christian tradition.

If the Huns were the epitome of all that was 'evil', the Goths had the advantage of founding a long-lasting kingdom in Hispania and of converting to Catholic Christianity. Their conversion from the heretical Arianism practised by most of the Germanic nations resulted in their entry into the 'accepted' tribes of Christendom. Furthermore, they produced a 'historian' named Jordanes, who wrote *A History of the Goths*, preserving information concerning the Gothic verbal histories. The outcome was that the Goths became simply one more of the kingdoms that arose on the ruins of the West, and the fact that they were accepted resulted in 'Gothic' becoming simply an architectural style. Possibly because of their acceptance, their leaders are unknown – largely due to them not having the label 'demon', as given to Attila.

The Vandals, on the other hand, were simply outcasts as far as contemporary writers were concerned. Although their King Gaiseric was a major figure throughout the majority of the fifth century, the fact that he remained staunchly Arian resulted in him being anathema to contemporary Romans, albeit obviously not as horrific as the pagan Attila. The fact that the Vandal kingdom in Africa only lasted for 111 years may also have been a factor in the fact that no Vandal historian comparable to Jordanes wrote a history of the Vandals. Without a favourable historian, and with a leader who failed to match Attila for detestation, it is necessary to rely on scanty Roman sources to piece together the story of the Vandals' most effective leader.

In this context, it should be noted that almost all of the information concerning the Vandals, and especially that with regard to religion, is filtered through the works of Nicene (Catholic) clergymen and anti-Vandal authors who had reason to depict them as the enemy of Catholicism. For example, Victor of Vita was probably writing during the persecution of Catholics declared by Huneric just before the latter's death in December 484. As a consequence, it is understandable that Victor's rhetoric is violently anti-Vandal, and his lurid descriptions of the sufferings of the Catholics are augmented by his depth of feelings against the Vandals. Yet Victor's need to vilify the Vandals means that his work must be used with care, as there is a real possibility that he has exaggerated Vandal actions in order to make them fit into his anti-Vandal rhetoric.

Victor isn't the only ancient writer who was interested in Gaiseric. Gaiseric receives far and away the most attention from Prosper, both because Prosper was probably 'in or around' Rome when it was sacked by the Vandals in 455, and Gaiseric was the only barbarian leader to actively seek to replace Nicene Christianity with the Arian 'impiety'.[2]

It was stated earlier that there is no history for the Vandals as there is for the Goths. Although strictly-speaking true, as no writer in Africa wrote a *History* which has survived, in Hispania, Isidore wrote a book, part of which purportedly covers the 'History of the Vandals'. Yet this does not relate evidence from the viewpoint of the Vandals: it rather describes the Goths pushing the Vandals out of Hispania, hence making the Goths look more 'impressive', especially as the Vandals were later able to defeat the Western Empire in Africa.[3] In effect, the book is simply a propaganda exercise intended to emphasize the power of the Goths, not give the story of the Vandals.

Despite the problems, there have been attempts to write the history of Gaiseric – for example *Genséric: Soleil barbare* by Henri Gourdin (Alif, 1999) – but these are rare and, as in this case, usually not published in English. The net result is that, although possibly more famous on the Continent, in English-speaking countries there has been little opportunity to read the story of Gaiseric without resorting to 'Roman' histories, where Gaiseric is simply one of many characters.

Gaiseric was born some time around 389 CE. As usual, the exact date is uncertain, and 389 is arrived at only by subtracting his attested age at the time of his death from the year in which he died.[4] This is obviously only an approximate calculation, and his actual year of birth could be one or two years either way. Throughout this book, a long list of names of both barbarians and Romans will attest to the confusion surrounding the last century of Imperial rule in the West. Gaiseric is the one constant throughout the period.

When Gaiseric was born, the Roman Empire was still the major political and military power in Europe, ruling lands as far apart as Scotland and the Sahara, and Portugal and Syria. Although the empire had been divided by the brothers Valentinian and Valens in 464, and for the vast majority of the fourth and fifth century it was to remain separated, the disunity had not yet proved to be a terminal difficulty. It would have been obvious to all of the tribesmen living beyond the frontiers that, although raids could acquire huge amounts of booty – as was being proved by the Huns fighting the Eastern Empire – the Roman Empire itself was a permanent fixture. The concept that either half of the empire could cease to exist would not have entered the minds of anyone other than the most pessimistic of Christian believers constantly expecting the apocalypse and their entry into the Kingdom of God.

When Gaiseric died in 477, the East still retained its aura of power, but the West had collapsed: from the position of holding the vast majority of Western Europe and the coasts of North Africa, along with all of the islands in the western Mediterranean, Gaiseric had seen Britain, the majority of western Africa, the Mediterranean islands apart from Sicily, as well as most of Gaul and the Iberian peninsula, fall into the hands of barbarian kings. All that remained of the mighty Western Roman Empire was Italy, most of Sicily, and a claim to part of the western Balkans.

The reasons for the collapse are complex and open to widely differing interpretations, largely revolving around the dual aspects of either seemingly never-ending Roman civil wars and internal collapse, or of barbarian invasion. In some cases, the reasons for the fall of the West have turned into a simple case of whether internal collapse encouraged barbarian invasion, or whether barbarian invasion caused internal collapse.

Needless to say, for the overwhelming majority of historians, the actions of any individual may have caused some of the problems faced by the West, but to claim that any one man caused the 'Fall' is seen as inherently simplistic. As noted above, if one man was to be named, the expected candidate for most would be Attila, King of the Huns. Yet his main activities were focused upon the East, and despite his invasion of Gaul in 451 and Italy in 452, his actions were only a minor factor in the overall 'Fall', so although his actions doubtless damaged the West, he must remain an active participant but not a major cause.

Specialists, however, would acknowledge that if anyone was to be given sole blame for the 'Fall', that man would be Gaiseric. During his early life, he took part in the invasion of Gaul and the crossing to Hispania. After coming to the throne, it was Gaiseric who led the Vandals into Africa and bankrupted the West by his seizure of the province of Africa Proconsularis and the surrounding regions. Without the money and food supplied from Africa, the West was unable to finance the military operations which would successfully defend the empire, and would struggle to feed itself should Gaiseric or his successors decide to withhold the grain supply to Rome.

Although he is now almost forgotten, Gaiseric was almost certainly one of the few individuals who made a direct impact upon history. This book is an attempt to rectify the situation and restore Gaiseric to a position where his life and times are better understood by an English-speaking audience.

Terminology

One of the main problems when analysing the fifth century remains that of nomenclature. Should Roman names be given in full Latin, or should the common abbreviation – should there be one – be used? For example, many historians drop the

'…us' from Roman names and the Latin letter 'i' is often converted to 'j'. Hence we have the names Hadrian instead of Hadrianus, or Trajan instead of Traianus. In addition, the Germanic names of many barbarian kings are rendered in different ways by the ancient sources, and the different spellings can cause confusion. Obviously, the most relevant here is Gaiseric himself, whose name is also given as Geiseric, Genseric or even Gizeric by different authors. Throughout this work – except for translations of sources which used alternate spellings – the version Gaiseric is being used due to the fact that this is the spelling used by Hydatius, whose work covers much of Gaiseric's early years and whose contacts in Hispania may have given him a spelling acceptable to Gaiseric himself.

There is also the problem of place names, both of towns and countries. The names of towns have obviously changed over the centuries, and one of the problems faced with relating ancient history to modern audiences is the decision whether to use the ancient names of places as given in the sources, or to use the modern place names familiar to today's readers. In this book, the decision has been made to use either form within the context of the text, relying on the maps to clarify the placement of the town. Sometimes, when both modern and ancient place names have been used within a chapter, the map will contain both place names, with a diagonal in between: for example, 'Arles/Arelate'.

With reference to the naming of modern countries, the ancient form has been used throughout as it is expected that the maps will give the reader the relevant information needed for understanding. This is in part because, over time, the outline of countries has changed and only the ancient boundaries have remained constant. Of more importance for the history of the Vandals, there remains the problem of Spain/Portugal. These two countries are relatively recent in origin and the division is not reflected in the Roman world: although in some modern works Portugal is connected to the ancient province of Lusitania, this correlation has not been deemed accurate enough to use the delineation, so the ancient term 'Hispania' has been used for the whole of the Iberian peninsula.

Finally, a note should be made concerning one further piece of terminology used. Throughout the text, the word 'barbarian' is used to describe several of the tribes that invaded the Roman Empire in the fifth century. The term has fallen out of use in recent times due to the assumed pejorative nature of the word: a quick check in a Thesaurus gives alternatives such as 'uncivilized', 'uncultured' and 'aggressive'. Sadly, no suitable replacement has gained acceptance, and so 'barbarian' has been retained. However, it should be noted that it is here used simply as a generic word to describe the various peoples of non-Roman origin inhabiting the empire but owing little or no loyalty to the emperor. It is always necessary to bear in mind that it is not used in a negative manner, simply as a 'catch-all' when no other word is available.

The Sources

Histories

The major difficulty faced by anyone attempting to tell Gaiseric's story is that the surviving evidence is either brief, giving few details with which to flesh out the story and provide a clear picture of Gaiseric's personality and actions, or it is fragmentary, as although some histories were written at the time, especially in the East, these only survive in excerpts, which are copies of earlier works, which themselves are epitomes of the original. For example, the 'fragments' of Priscus are taken from many later works. The question remains as to whether the later writer has used Priscus word-for-word or whether he has abbreviated, miscopied or misunderstood his source.

As a result, the personality of Gaiseric that emerges in the following pages is a composite of the crumbs of information given by the sources assembled into a coherent whole. There is no certainty as to whether the image obtained is accurate: all that can be stated is that the overall personality that emerges is consistent and gives a sensible explanation concerning Gaiseric's motivations and expectations.

One of the major sources of information should have been the many 'histories' written at the time, but as noted, these are now incomplete. The major Eastern histories that have been used include the fragments of Priscus, Malchus, Eunapius and Olympiodorus. Although these can be used, their fragmentary nature, plus the fact that the snippets that survive are obviously out of context, means that they need to be used with care. Unfortunately, many of these fragments cover events that are nowhere else recorded in detail, so there is little choice but to use them, whilst remaining wary of their contents.

Another major source is the *Wars* of Procopius. Unlike the others, these books exist almost in their entirety. However, Procopius was a later author, writing in the mid-sixth century, and his sources for events in the West in the previous century are not always accurate. Many of the tales he relates concerning the Vandals do not tally with more contemporary accounts. Furthermore, his political agenda in raising the profile of his hero Belisarius results in his work being very heavily biased, and even inaccurate at times, in order to emphasize Belisarius' exploits. As a result, the works of Procopius cannot be used without extreme care.

In the West, the major full-length works of Jordanes – the *Getica* (*History of the Goths*) and the *Romana* (*History of the Romans*) – cover much of the period. Writing in the mid-sixth century, Jordanes used the (lost) *Gothic History* of Cassiodorus as the foundation for the *Getica*. Sadly, his bias towards the Goths and his desire to distort events to fit with his theme of Gothic superiority, plus the fact that his work contains many errors, means that Jordanes needs to be carefully analyzed before being used.

The same is true of the works of Isidore of Seville. His *Historia de regibus Gothorum, Vandalorum et Suevorum* (*History of the Kings of the Goths, Vandals and Sueves*) and the *Chronica Maiora* (*Great Chronicle*) are major works, but again the author's bias towards the Goths, effectively asserting that they are the inheritors from the Jews and Romans of the title 'Chosen People of God', results in many major falsehoods, or at least an interpretation of events in a manner that would support his theme. As a consequence, his works – although useful in some ways – need to be approached with extreme care.

Serving under Theoderic I (r. 475–526), the first Ostrogothic king of Italy, the Roman Cassiodorus wrote a variety of works. Most of these are either lost or exist only in fragments. For example, and as noted above, his *Gothic History* survives only in the works of Jordanes, and his *Laudes* (*panegyrics*) only in very fragmentary form. However, his *Chronicle*, which covers the period under analysis, does survive, as does his *Variae Epistolae*, or *Letters*, usually abbreviated simply to *Variae*. These works contain some valuable information, but again care needs to be taken, as they were written during the reign of Theoderic and therefore can be biased towards the Goths.

Also worthy of mention is Paul the Deacon. Writing in the eighth century, he composed his *Historia Romana* (*History of Rome*), a continuation of the *Breviarium* of Eutropius, plus the *Historia Langobardum* (*History of the Lombards*). Both of these works, as with all of those written for later rulers, have serious flaws, but if used with caution, they may help to either fill gaps or corroborate evidence from other sources.

Chronicles

In the West, and unsurprisingly given the context of the collapse of the empire, our main source of evidence is the many surviving Chronicles. Usually Christian in nature, these purport to assign a year to the brief record of the events contained. Sadly, the dates given can easily become confused. For example, it is clear that the Chronicler Hydatius, writing in Spain in the middle of the fifth century, either had to guess at the date of events or simply ascribe them to the year in which he learned of them: it should be remembered that news of events in Italy and the East obviously arrived in Spain at a later date, and so it is uncertain whether Hydatius attempted to insert information in the correct entry or simply added it to the date of the entry when he heard the news.

A further problem is the fact that all too often the sources do not overlap, which results in there being neither corroborative nor contradictory data with which to judge the evidence, but also the appearance of *lacunae*, gaps in our knowledge which are not covered. In these cases, it has been necessary to either simply accept the evidence at face value, or, if possible, adopt a judgemental method based upon perceived chronological factors, confirming whether an event could or could not have happened in the timescale presented.

To add to the confusion, many times where the sources do record the same event they give conflicting evidence, especially with regard to the date. In most of these cases both sources have been recorded and, where necessary, an analysis is made to decide upon which date is preferable. However, more often than not this is impossible and both entries are simply recorded. Although in many ways an unsatisfactory approach, in a period where few sources survive it has made little difference to the overall text and thus has been deemed the only usable method.

The Western Chronicle tradition is mirrored in the East, for example in the works of John Malalas and John of Antioch. The *Chronographia* (*Chronicle*) of John Malalas, written in the mid-late fifth century, survives in a later abridgement, although a few fragments also survive. Although now seen as of little value, due to the inaccuracies present in parts of the text, it is likely that there are some facts within the text, so it can be used as a secondary validation for information found elsewhere.

The work of John of Antioch, the *Historia Chronike* was written in the early-mid sixth century, but has again been lost and now exists only in fragments. As with most of these works, its value is unclear as it has little context in which to place events, and so a chronology including the information has to be pieced together by comparison with other, more reliable sources. As a result, and as with the *Chronicle* of John Malalas, its primary use is as a secondary validation for information found elsewhere. On the other hand, the fragments that remain contain detail not found in other sources, so where possible these have been used in order to build a potentially more detailed picture.

Letters

Another source of information, especially with regards to events in Gaul, is the many letters produced by the ruling classes of the West, including several Popes. As noted above, a selection of those written by Cassiodorus have survived; however, the major author of letters in this period is undoubtedly Sidonius Apollinaris.

Many of his letters cover events in Gaul during the final days of the West, giving a contemporary chronology within which it may be possible to integrate other evidence concerning the Vandals. However, as usual, care needs to be taken. Sidonius adopts different tones at different times to different people, acting as a 'wind-vane' of the ebb and flow of the empire in Gaul, as well as demonstrating the intense pressure placed on the Gallic aristocracy in their struggle to adapt to the change in political masters. It is therefore necessary to analyse each letter in context to provide a framework in which to use the information.

Hagiographies

Apart from a tendency to prefer writing Chronicles rather than lengthy Histories, a further change due to the conversion of the Roman Empire to Christianity was the proliferation of *Hagiographies*: biographies of the lives of saints, usually following a standard formula in which the subject is attributed many miraculous deeds. Needless to say, some of these stories are a little far-fetched, their purpose being to laud the saint rather than to write objective history. Nevertheless, they can prove useful to the historian by giving details about the background conditions during which the saint lived.

For example, a major hagiography from the period is the *Vita Epiphanius/Epifanius* (*Life of Saint Epiphanius*, bishop of Pavia) composed by Ennodius. Epiphanius was used by emperors as an envoy to barbarian kings, and also appears to have played a major part during the civil war between Ricimer and Anthemius. Yet even here there are problems: in an attempt to establish the importance of his subject, Ennodius inflates the role played by Epiphanius, a factor discussed at the appropriate place in the text. The inherent bias of all of the hagiographies towards their subjects results in all of their narratives being open to at least a modicum of doubt, and as a result, as usual, these works can only be used in an historical context if their original purposes are understood and taken into account.

The *Notitia Dignitatum*

When assessing the military capabilities of the Late Empire, it is common for ancient historians to refer to the *Notitia Dignitatum* (*List of Officials*), a list ostensibly giving the name and location of military units throughout the West. Whilst it is true that the document is important for the information it gives, its shortcomings are often glossed over to allow it to be used. With reference to the last decades of the West, the most important of these revolves around the date of its compilation.

The Western section dates to around 420, the Eastern to around 395, but both contain data from before these dates, resulting in the duplication of entries.

Alongside this is the fact that no attempt was made in the document to give muster strengths for any of the units listed. As a result, the strengths of the units listed is completely unknown and must be estimated from other evidence, usually archaeological excavation of Late-Roman forts, but whether the forts excavated were typical of those built throughout the empire is again open to question.

What effect these issues have for the accuracy of the *Notitia* is unknown. Furthermore, the fact that the Western list was compiled so early results in its value for the period from 455 onwards being extremely dubious. By the later date, Britain had been lost, large parts of Gaul were under the control of the Goths and, most importantly, Africa had been lost to the Vandals. The loss of the vital revenues from Africa resulted in the empire becoming bankrupt, doubtless with a major effect on the recruitment and equipping of the army. As a result, by the death of Aetius in 455, it is certain that the information contained in the *Notitia* is long out of date and therefore of very dubious value. However, due to the fact that there is no comparable source for the late-fifth century, where absolutely necessary it has been used to give some idea of what resources *may* have been available to the empire. Obviously, these figures cannot be accepted at face value.

Conclusion

Although the above may give the reader the impression that nothing is certain concerning the life of Gaiseric, this is actually far from the case. The sheer number of sources for events between 390 and 480 (as demonstrated by the Abbreviations listed below) results in the major events being confirmed by a number of independent sources, with only some specific dates being under question. As a result, although there are many inconsistencies and gaps in our knowledge, what remains is still enough to fashion a fairly comprehensive chronology and hence to allow for a description of events which is more detailed than most students of the period realize. Whether there is enough evidence and certainty for the account which follows is left to the reader to determine.

Abbreviations to the sources used in the text

Addit. Ad. Prosp. Haun.	*Additamenta ad Chronicon Prosperi Hauniensis*
Ann. Rav.	*Annals of Ravenna*
Anon. Cusp	*Anonymus Cuspiani*
Anon. Val.	*Anonymus Valesianus*
Auct. Prosp. Haun. ordo prior.	*Auctarium Prosperi Hauniensis ordo Priori*
Auct. Prosp. Haun. ordo post.	*Auctarium Prosperi Hauniensis ordo Posterior*
Auct. Haun. ordo post. marg.	*Auctarium Prosperi Hauniensis ordo Posterior Marginialia*
Aust. Lett.	*Austrasian Letters*
Cand.	Candidus
Cass. *Chron.*	Cassiodorus, *Chronicle*
Cass. *Variae*	Cassiodorus, *Variae*
Cedr.	Cedrenus (Kedrenus), *Historiarum Compendium*
Chron. Caes.	*Chronicon Caesaraugusta (The Chronicle of Saragossa)*
Chron. Gall. 511	*Chronica Gallica a. DXI*
Chron. Pasch.	*Chronicon Paschale*
CIL	*Corpus Inscriptionem Latinarum*
CJ/ *Cod. Iust.*	*Codex Iustinianus*
Cod. Th.	*Codex Theodosianus*
Cons. Const.	*Consularia Constantinopolitana*
Cons. Ital.	*Consularia Italica*
Corrip.	Corripus
Dam. *Epit. Phot.*	Damascius, *Epitome Photiana* (see Dam. *V. Isid.*)
Dam. *fr.*	Damascius, *fragments*
Dam. *V. Isid.*	Damascius, *Vita Isidori*
Ennod. *Epist.*	Ennodius, *Epistulae*
Ennod. *Pan.*	Ennodius, *Panegyricus Theoderici*
Ennod. *Vit. Epiph.*	Ennodius, *Vita Epiphanius (Epifanius)*
Eugipp. *Vit. Sev.*	Eugippius, *Vita Severini*
Eugipp. *Ep. Ad Pasc.*	Eugippius, *Epistle ad Paschasius*
Evag./Evag, Schol.	Evagrius Scholasticus
Exc. Val.	*Excerpta Valesiana*

Fast. Vind. Prior.	*Fasti Vindobonenses Priores*
Fred. *Chron.*	Fredegar scholasticus, *Chronica*
Gel.	Pope Gelasius I, *Epistulae*
Greg. Tur, de Mir. S. Mart.	Gregory of Tours, *de Miraculis S. Martini*
Greg. Tur. *HF*	Gregory of Tours, *Historia Francorum*
Greg. Rom.	Gregory of Rome
Hilarus, *Ep.*	Pope Hilarus, *Epistulae*
Hyd.	Hydatius Lemicensis, *Chronicon*
ILS	*Inscriptiones Latinae Selectae*
Isid. *Hist. Goth.*	Isidore of Seville, *Historia Gothorum*
Joh. Ant. *fr.*	John of Antioch, *fragments*
Joh. Nik.	*John of Nikiu, The Chronicle of John of Nikiu*
Joh. Ruf.	John Rufus, *Plerophories*
Jord. *Get.*	Jordanes, *Getica*
Jord. *Rom.*	Jordanes, *Romana*
Land. Sag.	Landolfus Sagax, *Historia Romana*
Laterc. Imp. ad Iust.	*Laterculus Imperator ad Iustiniani*
Lib. Hist. Franc.	*Liber Historiae Francorum*
Lib. Pont.	*Liber Pontificalis*
Lup. Troy.	*Life of Lupus of Troyes*
Mal. *Chron.*	John Malalas, *Chronographia*
Mar. Av.	Marius Aventicensis, *Chronicle*
Marc. *com.*	Marcellinus *comes, Chronicle*
Mich. Syr.	Michael the Syrian, *Chronicle*
Nest. *Baz. Her.*	Nestorius, *The Bazaar of Heracleides*
Nic. Call.	Nicephorus Callistus Xanthopulus, *Historia Ecclesiastica*
Not. Dig.	*Notitia Dignitatum*
Nov. Anth.	Anthemius, *Novellae*
Nov. Maj.	Majorian, *Novellae*
Nov. Sev.	Severus, *Novellae*
Nov. Val.	Valentinian III, *Novellae*
Olymp.	Olympiodorus
Patr. Const.	*Patria Constantinopolitana*
Paul. Diac. *Rom.*	Paulus Diaconis (Paul the Deacon), *Historia Romana*
Paul. Diac. *De Gest. Lang.*	Paulus Diaconis (Paul the Deacon), *Historia Langobardorum*
Paul. Petric.	Paulinus Petricord (Paulinus of Perigueux), *Vita San Martini*

Phot. *Bibl.*	Photius, *Bibliotheca*
PLRE 2	*Prosopography of the Later Roman Empire, Volume 2*
Pol. Silv.	Polemius Silvius, *Laterculus Principum Romanorum*
Prisc.	Priscus, *Fragments*
Proc.	Procopius, *de Bello Gothico*
Prosp. Tiro	Prosper Tiro, *Chronicle*
Pseud. Zach. Rhet.	Pseudo Zacharias Rhetor, *Historia Ecclesiastica*
Sid. Ap. *Carm.*	Sidonius Apollinaris, *Carmina*
Sid Ap. *Ep.*	Sidonius Apollinaris, *Epistulae*
Suid.	Suidas, *Lexicon*
Theod. Lect	Theodorus Lector, *Epitome Historiae Ecclesiasticae*
Theoph. AM.	Theophanes, *Chronographia* (dates 'Anno Mundi')
Fl. Val. Th.	*Fl. Valila qui et Theodovius*
Veg. *Epit. Rei Mil.*	Publius Flavius Vegetius Renatus, *Epitoma rei militaris*
Vict. Tonn.	Victor Tonnennensis, *Chronicle*
Vict. Vit.	Victor Vitensis, *Historia Persecutionis Africanae Provinciae*
Vit. S. Dan. Styl.	*Vita Daniel Stylites*
Vit. S. Gen.	*Vita Sancta Genovefa*
V. S. Marcelli	*Vita et Conversatio S. Marcelli archimandritae monasterii Acoemetorum*
V. Lup.	*Vita Lupicini*
Zach. *HE*	Zachariah, *Historia Ecclesiastica*
Zintzen, *Damascii*	Zintzen, *Damascii vitae Isidori reliquiae* (see Bibliography)
Zon.	Zonaras, *Extracts of History*
Zos.	Zosimus, *Historia Nova*

Chapter 1

Vandal History and Gaiseric's Early Life

Gaiseric was born around AD 389: the exact date is unknown and must be calculated from later evidence.[1] The illegitimate son of 'King' Godigisel, and half brother of Godigisel's legitimate son Gunderic, it is alleged by the ancient sources that his mother was a slave.[2] Although it is possible that this was propaganda aimed at damaging his reputation, if his mother was a Roman who had been enslaved it would explain the claim that he had originally been a Nicene Catholic rather than an Arian.[3] The place of his birth is also unrecorded, although modern historians have sometimes guessed at the location.[4] All that is actually known is that at the time of his birth, the Vandals were living in Pannonia. This had not always been the case.

Until recently it has been assumed – following Jordanes, who was writing in the sixth century – that Gaiseric's people had their origins in the Baltic region:

> Now from this island of Scandza, as from a hive of races or a womb of nations, the Goths are said to have come forth long ago under their king, Berig by name. As soon as they disembarked from their ships and set foot on the land, they straightway gave their name to the place. And even to-day it is said to be called Gothiscandza. Soon they moved from here to the abodes of the Ulmerugi, who then dwelt on the shores of Ocean, where they pitched camp, joined battle with them and drove them from their homes. Then they subdued their neighbours, the Vandals, and thus added to their victories.
>
> Jordanes, *Getica*, 25–26

It would appear from this that the Vandals were a small group of peoples on the fringes of the Baltic who were easily defeated by the Goths. Seemingly complementing Jordanes, the earliest mention of a Germanic tribe known as '*Vandilii/Vandili*' is by Pliny the Elder in the late first century AD:

> There are five German races: the Vandili, parts of whom are the Burgundiones, the Varini, the Carini, and the Gutones.
>
> Pliny, *Natural History*, 4.28

Map 1: The Roman Empire on the Death of Theodosius, AD 395.

A tribe by the name of '*Vandilii*' are also mentioned by Tacitus in his *Germania*, also in the late first century (*c*.AD 98):

> Some, with the freedom of conjecture permitted by antiquity, assert that the god had several descendants, and the nation several appellations, as Marsi, Gambrivii, Suevi, Vandilii, and that these are genuine old names.
>
> Tacitus, *Germania*, 1.2

Since Jordanes' account places the Vandals on or near the shores of the Baltic Sea, many archaeologists associated the Vandals with the *Przeworsk* culture, an archaeological phenomenon based on similarities in finds – especially cremation burials – reaching from the Baltic through a large part of central Europe. The supposition was that the Vandals began life on the Baltic littoral before extensive migrations brought them to the borders of the Roman Empire.

However, recent work has brought these assumptions into question, with it being shown that even the basic concept of 'migrational waves … does not stand up to scrutiny'.[5] For example, the connection between the '*Vandilii*' in Pliny and Tacitus and the tribe who later invaded the Empire is extremely insecure, especially as neither Pliny nor Tacitus give a specific location to the *Vandilii*. Further, rather than being a single tribe, these two excerpts suggest that the *Vandilii* were almost certainly a large union of peoples existing during the first century AD, so there is no direct connection between these peoples and the two tribes (Asdings and Silings) later known as the Vandals apart from the coincidence of their names.[6]

In addition, a further reassessment has broken the association of the Vandals with the *Przeworsk* culture, since previous analysis of the archaeological evidence is now seen as being ambiguous at best. It has been recognized that, rather than beginning in the region of the Baltic and spreading south with the assumed Vandal 'migration', pottery and burial practices associated with the *Przeworsk* culture actually had many local origins and the perceived spread is simply a coincidence of local societies evolving similar forms rather than adopting them from an outside source.[7]

Likewise, it has always been supposed that, due to their later influence, the Vandals were a powerful and important feature of cross-border politics. Instead, it must now be accepted that, far from being a tribe of great power and prestige from its earliest days, between the second and the fifth century the Vandals were actually a small group of unimportant peoples – one of around fifty tribes on the Roman frontiers – that are barely mentioned in the historical sources and have left little individual residue in the archaeological record.[8]

In reality, the first 'secure' reference to the Vandals dates to the second century AD. During the reign of Marcus Aurelius, and probably in AD 171:[9]

> The Astingi [Asdings], led by their chieftains Raus and Raptus, came into Dacia with their entire households, hoping to secure both money and land in return for their alliance. But failing of their purpose, they left their wives and children under the protection of Clemens [the governor of the province], until they should acquire the land of the Costoboci by their arms; but upon conquering that people, they proceeded to injure Dacia no less than before. The Lacringi ... attacked them while off their guard and won a decisive victory. As a result, the Astingi committed no further acts of hostility against the Romans, but in response to urgent supplications addressed to Marcus they received from him both money and the privilege of asking for land in case they should inflict some injury upon those who were then fighting against him. Now this tribe really did fulfil some of its promises.
>
> Cassius Dio, *Roman History*, 72.12

The information ties in with the division of the Vandals into two distinct confederations: the Asdings and the Silings.[10] The 'alliance' of the Astingi (Asdings) with Rome, which was most likely a *foedus*, may have lasted for quite a time, as the next secure reference dates to around a century later, when in late summer 270 a Vandal warband invaded the Empire near Aquincum.[11] It is possible that the invaders could have been Silings rather than Asdings, although it should be noted that during this period the Asdings were probably settled in the region of the Upper Tisza River.[12] Alternative evidence suggests that at this time the Silings were settled in the region later known as Silesia.[13] Whatever the source of the attack, the Emperor Aurelian responded and the Vandals were quickly defeated.[14] This was followed in *c*.280 by a battle in which the Emperor Probus defeated a mixed force of Vandals and Burgundians, although again whether the 'Vandals' were Asdings or Silings is unclear.[15] In neither of these cases is the danger sufficient to form a major threat to the Empire.

However, in the fourth century, *c*.330–335, the Asding Vandals came under Gothic attack:

> Soon he [Geberich, king of the Goths] sought to enlarge his country's narrow bounds at the expense of the race of the Vandals and Visimar [Vidimar], their king. This Visimar was of the stock of the Asdingi ... At that time they dwelt in the land where the Gepidae now live, near the rivers Marisia, Miliare, Gilpil and the Grisia ... They then had on the east

the Goths, on the west the Marcomanni, on the north the Hermunduli and on the south the Hister, which is also called the Danube. At the time when the Vandals were dwelling in this region, war was begun against them by Geberich, king of the Goths, on the shore of the river Marisia which I have mentioned. Here the battle raged for a little while on equal terms. But soon Visimar himself ... was overthrown. Then the remnant of the Vandals who had escaped, collecting a band of their unwarlike folk, left their ill-fated country and asked the Emperor Constantine for Pannonia. Here they made their home for about sixty years and obeyed the commands of the emperors like subjects.

Jordanes, Getica, 22.113–15

Some historians have doubted the story as relayed by Jordanes; with good reason, as after the excerpt above Jordanes goes on to state:

A long time afterward they [the Asdings] were summoned thence by Stilicho, Master of the Soldiery, ex-Consul and Patrician, and took possession of Gaul. Here they plundered their neighbours and had no settled place of abode.

Jordanes, Getica, 22.115

Obviously, this story is contradicted by other sources, so it is clear that Jordanes is mistaken when he claims that Stilicho invited the Asdings into Gaul. On the other hand, supporting evidence from Peter the Patrician suggests that there was indeed an alliance between Constantine and a group of Vandals in the 330s.[16] As a result, it should probably be accepted that the Asdings did live in the Tisza basin and that at least some were driven out by a Gothic attack, moving to Pannonia under the auspices of the Emperor Constantine. Furthermore, it should be noted that the ease with which the Goths defeated the Vandals supports the idea that the Vandals remained a small, unimportant group of tribes.

Once their small size is accepted, there remains the question of whether they were settled in Pannonia I, Pannonia II or both (see Map 1). The chances are that, following earlier policies and learning from some of the mistakes made when allowing the Goths into the Empire, the Vandals were probably distributed across the two provinces in the hope that they would settle and merge with the loyal Roman inhabitants. If the hypothesis is correct, the attempt to integrate the Vandals was doomed to failure, not least because the Vandal leaders were not employed by Rome, instead remaining in control of at least some of the settlers. Again, this suggests that the Vandals were a small tribe and the Romans did not expect them to cause many problems for the Empire.

'Romanization'

Even prior to the settlement, along with the other 'Germanic' tribes along the northern frontier, the Vandals were slowly influenced by the spread of Roman goods via trade, especially with regard to jewellery and ceramics.[17] But whereas the trade and giving of 'gifts', or subsidies, to allied tribal leaders may have helped in the formation of large tribal groupings such as the Greuthungi, Tervingi, Alamanni and Franks, similar payments appear not to have helped the Vandals to form their own large alliance. This may be because before the fourth century any such support in the region appears to have been given to the Sarmatians. As a result, the Vandals remained divided into their two major branches, the Asdings in the south, where Gaiseric was born, and the Silings in the north-west, with only some of the Asdings later entering Pannonia. In part due to this division, the Vandals remained insignificant.[18]

Conversion to Arianism

Yet there was one way in which the Empire would have a major effect upon Vandal traditions. At an unknown date, the Vandals converted to Arianism. In the standard, Catholic/Nicene creed, Jesus is seen as being equal with God, part of the 'Trinity' of Father, Son and Holy Spirit. Arians believed differently. For them, it was clear that Jesus was created by God: God the Father was Unbegotten (eternal), whereas Jesus was Begotten (not eternal), and therefore God was superior to Jesus.[19] Jesus was 'like' God, but not the same. Obviously, this was opposed by the Nicenes as heresy.

In the middle of the fourth century AD, Arianism had a strong following in the Roman army. As a result, any barbarians serving in the army at this time would likely have been converted to Arianism rather than the Nicene creed. In addition, a Goth named Ulfilas (c.310–380) was converted to Arianism and was sent to preach to the Goths. It is likely that at the same time, missionaries were sent to other tribes, including the Vandals. The missionaries were helped by religious divisions within the Empire, and especially by the fact that Constantius II (337–361) was of a 'semi-Arian' persuasion, whilst Valens (364–378) was a committed Arian.[20] Both of these emperors may have actively encouraged barbarian conversions.

A further factor was that Ulfilas had translated the Bible into Gothic, meaning that the missionaries could now easily convert the Vandals, as they spoke a language similar to the Goths. However, many Vandals doubtless remained pagan, only becoming converts after they had entered the Empire in the early fifth century, in this being influenced by their new barbarian neighbours the (Visi-) Goths.[21] The choice would influence Vandalo-Roman relations in the future.

The Huns, the Goths and Adrianople

Not long after the Vandal settlement in Pannonia, a new political and military force arrived on the scene. Some time before AD 370, the Huns attacked and subjugated the Alans, after which many of the Alans joined the Huns in attacking the Greuthungi.[22] Unhappy with their suppression by the Huns, some Alans fled west and gained permission from the Empire to settle in Pannonia, near to the Asdings. Although Ermanaric, the King of the Greuthungi, resisted the Huns for a long time, he eventually committed suicide and his successor, Vithimer, was defeated and killed. The survivors fled and took refuge with the Tervingi.[23]

After further lengthy resistance, the Tervingi were also defeated and the majority fled to the Danube and, with the agreement of the Emperor Valens, in 376 crossed into Roman territory. Mistreated, they broke into open revolt and in 378 defeated the Roman army at the Battle of Adrianople. After a further four years of fighting, including a second defeat for the Romans at the Battle of Thessalonica in 380, in 382 the Goths finally signed a treaty with the Romans. This was the first time that the Romans had ever signed a treaty with a barbarian invader without first defeating them outright. Consequently, the Goths not only received land, but were allowed to maintain their political integrity under their own leaders.

Although the significance of the Roman defeat has been downplayed by recent historians, the effects of the battle have always been interpreted from the viewpoint of the Romans, and especially of the Roman army. Similarly, the implications of the treaty of 382 – introducing a foreign people intact into the Empire – have also been analysed almost solely from a Roman viewpoint. The impact of these events on the tribes living beyond the frontier is rarely considered.

The Impact of Adrianople

Under pressure from the expansion of Hunnic power, before 382 the border tribes would have seen the frontier with the Empire as the anvil upon which the hammer of the Huns would break them. The Gothic victory and subsequent treaty would have astonished the barbarians. Not only could the Empire be defeated in battle, but there was now the possibility of commanders and kings leading their men into the Empire and gaining employment whilst retaining leadership of their tribes: previously, tribes admitted to the Empire were almost always defeated, split, and the leader was appointed to command Roman units in a distant province, not left with his own men. If it was a choice between serving as underlings in the expanding Hun Empire, being brought under Gothic dominion, or taking the chance of crossing the frontier and accepting service in the Roman Empire, possibly retaining their identity, after 382 many would have seen the latter as the better option.[24]

Imperial Civil War

One of the most striking features of Late Imperial Rome was the number of civil wars fought, both between internal rivals in each division and between the two halves of the Empire. The confusion caused in the Empire by the Gothic War of 377–382 was quickly exacerbated by two civil wars: in 388, the Eastern Emperor Theodosius I invaded the West and defeated the usurper Magnus Maximus at the Battle of the Save; then in 394 he again mustered an army to defeat the usurper Eugenius at the Battle of the Frigidus. Needless to say, the restless barbarians on the borders took every opportunity to benefit from Imperial discord:

> For twenty years and more the blood of Romans has been shed daily between Constantinople and the Julian Alps. Scythia, Thrace, Macedonia, Dardania, Dacia, Thessaly, Achaia, Epirus, Dalmatia, the Pannonias – each and all of these have been sacked and pillaged and plundered by Goths and Sarmatians, Quadi and Alans, Huns and Vandals and Marcomanni. How many of God's matrons and virgins, virtuous and noble ladies, have been made the sport of these brutes! Bishops have been made captive, priests and those in minor orders have been put to death. Churches have been overthrown, horses have been stalled by the altars of Christ, the relics of martyrs have been dug up.
>
> Jerome, *Epistle*, 60.16

Even though the apocalyptic tone of Jerome's epistle doubtless exaggerated events, it is clear that the barbarians on the borders saw the time of Imperial civil war as a chance to raid the Empire and get away with it.

Gaiseric and the Asdings

At some point, probably early in the time between the two civil wars, Gaiseric was born in Pannonia. Sadly, due to the focus of Roman historians on the civil wars and their aftermath, events in Pannonia are poorly recorded and hence are slightly confusing:

> The Huns threw themselves on the Alans, the Alans upon the Goths, and the Goths upon the Taifali and Sarmatae.[25]
>
> Ambrose, *Expositio evangelii secundum Lucam*, 10.20
> (trans. Maenchen-Helfen, 1973, 20)

The fact that the Vandals are omitted from this description reinforces the theory that when Gaiseric was born at the end of the fourth century, the Vandals were two minor confederations lacking in political or military power. This would not change until long after they had left the lands of Pannonia far behind.

As a result of the conflicts described above, it has already been noted that Alans fleeing from the Huns arrived in Pannonia under Imperial direction. Accordingly, the Asdings came under increased territorial pressure, and it is possible that from this point on they began to feel the effects of overcrowding. In addition, Godigisel, the Asding king and father of Gaiseric, will also have been concerned that the Huns would spread their dominance over Pannonia.

Although in theory such an expansion would have been resisted by the Empire, in reality the two halves of the Roman Empire were drifting apart. Nowhere was this more apparent than with the eruption of another civil war between East and West. As already noted, in 394 Theodosius led his troops west for a second time, winning the Battle of the Frigidus and once more uniting the two halves of Empire. Sadly, he died in the new year and the reality of Imperial unity died with him.

As a consequence of these conflicts, Pannonia was becoming a no man's land between the two empires. It would be easy for the Huns to move into the vacuum thus created. If this was to happen, Godigisel would become a relative non-entity in the Hunnic polity and his people merely 'cannon fodder' in the wars of the Huns. Later evidence suggests that at least two groups of Alans who had earlier fled from the Huns and settled in Pannonia had the same fears.

Rather than remain and hope for the best, Godigisel's other option was to try and establish himself as a military leader within the Empire, with the political and financial benefits that came with Roman military status: the success of the Gothic leader Alaric (c.370–410) in obtaining Roman military titles after AD 395 may have given Godigisel a model for his actions. In 395, Alaric had revolted against the Eastern Empire and eventually obtained a military position within the Empire, at first just in the East.

Godigisel's decision was of greater urgency as, though a minor player in the region, the Vandals as a whole were facing another problem: according to Procopius, the 'trans-Danubian lands' of the Vandals had become insufficient to support their growing numbers.[26] This implies either that the Asdings had settlements on both sides of the Danube, not just within Pannonia, or, more likely, that the Silings were suffering from food shortages. It is likely that the Asdings too were suffering from famine, competing as they were with the newly settled Alans for land. Whatever the cause, at around 12 years of age, it is unlikely that Gaiseric was consulted about which option to take.

The Invasion of Raetia

There remained the question of where to cross the frontier. It was obvious that the Eastern Empire was too strong, so there was little choice but to attack the

West. Godigisel and his advisors made their decision: the Asdings, along with some Alan allies, invaded Raetia in 401.[27] Their opponent was the Roman *magister militum* Stilicho. Despite the fact that his father was a Vandal, Stilicho was a Roman citizen who displayed a staunch loyalty to Rome throughout his life.[28] A capable military commander, Stilicho quickly defeated the invasion. Some of the defeated tribesmen were then forced to accept service in the Roman Army. The balance of the Asdings and Alans were either settled in Italy or were forced to return to Pannonia. Ensuing events suggest that the latter is the most likely, at least for the majority.

The 'Vandal' invasion of Raetia, along with the later 'Gothic' assault on Italy, highlights some of the main factors hindering our understanding of barbarian attacks on the West: namely, the loyalty of individuals, the movement and composition of barbarian tribes, and the response of the Romans. Many recent assumptions concerning the formation of tribes are based around modern interpretations of nationhood. 'Peoples' are one nation and indivisible, yet all of the contemporary evidence shows that this was not the case with the tribes along the Roman frontier in the fourth and fifth centuries AD. Instead, tribal groupings were fluid and open to change at a moment's notice. For example, in the attack on Italy, the Asdings were joined by a group of Alans who were unwilling to be part of the Hunno-Alanic alliance that was dominating the area north of the Danube.

In the same way, although many historians have in the past highlighted the parentage of Stilicho, despite the fact that his father was a Vandal he had no sense of brotherhood with the Vandals and maintained his loyalty to Rome until his death in 408. This 'betrayal' of his 'nationhood' has many parallels in Roman history, and the ease with which many Germanic barbarians were employed by Rome against their fellow Germans has in the past been viewed with horror. However, recent work has demolished the 'pan-Germanic' notion of unity: not only did earlier modern historians ignore the fact that the Germanic tribes were often at war with each other, but they overlooked the fact that each singular tribe was a law unto itself. As a result, the concept of 'Germania' is no longer tenable. All of the German tribes had loyalty only to their own small tribe. Yet the theory of 'non-nationhood' goes further than the Germans. Even the Huns, as they fought against the Goths, were divided: Ammianus records that Ermanarich, the king of the Greuthungi, had mercenary Huns in his service fighting against the invaders.[29] Notions of peoples being united by a shared language and culture belong to a much later epoch than Late Antiquity.

Alaric

At the same time as the Vandals had invaded Raetia in 401, Alaric had nullified his agreement with the East by invading Italy. Some of the Vandals who had accepted service in the Western army fought against Alaric in the battles of Pollentia and Verona (both in 402). Despite these defeats, Alaric's threat remained high enough for him to be given a post in the Western hierarchy. Yet again the Empire had given a military post to a barbarian invader and allowed him to retain his own troops as his army. The example set by Adrianople and its aftermath had been greatly reinforced, as this time Alaric had been employed even after being defeated.

Radagaisus

Three years after the defeat of Alaric, Italy was invaded by a new enemy in 405, possibly hoping to follow in the examples of the Goths and Alaric. The origin of Radagaisus is unknown. Called 'King of the Goths', it is likely that he was the leader of a Gothic tribe from the north of the Danube, hoping to escape domination by the Huns.[30] According to Zosimus:

> Rhodogaisus [sic], having collected four hundred thousand of the Celts, and the German tribes that dwell beyond the Danube and the Rhine, made the preparations for passing over into Italy.

> Zosimus, 5.26.3

The use of 'Celt' and 'German' was, by this date, simply traditional literary terminology for non-Romans across the northern frontiers. However, the combination of both terms strongly suggests that Radagaisus was joined by members of other tribes willing to risk entry to the Empire. In addition, the inclusion of both the Rhine and the Danube in the claim is important. It suggests that he did not pass through Illyricum or Pannonia, as is sometimes claimed.[31] Instead, he probably crossed the northern border and ravaged Raetia before crossing the Alps and entering Italy before the snows fell.[32]

It is feasible that Radagaisus was joined by at least some of the Vandal tribes, in the same way as the Vandals had earlier been joined by the Alans. However, the evidence to support this theory is vague, simply a claim that 'Arian Christians' swelled his forces.[33] As large numbers of the Goths had already converted to Arianism, this may simply point to the inclusion of some Tervingi amongst his mainly Greuthungian forces. Despite the vast number claimed by Zosimus, it has been estimated that Radagaisus' forces were, at the most, about 20,000 men.

Over winter, Radagaisus and his army remained at large, devastating 'many cities'.[34] Stilicho was outnumbered and remained with his troops at Ticinum.[35] However, he sent orders for troops from the Rhine frontier to move to Italy to reinforce the *praesental* ('in the presence of the emperor') army there, as well as ordering a recruitment programme to bring his forces in Italy up to strength.[36] The frontiers of Gaul were left to the defence of the *foederati* (allies): the Franks and Alamanni.[37] Moreover, two edicts, dated 17 and 19 April 406, called on the inhabitants of Gaul to arm themselves for the peace of their country.[38] Stilicho was focusing upon Italy, and as a result the Gallic frontier had been stripped of a large proportion of its defenders, a factor that would later help the Vandals.

In 406, and possibly to ease supply difficulties, Radagaisus split his force into three, a move that was to prove a mistake. Stilicho defeated the core of the army led by Radagaisus himself, and Radagaisus was captured and executed. Allegedly, 12,000 of his men were accepted into the Roman Army, and some were settled in Italy, but the majority were enslaved. In fact, so many were sold into slavery that the slave markets in Rome were flooded and prices collapsed.[39] This implies that Radagaisus led a large number of people composed of both warriors and their dependants.

On hearing the news of Radagaisus' defeat, the other two groups appear to have lost heart. Stilicho gave orders to his Hun troops to attack at least one of the two groups, who were quickly defeated or chased from Italy, with some possibly escaping across the Alps into Gaul.[40] However, there was a later rumour that he had negotiated with the third group, so it is possible that at least one of them was simply persuaded to leave Italy peacefully, although the truth of the claim is open to doubt.[41] It is likely that the majority, if not all, returned to their homes outside the Empire.

Godigisel and the Invasion of Gaul

The attack of Radagaisus appears to have stirred the Asdings and Alans into action once more. Although impossible to prove, it is feasible that in either 405 or early 406, Godigisel planned to take advantage of Radagaisus' invasion of Italy by following his invasion route before offering his own services to Stilicho – who was short of troops – in the hope of being given a post similar to that occupied by the Gothic leader Alaric. However, the decisive victory of Stilicho over Radagaisus, plus the rumour that 12,000 of Radagaisus' men had joined the Romans, resulted in there being little chance of Stilicho accepting Godigisel's offer.

Unwilling to remain in Pannonia, Godigisel needed to decide upon a new target. It is likely that Gaiseric, now aged 17 or 18, was allowed to voice his opinions and took part in the decision. It should be noted, however, that there is no evidence that the invasion of Gaul was 'carried out by tribesmen forced out of their land by strangers whom they could not resist'.[42] It would appear that Godigisel was a shrewd leader who took the initiative in leading his people out of Pannonia, away from the dangers posed by living in a turbulent and violent region. Yet Procopius suggests that many of the Asdings did not wish to follow Godigisel in an emigration and remained behind.[43] Although not attested elsewhere, this would make sense: not all of the people who had been settled for generations would be willing to risk all in a confrontation with the Empire, so many probably remained in their homes, preferring to risk coming under non-Vandal rule.

The Asdings had doubtless heard of the transfer of Roman troops from the Rhine frontier to Italy to defeat Radagaisus, so it is possible that Godigisel determined to enter Gaul by way of the weakened frontier. In that way he could negotiate from a position of strength with the Gallic commander, in the hope of gaining employment. Accordingly, he decided to lead his people to the northern bank of the Danube before heading towards Gaul: staying within the Empire would not only give Stilicho notice of his intentions, but would give the Roman commander many chances to pin and defeat Godigisel in a similar manner to that in which he had defeated Radagaisus.

It has been suggested in the past that the forces that invaded Gaul were the remnants of the second of the three divisions that Radagaisus had led into Italy in 405–406. In this proposition, the group escaped over the Julian Alps and crossed the Danube before travelling through Germany and finally arriving at the Rhine.[44] Furthermore, it is proposed that the remnants of the third of Radagaisus' contingents crossed the Cottian Alps into Gaul and later rejoined their compatriots.[45] Although possible, this is a very complicated course of events and the account given above is probably the more likely.

With the decision made, the Asdings began their long journey.

Chapter 2

The Invasion of Gaul

Now the Vandals and the Alani, as we have said before, had been dwelling in both Pannonias by permission of the Roman Emperors. Yet fearing they would not be safe even here if the Goths should return, they crossed over into Gaul.

Jordanes, *Getica*, 31.161

T he precise course of events for what followed is unknown and several options present themselves. Possibly the most likely is that, upon hearing of the Asdings' decision to head west, several other tribes decided to join them. Interestingly, Jordanes claims that the Alans who joined the 'migration' were also from Pannonia. This implies that conditions in Pannonia were so precarious that many of the inhabitants wanted to leave, not just the Vandals.

It is unknown how many groups of Alans took part with the Asdings in the assault upon Raetia in AD 401, but once the Asdings began their journey to Gaul they were joined on the road by at least two separate Alan tribes, each with their own king: Goar and Respendial.[1] They too had decided that their hopes for the future lay in Gaul.

Furthermore, according to Jerome, the force eventually consisted of:

Quadi, Vandals, Sarmatians, Alans, Gepids, Herules, Saxons, Burgundians, Allemanni and – alas! For the commonweal! – even Pannonians.

Jerome, *Epistle*, 123.16

If accurate, this suggests that upon leaving Pannonia, the Asdings had been joined by at least some Sarmatians, Gepids and Heruls. Jerome even suggests that a few Roman citizens in Pannonia allied themselves with the Vandals, reinforcing the concept that conditions in Pannonia were harsh. All of Jerome's list is possible, but if so, the numbers of the other peoples involved in the migration were minimal, and it is just as likely that at least some are included by Jerome simply to maximize the tragedy that was about to befall Gaul.

The combined army began to force its way across Europe to the River Main. Whether Godigisel was in contact with the Siling Vandals from the start is

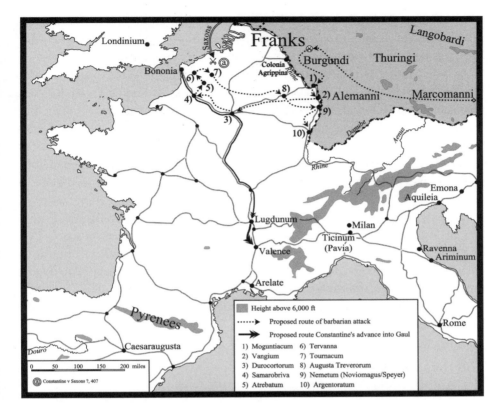

Map 2: The Invasion of Gaul.

unknown, but remains a possibility. Whatever the case, at some point at least one of the tribes of the Silings decided to join the western migration.[2]

But before meeting any recorded opposition, yet another barbarian group decided to join the migration: the Suevi. Their identity is rarely discussed, since they appear to be seen by many modern historians as being simply a contemporary tribal group living beyond the frontier. Yet this is almost certainly not the case. 'Suevi' appears to be a name given by contemporaries to a collection of peoples incorporating sections of the Marcomanni, Alamanni and Quadi. In their movement through '*barbaricum*', the migrating groups appear to have attracted support from at least two of these tribes: if only one tribal group had been included, that group would have been identified by its own name, not that of the composite group. One section was the Alamanni attested in Jerome, the second at least one tribe from either the Marcomanni and/or the Quadi.[3]

This meant that shortly before reaching the areas under the control of Roman *foederati*, Godigisel was in command of one of five main tribal groupings heading for the Rhine: Asding Vandals, Siling Vandals, Alans under Goar, Alans under Respendial and a composite group known as the Sueves. Gaiseric, the son of the king, was no doubt an important leader of the Asding army, although aged just 16.

As noted above, the Burgundians are included in the list of tribes attacking the Empire. However, in this instance, and given the long-standing treaty between themselves and Rome, this may be a mistake on the part of Jerome. Rather than invading Roman territory, it is far more likely that the invasion of their own lands by the migrating tribes forced many Burgundians to flee across the frontier in search of safety. A combination of ignorance and a desire to maximize the severity of events has led Jerome to erroneously include the Burgundians in the list of invaders.

If the theory proposed above that the Suevi in the list composed distinct groupings of at least two of the aforementioned tribes hoping to carve out new lives for themselves in the West, it would help to account for the lack of opposition recorded in the sources. After all, the Burgundians were too small a tribe to oppose the mass migration, and the Alamanni may have been unwilling to attack members of their own tribes. Whatever the case, the travelling tribes finally approached the Rhine crossings.

The Invading Forces*

The hypothesis outlined above concerning the origins of the tribes that were to cross into Gaul in 406 is a modern construction. Earlier historians appear to have followed Gibbon, who himself seems to have followed Jerome when the latter claimed: 'Savage tribes in countless numbers have overrun all parts of Gaul.'[4] Gibbon goes on to claim that the tribes that crossed the Danube were actually at least one third of the forces that Radagaisus led into Italy.[5] Sadly, there is no supporting evidence for Gibbons' theory concerning the invasion – although it remains a remote possibility.

These numbers have since been drastically reduced on logistical grounds, although some historians still refer to the invaders as a 'vast horde'.[6] However, most historians are – understandably – unwilling to commit to numbers, either avoiding the problem or stating merely that the numbers of the invaders should probably be in the tens rather than the hundreds of thousands.[7]

Yet there are also arguments that the initial invasion forces were composed largely of men of military age prepared to risk all to find a new life within the Empire.[8] The unwilling, too old or too young may have preferred to remain in their

---

* A variation of this analysis first appeared in *Stilicho: The Vandal Who Saved Rome* (Hughes, 2012). Readers who have read that book may wish to skip this section.

respective homelands. In this model, the core of the invading tribes was relatively small: only later were they to be swollen by new recruits and dependants joining them whilst they were in Gaul.

This explanation receives some support from the *Chronicle* of Prosper. A close reading of the *Chronicle* gives the impression that Prosper, writing in the mid-late fifth century, believed that little had changed between 406 and 418.[9] This is hardly likely had extremely large numbers of barbarians swept through Gaul and Spain, pillaging as they went. Instead, Prosper sees the collapse of Imperial rule as coming after 422. As a result, it is probably correct to assume that there is no need to see the invading forces as beginning with a vast number of people, although later they were to grow in size and become a more serious threat to the Empire.

The First Battle

Neither the exact direction taken by Godigisel and his followers, nor the reasons for the decisions made during their trek, are described by Roman sources. However, by analysing the few details given, it is possible to suggest a reasonable series of circumstances for their journey.

It is obvious from the fact that the migrants are recorded being far to the north along the Gallic frontier that they were trying to move themselves far from the main Roman army in Italy and from their traditional enemies, the Goths. In addition, having heard of Stilicho's removal of troops from Gaul, they appear determined, if at all possible, to travel on the far side of the Rhine so that they could avoid the risk of a battle against Roman forces stationed within the Empire, before taking their chances at the frontiers.

Yet it is also plausible that during their journey they may have become over-confident: the fact that there is no recorded resistance from either the Alamanni or the Burgundians, plus the fact that they had been joined by at least some of these tribes, may have resulted in them believing that they could travel as far as the ocean, picking up an ever-increasing army as they did so. This would explain why they travelled so far to the north before crossing the frontier. On the other hand, they may have simply been looking for an undefended crossing point into the Empire, and prior to this had failed to find one.

Whatever the case, the independent tribes arrived at different times on the banks of the Rhine. The Alans appear to have been travelling in close company with each other, yet as soon as they reached the crossing point, Goar, one of the Alanic kings, offered his services to the Romans. His offer was accepted and he appears to have crossed unhindered into the Empire with his people.[10] He is later attested as serving Aetius during the latter's tenure as leader of the West (433–454).[11]

Faced with Goar's defection, Respendial, the other Alan king, decided to retire from the frontier and join the Asding Vandal forces under Godigisel, who were advancing into areas defended by the Franks. His decision had a major impact upon the future of the invasion.

This was because the Asdings had met the first recorded resistance to the migration. Somewhere on the far banks of the Rhine, they were opposed by the Franks and a fierce battle took place.[12] Godigisel was killed, and the Asdings were on the point of being overwhelmed when the Alans under Respendial, retiring from the Rhine, arrived on the scene. Their unexpected appearance changed the course of the battle and the Franks were defeated.[13] Sadly, no other details of the encounter survive.

It is interesting that the sources for the battle only write that the Franks fought the Vandals, nowhere giving the Franks' 'federate' status.[14] Therefore, claims in modern works that the Franks were definitely allied to Rome are not conclusive. However, the fact that these events were reported in Rome suggest that the Franks were indeed those federates who had agreed to defend the Empire after the earlier recall of Roman forces to Italy by Stilicho, and that consequently the Franks informed the Empire of their defeat – hence the record in the sources.

Gunderic

Godigisel was succeeded by his legitimate son, Gunderic, who was to lead the Asdings for the next twenty-two years (406–428).[15] The resistance of the Franks caused Gunderic to change the direction of the march, although it did nothing to alter the desire to invade Gaul. The Asdings retreated south along the Rhine, leaving the territory of the Franks: they could not afford further expensive clashes before entering Imperial territory. Furthermore, it is likely that they were now short of supplies, as food would be scarce in December and much of their supplies would have been used during the journey, as a result of which they desperately needed to gain access to Imperial stores. Consequently, they moved back along the course of the Rhine before finally managing to break into the Empire in the region of Moguntiacum (mod. Mainz).

The Invasion of Gaul

The events surrounding the crossing are hard to follow, as the surviving sources do not give all of the information necessary for a clear understanding. As a consequence, even the date of the crossing has been questioned.[16] In addition, the accepted account that the Rhine was frozen is not upheld by any of our ancient sources, instead appearing to be a theory proposed by Gibbon, possibly to account for the lack of Roman presence at any of the bridges and crossings that should have been defended. The claim may, however, have been based upon the fact that the Rhine was liable to freeze in bad winters.[17]

Whatever the case, the four remaining groups – the Asdings, the Silings, the Alans of Respendial and the Sueves – now faced different dilemmas. Their arrival appears to have been a surprise, reinforcing the idea that their forces were small and relatively mobile. However, their small numbers meant that they faced resistance from the start. This may be the reason for their appearing to work to a more unified strategy: there is no clear indication that they operated as separate tribes once they entered Gaul.[18]

The only information we have concerning the attack of the barbarians on Gaul that includes any detail is found in the letters of Jerome, supplemented by a few sentences in the works of Salvian. Jerome states:

> The once noble city of Moguntiacum has been captured and destroyed. In its church many thousands have been massacred. The people of Vangium after standing a long siege have been extirpated. The powerful city of Rheims, the Ambiani, the Altrebatæ, the Belgians on the skirts of the world, Tournay, Spires, and Strasburg have fallen to Germany: while the provinces of Aquitaine and of the Nine Nations, of Lyons and of Narbonne are with the exception of a few cities one universal scene of desolation. And those which the sword spares without, famine ravages within. I cannot speak without tears of Toulouse which has been kept from falling hitherto by the merits of its reverend bishop Exuperius. Even the Spains are on the brink of ruin and tremble daily as they recall the invasion of the Cymry; and, while others suffer misfortunes once in actual fact, they suffer them continually in anticipation.
>
> Jerome, *Epistle*, 123.16

Sadly, this is the only information Jerome gives. To some extent, his depiction of the ravaging of Gaul is countered by Paulinus of Bezieres, who portrays the invasion more as a nuisance that is not being dealt with rather than severe and 'permanent economic destruction'.[19]

Yet the sequence in which the cities are listed may be the result of their attacks being listed in chronological order.[20] If true, by combining this with the sparse information found in Salvian it may be possible to recreate an itinerary for the attack. As a consequence, it could then be feasible to analyse the motives for their actions.[21] Yet it should be remembered that this is only theoretical, since it cannot be ascertained with certainty either that Jerome placed his list in chronological order or that it is extensive. However, with no other information available there is little alternative.

According to Jerome the first city to fall was Mainz, with the city itself being sacked and many of the inhabitants massacred. Yet despite the knowledge that many troops had been taken to Italy, the strength of the Roman forces in Gaul was unknown, so the Vandals probably expected to be attacked at any time. As a result, at the start the Vandals remained close to the safety of the frontier. However, and understandably, they also appear to have wanted to put some distance between themselves and the Franks. Therefore, after the sack of Mainz the Vandals moved south and attacked Vangium (Augusta Vangionum: Worms). Warned by the fate of Mainz, the citizens of Worms defended their walls and were subjected to a long siege. Their bravery was wasted, as the Asdings and their allies broke in and the city was sacked.

After the sack of Worms, the realization appears to have struck the invading peoples that there had been no response at all from the Roman Army. There also appears to have been no approach from the *magister militum per Gallias* – who may have been a man named Gaudentius, father of the later *magister militum* Aetius – either to offer service in the Roman Army or to demand that they cease their attacks. As a consequence, they decided to move further into Gaul.

The next town they came to was Durocortorum (Reims). Jerome now adopts a slightly different phraseology. Rather than describing the sack of cities, he notes that:

> The powerful city of Reims, the Ambiani, the Altrebatæ, the Belgians on the skirts of the world, Tournay, Spires, and Strasburg have fallen to Germany.
>
> Jerome, *Epistle*, 123.16

The change in tone is important, as it may signify a change in the barbarians' policy. In the interior of Gaul there would be no access to a safe border, and the siege of Worms had taken a long time and caused many casualties. Therefore, Gunderic – after consultation with the other leaders – appears to have realized that it would take less time and prove less costly in manpower simply to ravage the territory surrounding a city. In this way, the coalition could maintain the health of the people with plentiful supplies and at the same time maintain the pressure on Roman authorities to come to terms: a process made easier for Rome if Gaul had not been devastated. The weak forces left behind by Stilicho's demand for troops appear to have been either unwilling or unable to face the coalition in battle. This hypothesis has the advantage of explaining the speed with which the Vandals and their compatriots moved during the following months.

After ravaging the area around Reims, the coalition moved further to the north-west, away from the Franks and the Roman Army in Italy. The cities of Samarobriva

(Amiens), Atrebatum (Arras) and Tervanna (Therouanne) were all attacked and their surroundings plundered.

Civil War

Surprisingly, after the attack on Therouanne the coalition headed east, back towards the Franks and the frontier. Sadly, there is no explanation for their decision in any of the sources, so again there is the need to resort to speculation.

Either during or shortly after the attack on Therouanne, the coalition probably received two pieces of worrying news. One was that a Saxon warband was advancing into Gaul from the north-east.[22] The second, and far more disturbing, was that a large Roman army from Britannia had landed at Bononia (Boulogne). Believing this to be the expected Roman reaction to their invasion, the coalition took the safe course of heading in the direction of the frontier.

Unknown to the Vandals, this was not a campaign aimed at them. In 406, a revolt had broken out in Britain and an individual named Marcus had been declared emperor.[23] He was quickly assassinated and replaced by Gratian, a British native, but after a brief 'reign' of four months Gratian was in turn overthrown and replaced by Constantine III.[24] In 407, Constantine gathered an army and it was this force that landed at Boulogne.[25] However, Constantine's main target was acknowledgement as co-emperor with Honorius, not the coalition. Having set up his headquarters at Boulogne, Constantine quickly won the support of the army in northern Gaul.[26]

The arrival of Constantine at Bononia explains the change of direction adopted by the Vandals, who headed for the safety of the frontier. The move was justified: it would appear that Constantine learnt of the presence of an enemy near to Therouanne and dispatched an army to defeat it. Zosimus even goes so far as to state that Constantine defeated an enemy that later reorganised itself ready for a second attack.[27] Several possible 'enemies' have been mooted.[28] It is theoretically possible that he defeated the Vandals, but as this is not specifically reported it is unlikely. It is more likely that it was the invading Saxons who were defeated and that Constantine, having been told of only one enemy, now believed that the north of Gaul was clear.[29]

Gaul

Believing themselves to be under attack, the coalition headed back to the Rhine, plundering the lands of Tornacum (Tournai) as they went. When it became obvious that Constantine's attentions were focused on the south of Gaul, the coalition changed direction – possibly to the south-east. Salvian claims that at some point the coalition laid siege to Augusta Treverorum (Trier).[30] Salvian does not date the attack and the city is not mentioned by Jerome – probably because it success-fully resisted the invaders and so avoided being sacked – so it is unclear when the coalition attacked Trier. However, given the other available information and the assumption that Jerome is giving a chronological account, this would be a logical explanation for the date of the siege and of Jerome's failure to mention the city.

In the meantime, and believing that he had secured the northern frontier, Constantine headed south, establishing himself at Lyon. Becoming aware of Constantine's movements, and believing themselves to be the target, the coalition raised the siege of Trier and moved even further to the south-east. Surprisingly, they were ignored as Constantine moved south to capture Lyon.[31]

Regaining their composure, the coalition moved to devastate the region sur-rounding Nemetum (Speyer), before moving on to Argentoratum (Strasbourg). It may have been at around this time they attacked the house of Paulinus of Pella, but sadly he does not specify the house's location.[32] However, their continued depreda-tions at last brought them to the attention of Constantine in Arles.

Although Constantine's main aim was to be accepted as an equal by Honorius, his case would not be helped by the presence of large numbers of roaming barbar-ians in Gaul. Their attacks needed to be stopped, as not only would they under-mine his financial viability by reducing taxes in Gaul, but any failure to deal with the invaders could easily lead to discontent.

A Roman Alliance

The tribe of the Alans under Goar had previously pledged their loyalty to Honorius, and Constantine may have realised that, like the Alans, the other tribesmen would be willing to serve in the Roman Army: whether that of an usurper or the legiti-mate emperor would be immaterial. Accordingly, Constantine opened negotiations with the barbarian intruders. It should be noted that there is no specific link to any negotiations, but Orosius describes how Rome had made 'unreliable alliances' with barbarians and that these treaties were 'not strictly kept'.[33] There is no evidence that any other treaties were being broken at this time, so this can only relate to treaties with the coalition.

Yet in 407, Constantine would not have known that his potential new allies would be unreliable. Using a combination of threats and diplomacy, Constantine brought the invaders under control. The agreement solved two of his major prob-lems. Firstly, in order to face Honorius, he needed recruits, and it was cheaper and quicker to enrol the coalition than to enlist, equip and train raw recruits. Secondly, and just as important for political reasons, the treaty stopped the attacks on Gaul. The alliance also meant that he no longer needed to detach troops to protect his lines of communication. Constantine had now become a force to be reckoned with, with a large army at his command. The fact that he was able to quickly restore Roman administration in the north and that the mint at Trier began to strike coins in Constantine's name adds weight to the suggestion that the invaders had ceased to be a major problem.[34]

For the coalition, the treaty was a major breakthrough. The reasons for their decision are easy to understand. The coalition leaders would now find a place within the Imperial military bureaucracy, with the pay and prestige that such posts would provide. Furthermore, their men would now be supplied at the expense of the Empire, without the need to risk life and limb to take provisions from hostile Imperial citizens. However, there appears to have been one major omission from the treaty: nowhere is there any mention of land being assigned to the barbarians on a permanent basis. As a result, all four groups remained peripatetic mercenaries looking for a permanent home. In the meantime, they would have joined the Gallic army in southern Gaul, deployed to resist any forces emerging from Italy to overthrow the usurper.[35]

Barbarian recruitment

By the time of the treaty, it is likely that the invading armies had already begun to change. The evidence of *bacaudic* revolts, especially those in Gaul, points strongly to the idea that, like the British, many Gauls were unhappy about the level of protection the Empire offered, as well as the fact that they had little say in Imperial policies. Furthermore, the actions of Stilicho in withdrawing troops from Gaul to protect Italy, especially as their withdrawal had in part resulted in the successful barbarian invasions, would have caused deep distrust. Many in Gaul, whether nobles, ordinary citizens or slaves, would have been tempted to switch their allegiance, either in return for protection from the newcomers or simply in order to join them in their plundering. It may even be at this time that the invaders were joined by refugees, the last survivors of Radagaisus' attack on Italy who had by now crossed into Gaul.[36] As they grew in size, so their effects on districts they passed through grew to be ever more serious. A large army, with dependants, requires a large amount of provisions to survive. This in part helps to explain why Constantine was willing to enter negotiations. For the next two years, the coalition would serve Constantine. However, they had one desire that had been denied them: land of their own on which to settle in safety.

The Roman Civil War

In Italy, news of the invasion and rebellion doubtless caused confusion and concern. Yet it was not the barbarian invasion but the emergence of a usurper which was the main focus of the Italian court.[37] The Emperor Honorius and his *magister militum* Stilicho – who was, in effect, a fourth-century general – devoted their energies to defeating the usurpation.[38] In addition, after Constantine had recruited the coalition there was simply one enemy to defeat. In this context, it is certain that it was the defection of the Gallic armies to Constantine, rather than his employment of barbarians, that was the main concern in Italy. Yet due to the lack of reliable information before the end of the year, Stilicho was in no position to oppose the invaders in Gaul in 407. Reorganising his forces, Stilicho was forced to wait for the campaign season of 408 before opening hostilities.

In the meantime, Constantine had based himself in Lyon, where he received welcome news: the governors of the Hispanic provinces had recognized his right to the throne, no doubt due largely to the presence in Gaul of barbarian invaders who would pose a threat to Hispania should they cross the Pyrenees.[39] Constantine quickly sent *iudices* (judges) to Hispania, where, according to Orosius, they were obediently received.[40]

This move was opposed in at least some of the peninsula due to a long-standing loyalty to the Theodosian family. Two members of the Imperial family, Didymus and Verinianus, set about raising an army from their dependants.[41] The revolt would force Constantine to divide his forces, an action that would have a major effect on the future of the coalition.

408

In Gaul, Honorius' supporters had retreated to Arles, and it is possible that the coalition was stationed in this region in order to defend against any hostile move from the city.[42] However, the attack was to come from Italy, when a Goth named Sarus was appointed by Stilicho to command in Gaul with orders to defeat Constantine.[43] Crossing the Alps, Sarus advanced towards Lyon. Constantine was aware of his movements and sent his own *magister militum* Justinianus against Sarus. Sarus won a complete victory, killing Justinianus along with many of his men and capturing a 'vast amount of booty'.[44] Sarus followed up his victory by managing to surround Constantine while he was still in Valence and laying siege to the city.

Shortly afterwards, Constantine's other *magister*, Nebiogastes, arrived on the scene and came to an agreement with Sarus, the nature of which is unknown, before being treacherously killed.[45] Constantine had lost his main military commanders. Thankfully for Constantine, he had earlier sent Edobich, a Frank, and Gerontius, a Briton, to raise troops in the north of Gaul. After he had been besieged by Sarus for only seven days, they led their newly recruited force south, relieving the siege. Following the deaths of Justinianus and Nebiogastes, Constantine appointed Edobich and Gerontius as his new *magistri*. Sarus retreated across the Alps, where he was forced to buy passage from local *bacaudae*.[46] Constantine reacted aggressively to the attack and evicted the last remnants of Honorius' government from Gaul before establishing his capital at Arles.[47]

What part, if any, the Sueves, Alans, Asdings and Silings took in these affairs is not recorded. The fact that they are not mentioned in any of the sources suggests that they were stationed away from Lyon, and so not involved in the battles with Imperial forces. It is possible that they had been stationed in the vicinity of Toulouse in order to maintain control of the city and defend it from an attack from Arles: it is unlikely that Constantine would trust them to defend the frontier, either along the Rhine or the Alps, as in these locations they could be tempted to change allegiance and so help his enemies. In this case, Toulouse, far from the frontier, was a sensible place to station them.

Hispania[48]

Despite these successes, problems were mounting for Constantine. In Hispania, the rebellion of Didymus and Verinianus, relatives of the Emperor Honorius, had begun.[49] They quickly succeeded in establishing themselves in Hispania and set about attempting to seal the passes over the Pyrenees. Constantine swiftly elevated his eldest son, Constans, to *Caesar* and sent him with an army to Spain, along with the *magister* Gerontius.[50] Didymus and Verinianus won a victory against Constans in the Pyrenees, but were defeated and forced to cede the passes when Constans called up reinforcements from Gaul. Constans moved to Caesaraugusta to establish control of the peninsula, leaving Gerontius to pursue Didymus and Verinianus.[51]

After stiff resistance, Gerontius defeated the two rebels in Lusitania.[52] According to Orosius:

> With him [he had] certain barbarians, who had at one time been received as allies and drawn into military service, and who were called *Honoriaci*. They were the cause of the first misfortune that befell Spain. After killing the brothers who were trying to defend the Pyrenean Alps with their private forces, these barbarians received permission to plunder the Plains of Pallantia (*campi Pallentini*) as a reward for their victory.
> Orosius, *Historiarum Adversum Paganos Libri VII*, 7.40.78[53]

Although of uncertain location, the *campi Pallentini* was possibly in the region of Pallantia (Palencia) in Spain, in the Castilian *meseta* along the middle course of the River Duero (Douro). The area contains many sumptuous residential villas and was most likely the centre of Didymus' and Verinianus' estates. Once Hispania was pacified, Constans left Gerontius in Spain with Gallic troops to cover the passes over the Pyrenees, and returned to his father in Arles with Didymus and Verinianus as captives.[54]

Italy[55]

In Italy, the Gothic leader Alaric, who had been serving under Stilicho in Epirus, advanced with his forces and demanded 'expenses' and a higher rank from the emperor. After debate and confusion, Alaric was voted 4,000 pounds of gold to cover his losses. In addition, Stilicho now forced through the appointment of Alaric to command in the war against Constantine. This was, understandably, interpreted by the Senate as a betrayal and seen as giving a valid motive for a conspiracy against Stilicho.[56]

On 22 August 408, Stilicho was executed.[57] Upon his death, chaos and anarchy broke out in Italy: the Roman troops in Italy turned upon the Imperial federates, killing or enslaving their families.[58] The federate troops immediately joined their forces to Alaric.[59] After fruitless negotiations, Alaric invaded Italy in 408 and laid siege to Rome.[60] Eventually, the Roman citizens came to terms, agreeing to supply the Gothic forces with 'gifts' and at the same time sending an embassy to Honorius to promote Alaric's cause. Alaric withdrew to Ariminum.[61]

Gerontius

Although the confusion in Italy over the winter of 408–409 allowed Constantine to secure his rule in southern Gaul, problems erupted elsewhere. Three years after he had been declared emperor in Britain to protect the island, it was clear that his attention was focused upon Gaul and Italy, so Britain revolted against Constantine's rule. In addition, in late spring 409, Gerontius, Constantine's *magister* in Hispania, made a decision that would have a major impact upon the future of the young Gaiseric.

Chapter 3

Hispania

The rapid rise of Constantine, the removal of Stilicho and the continuing confusion prevalent in Italy seem to have given Gerontius in Hispania the belief that he could also rebel and set himself up in opposition to both Honorius and Constantine. Yet there may have been extenuating circumstances.

Either in late AD 408 or early 409, Constans, son and *Caesar* of Constantine, was allegedly ordered to return to Hispania by his father, possibly accompanied by a man named Justus, the replacement for Gerontius.[1] It was probably in response to his impending removal that Gerontius rebelled, proclaiming his *domesticus* Maximus as emperor at Tarraco.[2] However, he only had the support of the Hispanic army plus a few troops from the Gallic and/or British field armies that had accompanied him to Hispania. All of these were of dubious loyalty, a factor to be proved true later. In order to cement his position, he needed time to pacify Hispania, and also needed to augment his forces as soon as possible to become a serious contender. The answer to both of his problems was the barbarians in Gaul.

Obviously, to convert them to his cause he would need to offer them something beyond the agreement they had with Constantine. Gerontius may have offered the barbarians land in Hispania on which to settle in return for service in his army, although whether this was actually the case is unclear.[3] What he undoubtedly did offer was a haven further away from Italy and the threat of the Imperial army and Goths.[4] The proposal also meant that the Vandals and their allies would be able to move away from Gaul, where a major civil war was ongoing: they may have to fight again in Gaul, but their dependants would be safe in Hispania.

As noted in the previous chapter, the main source for events is the letter written by Jerome. It appears to be dated to 409 or 410.[5] Interestingly, after lamenting the sack of Argentoratum, Jerome becomes vague, except for acknowledging an attack on Toulouse. The implication here is that Jerome had knowledge of events in 406–407, but that in 409–410 news was only just arriving that the Vandals, Sueves and some Alans had reneged on their agreements and were again ravaging Gaul.[6] Whether land was offered or not, Gunderic, as well as many other barbarians, had seized their opportunity with both hands.[7]

Map 3: Gaul and Hispania.

Regrouping from their disparate postings, it would appear that the coalition set out to wreck southern Gaul, including Aquitaine, Narbonensis and
Novempopulum, and Jerome notes that when he wrote, Toulouse had not yet
fallen.[8] An obscure source may demonstrate the Roman view of events:

> By the sword, disease, hunger, chains, cold, heat: with a thousand dif-
> ferent ways one death snatches wretched men. War rages everywhere,

madness incites all, kings resort to arms against countless kings. Impious discord vents its rage on a world thrown into confusion: peace has left from the land: and what you see is the end.

Prosper of Aquitaine (?), Carmen ad Uxorem
(Ad Coniugem Suam), 25f.

It should be noted, however, that not all of the Vandals, Alans and Sueves accepted Gerontius' offer. For whatever reason, some chose to remain in Gaul and either joined the Imperial forces, served Constantine or focused on their own, unknown agenda.[9]

Apart from being intent upon enriching themselves, it is possible that Gerontius had ordered their actions in an attempt to weaken Constantine's political position. Having collected as much booty and all of the supplies that they could gather, they headed towards the Pyrenees.

Almost as if to prove that Gerontius was destined to be successful, at the same time as the Vandals prepared to leave for Hispania, the 'barbarians over the Rhine', the Franks and Burgundians, took advantage of the focus of all parties being on Italy, Hispania and southern Gaul to attack the Empire.[10] It may be at this time that the Franks seized further lands across the Rhine and the Burgundians settled the area later known as Burgundy.[11]

The loss of Hispania wasn't the only demoralizing event for Constantine. His focus on Italy and on gaining the acceptance of Honorius resulted in him neglecting to defend Britain, as well as northern Gaul.[12] Despairing of Constantine, the two areas revolted and refused to accept Constantine as emperor.[13] It is also possible that the Britons now sent envoys to Honorius asking for help. Honorius, beset on all sides by enemies, replied in the famous 'Rescript of Honorius' that the Britons needed to look after themselves.[14] For Constantine, the threat from the north was far more serious than that of Gerontius. For a short period, Gerontius was to be left to his own devices.

Accommodation

Constantine would have been surprised by the news of the defection of Britain, northern Gaul and Hispania and the reversion of the Vandals, Alans and Sueves to their previous tactics of ravage and plunder. With his power base shrinking, Constantine needed an accommodation with Honorius more than ever. In late summer 409, Constantine sent envoys to Italy asserting that he had been forced to claim the throne by his troops, and 'begged forgiveness' from Honorius 'for having seized power and promising help against the Visigoth Alaric in Italy'.[15] Honorius was under great pressure, both from Alaric and those opposed to Alaric's prospective employment. Honorius finally recognized Constantine III, in the process dispatching an 'imperial robe' as proof of Constantine's acceptance.[16] It is possible that Honorius also granted Constantine an honorary consulate at the same time. With peace now assured on the Gallic frontier, Honorius could concentrate on Alaric, and Constantine could theoretically restore the situation in Gaul, Hispania and Britain.

Unimpressed by events, Alaric broke off negotiations and returned to Rome, once again placing the city under siege. In a new twist, in December 409, Alaric persuaded the Praetorian Prefect of the City, Attalus, to accept the post of emperor.[17]

The Pyrenees

After spending at least part of the spring and summer ravaging southern Gaul, late in 409 the four barbarian tribes advanced towards the Pyrenees. The quality and quantity of the sources covering the entry of the migrating tribes into Hispania is extremely poor. As a consequence, it is necessary to rely on the few snippets of information available to investigate what happened when the barbarians reached the passes over the Pyrenees. Two possibilities are usually proposed for what occurred.

The first is that they simply forced an entry into Hispania against minimal opposition, as implied by Jordanes:

> Now the Vandals and the Alani, as we have said before, had been dwelling in both Pannonias by permission of the Roman Emperors. Yet fearing they would not be safe even here if the Goths should return, they crossed over into Gaul. But no long time [sic] after they had taken possession of Gaul they fled thence and shut themselves up in Spain, for they still remembered from the tales of their forefathers what ruin Geberich, king of the Goths, had long ago brought on their race, and how by his valour he had driven them from their native land.
>
> Jordanes, *Getica*, 31.161–62

In this version, the main reason for their wishing to cross the Pyrenees was to avoid the attention of the Goths, at this time in Italy. It is true that the Vandals had suffered at the hands of the Goths in the previous century, and in 409 the Goths were in Italy and in conflict with Rome, with Alaric demanding concessions and a post in the Imperial hierarchy. It is therefore possible to assume that they were indeed fearful that the Goths would be employed by Honorius to reconquer Gaul.

Other historians follow Orosius, who states that it was due to the actions of the unit named *Honoriaci*, the same as mentioned in Chapter 2. As already described, under orders they had sacked the 'Plains of Pallantia':

> Later, after the removal of the faithful and efficient peasant guard, they were entrusted with the defence of the [Pyrenees] and their passes. These *Honoriaci*, having had a taste of plunder and being allured by its abundance, planned to secure both freedom from punishment for their crimes and a wider scope for their wickedness. Therefore they betrayed their watch over the Pyrenees, left the passes open, and so loosed upon the provinces of Spain all the nations that were wandering through Gaul. They themselves even joined the latter.
>
> Orosius, *Historiarum Adversum Paganos Libri VII*, 7.40

Unfortunately, there are problems with the version given by Orosius. The main difficulty is that this description follows a traditional *topos* (an archetypal line of argument) amongst Roman writers which ascribed defeats and catastrophes to the giving of information harmful to Rome by, or even the outright defection of, traitors. In this case, the *Honoriaci* were the guilty party.[18]

In addition, Orosius later notes that:

> Whoever wished to go out and depart, found mercenaries, helpers, and defenders in the barbarians themselves. At that time they were voluntarily offering this help; and though after killing everybody they could have carried off everything, they demanded only a trifling payment as a fee for their services and for the transportation of loads.
>
> Orosius, 7.41

It would appear that Orosius has recognized that the invaders had not ravaged Hispania to the degree that is usually accepted, and had even turned to the service of citizens who could afford them – a far cry from the usual suggestion that once they had entered Hispania they simply looted all the places that they could.[19]

As a consequence, it is obvious that Jordanes' account contains too little information to be of much use, whereas that of Orosius must be suspect due to its adherence to traditional Roman literary forms and his later negation of his own description. Yet the fact that Orosius names the guilty party implies that he had access to some information concerning events in Spain not used by Jordanes. As a consequence, the version followed here is a variation on the theme proposed by Orosius, with part of the motive taken from Jordanes.

If the concept that the *Honoriaci* were 'traitors' is discounted, then there is need for an alternative explanation for their name being associated with the coalition. The hypothesis is that they did not 'treacherously' allow the barbarians to cross the Pyrenees, but, as implied above, had been ordered by Gerontius to grant the coalition access, a fact distorted by later historians.

Crossing into Hispania on either 28 September or 13 October 409, the barbarians joined Gerontius' forces and almost certainly helped him to quell any opposition to his usurpation in Hispania.[20] The concept that the barbarians were instead stationed on the passes over the Pyrenees is doubtful:[21] having already turned their back on Constantine and accepted Gerontius' offer, Gerontius will have known that their loyalty was dubious and so will have removed them from temptation.

In line with his policy of presenting events as 'apocalyptic', Hydatius describes the coalition as pillaging Hispania 'with a vicious slaughter'. They would almost certainly have faced opposition, both from those opposed to Gerontius as well as those who simply objected to the appearance of barbarians in Hispania. Their arrival, however, coincided with the beginning of a local famine which resulted in an ensuing pestilence – a coincidence used by Hydatius to promote his sense of 'apocalypse'.[22] Following Hydatius, Olympiodorus used events in Hispania to return to his favourite preoccupation of cannibalism.[23] The sense of catastrophe was mirrored by events in Italy, where, after more fruitless negotiations, Alaric laid siege to Rome for a second time.[24]

410

There are few, if any, events recorded in Hispania for the year following the arrival of the coalition. However, it is interesting to note that Hydatius records that the towns of the peninsula were spared from barbarian attack, but that their taxes were increased and stored food supplied to the army.[25] In addition, it is claimed by Orosius that some Roman citizens preferred living among the barbarians to paying Imperial taxes.[26] This implies a continuing bureaucratic administration in the provinces, and may also be evidence that during this year Gerontius was focused upon establishing his authority and boosting his treasury in preparation for a campaign in Gaul against Constantine – although obviously this is speculation. Bureaucratic continuity gives the lie to Salvian's hyperbolic claim that nothing remained of Hispania in the fifth century except its name.[27] The mint at Barcino began to strike coins in the name of Maximus, a sure sign of at least minimal support (see Plate 4).[28]

The fact that the coalition halted their attacks suggests that opposition in Hispania had finally been quelled, but Orosius' claim that citizens joined the coalition implies that any who refused to accept Gerontius' rule were welcomed into the coalition's ranks: this may have been exacerbated by the continuation of the pestilence and the outbreak of famine, as doubtless the 'government' was seen as being at fault for both calamities.[29] More importantly, it implies that the coalition were now working in tandem with Gerontius, another piece of evidence that Gerontius had indeed invited them into Hispania as allies.

Rome

In Italy, Alaric had retaken the initiative by laying siege to Ravenna. However, he soon lost patience with Attalus, his puppet emperor, and Alaric deposed him in disgust in summer 410.[30] He was advancing towards Ravenna in preparation for the opening of talks when he was attacked by the Goth named Sarus, who had previously been in Imperial employment against Constantine III. Although the attack was quickly defeated and was almost certainly on Sarus' own initiative, being an attempt to continue the vendetta that existed between the two men, Alaric saw it as being endorsed by Honorius. Furious, and finally giving up on his dreams of an Imperial post, Alaric returned to Rome. On 24 August 410, his troops were allowed to enter the city at the Salarian Gate and, for the first time in 800 years, the eternal city was sacked by barbarians.[31] In the process, Placidia, daughter of Theodosius and sister of Honorius, was captured.[32] Yet Alaric's success was to be short-lived: he died shortly afterwards and a major threat to the Empire was removed. He was succeeded by Athaulf, his brother-in-law.[33]

Constantine

In a surprising move, Constantine acted to support Honorius against the Goths, crossing the Alps and heading towards Ravenna.[34] Political events in Rome now played against him: Allobichus, the *magister militum* who had proposed the alliance between Honorius and Constantine, was executed.[35] Hearing the news in the region of Liverona, a city in Liguria, Constantine re-crossed the Alps and returned to Arles, where he appointed his son Constans as joint *Augustus* before sending him to Vienne, presumably to prepare for a campaign against Gerontius in the coming year.[36]

However, Constantine's focus on Italy had allowed Gerontius to take the initiative: advancing towards Vienne, he surrounded and laid siege to the city, trapping Constans before he could take any offensive action.

411

Constantine now faced war on at least two fronts. Although Gerontius was already laying siege to Vienne, the fallout from Allobichus' execution in Italy meant that the Roman forces in Italy would probably not be able to attack in 411. Yet the defection of the barbarian and Hispanic troops had left him short of men, and the defection of northern Gaul and Britain meant that he could not expect reinforcements from these areas. His only hope lay with securing the support of barbarians beyond the Rhine. Thankfully for Constantine, his *magister* Edobich was a Frank and was immediately sent to the Rhine to get help from the Franks and Alamanni.[37]

It was too late to save Vienne. After a short siege, the city was captured by Gerontius and Constans was killed.[38] Upon hearing of the death of his son, Constantine declared his other son Julian as *Augustus*. Gerontius, obviously a competent commander, wasted no time celebrating his victory. After the capture of Vienne, he led his troops straight on to Arles, where Constantine and Julian were placed under siege.[39] It seemed that Gerontius would soon replace Constantine as *Augustus* in Gaul.

Death of Gerontius

Unfortunately for Gerontius, in Italy, Honorius had appointed a new *magister militum*, an energetic and capable soldier by the name of Constantius, formerly a supporter of Stilicho.[40] Constantius acted fast. As the siege began in Gaul, Constantius took an army across the Alps and advanced on Arles. In the face of the Imperial army, Gerontius' troops deserted him and he fled back to Spain, where shortly afterwards his remaining troops mutinied and he was killed.[41] The usurper Maximus also fled to Hispania, but he appears to have joined one of the coalition groups: no doubt he distrusted the Roman forces and expected to be arrested and handed over to Constantius.

Interestingly, one of Gerontius' companions who remained loyal was an Alan.[42] This implies that the Alans in Hispania, and therefore possibly also the Asding Vandals, may have been a component in Gerontius' army during the invasion of Gaul, but if so their presence is not noted by the sources. However, it also implies that as soon as Gerontius had fled from Arles, the majority of the coalition troops deserted him and returned to Hispania on their own. The defection of his Gallic and Hispanic troops also deserves note. It is possible that these troops deserted him in part due to his favouring of his Alan allies over his Roman troops.

Whatever the case, it was probably after hearing of the death of Gerontius that the *Honoriaci* joined the Vandals. There was little chance of their being accepted by Constantius: they had supported Constantine, then transferred their loyalty to Gerontius, so may have felt it unlikely that Constantius would have trusted them enough to let them join his army.

Those barbarians who had either remained in or returned to Hispania now 'captured many forts and cities of Spain and Gaul together with officials of the usurper'.[43] Although sometimes used to demonstrate that they remained hostile to Rome and were simply wreaking havoc, the fact that they captured 'officials of the usurper' suggests a different connotation. Expecting whoever was victorious in the civil war in Gaul to then reorganise and lead a campaign into Hispania, it is possible that the towns and officials were captured to be used in negotiations with either Constantine III or Honorius in an attempt to secure a home for the coalition in Hispania. Although speculation, this theory explains subsequent events and Olympiodorus' mention of their capture of the officials.

In the meantime, Constantius took over the siege of Arles. When Edobichus returned from the Rhine frontier with reinforcements for Constantine, the relieving force was ambushed and defeated by Constantius, whereat Constantine lost hope.[44] He took refuge in a church and was ordained in the Church before surrendering to Constantius.[45] Constantine was then sent to Italy, but was murdered before he reached Honorius. His head was sent to Ravenna, where it was exhibited from 18 September 411.[46]

Although the new Roman *magister militum* Constantius may have been hoping that the defeat and deaths of both Gerontius and Constantine would allow him to regain control of Gaul and Hispania, even before the end of the siege he was to be disappointed. The siege of Arles had just entered its fourth month when news arrived from farther Gaul. The Alan leader Goar (who had entered Gaul in 406) and Burgundian king Gundahar had nominated a man named Jovinus to be emperor at Mainz.[47]

Using Jovinus' authority as a pretext, the Burgundians now set about establishing a settlement inside the Empire, their capital being Borbetomagus (Worms). The region later took their name and became modern Burgundy. This wasn't Constantius' only problem. Firstly, the continuous wars contributed to the outbreak of an enormous famine in Gaul.[48] Yet probably the greatest dilemma at this time was the continuing existence of the Goths in Italy. The presence of yet another usurper would normally have been the greatest threat to Honorius, but Jovinus was in the north of Gaul, so Constantius decided to deal with the Goths first.

412

Over the winter of 411–412, Constantius made preparations for a new campaign against the Goths in Italy. With the arrival of spring, he set his forces in motion. Under pressure, Athaulf led the Goths out of Italy and into southern Gaul.[49] Athaulf quickly allied himself with the usurper Jovinus, taking the opportunity to attack and kill his sworn enemy Sarus. Athaulf may now have seen himself as Jovinus' *magister militum*, and therefore part of the regime's decision-making process. Consequently, when Jovinus appointed his own brother Sebastianus as co-emperor, Athaulf was offended and opened negotiations with Honorius, and began to cooperate with Dardanus, the Prefect of Gaul.[50] The net result was that the Goths attacked the usurpers' forces, defeating their army and capturing Sebastianus, who was later executed.[51] Jovinus fled.

Heraclian

Constantius may have seen the removal of the Goths from Italy and the death of Jovinus as the end of his major problems. It was not to be: whilst these events were unfolding in Gaul, in Africa the *comes* Heraclian revolted and declared himself *Augustus*, before stopping the shipments of grain from Carthage to Rome.[52] In response, Heraclian was declared *hostis publicus* (enemy of the state) and condemned to death in July 412.[53]

Hispania

Under increasing pressure, Constantius almost certainly decided that he could not afford another usurpation in Hispania, where Maximus remained at large. Obviously, with the loss of his sponsor Gerontius and the defection of Gerontius' army, Maximus now had little chance of maintaining his position as '*Augustus*'. Further reinforcing the concept that Gerontius had made an agreement with the Vandals, Alans and Sueves, Maximus had fled into exile amongst the coalition.[54] Although his fate is uncertain, it is possible that he would have a further role to play in Imperial history.

Constantius now sent envoys to the coalition. The permanent removal of Maximus as a threat was certainly one clause demanded by the envoys for peace. Another may have been assurances that the coalition would not join the Goths, who were now in southern Gaul: should such an alliance be formed, the Empire would be in serious danger of losing both Gaul and Hispania.

For their part, the coalition still wanted a treaty with the emperor in order to have land on which to settle without the threat of Imperial attack. In addition, if the theory that the Vandals and the Goths had a long-standing enmity is correct, then at least one of the tribes would have wanted an alliance with the Empire against the Goths.

The Treaty of 412

Probably starting late in 411 – Orosius claims that the barbarians ravaged Hispania for two years (409–411) – negotiations were begun.[55] Finally, in 412, an agreement was reached in which the four tribes were given land to settle in return for guarantees of peace, possibly in return agreeing to serve as *foederati*.[56] It is also possible that as part of the accords, they had to hand over to the Romans the 'officials of the usurper' whom they had captured in 411, as noted earlier.[57] However, Maximus was not surrendered and remained at large with one of the tribes.

It should be noted that not all historians accept that a treaty was signed in 412. One even states that as there is no direct evidence of a treaty with the Sueves, the concept of a treaty by 'eminent historians shows a radical fault in the train of reasoning'.[58] However, the same historian then states that it is obvious that there was no treaty, as the later history of Hispania is full of accounts of Suevic attacks on Roman citizens. This observation fails to take into account the fact that the Romans were the first to attack, in 420, so breaking the assumed treaty (see Chapter 6). As a result, the concept of a treaty is accepted here, and this assumption will guide analysis of events from this point forward.

What is accepted is that the barbarians divided Hispania 'by lot', in accordance with the established translation of the passage in Hydatius.[59] Yet problems remain with this translation, especially once it is noted that the largest tribes received the best areas. As a result, the further hypothesis accepted here is that the tribes were settled as *foederati* according to their strength and the amount of land needed for their survival. (For a more detailed analysis of the reasons behind this decision, see Appendix I.)

Whatever the reality of the situation, the tribes were accepted in Hispania and land was divided in peace.[60] The Alans were settled in parts of Lusitania and Carthaginiensis, the Siling Vandals in Baetica, and the Asdings plus the Sueves in Gallaecia, with the Sueves being apportioned lands nearest to the ocean.[61]

It is possible that the tribesmen had some say in where they were to be settled. It is noteworthy that all four territories were on the far side of the peninsula to the Mediterranean and to Gaul, and it may be that fear of Gothic attack still loomed large, especially in the minds of the Vandals. News of events in Gaul and Athaulf's execution of Sebastianus would have reached them in Hispania, and the knowledge that Athaulf and his Goths were close to making an agreement with the Imperial government may have caused long-submerged fears to resurface. They wanted lands as far away from potential attack as possible.

Yet despite some modern assumptions, it should be noted that the settlements were relatively small, with the vast majority of Gallaecia, Lusitania and Baetica remaining firmly under Roman control. Constantius retained full possession of the important province of Tarraconensis and the majority of Carthaginiensis and Baetica. The situation in Gallaecia, where two tribes were settled, is unclear, but from later events it is certain that not all of Gallaecia was allotted to coalition settlers.

Interestingly, none of the surviving sources describe the fate of Maximus, although it should be noted that a man of the same (common) name emerges later in Hispania. It is possible that the later Maximus is the same man, harboured by at least one of the tribes in the hope that the threat of rebellion would ensure that the Romans stuck to their treaty.

After eight years of wandering, the tribes were finally able to settle in a land far from the threat of the Huns, although the danger of attack by the Goths may have remained a constant worry. However, the treaty with the Empire may have given them hope that they could at last put down roots in peace.

Chapter 4

The Empire Strikes Back

413

S adly for the Asdings, affairs in Gaul would upset their hopes. During the campaign season of AD 413, Athaulf and his Goths continued their war against the usurper Jovinus, and at an unknown date trapped him in Valentia (Valence). Jovinus was besieged before, in late summer or early autumn, the city was taken and Jovinus was captured before being sent to Dardanus at Narbo (Narbonne). In autumn 413, Dardanus had Jovinus executed and his head was sent to Italy.[1] It is generally accepted that the heads of both Jovinus and Sebastianus were later exposed at Carthage; however, it has been suggested that this is unlikely, and it is probable that the heads were sent to Carthago (Cartagena) in Hispania in order to impress Honorius' relatives and the peoples of Spain with the idea that the Empire was recovering.[2]

Following their defeat of Jovinus, Athaulf and the Goths appear to have come to an agreement with Rome. Included was a demand from Honorius and Constantius that Placidia be freed: it may be possible that even at this early time, Constantius desired to marry Placidia in order to become related to the Imperial family – his predecessor Stilicho had also been related to the emperor by marriage.[3] Negotiations may also have been undertaken with the Burgundians, who were allowed to remain in that part of Gaul they had acquired when supporting Jovinus. With the Goths defeating Jovinus, Constantius was more focused on the actions of Heraclian, who was a threat to the emperor and himself, than on eliminating the coalition of barbarians in Gaul.[4]

Heraclian

At an unknown date, Heraclian finally acted. He gathered his forces, allegedly including 3,700 ships, and headed towards Italy.[5] Constantius may have been taken unawares by Heraclian's invasion, as Imperial opposition was led by a *comes* (count) named Marinus, or it may be that Heraclian landed in the area that Marinus had been ordered to defend.[6] At the head of his army, Marinus faced Heraclian and the African forces in battle near Utriculum (possibly near to modern Otricoli – see Map 3). The invasion was defeated and Heraclian fled back to Carthage: according

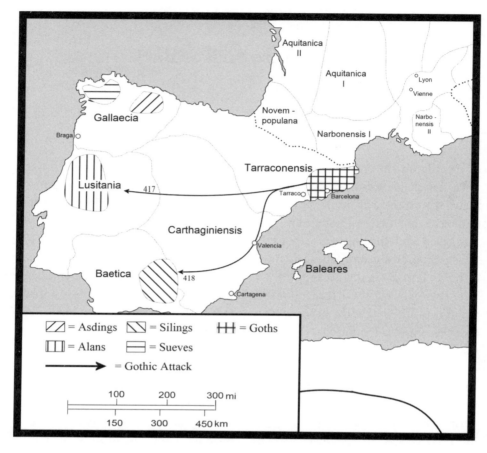

Map 4: Hispania: the placement of the settlements is approximate.

to Hydatius, 50,000 men were killed in the battle, although doubtless this is an exaggeration.[7] This event would have little impact on the fate of the Vandals, except for the fact that during the battle a large proportion of the African troops would have been amongst the casualties, and it is further possible that some of the defeated troops were enrolled in the Italian army rather than being allowed to return to Africa. The loss thus represented a great drain on African resources, leaving Africa short of men. This would have great repercussions for the future of the Vandals.

Athaulf and Placidia

With Heraclian defeated, attention returned to the Goths. As part of the newly signed agreement the Goths had demanded large amounts of grain with which to feed themselves, but with the grain supply from Africa interrupted due to Heraclian's revolt and invasion of Italy, Rome was unable to meet their demands.[8] Consequently, Athaulf again began offensive operations.[9] An attempt to capture Marseilles failed, and Athaulf was allegedly injured in the assault by a man named Bonifacius, who would play an important part in the Vandals' future.[10] After the failure at Marseilles, however, Athaulf managed to capture Bordeaux, Toulouse and Narbonne, making the latter his capital.[11]

414

Yet Athaulf still appears to have desired an accommodation with Rome. In this context, his next action has caused controversy amongst modern historians. The exact circumstances surrounding the event are unknown, but in January 414 Athaulf managed to persuade Placidia to accept him as her husband.[12] It is possible that there was an attraction between the two, but Athaulf was, above all, the leader of a barbarian people at war with Rome. It is possible that he was hoping that the marriage would help him negotiate peace with Honorius, with Placidia acting as mediator.[13]

Whatever the case, the marriage was celebrated in Narbonne, and Attalus, who had previously been 'emperor' under Alaric, gave an *Epithalamium* (a poem written in honour of the bride).[14] Interestingly, contemporary writers see in the event a fulfilment of prophecies found in the Bible, further evidence that the sources have to be used with caution since they interpret events to suit their own purposes.[15]

However, the move appears to have backfired. As noted earlier, Constantius may also have planned to marry Placidia – at least, this is what later events imply. The marriage of Athaulf and Placidia would obviously have been a blow to Constantius' plans. Negotiations quickly broke down and Athaulf, following the example set by his predecessor Alaric, set up Attalus as emperor in opposition to Honorius.[16] Thankfully for Constantius, as a balance to the bad news, at some point in early spring intelligence arrived from Africa: on 7 March 414, the usurper Heraclian had been put to death at Carthage.[17]

With the threat from Africa removed, Constantius was able to set up a blockade of the Goths by both land and sea, ensuring that the barbarians would not have enough food to survive. In this way, he probably hoped that even if Athaulf did not submit, at least some of the Goths would rebel against their leader, thus weakening his forces. The duration of the siege is not known, but it may have lasted until the end of the year. If so, it was probably during the course of the siege that Placidia gave birth to a boy, son of a barbarian king and a Roman 'princess'. As if to emphasize the baby's Imperial pretensions, he was given the name Theodosius in honour of his grandfather the emperor.[18]

The Goths and Africa

One other pivotal event did take place, probably in 414: a group of Goths captured some ships and attempted to sail to Africa. There are two different sources for this event. One is Isidore of Seville, the other is Orosius. Isidore specifically states that the event took place after the Goths had defeated both the Siling Vandals and Alans in Hispania, and therefore cannot be earlier than 418:

> When the war in Spain was ended by Wallia and he was preparing to cross to Africa with the fleet which he had equipped, he was overwhelmed by the force of a very severe storm in the Strait of Oceanus; and still remembering the shipwreck in the reign of Alaric, he avoided the danger of sailing and went back to Gaul.
>
> Isidore of Seville, *History of the Goths*, 22

Totally contrary to this tale, Orosius claims that:

> Thereupon Wallia succeeded to the kingdom [in 415] ... He was especially terrified by God's judgement, because a large band of Goths, provided with arms and ships, had tried to cross into Africa a year before [414] but had been caught in a storm within twelve miles of the Strait of Gades and had perished miserably.
>
> Orosius, 7.43.11–12

The specific divergence in chronology, with Isidore ascribing the event to the reign of Wallia whereas Orosius dates it to before his accession, has allowed modern historians to choose from either of these sources to support their theories.[19] However, there is one major factor that has resulted in the evidence as given by Orosius being accepted and the event being dated to 414. Orosius almost certainly wrote his book in 417, and his fate after this date is uncertain. Consequently, his account could not possibly have covered events after the later end of the war with the Silings and Alans. Consequently, the evidence provided by Orosius is preferred, and it is almost certain that in 414 a group of Goths managed to secure some boats and attempted to cross to Africa, only to be shipwrecked and drowned in the Straits of Gibraltar.

The importance attached to this event is that news of this would certainly have reached Constantius: after all, it was commented upon by at least two 'Roman' sources and so must have been common knowledge amongst the Romans. Once he had learned of the attempt, Constantius (and Honorius) would have been aware that at least one group of barbarians was still intent upon reaching the relative safety of Africa. This may have affected his later dealings with the Goths.

415

The birth of Theodosius had no effect on Roman policy towards the Goths. As the effect of the blockade increased, the Goths had no choice but to either surrender or attempt to break out. The idea of surrender was unacceptable, and the Goths broke out to the south.[20] In the new year of 415 at the latest, they crossed the Pyrenees and descended into northern Hispania.[21] However, not all of the Goths managed to escape. At least some of them were trapped and either captured or killed by Roman forces. Amongst the captives was Attalus, Athaulf's 'puppet emperor', who was sent by Constantius to Honorius at Ravenna before being exiled to the island of Lipara, to the north of Sicily.[22]

Unfortunately for the Goths, who had been suffering the effects of Constantius' blockade, when they entered Hispania they found a country ravaged by famine.[23] The situation may have been caused, or at least exacerbated, by the loss of farming land to the Vandals, Sueves and Alans. Many people would doubtless have taken refuge in towns, where there was a greater chance of accessing imported food, but ironically this may have made the situation worse, as it reduced the production of food. In addition, the increased population meant that in towns the effect of the famine was thus greatly magnified.

At an unknown date in 415, the Goths managed to capture the city of Barcelona. Sadly for Athaulf and Placidia, shortly afterwards their son Theodosius died.[24] The cause is unknown, but doubtless the long journey and the effects of hunger played a part in the child's death. His grieving parents buried him outside the walls of Barcelona in a silver-plated coffin.[25]

War

Although he had evaded the immediate attention of the Roman army, upon his arrival in Hispania Athaulf encountered the tribes who had earlier entered the peninsula. Desperate for food, the Goths began to buy supplies from the Siling Vandals: it is unlikely that the Asdings were involved in these exchanges due to the long distances involved and the possible lack of surplus food being available for trade in the poorer arable regions of Gallaecia. Displaying a distinct lack of common sense, the Silings began to mock the Goths, calling them:

> *Truli* because when they were oppressed by hunger they bought grain from the Vandals at one *solidus* per *trula*. A *trula* is one third of a *sextarius*.[26]
>
> Olympiodorus (fragment), 29.1

Old grievances quickly reawakened, and the Goths and Siling Vandals – at this time the Silings were probably allied with and subservient to the Alans under their king, Addax – quickly became engaged in war.[27] According to Jordanes, Athaulf, having established his capital at Barcelona, left his treasure and the unfit in the city and began a campaign against the Vandals. Sadly, Jordanes does not include any details concerning the nature of either the outbreak or the course of the conflict.[28]

At this point affairs took an unexpected twist. Athaulf was assassinated – according to Jordanes by one 'Euervulf, a man whose short stature he had been wont to mock'; according to Olympiodorus by a man named Dubius, one of Sarus' followers.[29] Immediately following the death of Athaulf, a man named Sigeric, allegedly a relative of Sarus, was made king, but he quickly became unpopular and within only seven days he too was assassinated.[30]

Wallia

After the short reign of Sigeric, the Goths needed a new leader. Their choice fell upon a previously unknown man named Wallia.[31] His greatest problem was the continuing wars on two fronts, with the Romans to the north and the Vandals/Alans to the south. Wallia understood that, although he had been 'made ruler by the Goths for the sake of war', the Goths needed peace on at least one front in order to survive as a separate political entity.[32] Accordingly, over the winter of 415 to 416 he entered into negotiations with Honorius and Constantius. The details are nowhere preserved, but modern historians have attempted to deduce the contents from later events.

The difficulty lies in the interpretation and dating of these events, which are confusing and sometimes contradictory. As a result, the conclusion reached here differs from that usually offered; however, it should be noted that both depend upon the same sources and both are equally valid.

Treaty

In exchange for 600,000 bushels of wheat, the Goths agreed to a peace with Rome.[33] In return, they were to restore Placidia to her brother Honorius.[34] Furthermore, it would appear that they agreed to serve as *foederati* in a Roman-sponsored continuation of their campaign against the Alans and Siling Vandals.

The reasons for the treaty on the part of the Goths are obvious: reduced by hunger and with a continuing blockade limiting their supplies, as well as with war on two fronts, they desperately needed relief. This they achieved. Yet the reason behind the Roman desire to set them on the Vandals and Alans is taken as being the barbarians' 'illegal' occupation of Roman territory. Yet if they had been allowed by treaty to settle, as posited earlier, this theory does not hold water. Instead, an alternative needs to be found. The most appealing but simplistic is that Constantius was unhappy with the settlements in Hispania, as they had been conceded under extreme pressure from a Rome under attack from barbarians and rebellions. Now that the threat had receded, Constantius may have felt that the time had come to redress the balance. This is eminently plausible, especially when the added benefit of barbarian killing barbarian is added to the equation.

It is even possible that the campaigns were intended to 're-establish imperial control over the city of Mérida and the rich grain-producing lands of Southern Spain'.[35] This remains a possibility, and must at least be included as part of the overriding aims of the projected military operation.

On the other hand, a further – and possibly more important in the mindset of the Roman court – pretext offers itself. All of the usurpers who had arisen between 405 and 415 had been defeated and executed – with one exception: Maximus, Gerontius' puppet, who had fled to the coalition after his benefactor's defeat. It would appear that Maximus had stayed with either the Siling Vandals or the Alans – and given earlier evidence, most likely the Alans – who had refused to hand him over to the Romans, preferring instead to keep him as an omnipresent threat for use when negotiating. Constantius may have seen the ongoing war between the Alans and Goths as a simple way of reducing the threat of the Alans, as well as hopefully removing that of Maximus. Accordingly, in the same year as the treaty, Constantius called on the Goths to conduct the campaign against the Silings and Alans in the name of Rome.[36] By entering into a *foedus* (treaty), the Goths now had the advantage of being able to utilize Roman supply bases during their campaigns in the peninsula.

However, despite modern claims, there is no evidence for the assumption that they were also to wage war on either the Asding Vandals or Sueves in return for land in Gaul.[37] That eventuality was dependent upon later events. Instead, the lack of evidence to support the claim may reinforce the concept that the main Roman reason for the campaign was to remove the threat posed by the usurper Maximus by attacking the alliance between the Alans and Silings, the group who were giving him sanctuary.

The Campaigns

It is sometimes assumed that, at Roman instigation, the Goths fought a single campaign against the Alans and Siling Vandals. Although a possibility, the definitive outcome of the campaign plus the evidence given by Hydatius suggest that it may have taken at least two separate campaigns, one to destroy each of the two kingdoms. If this is correct, some otherwise confusing information becomes easier to understand. (See below on the treaty of 419 attested by Prosper.)

417

Beginning either in late 416 or, more likely given the logistical requirements, with the opening of the campaign season of 417, the Goths launched a major attack upon the Alans and Silings.[38] Led by their king, Addax, the Alans at this time may have had some form of hegemony over the other tribes in Hispania – although this may only have been in the form of a loose confederation, with the largest group having the final say.[39]

The Goths began the war with a devastating attack on the nearest target, the Alans: Hydatius records the slaughter of a vast number of barbarians in an entry dated to 417.[40] Addax was killed and his army decimated.[41] Although the Alans are not specifically named in the first assault, the theory is supported by a close reading of Hydatius.[42] The violence of the attack almost certainly stimulated a political response from the other members of the original coalition:

> However, the other kings, those of the Alans, the Vandals, and the Suebi, had made a bargain with us on the same terms, sending this message to the emperor Honorius: 'Do you be at peace with us all and receive hostages of all; we struggle with one another, we perish to our own loss, but we conquer for you, indeed with permanent gain to your state, if we should both perish.' Who would believe these things if they were not proven by the facts? Thus it is that we are informed by frequent and trustworthy messages that warfare among the barbarian nations is now being carried on daily in Spain and that much blood is being shed on both sides; especially is it reported that Wallia, the king of the Goths, is intent upon bringing about peace.
>
> Orosius, 7. 43

The dating of the embassies is problematic. The first sentence implies that the embassies arrived after the treaty with the Goths, but the final sentence suggests that they should be dated prior to Wallia's agreement with Constantius. Certainty is impossible, but the assumption here is that the first sentence is accurate and that the final sentence is implying that Wallia is 'intent upon bringing about peace' on Roman terms.

Whilst these events were transpiring in Hispania, in Gaul the *magister* Constantius scored a major political coup over any opponents in the Senate. Possibly using his predecessor Stilicho as a role model, Constantius married the newly released Placida, sister of Honorius, in Narbonne.[43] The move placed Constantius far above his opponents and ensured that, at least for the foreseeable future, his would be the opinion that would be listened to by Honorius.

418

After destroying the bulk of the Alan army in the first year, the Goths mounted a second campaign in 418, this time aiming to decimate the Siling Vandals.[44] Although not stated, it is possible that Maximus had fled from the first attack to the 'safety' of the Siling Vandals. If true, this explains why Constantius unleashed the Goths for a second campaign. The campaign was a success: the Siling Vandals were destroyed as a separate people, with Maximus then fleeing to Gallaecia.[45]

Vandal Consolidation

As noted in the previous chapter, the settlements of the four barbarian tribes in Hispania were not as widespread as sometimes claimed. The strongest two tribes, the Alans and Siling Vandals, had been not only defeated but destroyed by the single tribe of the Goths. In addition, this Gothic force was later to be settled in only a small part of Gaul. The ramifications of this analysis negate earlier preconceptions concerning the barbarians' strength.

The implication is that the four tribes who had invaded Hispania were not given whole provinces, but only some of the land within these provinces. This hypothesis is reinforced by later events, where the Sueves are continuously seen as attacking Roman territory in Gallaecia, which would not be possible if the whole territory had been divided between them and the Asding Vandals, as is usually claimed.

Ironically, however, the destruction of both the Siling Vandals and Alans was to benefit the Asdings. The first stage in this reversal of fortunes was the amalgamation of the defeated tribes with the Asdings:

> [Wallia] destroyed by war all the Silingian Vandals in Baetica; and he killed so many of the Alani, who ruled over Vandals and Suevi, that when their king Attax was killed, the few who survived forgot the name of their kingdom and placed themselves under the rule of Gunderic, king of the Vandals who lived in Galicia.
>
> Isidore of Seville, *History of the Goths*, 21[46]

At a stroke, Gunderic had gone from being one of the weakest of the barbarian kings in Hispania to being by far the strongest. Yet the initiative lay with Rome, and the question remained as to what their next move would be.

419

The earlier attempt by at least some Goths to cross to Africa meant that Constantius now realised that, above all, the Goths needed land to settle. The simplest method would have been to allow them to settle the lands recently conquered in Hispania, but there was a problem with such a deal. There was no guarantee that the Goths would remain settled: at least some of them could easily make a further attempt to cross the Straits of Gibraltar. Furthermore, settled in Hispania, the Goths were a long way from Italy and the army, so there was no certainty that they would not attempt to assert their independence in opposition to Rome. What Constantius needed was a settlement that was within easy reach of Roman forces but which did not threaten the Empire.

Therefore, it is probably only after the campaigns against the Silings and Alans that Constantius realised that the Goths needed to be settled in Gaul. In this context, the suggestion that he 'recalled' them from Hispania makes more sense.[47] Any attempt by the Goths to settle in Hispania would face opposition from the newly enlarged Asdings, the Sueves and the Empire, and so at this stage Wallia would still be submissive to Roman decisions.

> On account of his service in gaining victory, Lower Aquitania together with certain towns in the neighbouring provinces that stretched to the Atlantic Ocean was given to him by the emperor.
>
> Isidore of Seville, *History of the Goths*, 21

Over the winter of 418–419, a new treaty was arranged in which the Goths received lands in south-western Gaul, possibly in return remaining *foederati* – agreeing to supply men to serve in Roman armies. Here they would be under the close supervision of the Roman Gallic army and would be readily available for campaigns both in Hispania and on the Rhine frontier.[48] The fact that a new treaty was needed and that this took some time to organise helps to explain the confusion over whether the date for the settlement was 418 or 419.

Sadly for Wallia, he did not see the full fruits of his negotiations. He died in 419 and it was his successor, Theoderic (I), who oversaw the final settlement of the Goths in Gaul.[49]

Hispania

Yet the Goths were not the only problem for Constantius. The exact nature of events is unclear due to the poor quality of the sources. In this case, recent work has revealed a new line of inquiry.[50] Although Hydatius tells of the stationing of a Roman army in Hispania, strangely he still makes no mention of the usurper Maximus.[51] Analysis of recently discovered letters suggests that, after 25 July 419, Maximus, who had previously been proclaimed emperor by Gerontius, was proclaimed emperor again.[52]

There is no indication of who was supporting the usurper, but other factors suggest that he had fled when the Goths attacked the Alans and Siling Vandals. Sadly, as Hydatius does not mention Maximus at all, it is nowhere clearly stated where he gained support. It is usually accepted that he joined the Vandals and that the war between the Vandals and Sueves was due to the Sueves' refusal to accept Maximus.[53]

However, this does not take into account all of the evidence given by Hydatius, which may possibly imply that instead Maximus escaped and joined the Sueves, the group at the farthest edge of the Empire. The reasoning behind this assumption will become clear during analysis of the events of 420.

Once amongst the Sueves, Maximus was declared emperor once again.[54] Obviously, neither Honorius nor Constantius could tolerate the affront to Roman dignity, yet it was too late to organise a campaign for 419. Orders were issued and preparations begun for a campaign in 420. Yet amidst the continuing confusion, Constantius received some good news: on 2 July 419, Placidia gave birth to a son, named Valentinian.[55]

420

Again, the sources give little indication as to what happened in Hispania in 420, but it is likely that the Sueves demanded that the Vandals, including the survivors of the Gothic attacks, join the rebellion. But rather than join the revolt, war began between the Sueves and Vandals.[56]

As previously noted, Hydatius makes no mention of Maximus, simply stating: 'After a dispute had arisen between Gunderic, king of the Vandals, and Hermeric, king of the Sueves, the Sueves were besieged in the Erbasian Mountains by the Vandals.'[57] Sadly, the 'Erbasian Mountains' are unidentified, as a result of which it is unknown whether the Vandals invaded Suevian territory or vice versa.

In the meantime, the Roman *comes* Asterius had been 'given command of a very great army and the outcome of a very great war'.[58] Sadly, the relevant passage in Hydatius is confusing and open to interpretation:

> The Vandals were dissuaded from their siege of the Sueves by pressure from Asterius, the *comes Hispaniarum*, and after some men under the command of the *vicarius* Maurocellus were killed in their flight from Braga, the rest of [the Vandals] left Gallaecia behind and crossed into Baetica.
>
> Hydatius, 66 [74] s.a. 420[59]

The first thing of note here is that nowhere is Asterius given credit for defeating the Vandals in a set-piece battle: instead, it is the threat of attack from both the Romans outside and the Sueves inside the siege lines that forced the Vandals to raise the siege.

On the contrary, the *vicarius* (deputy commander) Maurocellus was apparently defeated as he fled from Braga, a city under the control of the Sueves, although why this should be is not noted. Shortly after the conflict, the Vandals left Gallaecia and moved to the far south of Hispania, to Baetica, possibly to the regions previously held by the Silings. Yet it should be noted that many years after the move, the Vandals were recorded by Hydatius attacking Hispalis (Seville), the main city in the province. Consequently, the modern assumption that they immediately took control of the whole province is mistaken.

Yet despite the defeat of Maurocellus and the loss of Baetica to the Vandals, Asterius was unaccountably honoured with the title of *patricius* (from *patres*, 'father', the highest rank after the emperor) shortly after the campaign.[60] Thanks to his being rewarded for the campaign, the whole episode is usually interpreted as a major victory for the Romans, with dissenting historians being few.[61] This is confusing, unless Asterius had accomplished his mission.

In this context, of more importance is the phrase 'after some men under the command of the *vicarius* Maurocellus were killed in their flight from Braga, the rest of [the Vandals] left Gallaecia behind'. The implication here is that Maurocellus had been to Braga, the capital of the Suebian territory, and had fled from there in some haste, being attacked and losing some men in the process. Why a Roman force would be present at the Suebian capital is nowhere explained.

The only narrative which fills all of the known facts as well as explaining later events is that the main force under Asterius was advancing towards the Erbasian mountains, but that the main objective was not the Vandals, but Maximus, as barbarians were always less important than usurpers in the priorities of the Roman government.[62]

Only as he approached the mountains did Asterius learn that Maximus was being supported by the Sueves, and that he had remained in Braga. Aware that the majority of the Suevic forces were trapped by the Vandals, Asterius detached a small force under Maurocellus to attempt the capture of Maximus. In the meantime, Asterius advanced a little nearer to the mountains, pinning both the Vandals and Sueves and so giving Maurocellus time to fulfil his mission.

Threatened by the Romans in their rear, the Vandals had little option but to raise the siege. Yet there needs to be an explanation for Asterius' failure to use his military supremacy to inflict a defeat on either the Sueves or Vandals. This is because his orders were the elimination of Maximus, not a risky military engagement.

Instead, Maurocellus managed to infiltrate Braga and capture Maximus, being attacked by Sueves from the city as he escaped but still managing to evade capture, with the loss of only a few men. Despite the fact that the Vandals then moved south and were now at large in Hispania, rather than being pinned in the north-west corner of the peninsula, the elimination of Maximus with so few losses is the main reason why Asterius was rewarded with the title of *patricius*. Maximus himself was sent to Honorius, probably in late 420 or early 421, where he was included in Honorius' parade celebrating his thirty years of rule before being executed.[63]

421

The new year would have been one of great optimism for Rome. The Goths had been defeated and forced to accept terms equal to those imposed by Theodosius in 382. Not only had they been removed as a threat, but they had then been used to destroy two barbarian groups that had earlier invaded the Empire. In addition, the last of the usurpers had been captured and Honorius was once again the sole Roman emperor in the West, with no threat of usurpation. The West was well on the way to recovery.

However, Honorius remained childless and there was a need to ensure a smooth succession should anything happen to him. In these circumstances, the next requirement was clear. On 8 February 421, the *magister* Constantius, brother-in-law of the emperor, was declared joint *Augustus*.[64] This was bad news for the Vandals. Constantius was an able military commander, and it was likely that he would conduct at least one campaign against the tribe who had moved from their settlement in Gallaecia and 'illegally' settled in Baetica.

Yet it may be that they need not have worried: there are reports that Theodosius, the Eastern Emperor, did not approve of Constantius' elevation, and Philostorgius claims that in order to enforce his position, Constantius immediately began to prepare for war with the East.[65] Whether the story of Constantius' plans for war are true or not, the fact that Theodosius was not prepared to accept Constantius as co-emperor confirms that East and West were not in accord, a circumstance that was not lost on Gaiseric – at least if his later actions are interpreted in a certain way (see 'The Vandals' in Chapter 5). The question of whether Constantius was preparing for war or not is, in fact, immaterial: before any war could begin, Constantius died after a reign of only seven months.[66]

It is also likely that it was only in the new year that the Vandals made their move to the south. They would have been wary of Asterius and his army and would have waited until the coast was clear before making their move, rather than risk being attacked when they were vulnerable en route to Baetica, a region well-known by the survivors of the Siling Vandals.

422

Despite the death of his co-emperor, January of the new year saw public festivities to mark the *tricennalia* of Honorius. The fallen usurper Maximus was displayed during these ceremonies, doubtless to emphasize the power of the emperor, who now ruled alone without the presence of a domineering *magister militum*.

Yet there were problems for Honorius. Not least of these was the fact that an alien enemy was at large in Hispania. At some time, possibly after Constantius had been made emperor, a man named Castinus had been promoted to the post of *magister militum*. Castinus was sent to Hispania to command an army, which included a contingent of Gothic *foederati* from Gaul. Bonifacius, who had earlier allegedly wounded Athaulf at Marseilles and who was a protégé of Placidia, was to accompany Castinus – possibly in order to keep the *magister* under close surveillance. However, the two men argued and Bonifacius left the army.[67]

It is usually claimed that he simply moved from Hispania to Africa, but Hydatius claims otherwise: 'Bonifacius left the Palace and invaded Africa'.[68] Bonifacius clearly returned to report to his mentor Placidia in 'the Palace' before leaving for Africa. However, the use of the word '*invadit*' (invaded, entered) is a little odd. Other words could have been used if Bonifacius had simply been sent to Africa, so there must have been a reason for Hydatius' choice. Interestingly, Bonifacius gained a reputation as a commander whilst in Africa, so it is possible that he was sent with a detachment of troops in order to clear rebels and bandits from the region.

In the meantime, Castinus carried on with the campaign, probably because he saw the Vandals as an easy target: they had only 'fought two or three pitched battles in the previous fifteen years and had lost them all'.[69] Probably solely by manoeuvre, he managed to place the Vandals under siege, although it is nowhere made clear whether or not this was the siege of a city. However, although they were soon close to surrender, Castinus decided that he needed to gain a complete military victory, possibly due to the need to improve his standing thanks to the political machinations at court involving Honorius, Placidia and Bonifacius. His strategy backfired: he was allegedly betrayed by his Gothic *foederati*, and was defeated and forced to retire to Tarraco (Tarragona).[70] According to the *Gallic Chronicle of 452*, he lost 20,000 men, although this number is open to question.[71] Sadly, Hydatius, the source for these events, does not clarify why or how he was 'betrayed' by the *foederati*. However, as Bonifacius had abandoned the army due to Castinus' 'haughty and inept exercise of command', it is possible that the Goths were reacting to their poor treatment by the general. On the other hand, Possidius later claims that there was a Gothic contingent amongst the Vandals and it may be that the Goths preferred to join the Vandals rather than serve the Empire.[72]

Whatever the case, the unexpected victory was a major turning point in the history of the Vandals.

Chapter 5

Freedom

E vents in the years immediately following 422 further conspired to help the Vandals in their quest for freedom from attack. After the death of Constantius III – husband of Placidia – questions began to arise concerning the scandalous manner in which Honorius and Placidia, brother and sister, were behaving towards each other, especially the closeness of their 'embraces'.[1] However, things quickly changed: the return of Bonifacius from Hispania and his report concerning Castinus' behaviour, plus the unexpected defeat of Castinus' army, caused a rift between Placidia and Honorius. Either in late 422 or early 423, Placidia took her son Valentinian to the safety of the Eastern court at Constantinople. The estrangement would have great ramifications for the future, especially as Bonifacius in Africa gave his support to Placidia over Honorius.

Yet it also had an immediate impact, in that affairs at court were dominated by the fallout of the incident, the net result probably being that no action was initiated against the Vandals either in 422 or for the campaign season of 423. Yet it should be noted that any plans for the new year of 423 may have been disrupted.

423

On 27 August 423, Honorius died in Ravenna, perhaps of dropsy (oedema).[2] The exact form of 'dropsy' isn't specified, but the two most common causes were probably congestive heart failure or kidney disease. Neither of these would be instantaneous, and this in part explains the relative inactivity of the court in this year, since the court remained in limbo as the emperor's health deteriorated. Theodosius II in the East was now sole emperor and needed to designate a new emperor for the West. He hesitated, and Castinus took his chance. He would have known both that Valentinian was the most obvious successor, and also that should Valentinian become emperor, Valentinian's mother, Placidia, would not hesitate to remove him as *magister militum*.

On 20 November, Castinus used his role as *magister militum* to appoint a man name John, the *primicerius notariorum* (chief notary, head of the 'civil service'), to the throne.[3] Opinion quickly became divided. Gaul, Italy and the 'free' regions of Hispania threw their support behind John. Individuals were also forced to choose. For example, a man named Aetius chose to support John and was made *cura palatii* (curate of the Palace). But in Africa, Bonifacius refused to acknowledge John's elevation and withheld the grain fleet destined for Rome.[4]

Bonifacius had used his time in Africa well. He had 'freed Africa from attack' by barbarians and bandits and was now recognized as a capable military commander.[5] The loss of Africa was obviously a major blow to John's attempt to hold the crown, and over the winter he took steps to organize a campaign to retake the area. Bonifacius' response was to rebuild the city walls of Carthage in preparation for an attack.

However, the level of support in the West meant nothing as, despite an embassy being sent, in the East Theodosius refused to acknowledge John's position.[6]

424

Over the course of 424, envoys would have been passing between East and West, between the West and the Goths, Sueves and Vandals, and between Bonifacius in Africa and Placidia in Constantinople. It is possible that, frustrated by the lack of response from the East and by Bonifacius' withholding of the grain supply for Rome, in the summer of 424 John launched an expedition to take Africa.[7] The campaign is nowhere described, but appears to have been a complete failure and only served to weaken John's position.

Late in 424, Theodosius finally began to move. On 23 October, he bowed to the inevitable, nominated his cousin Valentinian as *Caesar* and sent an Eastern army to invade the West under the command of his *magister militum* Ardabur and Ardabur's son, Aspar.[8] The usurper John's response was to seek allies for the West. Accordingly, John sent his *cura palatii* Aetius, who had spent time amongst the Huns as a hostage, back to the Huns in the hope of recruiting an army.

425

John was too late. Before Aetius could return, John was defeated, captured and shortly afterwards executed in Ravenna.[9] Rather than being executed, it seems that *magister militum* Castinus was sent into exile.[10] Three days later, Aetius returned to Italy with a large force of Huns.[11] After a brief skirmish, Aetius and Placidia opened negotiations: the Huns were paid off and returned home, whilst Aetius was given a military command in Gaul as part of the new Imperial regime.

On 23 October 425, the infant Valentinian III was crowned Roman Emperor.[12] Placidia became the de facto regent, but circumstances dictated that she had to play a dangerous political game. To lead the army as *magister militum*, she had a man named Felix, who appears to have come from the Eastern Empire and have been nominated by Theodosius.[13] As such, he had little if any support in the West. In Africa, she had Bonifacius, who had supported her and her son throughout her exile, while in Gaul, she had Aetius, who had supported her opponent John, but whose position was strong thanks to his connections at court and amongst the Huns. To make matters worse, the three men opposed each other and were the focus of court politics that were destined to weaken the West when it needed to be strong.

Over the course of the remainder of 425 and 426, tensions simmered beneath the surface, only tempered by the fact that Felix was in Italy, Aetius in Gaul and Bonifacius in Africa; the three men did not have much in the way of face-to-face contact, except when Aetius delivered reports to court. This was because during this period, Aetius was using the Gallic army to stabilize affairs in Gaul, including keeping the Gothic King Theoderic in check.

Civil War: Felix, Bonifacius and Aetius

In 427, matters did finally come to a head. In a complex series of manoeuvres, Felix managed to implicate Bonifacius in an attempt to seize the throne.[14] Placidia agreed to allow an army, led by Mavortius, Gallio and Sanoeces, to be sent to Africa, but Mavortius and Gallio were killed when Sanoeces defected to Bonifacius. The treachery did not benefit Sanoeces: shortly afterwards he was killed by Bonifacius and his troops swelled the ranks of the African army.

The defeat of the first campaign against Bonifacius was a major blow, both in terms of men and morale. Nevertheless, a second expedition was organized, probably in 428, this time under the command of a man named Sigisvult, who was to have a long Imperial career.[15] Realizing that an alliance with the now Mediterranean-based Vandals could help to defeat the enemy, either Felix or Sigisvult may have made a complete U-turn and attempted to recruit at least some of the Vandals to their cause, though whether these were the Vandals living in Hispania or tribesmen left behind in the Tisza basin or Pannonia remains unknown.

The imminent dispatch of a second expedition will also have worried Bonifacius. So at the same time, and possibly with more hope of success, Bonifacius may also have attempted to gain the alliance of at least some of the Vandals in Hispania:

> Thereafter access to the sea was gained by peoples who were unacquainted with ships until they were called in by the rival sides to give assistance.
>
> Prosper, *Tiro* s.a. 427

It is possible that Prosper's statement reflects the enrolment of Gothic reinforcement by Bonifacius, possibly the troops previously led by Sanoeces, the commander killed by Bonifacius.[16] Yet there may still be some truth in the concept that Vandals were included amongst those recruited by Bonifacius:

> But Bonifacius, since it did not seem to him that he was able to array himself against the emperor ... began to lay plans so that, if possible, he might have a defensive alliance with the Vandals, who ... had established themselves in [Hispania] not far from Libya. There Godigisclus had died and the royal power had fallen to his sons, Gontharis [Gunderic] ... and Gizeric [Gaiseric]. Boniface accordingly sent to Spain ... his ... most intimate friends and gained the adherence of each of the sons of Godigisclus on terms of complete equality, it being agreed that each one of the three, holding a third part of Libya, should rule over his own subjects; but if a foe should come against any one of them to make war, that they should in common ward off the aggressors.
>
> Procopius, *The Vandalic War*, 1.3.22f.

There are obviously several problems with this passage. Not least is the fact that Procopius claims that Gunderic and Gaiseric were kings of the Vandals. This implies that the embassy took place prior to 428 and the death of Gunderic, yet Hydatius strangely makes no mention of such an event. Further, the more contemporary evidence of Hydatius clearly states that Gaiseric was the successor of Gunderic, not co-ruler, with the implication being that no such embassy can ever have taken place.[17]

However, it is possible that Procopius' account contains a grain of truth. In either late 427 or early 428, envoys arrived in Hispania from Bonifacius asking for support. During the negotiations, Gunderic died. Doubtless there were many individuals – heads of families or extended families – that were unhappy with Gaiseric's accession, whether due to political or personal disagreement. These individuals, families or extended families may have felt that accepting employment within the Imperial structure, whether it be a legitimate ruler or a usurper, was better than remaining under the command of the illegitimate successor to Gunderic. The suggestion would help explain why these people(s) are stated as having been hired during the kings' 'joint tenure', as the negotiations continued after Gunderic's death. As a result, it would appear that at least a small force of Vandals agreed to join the African army and fight for Bonifacius against Sigisvult.

In addition, there is the claim that Bonifacius agreed a treaty to share Africa with the Vandals. Obviously, there would have been little difficulty in settling the Vandals in some remote area after they had arrived without the need for a risky conflict. Yet the fact that the Vandals under Gunderic made no attempt to cross to Africa, and that it was only in 429 that Gaiseric finally crossed, implies that the claim is false and is simply a standard attempt to ascribe Roman defeats to 'treachery' on behalf of individuals or 'traitorous groups', in this case Bonifacius. It almost certainly had nothing to do with Gaiseric's later invasion of Africa, as is sometimes implied, as otherwise the Vandals would have arrived at Carthage far more quickly than they did.[18]

It may also be seen as unlikely that the Vandals would agree to fight alongside the Goths, who had only the decade before so ravaged the Vandals who were now serving in the Imperial army. However, it should be noted that it was later accepted that the 'Vandals' had amongst them a contingent of Goths, so the rivalry may have been specifically related to families/tribes rather than the Vandals or Goths as a whole.[19]

The invitation is sometimes seen as being a motive for Gaiseric's later decision to cross to Africa, but this is an unnecessary complication. Africa had been a tempting target for barbarian settlement since at least 410, when Alaric had attempted to cross the Mediterranean and failed. His successor, Wallia, had also contemplated the crossing in 415.[20] That Gaiseric should consider it with his newly acquired fleet (see below) is only natural. In fact, the whole episode can be seen as envisioned by Gaiseric without outside encouragement, as will be seen.

It has also been suggested that Aetius was responsible for the Vandals crossing to Africa. This would date to after the loss of an unnamed battle alongside the Sueves in Spain.[21] This is extremely unlikely, as at this point Aetius was in no position to travel to the south of Spain, being embroiled as he was in events in Gaul and Ravenna, or negotiate with the Vandals, since his office was that of *magister militum per Gallias*.

Whatever the case, there was no recorded battle between Bonifacius and Sigisvult, and not long after the arrival of the latter, if not before, negotiations were opened between Placidia and Bonifacius. The truth of the conspiracy was revealed and Bonifacius was restored to Imperial favour. This was only just in time, as Africa was under serious barbarian threat for the first time in centuries.

The Vandals

Whilst these events had been unfolding in Italy and Africa, affairs in Hispania had taken an unexpected turn. The defeat of Castinus in 422 was to be a major watershed in the affairs of the Vandals:

> Castinus' defeat might justly be regarded as one of the most significant battles in the history of the Western Roman Empire ... At one stroke, the Hasding Vandals were transformed in the most unlikely fashion from a fugitive group, simply awaiting their coup-de-grâce, to undisputed masters of southern Spain.
> Merrills and Miles (2014), pp.46–47

The victory would have had one further effect: it would have encouraged many disaffected Romans, and free or enslaved barbarians, to swell Vandal numbers.[22]

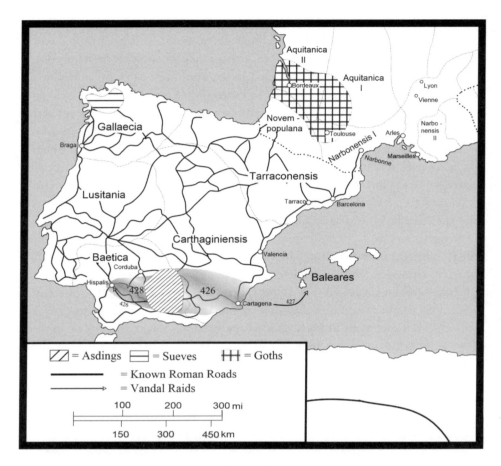

Map 5: The Move to Baetica and Later Expansion.

Not long after the battle, the Vandals migrated south to Baetica. There were doubtless many motives behind the move, including the need to find more fertile lands to support a growing population and the desire to move away from the hostile Sueves. Yet the most obvious was the fact that in Gallaecia the Vandals were vulnerable to attack. The greatest threat to the Vandals was a renewal of the alliance between the Romans and Goths which had already destroyed the Silings and Alans. The assault by Castinus' forces, which included Gothic *foederati*, was proof that Gallaecia was unsafe. Although the Siling Vandals had been settled in Baetica and almost wiped out by the Goths, the region was still far less open to attack than Gallaecia, especially if the Romans managed to form an alliance with the Sueves.

The move from Gallaecia to Baetica did not, as is usually implied, result in the Vandals immediately conquering the whole province. Instead, a people moving to find safe haven would have settled in areas where there were fewer Romans to fight and where access was slightly more difficult for an avenging Roman army. Consequently, the most likely region for them to settle was to the east and south-east of Corduba (Cordoba). They may even have moved to the places abandoned by the Siling Vandals after their defeat by the Goths. The nature of the new settlement almost certainly followed the same criteria as that of 412.

There is no indication in the sources of the precise date. However, there is one factor that is almost always overlooked when any analysis of the Vandals' motives is assessed. On 27 August 423, Honorius died in Ravenna. The news of his death, plus the elevation of John to the throne and the ensuing chaos in Italy and Constantinople, would have given the Vandals a window in which to operate. Therefore, it is plausible that the move took place either in late 423 or, more likely, in 424. It is probably safe to assume that during the remainder of 424, the Vandals spent most of their time evicting Romans from their homes, constructing their own houses in deserted areas, growing crops and breeding and raising new livestock. Consequently, it would only have been in either late 424 or more likely in 425 that Gunderic would have been able to make a first attempt at expanding his realm.

What specific actions the Vandals were actually undertaking between their resettlement and 428 is almost completely unknown. It is possible that Gunderic did not have an overall strategy, instead attacking regions at random, or that his policy is no longer visible due to the paucity of the sources. However, using the few notices in the *Chronicles*, it is possible to reconstruct a viable plan, although it should be noted that this is obviously highly conjectural.

Expansion

Hydatius gives hints as to Vandal activities in two entries (dated to 425 and 428), but their exact meanings are vague and open to widely differing interpretation: for example, there is no concord over which date the events recorded actually took place. They read as follows:

> The Vandals pillaged the Balearic Islands and when they had sacked Carthago Spartaria [Cartagena] and Hispalis [Seville], and pillaged Spain, they invaded Mauretania.
>
> Hydatius, *Chronica*, 77 [86], s.a. 425 (trans. Burgess)

> Gunderic, the king of the Vandals, captured Hispalis, but soon after, when with overweening impiety he tried to lay hands on the church of that very city, by the will of God he was seized by a demon and died.
>
> Hydatius, *Chronica*, 79 [89], s.a. 428, (trans. Burgess)

In the entry for 425, Hydatius is obviously conflating events from several years as the Vandals only invaded Mauretania in 429, unless he is referring to an earlier raid that is otherwise unrecorded. Hydatius also appears to chronicle two attacks on Seville. The entry for 428 may be a repetition in order to clarify events, yet the fact that the second entry records that Gunderic died 'soon after' the capture suggests that the Vandals did indeed attack the city twice.

The question that then arises is if Gunderic had captured the city in or around 425, why did he need to take it again in 428? There is an explanation to this dilemma. In the ancient world, when a chronicler used the word 'city', he may not have meant just the walled settlement, but also the surrounding countryside that supported the central metropolitan area. If Hydatius follows this tradition, it may indicate that the first entry recording that the Vandals 'sacked' the city may instead indicate that the Vandals simply looted the region around the city whilst the inhabitants cowered behind the walls. This hypothesis would explain why Hydatius repeats the information: in 428, the city itself was captured, at which point Gunderic attempted to 'lay hands on the church'. Although hypothesis, this is a simple way of explaining the apparent complexity in Hydatius' *Chronicle*.

Having established that there were two separate attacks on Seville, there remains a second problem. The wording (or at least the translation) implies that the Balearics were pillaged prior to the attack on Cartagena, an entry which has confused historians ever since. In order to further establish a chronology for events, it is first necessary to determine whether the Balearics were indeed attacked first.

Prior to 422, the Vandals were in Gallaecia, and it is extremely unlikely that any ships they had at that time were sent around the coast of Hispania after their migration to Baetica. It is possible that they captured unnamed minor ports between 422 and 425, and so managed to scrape together a scratch force of ships with which to attack the islands, but this seems improbable, given the likely area of their settlement (see Map 5).

Consequently, it seems more likely that the attack on the Balearic Islands only took place after the Vandals had laid their hands on a number of large, seaworthy vessels. The most obvious source would be the port of Cartagena, one of the most important ports in the western Mediterranean. Given the context, it is probably safer to assume that the crossing to the Balearics (and the possible attack on Mauretania Tingitana) took place after the assault on Cartagena and the capture of a number of ships.

Despite the fact the Gunderic took the initiative and attacked Roman territory, defence may have been at the forefront of his mind throughout this period. Given the probable location of the Vandals, the main route of any attack would most likely be down the coastal roads towards Cartagena, which would act as the main base for the Romano–Gothic forces – see Map 5. Obviously, the easiest way in which to forestall any such attack was to make a pre-emptive strike against Cartagena. In addition to the simple capture of the city, the loss of the main port in the region would make the logistics of an attack into Baetica difficult for Rome.

Consequently, when Gunderic learned of the Romano-Gothic war, and that Theoderic was besieging Arles, the Vandals moved into Carthaginiensis in 426 and attacked Cartagena, seizing the port and the ships in the harbour. At this point, Gunderic discovered that this was the main naval force in the western Mediterranean. Therefore, either later in 426 or in 427, the Vandals launched a raid on the Balearic Islands – and possibly on Mauretania, although the latter is unclear. It is likely that with more than one attack being launched, Gaiseric took command of one of the invading armies. It is possible, given his acknowledged later ability, that he was in command of the raid on the Balearics. This would help explain his actions in 460 prior to the Battle of Elche.

At around the same time as the attack on Cartagena, a small force was sent to the region of Seville. In this model, it is assumed that the sacking of Cartagena was slightly different from that of Seville: whereas the former city was captured along with the harbour and any ships that were present, only the territory of the latter was attacked, the city itself remaining secure. This would make sense, given the comparatively small numbers of warriors available to the Vandals. It may also demonstrate the strategy employed by Gunderic, with a small strike force hoping to disrupt any possible attack from Seville while the main Vandal force was occupied in taking Cartagena. This would emphasize that the Vandals were still fearful of a Roman counter-attack – although it should be noted that this is conjecture of the highest order.

It is possible that the Romans did respond to the Vandals' attack. In a problematic entry, Jordanes claims:

> Now in the twelfth year of Wallia's reign the Huns were driven out of Pannonia by the Romans and Goths, almost fifty years after they had taken possession of it. Then Wallia found that the Vandals had come forth with bold audacity from the interior of Galicia, whither Athaulf had long ago driven them, and were devastating and plundering everywhere in his own territories, namely in the land of Spain. So he made no delay but moved his army against them at once, at about the time when Hierius and Ardabures had become consuls.
>
> Jordanes, *Getica*, 166

There are many challenges with this entry. Firstly, as Wallia reigned between 415 and 419, he did not have a twelfth regnal year. It is therefore clear that Jordanes' account is open to question. However, in the last sentence he notes that Hierius and Ardabures were consuls 'at about that time'. Hierius and Ardabures were consuls in 427, and that year could mark the twelfth year of Wallia's reign – had he survived – which began in 415. Therefore, it is possible that Jordanes is recording events that belong to the later reign of Theoderic I, and concerns attempts to control the Vandals during a period of Vandal aggression, and he has simply confused the rulers.

There remains the question of when and why the Goths in Gaul would have committed to a campaign against the Vandals. With reference to the date, the most obvious set of circumstances would occur in 427–428. In 426, Theoderic and the Goths had laid siege to Arles in southern Gaul. Aetius, the Roman *magister militum per Gallias*, succeeded in forcing the Goths to withdraw from the siege and then appears to have agreed a treaty with them. However, Aetius' presence was needed along the Rhine, where the Franks had slowly infiltrated the frontier and needed to be evicted from Imperial territory.[23]

Aetius would have neither the resources to commit to campaigns on two fronts, nor permission to intervene in Hispania, as his sphere of military operations as *magister militum per Gallias* was solely Gaul. It is probable that the treaty was overseen by Felix, the *magister peditum* (master of the infantry: the senior military commander in the West), rather than Aetius. Since Felix had greater authority, it is possible that, as part of the new agreement, the Goths may have agreed to lead a campaign in Hispania.

Due to the circumstances just outlined, the chances are that any such campaign would have taken place in 427. Yet the fact that any war which took place is not mentioned by any other sources implies that it was not a major event, and that no battles were fought. It is in fact more likely that the campaign was recalled before it had reached its intended target – hence the lack of any supporting evidence. This was doubtless due to the fact that news arrived in Europe that Bonifacius had revolted in Africa. The West would need all of its troops and allies in order to retake Carthage. Although the proposition concerning this whole campaign must remain complete hypothesis, it would help to explain later events in Hispania.

Having seen a minor Gothic campaign recalled in 427, and with the West once more embroiled in a civil war, Gunderic may have become more ambitious. With Cartagena already in his hands, he now turned his attention landward. What he needed was a major city that was not vulnerable to a seaborne attack to act as his capital. His target was Seville. In 428, he captured the city and began the preparations needed to make it into a capital worthy of the Vandals, one to at least rival Toulouse, the capital of the Vandals' traditional enemy.

One of the vital amenities that were needed was a church for his Arian followers to use for worship. As a result, he attempted to convert the Catholic Church in the city to an Arian church.[24] The attempt was short-lived: not long after his attempt to seize the church in Hispalis, he unexpectedly died. As he died without nominating an heir, the crown passed to his illegitimate half-brother, Gaiseric.

Chapter 6

Gaiseric

The new king was the half-brother of the newly deceased Gunderic. Although this is the first time that he is specifically mentioned in the sources, he had taken part in everything the Vandals had done since the decision to move from Pannonia had been made.

Two ancient sources – Sidonius Apollinaris and Procopius – claim that his mother was a slave.[1] This is a distinct possibility, but as Sidonius Apollinaris is the only *contemporary* source to mention Gaiseric's parentage, and as Gaiseric was one of the Empire's major opponents – and thus a target for ridicule by propaganda – this must remain a probability rather than a certainty. However, if true, it attests to the fact that his ability as a politician and general was recognized by those around him: 'His ability was so exceptional that his irregular birth ... did not diminish his influence and prestige.'[2] It is also claimed by Procopius that the two siblings had shared the kingship prior to Gunderic's death, but there is no evidence for this in contemporary sources.[3]

We actually know very little about the man who would go on to become the most effective enemy of the Roman Empire. Born around AD 389, by 428 he was approximately 30 years of age. Apart from having to guess at his age, the only pieces of information we have are a snippet from Hydatius, a hint of his personality from Procopius and a brief physical description from Jordanes. According to Hydatius, Gaiseric had begun life as a Catholic, but had later converted to Arianism, thus becoming an 'apostate'.[4] Although a possibility if, as noted earlier, his mother was a Roman slave, even Hydatius is forced to admit that this is a 'story that some relate', so may be a propaganda invention to create a 'demonic' image of Gaiseric in the eyes of Hydatius' Catholic Roman readers.

In his description of a peace treaty between Rome and the Vandals, Procopius portrays Gaiseric as a man with 'foresight worth recounting', who was 'not lifted up by the good fortune he had enjoyed, but rather became moderate because of what he feared', and as someone who 'showed himself a brave man in the battle'.[5] Procopius also compares Gaiseric favourably to Theoderic the Great, the king of the Ostrogoths in Italy.[6]

The portrayal is in some ways reinforced by Jordanes, who gives slightly more detail in his description of the new king:

> Gaiseric, still famous in the City for the disaster of the Romans, was a man of moderate height and lame in consequence of a fall from his horse. He was a man of deep thought and few words, holding luxury in disdain, furious in his anger, greedy for gain, shrewd in winning over the barbarians and skilled in sowing the seeds of dissension to arouse enmity.
>
> Jordanes, *Getica*, 168

Although this portrayal includes the attributes of scorning luxury, being quick to anger and of having a propensity for greed – typical of Roman writers when describing barbarians – the depiction of Gaiseric as 'a man of deep thought' and 'skilled at sowing the seeds of dissension' may be more accurate than expected. The story of his life shows many occasions when he appears to have been remarkably intelligent, a shrewd strategist and an excellent diplomat who used the maxim 'divide and conquer' to his great advantage.

On the other hand, this is the only mention of Gaiseric having a physical infirmity. Although it is possible that he had been made lame by a fall from his horse, as this is nowhere else attested, the description must be assumed to be a possibility, rather than a fact.

It is possible, given later examples, that Gaiseric – and possibly even Gunderic before him – had adopted the title *Rex Vandalorum et Alanorum* (King of the Vandals and Alans), but this is not specifically noted in contemporary accounts. Direct evidence of the title only comes from the later reigns of Huneric and Gelimer.[7] Yet even if the title was only assumed by later kings, it is clear that during the reigns of Gunderic and Gaiseric, the Siling Vandals quickly lost their identity as a sub-group, simply being absorbed by the Asdings. The same may be said of other people who joined the coalition, whether free Roman, barbarian or ex-slave. However, the Alans appear to have retained their individual customs and so maintained themselves as a separate entity within the coalition.

428

Gaiseric inherited a 'kingdom' that in only a short time had gone from being a nonentity on the northern fringes of Hispania to one which held a large swathe of territory in southern Hispania, including at least two major cities, one of which was a key Mediterranean port. At this point, the concept of the Vandals having a major effect on the Empire's future remained inconceivable, despite their control of a large part of southern Hispania – 'at this time the move to Africa was not an obvious step'.[8] This was probably because even at the time it was noted that Gaiseric only ruled 'a relatively small tribe'.[9] Yet over the next few years, the Vandals were to emerge as a major political force.

Given the fact that the Vandals probably captured Seville during the campaign season of 428, this would mean that Gaiseric came to power in mid- to late-428. There can be little doubt that he spent the rest of the year establishing firm control of his kingdom. Yet he was clearly not content just to rule in the south of Hispania. Over the course of the winter and into the new year, Gaiseric had already begun preparations for a new adventure: the crossing of the Straits of Gibraltar and the move to Africa.

The African Question

Having dismissed the alleged treaty with Bonifacius (see Chapter 5), there remains the question as to why Gaiseric took the major step of committing his people to the crossing to Africa. Whether Gunderic had also planned to cross the Straits is completely unknown. It may be that the capture of the ships at Cartagena, plus the realization that there was no other Roman fleet in the area to oppose a crossing, had resulted in Gunderic deciding that the crossing to Africa was feasible. On the other hand, the attempt to convert the Church in Seville into an Arian foundation implies that Seville was to be a Vandal city for several years to come, which in turn suggests that Gunderic planned to spend some time in southern Hispania.

It is feasible that during the alleged raid on the province of Tingitana, the Vandals became aware that Roman West Africa was only lightly defended. Of more significance, there were major links between Baetica and Tingitana, both economically and politically, as Tingitana was part of the Diocese of Hispania, not, as might have been expected, that of Africa.[10] This may have made gaining information about the region easier, enhancing Gunderic's perception of Africa as poorly defended but economically profitable. The lack of opposition to the Vandal fleet, plus intelligence that Mauretania Tingitana was only lightly defended, ensured that Gaiseric would at least consider the possibility.

These were not the only relevant motives for the decision. As noted in Chapter 5, it is possible that a Gothic campaign had materialized in 427. Although of limited strength and duration, it may have convinced Gaiseric that as long as the Vandals remained in Hispania, they would be vulnerable to attack by the Romans, Goths, Sueves or, even more to be feared, an alliance of the three. More than anything, the Vandals needed to move to a place where they would be free from attack by the Goths and Sueves.

A second motive is that the Vandals had already defeated one major Roman attack in 422, so the Roman Army was almost certainly less-feared than either the Goths or Sueves. Furthermore, the major Roman armies were needed to maintain the Empire's position in Italy and Gaul. Therefore, it may have been felt that once in Africa, the Vandals would have more chance of gaining a treaty, as the Romans would be unable to mount a major counter-attack with their armies needed elsewhere.

A third motive is that from at least the time of Alaric, king of the Goths (d. 410), there had been a desire amongst barbarian invaders of the Empire to reach Africa, probably due to the perception that it was a region rich in resources and only lightly defended.[11] Information received in Seville would only have enhanced this observation.

Yet the major factor would have been that Gaiseric was encouraged by news of the ongoing civil war between Bonifacius and the Imperial forces. Gaiseric would have already learned of the defeat of the first expedition under Mavortius, Gallio and Sanoeces, and the arrival of a new expedition under Sigisvult. He would obviously have expected the opposing Roman armies to face each other in battle, leaving the Vandals free to advance along the northern coast.

In addition, news would by now have arrived in Hispania of further events in Africa. Adding to Bonifacius' problems, the civil war had encouraged some of the African tribes to rebel and attack the Romans. In a letter dated to 427, Augustine complained to Bonifacius:

> But what shall I say of the devastation of Africa at this hour by hordes of African barbarians, to whom no resistance is offered, while you are engrossed with such embarrassments in your own circumstances, and are taking no measures for averting this calamity? Who would ever have believed, who would have feared, after Bonifacius had become a Count of the Empire and of Africa, and had been placed in command in Africa with so large an army and so great authority, that the same man who formerly, as Tribune, kept all these barbarous tribes in peace, by storming their strongholds, and menacing them with his small band of brave confederates, should now have suffered the barbarians to be so bold, to encroach so far, to destroy and plunder so much, and to turn into deserts such vast regions once densely peopled? Where were any found that did not predict that, as soon as you obtained the authority of Count, the African hordes would be not only checked, but made tributaries to the Roman Empire? And now, how completely the event has disappointed men's hopes you yourself perceive; in fact, I need say nothing more on this subject, because your own reflection must suggest much more than I can put in words.
>
> Augustine, *Epistle*, 220.7

With all of these factors in mind, Gaiseric made the easiest of his political decisions: he would cross to Africa with his people and attempt to carve out a kingdom there, free from attack by the Goths or Sueves.

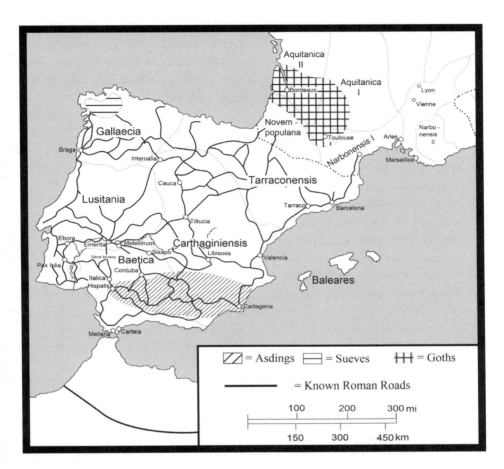

Map 6: Heremigarius and the Emigration.

429

When he presented this idea to his people, he may have received a surprise. It is usually accepted that Gaiseric led the whole of the Vandals and Alans to Africa. However, it is possible that some of them had no desire to go on yet another long exodus, and instead wished to remain in Hispania.[12] These may have now separated from the main body of the Vandals under the leadership of an individual named Andevotus, who is attested as being active in Hispania in the next decade.[13] Andevotus is otherwise unknown; he may not have been associated with the Vandals, and may instead have been an (Ostro)Goth.[14] On the other hand, by this time the Vandals were no longer a distinct 'ethnic' group, but rather composed of a core of true Vandals alongside many former slaves, ex-Roman citizens, Alans, Goths and others of unknown origin. As a result, it is possible that, although not originally a Vandal himself, Andevotus may still have been the leader of a group of people who had originally been part of the 'Vandal confederacy'.

However, the main body at least of the people agreed to follow Gaiseric. With his heart set on a move to Africa, he began to move his people and his fleet towards the Straits of Gibraltar. At this point, Gaiseric received disturbing news:

> In the month of May, King Gaiseric abandoned [Hispania] and with all the Vandals and their families crossed over from the shores of the province of Baetica to Mauretania and Africa. Before crossing, he was warned that the Sueve Heremigarius was passing through the neighbouring provinces and pillaging them as he went. Gaiseric therefore doubled back with some of his men and followed the Sueve as he plundered in Lusitania. Not far from Emerita, which Heremigarius had scorned, thereby causing an affront to the holy martyr Eulalia, Gaiseric slaughtered the accursed soldiers who were with the Sueve, but Heremigarius, who thought that he had saved himself by turning to flight more swiftly than the wind, was cast headlong into the river Ana by the hand of God and died ... Soon afterwards Gaiseric sailed off to his original destination.
>
> Hydatius, *Chronicle*, 80 [90] s.a. 429

This passage has confused historians for many years. It is usually assumed that the Vandals were already at the crossing place when news arrived of Heremigarius' presence in Lusitania. Although described by Hydatius as 'king of the Sueves', it is more likely that he was either a son of Hermeric, the actual king at this time, or an unrelated noble.[15] The question then is why Gaiseric, poised to cross to Africa, travelled so far out of his way to defeat the Sueves? A close scrutiny of the passage, plus analysis of when, how and from where the Vandals began their move, suggests a completely different series of events.

It is almost certain that the main body of the migrants met up at Seville (Hispalis) prior to moving towards the crossing point. Seville, a major town at the centre of a road network, had the logistics necessary for the massing of large numbers of people and the supplies necessary for the long journey ahead. Although many migrants would have joined the journey en route, it is from Seville that the main body began the journey.

The problems with the passage in Hydatius lies with a common difficulty with ancient Chronicles: the inclusion in one entry of several events which are not in chronological order. It is therefore necessary to analyze the passage one sentence at a time.

The first sentence simply records the crossing of the Vandals from Baetica to Africa. As all of the shortest crossings are from Baetica, rather than one of the other provinces, this statement needs no further analysis. Hydatius does give us the month of May as the date for the crossing, but sadly there is no mention of a specific location for either the departure or landing points.

The second sentence contains the first piece of information that can cause difficulty: 'Before crossing, he was warned …' The only chronological reference here is that the attack on Heremigarius came before the crossing. However, it is not stated how long before, and although it is usually accepted that the Vandals had arrived at the Straits prior to receiving the news, it is also possible that it arrived before their arrival at the Straits.

This concept may be reinforced by the wording used by Hydatius in the third sentence, where he states that 'Gaiseric therefore doubled back with some of his men and followed the Sueve as he plundered in Lusitania'. To 'double back' usually suggests a forward movement that is then reversed. It would therefore appear that news of Heremigarius' raid arrived whilst the Vandals were still on the move.

There remains the question of why Gaiseric took the time to double back and attack Heremigarius. A hint of the reason can be found in the latter part of the second sentence: 'Heremigarius was passing through the neighbouring provinces and pillaging them as he went.' There were only two provinces that had borders with Baetica: Lusitania and Carthaginiensis. This implies that Heremigarius was raiding both provinces to the north of Baetica. Interestingly, Hydatius later includes a small piece of relevant information when he states that Heremigarius 'scorned' Emerita. Unless he took a very long detour to the north around Emerita, this implies that he must have turned south and entered Baetica. This would pose a distinct threat to the Vandals as they moved.

All of the above suggests that Heremigarius led his forces south from Gallaecia into Carthaginiensis – doubtless encouraged by the unrest provoked by the Vandals' capture of Cartagena and Seville. If, as is probable, he used the Roman roads to ease his travels, then his possible route can be traced as he travelled first south and then across the region from east to west.

A potential itinerary would have taken Heremigarius from Gallaecia via Intercalia, Cauca and Titulcia, possibly as far as Libisoba. At this point, learning of the gathering of the Vandals ready for the crossing, he may have changed direction, hoping to take advantage of the Vandals' actions, travelling west via Sisapo and Metellinum towards Emerita, before skirting the latter – where he could expect strong resistance as it was still in Roman hands and therefore may have had a strong garrison – before turning south to Uguitunia. He may have travelled south as far as Italica, but it is more likely that he instead turned west at Uguitunia. It was either at Uguitunia or Italica that he probably learned of Gaiseric's approach and fled west, entering Lusitania.

If the above journey is in any way accurate, it would have been when Heremigarius reached the region of Metellinum or Emerita that Gaiseric learned of his presence. At this point it is necessary to refer back to Hydatius' account: 'Gaiseric therefore doubled back with some of his men and followed the Sueve as he plundered in Lusitania. Not far from Emerita … Gaiseric slaughtered the accursed soldiers who were with the Sueve, but Heremigarius, who thought that he had saved himself by turning to flight more swiftly than the wind, was cast headlong into the river Ana by the hand of God.'

The main Roman road from this region runs west to Pax Iulia. Heremigarius would not have attempted to cross the Sierra Morena, as it would be easy to be trapped in the unknown hills and mountains. Instead he would have kept to the main roads. He may have hoped that a rapid flight towards Lusitania would have caused Gaiseric to give up the chase. If so, he was to be disappointed: Gaiseric remained in close pursuit. At Pax Iulia, Heremigarius took the northern road towards Ebora and then the route north-east to Emerita.

Almost certainly laden with booty, Heremigarius would have stood no chance of evading the fast-moving pursuers. Near to Emerita, Gaiseric caught him and his forces were quickly defeated, Heremigarius himself drowning as he tried to cross the River Ana.

There remains the question as to why Gaiseric took such drastic action? Although the route taken by Heremigarius would have threatened his rear, once the Sueves began to leave the region during the pursuit, Gaiseric could have halted his troops and returned to the main body.

There is no doubt that Gaiseric did not have enough ships to ferry the Vandals to Africa in one crossing, and it would take a long time for the ships to cross to Africa. There would then be the need to disembark the passengers before the ships returned to Hispania for a second trip – and possibly even a third or many more. If Gaiseric was to begin crossing to Africa, the Vandals awaiting the return of ships for their own turn to cross would be vulnerable to attack. Although the Sueves were a long way from the crossing point, given the time necessary for the return of the ships it was plausible that the Sueves could return and attack the remaining Vandals. This was an unacceptable risk and explains why Gaiseric took the decision to chase the Sueves until they had been destroyed.

The Crossing

Several different dates are given by the ancient sources for the Vandals' crossing to Africa, as a result of which the dating of the crossing is insecure.[16] Yet the fact that Hydatius is a contemporary source living in Hispania means that his date is usually accepted – especially as, unlike some of the others, it gives adequate time for all of

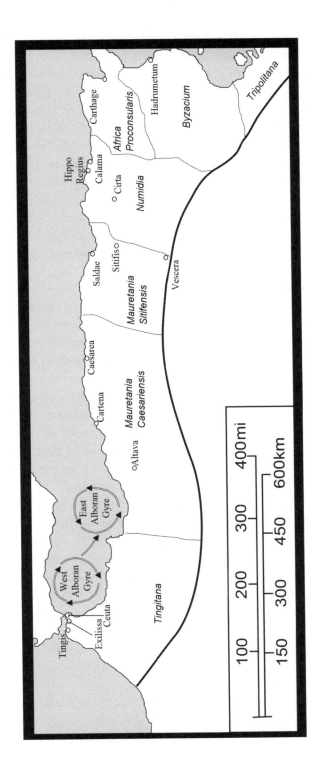

Map 7: The Vandals Cross to Africa.

the other events chronicled to take place.[17] As a result, what follows is based upon the date of May 429 for the crossing.

According to Victor of Vita, the Vandals at the crossing into Africa were organized into eighty '*thusundifaths*', each of 1,000 people. This figure was accepted during the nineteenth and early-twentieth centuries, but it has recently been questioned with reference to logistical analysis.[18] In addition, it has been noticed that Victor also states that the total claimed by Gaiseric was propaganda, being an attempt to convince onlookers that the forces crossing to Africa were larger than they actually were: Gaiseric had already shown himself an able propagandist with a view on future possibilities.[19] As a result, it is clear that the whole population was certainly less than 80,000 – perhaps around 70,000, or possibly even lower. Possibly more accurate, writing in the sixth century, Procopius noted the claim that there were 80,0000 Vandals, but suggested that the actual number was 50,000.[20]

Accepting the number of 80,000 at face value, but even downscaling the figure to around 50,000 people, the transfer of so large a number, along with their supplies, possessions and possibly even some of their flocks, would not have been a speedy operation as Gaiseric did not have a large number of ships. As a result, it is likely that the crossing took many return journeys, and so could easily have extended into June or even July 429.

Given the timescale involved, it may seem surprising that the Romans did not gather a fleet with which to oppose the Vandals. However, even if the news had reached either Italy or Carthage in time, the main fleet from the Western Mediterranean – minus the ships captured by the Vandals in Hispania – was being used to transport, guard and supply the forces being used by Sigisvult for the war against Bonifacius. The Vandals were completely unopposed.

The sources fail to give a precise location for either the place of departure or that of landing. As a result, it is necessary to resort to speculation. There are several places in southern Hispania that could have been the stepping-off point for the crossing, but two stand out more than the others simply due to their extreme southern location giving the shortest route across the Straits.

One is Carteia, a city on the southern extremity of the Bay of Gibraltar. This would allow the Vandals access to the Straits from a small port, where embarkation would be easier. The only difficulty here is that the city had a defensible wall and there is no indication in the sources of the city either being under Vandal control or of any attack being mounted before the crossing, which may have been of interest to a chronicler such as Hydatius.

A second possibility, and perhaps the most likely, is Mellaria (near Talifa). Although its precise location is open to question, interestingly, Pliny the Elder in his *Natural History* notes that the narrowest part of the Strait was between

Mellaria and the *Promonturium Album* (White Promontory) on the coast of Africa.[21] Mellaria also may have had a wall and have been defended, and so liable to the same caveats as Carteia. On the other hand, the Vandals would have known that this was supposedly the nearest place to Africa and therefore the best location to begin the transportation of large numbers of people. Consequently, it will be assumed that the Vandals followed the Roman roads round to Mellaria, with its small port, and from there began the long process of shipping the whole population across the Straits.

There remains the problem of locating a suitable landing place in Africa. Here, the knowledge gained from the close connections between Mauretania Tingitana and Baetica would have helped the Vandals. What they needed was a secure landing area which was safe from attack by any Roman forces in Tingitana.

There are few places in the region that qualify, simply because the most obvious were already populated and defended by Romans. However, there was one place that was suitable because it was midway between Tingis (Tangier) and Abyla (Ceuta – at that time possibly including a Roman fortress named *Castellum ad Septem Fratres*). It was thus the safest place from an immediate attack by Roman forces either in the city or the fortress.

The place was called Exilissa (Qasr al-Saghir), a bay protected by a natural buttress.[22] Access to the town by land was difficult, meaning that the Vandals would have time to transport a large number of people across the Straits before they were attacked by any Roman defenders. Of more importance, the Vandals would be able to travel between the two ports without needing to traverse the Straits themselves. Although they may have considered crossing the western Mediterranean, they may have been warned that sailing could be difficult thanks to the Alboran Gyres, a pair of large water currents formed by the entry of Atlantic waters into the Mediterranean, although this is open to question. Whatever the case, the Vandals probably spent a long time ferrying their peoples and belongings between Hispania and Africa.

The Vandal Army

A population of 50,000 would have given the Vandals an army of, at the most, around 20,000 fighting men.[23] The composition of this force is unknown, but it is likely that at least some horses would have been ferried to Africa, as the fame of the Alans rested upon their horsemanship, and without their horses they may have refused to cross the Straits. The same goes for the Vandal noblemen: the need to ferry horses for the Alans would have resulted in a great amount of pressure being placed on Gaiseric by his nobles to ensure that their mounts were also carried across the Straits.

As a result, it is clear that the Vandals would have access to a fair proportion of cavalry, with the nobles mounted and fighting as impact cavalry. Modern assumptions tend to categorize cavalry largely by their weaponry. The majority of the Alans were probably armed with bows and swords, with some possibly also bearing spears or lances. As a result, it is usually assumed that the Alans were skirmishing cavalry who would use their bows in an attempt to weaken and disorder the enemy. However, they could almost certainly have also fought in closer order as impact troops. Therefore, the cavalry were certainly able to hold their own against all Roman cavalry, except for the very heavily armed and trained.

The cavalry would have numbered around 2,000 at most: any more would have severely limited the ability of the Vandals to cross the Straits. This number of horses would also mean that the crossing took a long time and helps explain why Gaiseric was intent upon removing any threat to the Vandals in Hispania as they crossed.

If the Vandals numbered around 20,000, this would mean that the remaining 18,000 were infantry, with the majority armed with a spear, sword and possibly a seax (short sword or dagger) or other short stabbing weapon as a last-minute backup. Some of these troops, especially the young, may have been employed as skirmishers, operating in front of the main body in battle to disrupt enemy formations. There may also have been archers and slingers in the army, but if so, the numbers of these troops is completely unknown.

Whatever the numbers and proportions, the fact that the army was by chance a well-balanced force, with both cavalry and infantry able to skirmish, meant that as the Vandals advanced along the North African coastline, they would be able to put out a line of scouts in front of the main force. In this way they would be able to detect any opposition, as well as locate both loot and supplies as they moved.

Into Africa

Landing in Mauretania Tingitana, Gaiseric may have expected to face at least token resistance, but previous experience would have shown that a major counter-attack was most unlikely. According to the *Notitia Dignitatum*, the *comes Tingitana* had a maximum of 5,000–7,000 men: but many were second-class troops, so only a maximum of around 1,500 would have been capable of facing Gaiseric's battle-hardened veterans.[24] Unsurprisingly, the local commander made no attempt to stop the Vandals. However, he undoubtedly sent news of the crossing to both Carthage and Italy.

Victor of Vita states that 'news of this [number of 80,000] had spread widely', but that he was informing people of the true nature of the crossing.[25] It made little difference: as the Vandals advanced, petrified bishops were to write to Augustine, bishop of Hippo, to ask him whether it was right to allow their flocks to flee from the approaching danger and for themselves to abandon their sees.[26] Augustine – later Saint Augustine – replied that 'the bishop should let the people flee, but not abandon his post so long as his presence was needed'. It would appear that Gaiseric's propaganda had worked: rumour had spread in Africa that the Vandals had crossed with 80,000 fighting men, causing a panic which the Vandals were to take full advantage of.

After the landing in Africa, Gaiseric regrouped his people. This would have taken some time to organize, so it is unlikely that they began to move east before the end of June, if not later. As they travelled, they devastated the surrounding regions, committing the usual ravages by invading armies of plunder and rape.[27] Apart from personal gratification, this was both to cause panic and part of their constant need for supplies:[28]

> But a short time after this it came about, in accordance with the divine will and command, that a great host of savage foes, Vandals and Alans, with some of the Gothic tribe interspersed, and various other peoples, armed with all kinds of weapons and well trained in warfare, came by ship from the regions of Spain across the sea and poured into Africa and overran it. And everywhere through the regions of Mauretania, even crossing over to other of our provinces and territories, raging with cruelty and barbarity, they completely devastated everything they could by their pillage, murder and varied tortures, conflagrations and other innumerable and unspeakable crimes, sparing neither sex nor age, nor even the priests or ministers of God, nor yet the ornaments or vessels of the churches nor even the buildings.
>
> Possidius, *Vita S. Augustini*, 28

The claim by Possidius that the invaders included 'some of the Gothic tribe' implies that at some point a large number of Goths had joined the Vandals. The most obvious supply of such recruits dates to 422, when the Romans under Castinus had attacked the Vandals, but Castinus had been defeated due to the 'treachery' of his Gothic auxiliaries.[29] Hydatius gives no clue as to the form of this 'treachery', but given later events, and the fact that there is no mention of any other Gothic force joining the Vandals, the likelihood is that in 422 the Gothic auxiliaries had defected to the Vandals, remaining a separate group, and joining in the crossing to Africa.

However, it is also claimed that they were the entourage of Bonifacius' wife, Pelagia, who is described as a 'Gothic princess' by both Merobaudes and Sidonius Apollinaris.[30] The suggestion is that upon her marriage, she was probably followed by a small band of loyal retainers. These, for an unknown reason, may have then rebelled and joined Gaiseric. However, as no cause for their rebellion is forthcoming, this must be deemed unlikely. There is a further suggestion that they were followers of Sanoeces, who, after their leader's death at the hands of Bonifacius, took the first opportunity to desert to the Vandals.[31] As they had good reason for betraying Bonifacius, this must remain a viable alternative. Finally, it has also been suggested that the Gothic contingent were troops left behind to help in the defence of Africa by Sigisvult when he returned to Italy, but who had rebelled and joined the Vandals. Again, as with the proposal that they were Pelagia's entourage, no reason is given for their betrayal, so this must remain unlikely.

Possidius carries on with a list of the depredations of the Vandals:

> cities overthrown in destruction, and the resident citizens, together with the buildings on their lands, partly annihilated by the enemy's slaughter and others driven into flight and dispersed ... churches stripped of priests and ministers, and holy virgins and all the monastics scattered in every direction ... some succumb to torture and others slain by the sword, while still others in captivity, losing their innocence and faith both in soul and body, received from their foes the harsh and evil treatment of slaves ... the hymns and praises of God perish from the churches; the church buildings in many places consumed by fire; the regular services which were due to God cease from their appointed places; the holy sacraments no longer desired, or if someone did desire them, no one could easily be found to administer them. When they gathered in flight amid the mountain forests, in the caves and caverns of the rocks or in any other kind of retreat, some were captured and put to death while others were robbed and deprived of the necessary means of sustenance so that they gradually perished of hunger. Even the bishops of the churches and the clergy who, by the help of God, did not chance to meet the foe or, if they did meet them, escaped their hands, he saw despoiled and stripped of all their goods and begging in abject poverty, nor could they all be furnished with that by which they might be relieved.
>
> Possidius, *Vita S. Augustini*, 28

Although the passage has previously been accepted at face value, more modern analysis has concluded that the description is almost certainly exaggerated. For example, Possidius, the Catholic bishop of Calama, was himself later exiled by the Arian heretic Gaiseric; hence the overly dramatic invective against the Vandals. On the other hand, it is possible that Optatus, bishop of Vescera in Mauretania Sitifensis, fled to Rome as the Vandals advanced on the city, so it is at least understandable that garbled accounts of Vandal atrocities were spread from a very early stage of the invasion.[32] Yet given the time it took to traverse the North African coastline, they would certainly have not had the time to devastate the region in this manner. The distance is around 1,000 miles (1,600km), and it was only in the following year, 430, that they arrived in the region of Hippo. The question which then arises is why the Romans failed to oppose them during their long journey. The answer to that lies in events which were taking place simultaneously in Carthage.

Bonifacius

Whilst the Vandals had been ferrying their people across the Straits of Gibraltar in 429, an envoy from Placidia had reached Bonifacius. A man named Darius arrived and a truce had been called to allow negotiations to take place. Either before or shortly after the Vandal migration, the truth concerning Bonifacius' disgrace had emerged, and Placidia and Bonifacius had become reconciled. It would appear from events that Sigisvult had returned to Italy, but not before leaving some of his Gothic *foederati* behind to help in the defence of Africa.

When the news reached Gaiseric, he no doubt decided that caution was the best strategy. Ordering his fleet to move along the north coast of Africa – possibly keeping it filled with provisions and so keeping his baggage train to a minimum – Gaiseric kept pace with the fleet but would certainly have maintained a screen of scouts, both to keep him informed of the regional topography and to warn him of any impending attack by Roman troops. Furthermore, he would have continuously had a proportion of his troops out foraging for the supplies needed to keep such a large number of people constantly supplied. However, the main factor restricting the manoeuvrability of the Vandals was the slow pace of the women, children, elderly and any baggage animals and wagons being used.

The actual route of their advance is unknown, but there can be little doubt that it followed the course of the Roman roads along the northern coast of Africa. He may also have stopped to attack or at least plunder the hinterland of the cities that were on the route of his march, including Cartena, Caesarea, Saldae and possibly Sitifis, further inland. Alongside the earlier description given by Possidius, Victor of Vita describes the massive devastation of cities and demolition of buildings, but it is clear from alternative evidence that he exaggerates the destructive impact of the Vandals: little if any other literary or archaeological evidence of destruction survives.[33]

Possibly the only direct evidence for the Vandals' march is a funerary inscription from Altava, dating to August 429, which includes the mention of the deceased being 'struck down' by a 'barbarian':[34]

--- --- ---

1   KALSEM
    ANNOPROCCCXC

3   GLADIOP*ABARBAROS

---discessit ---]
Kal(endas) se(pte)m[bres]
Anno pro(uinciae) cccxc
Gladio p(ercessus) a barbaros

It is likely that the 'barbarians' in question were the Vandals on their long journey across North Africa. However, the description by Augustine of the 'devastation of Africa at this hour by hordes of African barbarians' means that the attribution is insecure.[35]

Whether the Vandals were responsible for the individual's death or not, they continued their migration across Africa until they finally arrived in Africa Proconsularis. Bypassing Cirta, they appear to have headed towards Hippo Regius (Annaba).[36] At this point they halted. Darius, the man who had negotiated a peace between Bonifacius and Sigisvult, convinced the Vandals to accept a truce and halt their advance.[37] It is possible that Verimodus, the son of Darius, may have acted as a hostage.[38]

The Battle and Siege of Hippo Regius

The truce was short-lived: whatever the Romans offered in exchange for peace was unacceptable to Gaiseric. Early in 430, the Vandals continued their journey – doubtless much to the disappointment of Darius – and approached Hippo Regius. Confident in his own military ability and the superiority of his troops over 'barbarians', Bonifacius led his men out and met the Vandals in battle.

The size and deployment of the opposing forces are completely unknown. If the figures quoted above for the Vandal crossing to Africa are correct, then the Vandals mustered at most between 15,000 and 20,000 fighting men. The number of troops in Bonifacius' Roman army is completely unknown. In theory, the *Notitia Dignitatum* can be used to calculate the force. According to the *Notitia Dignitatum*, the commander in Africa should have had thirty-one *comitatenses* (field) units and twenty-two *limitanei* (garrison) units stationed in Tripolitania and Numidia. This gives a total of approximately 35,000 men.[39] Yet by this time the *Notitia*, compiled around 420, was completely out of date, partly due to the passage of time, but mostly due to the fact that the army had been in constant use since Bonifacius took command in Africa in 422–423.

Since then, the army had been employed when Bonifacius first took control to defeat the Moorish rebels and again to defend against the Moors when they rebelled for a second time due to the outbreak of the civil war. It had then fought in the civil war, no doubt incurring some losses, but also possibly received troops as reinforcements: the Goths of Sanoeces and possibly even some of the troops brought in by Sigisvult. As a result, any attempt to estimate the strength of the Roman forces is merely guesswork. All that can be said with certainty is that if it was outnumbered by the Vandals, it was not by much – otherwise, Bonifacius may not have risked a battle.

However, the majority of these troops were used to dealing with minor border raids and supervision of the movement of nomadic tribes through the provinces. These men were not of the same quality as the Vandal and Alan warriors who had been fighting across Western Europe for the previous twenty years. Yet it may be that numbers were not to be the determining factor in the upcoming battle: it is likely that the outcome was to be determined by the quality of the opposing commanders.[40]

Bonifacius had a good reputation as a general, and was renowned for having injured Athaulf, the Gothic king, during Athaulf's attempt to take Marseille in 413. However, whether it was because he was unexpectedly outnumbered, or because Gaiseric was a general of exceptional talent, Bonifacius was defeated in battle. The survivors, including Bonifacius, retired to the safety of Hippo.[41]

Gaiseric, taking full advantage of his victory, called up his ships and, in May or June 430, the city was laid under siege:[42]

> [The] enemy also came to besiege the city of the Hippo-Regians which had so far maintained its position. With its defence at this time ... Count Boniface had been entrusted with an army of allied Goths. For almost fourteen months they shut up and besieged the city; and they even cut off its sea-coast by blockade. We ourselves with other of our fellow-bishops from the neighbouring regions took refuge in this city and remained in it during the whole time of the siege.
>
> Possidius, *Vita S. Augustini*, 28

Interestingly, and counter to the arguments that the Goths in Gaiseric's army had deserted Bonifacius', Possidius claims that the main force defending the city was Goths.

The siege soon became a desperate affair. Unlike most other sieges of coastal towns by barbarians, the Vandals were able to completely cut all supply lines into the city due to their possession of a fleet.[43] As the siege continued, the priests in the city, including Augustine, prayed for help.[44] However, on 28 August 430, in the third month of the siege, Augustine died.[45] Despite the loss of a great source of moral strength, Bonifacius continued to lead the resistance.

Sadly for Gaiseric, the Vandals themselves were suffering. The besiegers were not just an army: they included very large numbers of the old, women and children, non-combatants who weakened the attack by using supplies that would have allowed the besiegers to last longer than the besieged. The Vandals quickly began to feel the effects of the siege as much as those trapped inside Hippo. Despite these problems, the siege was maintained. Stretched on all fronts, and unsure of events in Africa, the West was unable to send troops to help Bonifacius: instead, Rome appears to have relied upon appeals to the East to supply the troops needed.

Aspar

After fourteen months of siege, hunger and the inevitable diseases were ravaging both the city inhabitants and the Vandals outside the walls.[46] The Vandals appear, like most German tribesmen, to have been poor in the art of siege warfare. Running out of provisions themselves, and with disease spreading amongst their dependants, they raised the siege in July or August.[47]

The move was none too soon. In the early months of 431, the Eastern Empire had decided that the Vandals were enough of a threat to help the West, and an expedition was prepared for Africa.[48] As a result, and unannounced, the Eastern *magister utriusque militiae* Aspar arrived with reinforcements from both East and West.[49] Aspar, son of the Eastern *magister militum* Ardabur, had already played a role in Western affairs, taking control of part of the invasion force which had overthrown the usurper John in 425. Aspar's arrival is evidence of continued negotiations between East and West concerning the condition of Africa, possibly under Aetius' direction, and illustrates that the two halves of the Empire still saw themselves as being united in their rule.[50]

432: The Second Battle of Hippo Regius

Heartened by the arrival of reinforcements, Bonifacius, accompanied by Aspar, led the joint forces to meet the Vandals in early 432. Somewhere to the west of Hippo Regius, the two sides met in a second battle. The Vandals were again victorious, forcing the Romans to retreat.[51] It is after this defeat that the future emperor Marcian, at the time serving as Aspar's *domesticus*, was captured by Gaiseric.[52] According to later legend, Gaiseric witnessed an omen that Marcian was destined to be emperor, and as a consequence he was released after having promised never to attack the Vandals.[53] However, this episode would appear to be a later invention to excuse Marcian's refusal to attack the Vandals after he became emperor in 450.[54] Instead, it has been proposed that after his capture and release, Marcian became the official Roman envoy between Aspar and Gaiseric, during which period Gaiseric impressed Aspar and Marcian with his personality and ability.[55] A Vandal named John, who later rose to prominence in the East, may have been the Vandal envoy.[56]

Unlike the previous battle, Bonifacius bypassed Hippo after the defeat, almost certainly because he did not want to experience a second siege. The decision left Hippo undefended: '[T]he city of Hippo, abandoned by its inhabitants, was burned by the enemy.'[57] It is to be expected that the sack of the city was particularly savage due to the suffering caused amongst the Vandals by its earlier refusal to surrender. Vandal raiding parties were then dispatched to ravage the whole of the province, most likely simply in their continuous search for supplies. Apparently, the only cities that escaped without major damage were Cirta, Hippo and Carthage. This suggests that Bonifacius was able to organize garrisons to defend these major strategic points, and that Gaiseric was unwilling to risk an attack that could weaken his position, at least without good reason.

Unknown to the Vandals, their defeat of Bonifacius and Aspar was to be another major turning point in their history: shortly afterwards, a new outbreak of internal intrigue was to leave the Vandals free from attack in Africa. Instead, the Roman troops in the region, led by the Eastern general Aspar, would attempt simply to limit Vandal attacks, but there would be no threat of a major battle. Instead, Roman eyes turned back to Italy.

Chapter 7

Settlement

Whilst the Vandals had been fighting Bonifacius, developments were occurring elsewhere in the Western Empire that would drastically affect their future. In AD 427, a Roman civil war had begun after accusations were made, probably by the *magister militum* Felix, concerning Bonifacius' desire to become emperor. Once the truth that the accusations were baseless became known, Placidia had made Aetius *magister militum*, possibly as a counter-balance to Felix.[1]

However, little could be done to help Bonifacius against the Vandals, as Aetius had been forced to undertake 430 fighting successful campaigns against invading tribesmen in Gaul and Raetia.[2] Also in 430, at around the same time as the Vandals had defeated Bonifacius and besieged Hippo, the *magister militum* Felix was killed, possibly with the collusion of Placidia.[3] Aetius was now the sole *magister militum*.

431

In the new year, the confusion caused by Felix's death, plus reports that the Vandals had defeated Bonifacius in Africa, caused warfare to erupt yet again in Europe. There was rebellion in Noricum, and Aetius was forced to crush the insurgents rather than send aid to help defeat the Vandals in Africa.[4]

In addition, the Franks had invaded Gaul. There was not enough time left in the campaign season for a Gallic campaign, and instead Aetius simply prepared his forces for war in 432.[5] In addition, an embassy led by Bishop Hydatius of Aquae Flaviae arrived and Aetius was told that the Sueves were once again ravaging Gallaecia.[6]

These commitments explain why Aetius did not send help to Bonifacius. Instead either he, or more likely Placidia, had negotiated with the East, and Aspar had been sent to Africa – with little positive effect. The mood in Italy would have been bad when news arrived of the Vandals' victory in the Second Battle of Hippo Regius.

432: Civil War

Early in 432, Aetius retook the cities of Tournai and Cambrai from the Franks, and shortly after he concluded a treaty with the Frankish King Clodio.[7] During his absence on campaign, Placidia made a fateful decision: as Aetius was gaining victories in Gaul, she recalled Bonifacius from Africa.[8] Accompanied by at least some of the African army, as well as his *bucellarii*, Bonifacius headed for Italy. The war against the Vandals was left to Aspar: Eastern sources claim that Aspar left when Bonifacius set sail for Italy, but evidence from the West clearly shows that Aspar remained in Africa, probably until 434.[9]

The Battle of Rimini

Bonifacius landed in Italy and was given the title *comes et magister utriusque militiae*.[10] At the same time, he was invested with the title of *patricius*.[11] The man titled *magister militum et patricius* usually had the greatest military and political power in the West.[12] Bonifacius was to replace Aetius as the most powerful man in the West, as confirmed by Hydatius, who states that when Bonifacius was recalled, Aetius was 'deposed' (*depulso*).[13]

In Gaul, Aetius may have been preparing for a campaign against the Sueves in Spain when news arrived of these developments. He decided that the best form of defence was attack, and headed for Italy. Bonifacius also massed his forces and prepared to meet Aetius in battle.

The two armies met outside Rimini.[14] Bonifacius was completely victorious and Aetius was forced to surrender.[15] Following his defeat, Aetius relinquished power and retired to his estates in Italy.[16] However, Bonifacius died shortly after.[17] His son-in-law Sebastian became *comes et magister utriusque militiae*.[18] For reasons that are unclear, there was an attempt to assassinate Aetius, who in response fled to the Huns.[19]

With confusion reigning in Italy, Aspar had little option but to use his Eastern troops, plus any men left behind by Bonifacius, to minimize the damage being caused by Gaiseric. It is possible that the widespread destruction recorded in the sources mainly dates from this phase of the war, since they would have mounted foraging expeditions that would have scoured much of Africa for supplies, but the timescale of events is sadly unrecorded. What is likely, given later events, is that Gaiseric set his court in Hippo, and from there awaited events in Europe.[20]

433

In the new year, Aetius returned to Italy, probably accompanied by a large force of Huns.[21] Aetius was restored to his previous position as *comes et magister utriusque militiae* without having to fight a battle.[22] He quickly resumed his duties in Italy and sent envoys far and wide to announce his return. For example, a new peace treaty with the Sueves was ratified at some point in 433.[23] At around the same time, Aetius married Pelagia, Bonifacius' widow.[24]

434

Aetius doubtless spent the majority of 434 settling affairs in Italy.[25] He also had to deal with returning envoys, sent out the year before. In many cases negotiations had failed. The civil war had resulted in barbarian tribes both within and outside the Empire attempting to expand their spheres of influence. Aetius would need his forces to crush these invasions, and the necessary campaigns would take several years. Aetius had to decide where to focus his attention.

It is likely that external events made the decision for him. In the East, relations between Constantinople and the Huns were breaking down. As the Huns were likely to resort to violence to attain their ends, Aetius was informed that Aspar was being recalled to face the Huns. As a reward for his efforts in Africa, Aspar was awarded the post of consul for 434. Despite being an Eastern general, in recognition of his services to the West he was the West's nomination.[26] The loss of Aspar and his Eastern troops would leave Africa vulnerable to attack by the Vandals.

With the Huns threatening in the East, Aetius did not have the option of an African campaign to defeat Gaiseric. In addition, the *praesental* army was needed in Gaul, where war with the Burgundians had broken out. As a consequence, Aetius led a campaign against the Burgundians in person, and, recognizing the futility of organizing an African campaign without Eastern support, he sent Trygetius, a man of some importance who had previously been *comes rei privatae*, to negotiate terms with the Vandals.[27] Trygetius would have had 'specific instructions about points to secure from the Vandals'.[28]

The Treaty of 435

Negotiations continued over the winter months into the new year. Finally, on 11 February 435, a peace treaty was agreed at Hippo Regius.[29] The Vandals were given 'a part of Africa to live in'.[30] The fact that the treaty was signed at Hippo implies that after the sack of the city, Gaiseric had chosen Hippo as his base, as it would remain from 435 to 439.[31] The treaty was a major political coup for Gaiseric. At a stroke, the Vandals were to go from being an enemy worthy only of destruction to a people settled within the Empire on legal terms. It may be at this time that Gaiseric was the first king to adopt the title of *Rex Vandalorum et Alanorum* (King of the Vandals and Alans). Yet as this title is only first attested during the reign of his son and successor Huneric in 483, it remains only a possibility rather than a certainty. However, as Gaiseric was the first king to need charters, it is probable that he used some form of title.[32]

There remains the question of why the Romans accepted a treaty with an enemy that was at large in a vital area for the Empire. The first reason is that Africa

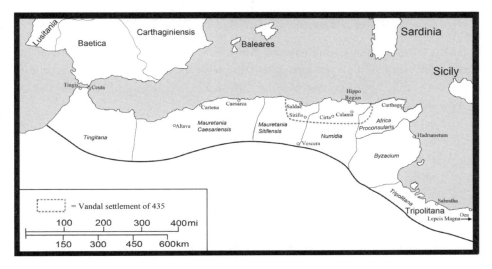

Map 8: The Vandal Settlement of 435. Note that the exact boundaries are unclear.

actually *was* vital to the Empire. Without the tax revenues from the region, and without the grain supply sent to Rome from Carthage, the West would have great difficulty in remaining economically viable. Obviously, they wanted to protect Africa from the Vandals, but the withdrawal of Aspar to the East meant that they did not have an army to hand with which to defeat Gaiseric: after three civil wars in twelve years, and the ensuing losses in men, equipment and finance, the West was extremely weak and needed time to recuperate.[33] Yet pressure on the European frontiers meant that this would not be forthcoming. In addition, the enemies in the north, unlike the Vandals, were a direct military threat to Italy. Consequently, it was 'highly desirable for the Empire to secure by treaty a recognition of the status quo in North Africa'.[34]

For the Vandals, the signing of a treaty was probably a welcome relief. Although in a strong position, the fact that Aspar had earlier been freed from commitments in the East to fight in Africa was a clear acknowledgement that even to the East Empire, the security of Africa was a priority. Despite the fact that Aspar had been recalled due to increasing tensions between Constantinople and the Huns, should the two opponents reach an agreement, it would be expected that Aspar, or another Eastern commander, would return to Africa with an Eastern army.

For Gaiseric, peace would be a reprieve from the pressures of war. In addition, the Vandals had shown with the overlong siege of Hippo that they did not have the skills needed for siege warfare. The only city that stood between them and total domination in Africa was Carthage, but it was clear that they stood little chance of taking it by storm, and a long siege would both weaken the Vandals and give the

Empire time to organize a major campaign of reconquest. Peace was a necessity, not a luxury.[35]

Sadly, none of the existing sources give a clear description of the terms of the treaty. The result is that modern historians have used the few clues available to construct viable, but often contradictory, theories – yet it should be noted that all of these are hypotheses, not factual accounts.

The first of the sources to be analyzed is Procopius. He writes simply that:

> At that time Gizeric [Gaiseric], after conquering Aspar and Boniface in battle, displayed a foresight worth recounting, whereby he made his fortune most thoroughly secure. For fearing lest, if once again an army should come against him from both Rome and Byzantium, the Vandals might not be able to use the same strength and enjoy the same fortune … he was not lifted up by the good fortune he had enjoyed, but rather became moderate because of what he feared, and so he made a treaty with the Emperor Valentinian providing that each year he should pay to the emperor tribute from Libya, and he delivered one of his sons, Honoric, as a hostage to make this agreement binding. So Gizeric showed himself a brave man in the battle and guarded the victory as securely as possible.
>
> Procopius, *B.V.*, 4.12–14

Apart from the description of Gaiseric's abilities, there are possibly two clauses of the treaty covered by Procopius. One is that Gaiseric 'should pay to the emperor tribute from Libya', the other that his son Honoric (Huneric) would act 'as a hostage to make this agreement binding'.

Both of these are plausible, especially the sending of Huneric as a hostage to Rome. The Vandals clearly had the upper hand in Africa, with a large experienced army that the Romans could not evict without a major campaign. In this context, it may be that Gaiseric was allowing the Romans to save face by giving Huneric as a hostage, meaning that Rome could present the treaty in the best possible light when it was announced.[36] However, without further evidence, this remains feasible, but possibly unlikely.

This is because there is a further major difficulty with accepting Procopius at face value: at no other point does Procopius mention a treaty with the Vandals. Yet it is certain that a further treaty was signed between Valentinian and Gaiseric. As a result, it is accepted that Procopius is here describing the later treaty, not that of 435.[37]

The other source of events is Prosper:[38]

> Peace was made with the Vandals and a part of Africa was given to them to dwell in [*Pax facta cum Wandalis data eis ad habitandum Africae portione*].
>
> Prosper, 1321 s.a. 435

Although the wording simply states that the Vandals were given 'a part of Africa', the terminology is a 'regular means of describing a treaty involving *foederati*'.[39] Such treaties typically offered 'land, subsidies and some practical autonomy … but placed them in a subordinate position to the western empire, and demanded military service in return'.[40] As a result, it is possible to determine that the Vandals were settled in Africa, and that they agreed to supply men to serve as *foederati* (troops supplied by a *foedus* – treaty) in the Roman Army in return. However, due to the Vandals' strong bargaining position, it is almost certain that these troops remained in Africa and were not sent to Europe.

The *foederati* would have been billeted on Roman households following the *hospitalitas* system during their service.[41] A law concerning such billeting describes a 'tripartite division', where two-thirds of the house is retained by the householder, with one-third apportioned to the soldier.[42] In addition, the troops would have received pay in the form of *annonae Foederaticae* (money for *foederati*).[43]

It is also possible that Gaiseric took an oath to 'not make further territorial encroachment' at this time, though the attribution is far from clear.[44] If this hypothesis is true, then it is almost certain that at least some of the Vandals were given land and billets according to traditional Roman methods.[45] As a result, the treaty would appear to be similar in some respects to that accorded to the Goths in Aquitaine in 419, where the Goths were given territory in return for military service as *foederati*. However, there were two major differences.

One was due to the nature of the Vandal takeover. It is usually accepted that treaties with barbarians were simple affairs where the barbarians were settled on Roman terms – for example, the Goths, Burgundians or Alan settlements in Gaul. However, in these cases the Romans were the dominant force and the itinerant people were settled in areas different from those they had ravaged. In addition, any land allocated to the barbarians was under Roman supervision and Roman rules.

In contrast, the Vandals had been in Mauretania and Africa Proconsularis from at least 430. Although opposed first by Bonifacius and later by Aspar, there are no accounts of any battles taking place apart from the two Roman defeats. This implies that after the capture of Hippo, the Vandals and Romans had settled into an uneasy status quo, with both sides unwilling to resume hostilities: the Vandals were in no position to lay siege to Carthage, and, after two defeats, Aspar was in no position to attack the Vandals.

Although the Vandals doubtless continued to take some of what they needed from Roman territory to survive, it would have been easier for the majority of the Vandal families to settle and begin to grow their own food. This could have been on *agri deserti* (deserted farmland), on land taken from farmers who had been killed or who had fled from the approaching Vandals, or on that appropriated from sur-viving Roman landowners.

The need to clarify the situation regarding already-settled Vandals, as well as the more traditional *foedus*, helps in part to explain the protracted nature of the negotiations between the Vandals and Rome. Furthermore, it would also account for the confusion in the sources: the different and mystifying forms of settlement would not be easily explained by accounts in a simple chronicle.

However, the protracted nature of the talks may have had one small benefit for the Empire: it is possible that Saint Augustine's library at Hippo was transferred to Rome shortly after the entente between Gaiseric and Valentinian III was agreed.[46] This would make sense, as the Nicenes in the region would be worried that the Arian Vandals would destroy some or all of the texts that did not support their religious position. The move has been dated by some historians to *c*.440, but it is more likely that it dates to 435, when the Vandals took control of Hippo: a later date means that the Vandals would have had several years in which to destroy all or part of the library.

In the same context, it was later noted by Bede that Augustine's body was taken to Sardinia 'on account of the barbarians'.[47] Although it is tempting to date this transfer to the same as that of the library, it is more likely that this refers to the late-seventh century and the Arab invasion rather than the Vandal invasion of the fifth century.[48]

Gaiseric *Dux*

The second difference, and possibly the most important for later events, was that due to the weaker status of the Empire, Gaiseric, unlike Theoderic, appears to have been given a military post.[49] The wording of references to the treaty imply that Gaiseric was given an official post within the Empire. For example, when describ-ing the eviction of the bishops, Prosper does not state that Gaiseric exceeded his legal powers. This implies that Gaiseric had the rights of a military commander and Roman official to order ecclesiastical affairs.[50] The hypothesis may gain confir-mation by a famous and oft-quoted passage in Victor of Vita:

> In his cunning duke Geiseric [*Geiserici ducis*], intending to make the rep-utation of his people a source of dread, ordered then and there that the entire crowd was to be counted, even those who had come from the womb into the light that very day.
>
> Victor of Vita, 1.2.

Although the majority of interest in the passage concerns Victor's claim concern-ing the number of Vandals who crossed to Africa, it is interesting to note that Victor calls Gaiseric '*Geiserici ducis*' ('*dux*', duke), not *rex* or a similar Latin term.[51] The most likely explanation for this is that in the treaty of 435, Gaiseric, following the example of previous barbarian leaders such as Alaric, had demanded an official post as part of the peace agreements. He was given the title *dux*, probably with responsibility for the areas of Africa allocated to the Vandals. Victor, who hated the Vandals, later used this title anachronistically to highlight the treacherous nature of Gaiseric.

The Vandal Kingdom

There remains the question of which parts of Africa were delegated to the Vandals. Several differing possibilities have been proposed, including claims that: the Vandals were given 'Numidia and the Mauretanias';[52] they gained control of 'large areas of Numidia and Mauretania Sitifensis, including Calama and Sitifis';[53] they were given 'The province of Africa – except the city of Carthage – the province of Byzacena, and a part of Numidia';[54] or simply that they were allocated territories 'probably along the coast of Numidia'.[55] What is clear from their use of ships to maintain a full blockade of Hippo during the siege, is that they had a fleet capable of holding its own, although exact numbers are nowhere stated and impossible to estimate. As a result, the coast of North Africa from the region of Hippo to the west was a Vandal-dominated sea.

The suggestions listed above can easily lead to confusion, yet it is possible that slightly more detail can be inferred from a later statement by Prosper, where, in an entry dated to 437, he notes that: '[Gaiseric] persecuted some of our bishops, of whom the most famous were Possidius, Novatus, and Severianus.'[56] It has been suggested that Possidius was bishop of Calama, Severianus of Cera and Novatus of Sitifis.[57] The latter is possibly reinforced by an inscription and definitely reinforced by a letter of Augustine to a man named Darius.[58]

This implies that the Vandals were settled in parts of Mauretania Sitifiensis, Numidia and western Africa Proconsularis, with their capital at Hippo Regius.[59] This information is supported to some degree by a *Novel* ('New Law') of Valentinian. Although dated to 445, it refers to the poor condition of some of those parts of Africa that had been under the control of the Vandals between 435 and 439.[60]

Whether he had been given a post or not, Gaiseric had succeeded in securing a place for his people, far from the Goths and Sueves. Although it was not entirely secure from Roman attack, the fact that a Roman army would need to be ferried across the Mediterranean, which would require a large amount of resources and time, and would leave Gaul and Italy relatively undefended, must have limited the threat posed by the Romans. He knew that he would now have time to organize his people on a more permanent basis.

Securing a position

With his position in Africa recognized by Rome, Gaiseric now had to secure his position within his newly conquered realm. The manner in which he achieved this, and the way in which the Vandals conducted themselves in their new territories, is unknown. Instead, it is necessary to rely on the hostile references given by Roman opponents, who are heavily biased due to both the Vandals' invasion and their Arianism. Accordingly, these need to be treated with extreme caution, although in the past they have at times been accepted at almost face value.

Possibly the most useful source for this early period is the *Vita Augustae* (*Life of Saint Augustine*) by Possidius. Augustine had died during the Vandals' siege of Hippo in 430, so in theory the events described by Possidius (see above, 'Into Africa', Chapter 6) as being seen by Augustine must have occurred prior to 430. However, as this is a hagiography many of the actions attributed to the Vandals may date to 435–439, or even later, so the description should not be taken literally.

In many ways, Victor of Vita simply follows Possidius' writings, but his work is far more scathing and there is little concept that the Vandals were anything other than vicious barbarians intent on ravaging Africa. However, not only is he writing sixty years after the Vandal crossing, but after the anti-Catholic persecutions of Gaiseric's successors.[61] As a result, his writings need to be closely analyzed before being used.

Interestingly, in the passage quoted earlier on pages 61 and 62, Possidius depicts the effects of the Vandal attacks on 'Mauretania, even crossing over to other of our provinces and territories'. Therefore, it is clear that he is attempting to maintain chronological accuracy, as he does not refer to the Vandal attack on Carthage or their domination of Africa Proconsularis.

Despite the description of savagery and the ransacking of holy places, there are hints within the text that Possidius himself knew that he was in danger of going too far with his portrayal. For example, he states that Augustine 'saw cities overthrown in destruction, and the resident citizens, together with the buildings on their lands, partly annihilated'. The fact that Possidius accepts that some buildings and the people who inhabited them were only 'partly annihilated', may be an acknowledgement that the Vandals were not as destructive as is usually depicted.

In addition, he notes that at times 'the holy sacraments [were] no longer desired, or if someone did desire them, no one could easily be found to administer them'. Again, the acceptance that there were people who had survived the attacks who could not find clergymen to administer religious rites goes against the traditional picture of the citizens of Africa being enslaved or killed by the savagery of the marauding Vandals.

In fact, if the description as given is slightly amended, it is likely that a more realistic picture can emerge. Many of the Vandals did ransack, kill, rape and torture many of the inhabitants, but this may not have been as widespread or as destructive as previously thought. Instead, it may be better to see the Vandal depredations as largely restricted to the need to secure supplies for survival, with the traditional horrors of enemy attack being restricted to only a proportion of the population, rather than being extremely extensive, and being carried out by the more brutal and vengeful parts of the Vandal army.

However, there is one major distinction to be made: it is likely that the attacks upon the Catholic Church were indeed widespread and intended to either kill or terrify the priesthood into fleeing. This analysis is supported by a passage in Victor of Vita:

> In particular, they gave vent to their wicked ferocity with great strength against the churches and basilicas of the saints, cemeteries and monasteries, so that they burned houses of prayer with fires greater than those they used against the cities and all the towns.
>
> Victor of Vita, *Historia Persecutionis Africanae*, 1.4

The Vandals were Arians and the Catholics viewed them as heretics. As a result, it would have been obvious to Gaiseric that the removal of the military hierarchy from Roman territory was only one aspect of his attempted conquest: the Catholic Church could easily replace the military command as the focus of anti-Vandal actions and propaganda. Accordingly, he would have given the order to remove local bishops and priests using whatever means necessary, and the methods used were likely those most appropriate to the local Vandal commanders. This would account for the death of the bishops in some cases, but them being allowed to flee in others: despite their Arian apostasy, it is probable that at least some Vandals saw the killing of Christian men-of-god as sacrilegious and therefore forced the Catholics out, whereas others simply killed the inhabitants of churches and monasteries without a second thought.

There is an additional aspect to Gaiseric's 'persecution' of Catholics. A large proportion of the population in Africa was not Catholic, but members of the Donatist schism.[62] There had been a major religious division in Africa following Diocletian's persecutions between 303 and 305, and Gaiseric may have seen his actions against Catholics as a way of gaining the support of the Donatists. On the other hand, this may simply have been a happy coincidence of policy benefiting the Donatists without Gaiseric understanding the implications of his actions.

According to Possidius, only the churches of Carthage, Hippo and Cirta survived.[63] Obviously, Carthage had never been taken, but the statement that the churches of Hippo and Cirta remained untouched needs some explanation. Hippo had been captured after the defeat of Bonifacius and Aspar, and it is surprising that the church there was not destroyed in the sacking of the city. It may be that Gaiseric had already determined to use the city as his base and recognized that in this instance the loss of their church could anger the inhabitants to the point of open rebellion. In this case, the church's survival is not surprising.

On the other hand, the continuation of the church in Cirta may imply that during the warfare between 430 and 434, Cirta had either remained safe from Vandal attack or had managed to resist a Vandal siege. Given that the Vandals may have been wary of an attack by Aspar and the Roman army if they were to lay siege to a town, the former is most likely. In fact, it is possible that Cirta remained in Roman hands until the signing of the treaty in 435. This would help to explain why the church survived.

New Policies

The settlement of the people, the assignment of political and military posts, and the distribution of the troops to billets around the newly won territory would all have taken time. This may help to explain why there is little mention in the Roman sources of any events concerning the Vandals. Instead, they are focused mainly on the ongoing conflicts with the Goths and Burgundians in Gaul.

Yet it would appear from an early stage that Gaiseric was intent upon taking advantage of Roman weakness and their ongoing conflicts. It is difficult to interpret Gaiseric's policies from the few notices in the surviving sources. These note nothing specific between 435 and 437, as would be expected if Gaiseric was cementing his position. Yet given his later actions and some undated evidence from the sources, it may be possible to deduce his strategy.

According to Jordanes. the unnamed daughter of Theoderic, king of the Goths in Gaul, had married Huneric, son of Gaiseric. If this information is accurate, it implies that at some point there was an alliance between the Goths and Vandals that was cemented in the traditional manner by a marriage union between the two 'royal' families.

It is possible that the marriage was organized in 431, but it is extremely doubtful if at this point, with the Vandals simply a rebellious group in Africa being held to a stalemate, that Theoderic would have seen them as a potentially valuable ally, nor that Gaiseric would have been able to overcome the long-standing enmity between the majority of his people and the Goths.

On the other hand, after the treaty of 435, the Vandals were now a powerful international group, equal to that of the Goths. It is interesting to note that throughout the period of Gaiseric's life, there is circumstantial evidence of barbarian envoys passing between each other's courts, as well as travelling to Rome and Constantinople. Although hypothesis, it is tempting to interpret the marriage as an alliance or agreement between Theoderic and Gaiseric that the Goths would not be deployed against the Vandals in Africa and that the Vandals would not send any troops to help Rome in Gaul.

Circumstantial support can be found in simultaneous events in Gaul. Probably after the conclusion of an agreement or alliance, both the Goths and Burgundians reopened the war with Rome.[64] Both groups would be encouraged by the fact that the Vandals had just signed a treaty with Rome, a sign that Rome's power was declining, but that they would only have to face the Roman Army, not the Vandals. In a similar way, Gaiseric's actions immediately after the outbreak of the war support the concept that the two leaders worked in the knowledge that they were under no threat of attack from each other.

An event recorded by Procopius reinforces the hypothesis that envoys were constantly passing between barbarian groups. According to Procopius, after the Vandal settlement in Libya, the Vandals who had remained in the region of the Upper Tisza River realized that they had a comfortable life, largely due to their low population for the area of land they controlled. Fearful that the Vandals would be evicted from Africa and return to their ancient homes – so putting pressure on resources – they sent an envoy asking that Gaiseric renounce claims to be the king of the Vandals everywhere. After much deliberation, Gaiseric refused the request, so remaining titular king of 'all of the migrating Vandals' and leaving open his return to Europe should the Romans reconquer Libya.[65] Although attested nowhere else, and so of extremely dubious accuracy, the fact that Procopius does not treat the envoys as an abnormal occurrence suggests that many envoys passed around the West but are simply not recorded.

437

In 437, Gaiseric began a more aggressive policy, and appears to have been attempting to consolidate Arianism as the predominant religion in his territories. As previously noted, according to Prosper, '[Gaiseric] persecuted some of our bishops, of whom the most famous were Possidius [bishop of Calama], Novatus [bishop of Sitifis], and Severianus [bishop of Cera].'[66] As also noted earlier, it is possible that Gaiseric was acting within his legal authority with this action.[67] Whatever the case, there was little danger of Rome taking any action over the matter: at this time they were busy dealing with the Burgundians and Goths, as the latter had earlier laid siege to Narbonne and fighting was continuing.[68] At the same time, four Hispanic functionaries – possibly named Arcadius, Paschasius, Probus and Eutychius – who had previously been 'valued and distinguished by virtue of their wisdom and faithful service', lost their property and then their lives for refusing to convert.[69] Prosper's testimony may be accurate, but as is usual this is the only mention of the functionaries, so certainty is impossible. It may even be that they were executed not only for refusing to convert, but for opposing Gaiseric's elimination of their co-religionist bishops.

In this context, a further short entry in Prosper's Chronicle takes on a new relevance: 'In the same year [437] barbarian deserters of the federates took to piracy.'[70] The only federates in the region were the Vandals, and it is interesting to note that Prosper calls them 'deserters'. This may have been the official line coming from Gaiseric when Roman envoys questioned the attacks, and some modern historians have accepted this concept, claiming that the attacks demonstrated 'Gaiseric's indifference to his military responsibilities'.[71] On the other hand, given Gaiseric's later actions and his obvious political ability, it is more likely that the attacks were sanctioned by Gaiseric. This was in part in the belief that the booty taken would help to improve the Vandals' financial situation in Africa, and also possibly to demonstrate to his allies that he was playing his part in the alliance against Rome, but mainly it was to test Rome's strength and ability to respond to attack in the Mediterranean.[72] By refusing to accept responsibility for the attacks, Gaiseric kept open his option to stop the attacks should the Roman response be strong.

His caution is understandable. In 437, the Roman Army recovered at least some of its dominance in Gaul: the Gothic siege of Narbonne was raised and 20,000 Burgundians were allegedly 'slain by Aetius'.[73]

438

However, Rome was almost totally focused upon the war with the Goths. Accordingly, in the following year the Vandal attacks resumed – 'the same pirates plundered many islands, especially Sicily'.[74] According to Marcellinus *comes*, the attackers were led by a man named Contradis, whose name may be a Latinization of the Vandal-sounding name Guntharix.[75]

The fact that Sicily bore the brunt of the attacks is open to interpretation. One factor was that the island had been almost totally untouched for many years, and so was a rich target. Yet it is tempting to interpret the attacks in a different way. With Rome still focused upon Gaul, Gaiseric may have seen a strong attack on Sicily as being of value in two ways. One was the rich booty to be gained from the island, and doubtless Gaiseric would claim his share. The other was to determine how the Romans would react to an assault on one of their major sources of food and revenue. Although the war against the Goths had swung in Rome's favour, and Hydatius records a Roman victory in which 8,000 Goths were killed, there is no record of any military activity against the 'pirates'.[76]

Any response to the attacks was on a purely diplomatic level, and it is interesting to note that Prosper clearly acknowledges both the lack of opposition to the attacks and the focus remaining on Gaul in an entry dated to 439: 'Since Aetius was concerned with matters that were being settled in Gaul, Gaiseric had nothing to fear from losing his friendship.'[77]

Yet this does not mean that everything was going well for the alliance: Aetius had taken his forces into Gaul and inflicted a heavy defeat upon the Goths, despite which the war continued.[78] Because the Goths continued to fight after the defeat, in either late 438 or 439, Gaiseric came to a major decision. It was obvious that his position in Africa was not under threat and the 'pirates' had faced little in the way of opposition during their attacks on the Mediterranean islands in 437 and 438. Furthermore, in early-mid-439, the Goths gained a victory over a Roman army.[79]

Therefore, in mid-late 439, Gaiseric made the defining action of his life.

Chapter 8

Conquest

Africa

From an early date, Africa – meaning the province of Africa Proconsularis – had become synonymous with peace and prosperity, at least amongst many of the barbarian invaders of the West. This can be demonstrated quite simply by noting that leaders from Alaric onwards had attempted to cross to Africa. In this context, Gaiseric had been simply following in the tradition of earlier invaders. Yet whereas today Africa denotes the continent, in antiquity the label only applied to a specific area. In Roman times, the term 'Africa' was usually applied to the province created in 146 BC after the defeat of Carthage. After this, the Romans conquered more areas of the North African coast, and these became the provinces of Tripolitania, Byzacium, Numidia, Mauretania Sitifensis, Mauretania Caesariensis and Tingitana. Tingitana eventually became part of the Diocese of Hispania, but the rest were included as part of the Diocese of Africa, with its capital at Carthage.

The province of Africa was known as Africa Proconsularis. Along with Egypt, Africa was the breadbasket of the early Roman Empire. African grain had been taken, as part of Africa's tax, to feed the citizens of Rome and Italy. Egypt had also supplied grain, but after the foundation of Constantinople this had been diverted to Constantine's new city. Since then, Rome had come to rely almost completely on the African grain supply to feed its citizens, and two-thirds of Africa's annual harvest was exported to Rome. Control of the grain shipments to Rome was vital, and from early in the Empire's history the governor of the province had been a proconsul rather than a senator – hence the name Africa Proconsularis – as a senator might use the region as the starting point for a revolt against the emperor.

In the beginning, the main commodity exported from Africa was grain. However, from the late second century, olive oil production had increased in importance, and the anonymous author of *Expositio totius mundi et rerum* noted that Africa was wealthy in all things, including grain, fruit, trees, slaves and textiles, but 'it virtually exceeds all others in the use of the olive'.[1] The interior of the provinces of Numidia, Byzacena and Tripolitania – especially the territories of Lepcis Magna, Oea and Sabratha (see Map 9) – were now used for olive production. The other major commodity exported from Africa was African red slip ware, a distinctive form of pottery that is now used by archaeologists as evidence for trade patterns from Africa to the wider Mediterranean area. However in the early fifth century, all of these goods were mainly destined for the market of Rome and Italy.

The fact that the city of Rome was dependent on African grain meant that the citizens of Africa had a ready market for their goods. Furthermore, to ensure quick delivery of the grain, the Imperial government maintained the transport facilities in Africa and its surrounding provinces at the highest standard. This infrastructure was highly beneficial to those wishing to export other goods. In addition, thanks to the favourable lease laws employed in Africa, there was a huge production of surpluses, which were transported along government-maintained highways to the Mediterranean for shipment to Rome and throughout the Mediterranean.

A final reason for the prosperity of the African provinces was that they had not been exposed to war. Although there may have been local troubles in the area, the troops stationed in Africa were mainly there to control the movement of the local nomadic tribes as they migrated between their winter and summer pastures, ensuring that they did not stray onto settled lands and cause damage.

Despite this advantageous position, Africa was not exempt from the changes being seen in other parts of the West. As elsewhere, the local councillors were becoming reluctant to serve on their local councils, since the financial burden was very high; partially as a result, in many areas the forum, the focal point of towns and cities, had either fallen out of use or at least had become much reduced in size. The functions of the forum were now being replaced by buildings connected to churches, signalling the rise in attachment to Christianity and the loss of attachment to pagan institutions. Additionally, large houses were now beginning to be divided into smaller units, and shop fronts were appearing along street frontages, replacing the shopping area of the forum.[2]

There were also areas of dispute. As already noted, the main cause of unrest was Christianity. There was a large community of Donatists in Africa who were in opposition to the Catholic majority. The disagreement went back to the previous century, when Diocletian (AD 284–305) had ordered a persecution of Christians in the Empire between 303 and 305. Many Christian clergymen had been killed in the persecution, but some had surrendered, giving up their copies of the scriptures and in some cases betraying fellow Christians to the authorities. These men were known as *traditores* (the ones who handed over).

After the end of the persecution, and particularly following Constantine the Great's edict of toleration, many of these men had been allowed to return to their former positions. A large number of Christians refused to accept the authority of these men, seeing them as traitors to the faith. When a new bishop of Carthage was consecrated by a *traditor*, his opponents refused to accept him. Eventually, in 313, a man named Donatus (after whom the movement was named) was elected as bishop and the controversy broadened due to the fact that Donatus was an anti-*traditor*.

As Bishop of Carthage, Donatus wielded great power and was able to appeal against the appointment of *traditors*, but in 313 a commission found against the Donatists. Despite this, the movement continued, especially in Africa, leading to widespread division, even after Donatus' death in 355. This was largely due to the Donatist priests being local men who spoke local languages and dialects, endearing them to the provincial population outside the big cities. On the other hand, Catholic priests tended to speak only Latin and so had more of a following in the cities.

The Donatist cause was not helped by the rise of the *Circumcellians*. These were groups from the lowest levels of society who developed anti-Roman biases and were prone to rebellion. They were usually Donatists and their infamy resulted in Donatism being associated with rebels and bandits. As a result, in the early fifth century, there began a persecution of the Donatists in Africa, which Saint Augustine thought to be harsh and ill-judged.[3]

In June 411, a conference took place in Carthage which found against the Donatists. Slowly, under pressure, Donatist adherents began to convert to Catholicism. Yet by the 430s, there were still many strong adherents to the cause who were unhappy with the course of events: religious division continued.

As a final point, although Roman Africa tends to be studied as a single entity, it should be noted that only in Africa Proconsularis was Latin a common language. The other provinces were not the same, and there were at least three languages in use in the area. Furthermore, there was a distinct cultural division between Romanized Carthage and the rural countryside.[4]

These divisions may have been surprising to Gaiseric when he took control of parts of the region after 435. Although he may have expected to be seen as a barbarian outsider, and is described as such by Catholic and aristocratic literature, the Vandals may have been seen as 'saviours' by those members of the population unhappy with Catholic Imperial rule.[5]

In this context, and although the treaty of 435 was in many ways unwelcome in the area – given the fact that the resources of the West were becoming increasingly strained from both internal and external threats – the treaty had had one major advantage: it had saved most of Numidia, Byzacena and Africa Proconsularis – including Carthage, the point of export for most African grain – from the Vandals.[6] Although there was political and religious confusion following the Vandal invasion, the actual damage to the economy was limited and there is little doubt that after 435 grain exports to Rome were resumed.

The net result of these factors was that, despite the arrival of the Vandals in parts of the Empire, the provinces of North Africa maintained extremely high productivity but were low on maintenance, and thus were the major net contributor to the financial stability of the West. Furthermore, it has been estimated that surplus revenues from Africa were vital to the maintenance of the armed forces.[7] However, this should not be overestimated. The largest estates were owned by relatively few men, absentee landlords who were the most powerful and influential in Italy. These individuals did not want men from their estates being conscripted into the army, nor did they want to pay the taxes necessary to furnish new recruits. Although Africa was vital to the economy, the political power of the major landowners was a source of constant friction between the emperor, the *magister militum* and the Senate.

439

The chronology of events in 439 is unknown: all that survives in the sources are brief statements of events dated to the year, with no attempt being made to link these to a chronological narrative. As a result, it is necessary to evaluate all of the information available before an attempt is made to construct a viable narrative.

It is known that during the campaign season, the war in Gaul between the Romans and Goths continued. However, following the defeat in 438, Aetius managed to recover the situation and at some point inflicted a defeat upon the Goths.[8] Sadly, Merobaudes does not give a date for the victory, but – as will be shown below – it is likely that this took place in mid-late summer.

News that the war between the Goths and Romans remained ongoing may have made Gaiseric decide upon his next and greatest gamble. As noted earlier, the piracy of 'barbarian deserters' and the persecution of Catholic priests, as well as – possibly – the local nobility, implies that Gaiseric was not content with his current position, especially since the hostility towards clergy and nobles could mean that he was aiming at removing all of those individuals who could lead indigenous resistance to his aims.[9] Possibly supporting this theory, he replaced the departing Roman nobles and priests with Vandal nobles and Arian clergymen.[10] He now cast covetous eyes on the nearby metropolis.

Carthage

The city of Carthage was the third largest of the Empire, only Constantinople and Rome having greater populations. By the end of the fourth century, it has been estimated that the city may have had a population as high as 100,000.[11] The main tasks of Carthage were to act as the administrative centre of Africa Proconsularis and to be the main port for the distribution of goods brought from the interior and from smaller ports along the coast. As an Imperial port, the emperor was able

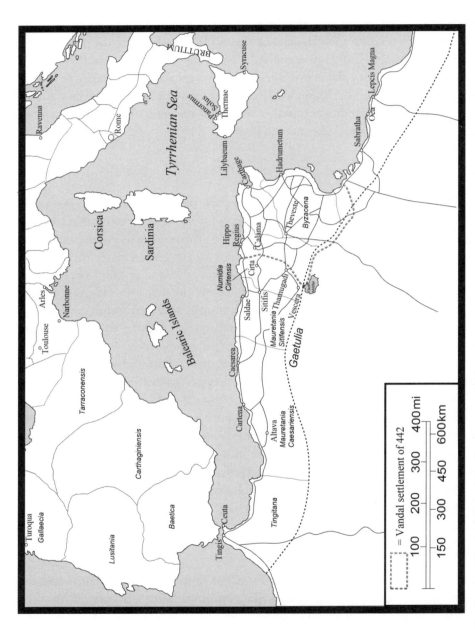

Map 9: The Romano–Vandal War and the Settlement of 442.

to impose taxes on goods being exported, but if the port was under the control of somebody other than the emperor, that person would become fantastically rich.

The condition of the Roman army in Africa is completely unknown, but Gaiseric doubtless had informants keeping him updated on events in Africa, and especially in Carthage. Twice defeated by Gaiseric – once even after the army had been reinforced by troops from the East – confidence would have been low. In addition, the Eastern reinforcements had returned home with Aspar, and it is unlikely that the troops which Bonifacius had taken to Italy to face Aetius in 432 were ever returned to Africa. Consequently, it is clear that Gaiseric was facing a very weak army, and it is probable that Aetius was relying upon Gaiseric's forces to fill the gaps and maintain peace as a garrison in the region.

It was obvious to Gaiseric that Aetius' attention remained focused upon the war against the Goths. The temptation was thus too much. Gaiseric decided that if he did not act whilst the main Roman army was occupied, he might never again get the chance. In a bold and unprecedented move, Gaiseric now took the last, fateful step on the journey of the Vandals. In an act of supreme political daring, he led his army out of the areas allotted to them and advanced towards Carthage, breaking the treaty of friendship he had agreed with Rome.[12]

On 19 October 439, Gaiseric arrived outside the walls of Carthage.[13] There is little primary information for the manner of Gaiseric's attack on Carthage, the main evidence being that he took the city by a 'stratagem' or 'trickery'.[14] The most obvious way for him to capture the city was to use his (theoretical) position as a military official of the Empire to gain entry to the city with a small bodyguard. After securing at least one of the gates, he could then arrange for the main body of troops to enter and secure the city.

Whatever method he used, once inside, he unleashed the Vandals. The Vandal sack of Carthage is usually seen as being a vicious episode. Prosper claims that Gaiseric:

> Put its citizens to various kinds of torture and took all their wealth as his own. Nor did he refrain from spoiling the churches. Emptying them of their sacred vessels, and depriving them of the attention of their priests, he ordered that they no longer be places of divine worship but quarters for his people. He was harsh towards the entire captive population but particularly hostile to the nobility and clergy so that no one could tell whether he was waging war more against man or God.
>
> Prosper, s.a. 439

This passage is illuminating, if interpreted correctly. It is clear that the aristocracy were targeted by Gaiseric in order to remove them and replace them with Gaiseric's own nobles.[15] Many of the landowners fled to Italy. Those who left had their lands confiscated by the Vandals.[16] The events are similarly described by Victor of Vita, who notes that the 'old class of freemen, freeborn, and noble' were condemned to slavery.[17]

The same can be said of the Church. Prosper notes that sacred vessels were taken from Catholic churches, which were seen as viable targets by the Arian Vandals.[18] Prosper also states that Gaiseric wanted his people to settle in the newly abandoned churches. In this context it is likely that the phrase 'his people' should really refer to the Vandal Arian clergy. The claim is reinforced by Hydatius, who states that Gaiseric immediately began a persecution of the 'Catholics'.[19]

These accounts combine to paint a picture of a violent sack of the city, yet this may be misleading. The dual attack on the Catholic Church and the aristocracy probably had three aims. One was to remove the leading clergy and aristocrats who could lead resistance to Gaiseric's takeover. A second was to release lands which could then be used to reward Gaiseric's loyal followers, including the Arian priests. Thirdly, the persecution of Catholic clergy would result in the Donatists, and other Christian sects who had been recently persecuted, transferring their loyalty to Gaiseric.

Consequently, it is probably far better to accept that, on the whole, the 'sack' of Carthage was more an exercise in evicting the clergymen and aristocracy – the potential leaders of resistance – from Carthage rather than a wholesale destruction of the city, although the Vandal warriors were no doubt let loose to enter the city and spread terror and disruption, ensuring that there would be no attempt at defence by the population.

After the first attack was over, the troops at large gained at least some of its booty for themselves, but not too much: Gaiseric was later able to pass a decree ordering 'that each person [citizen of Carthage] was to bring forward whatever gold, silver, gems and items of costly clothing he had'; hardly necessary or likely to be successful if the city had been ransacked as described in the sources, since the vast majority of these goods would then have been taken by Vandal troops.[20]

A large number of the Catholic clergy and Roman aristocracy fled from Africa, arriving in Italy as refugees.[21] Their horror stories doubtless heavily influenced Prosper's account of the capture of Carthage. In the meantime, the lands in Africa Proconsularis owned by absentee landlords who had always lived in Italy were also seized by Gaiseric.[22] However, there is little evidence that once the initial conquest was over, Gaiseric ordered a full persecution of Catholics.[23]

Gaiseric had reached his decision to attack at just the right time. Late in the campaign season, a peace treaty was agreed between Rome and the Goths.[24] It is usually assumed that the treaty was signed as a result of Gaiseric's capture of Africa: once the news arrived in Italy, all other conflicts and negotiations would obviously be rushed through in order to free up the resources – especially the army – necessary to deal with the emergency. Carthage fell on 19 October, and it is possible that Aetius in Gaul did not hear about the disaster until late October or early November. If so, then the negotiations with the Goths were conducted with extreme speed in order for them to be concluded before the end of the year. Aetius was aided in this by having recently inflicted a heavy defeat upon the Goths, who could now be expected to accept terms.

Theoderic, the Gothic king, doubtless also learned of the fall of Carthage, so despite the defeat he was able to use this information in his negotiations in order to maintain the status quo: the Goths were not humiliated by the peace terms, instead appearing to revert to the status they held prior to the opening of hostilities. However, if this was the case, there appears to have been one factor that enraged Gaiseric: as part of the treaty, it is probable that Goths once again agreed to serve in Roman armies, without limits on their deployment. If so, this made a break between Gaiseric and Theoderic inevitable.

The break may have been confirmed by the removal of Theoderic's daughter as the wife of Huneric, although it should be noted that historians disagree over the date of the affair.[25] At an unspecified date, Theoderic's unnamed daughter was accused of attempting to poison Huneric. But the plot was discovered, and she was mutilated – her nose and ears were cut off – and sent back to her father.[26] It is possible that, following the treaty with Rome, Theoderic sent messengers to his daughter encouraging her to poison her husband. Yet this would be a strange decision: it would put his daughter in extreme danger, and the benefits of such an act are hard to define. On the other hand, the use of poison was one of the few acceptable reasons for a divorce, so Gaiseric may have simply been using this as an excuse to rid himself of an embarrassing reminder of a failed alliance. In addition, it would also remove a possible spy who could pass on Vandal secrets to the enemy, the Goths and their Roman allies. Whatever the truth, Huneric was once again single and available for a political marriage.

Italy

Understandably, the capture of Carthage was a major blow to the Empire. In one fell swoop, Gaiseric had stripped the West, and especially Italy, of its major grain supplies and a large part of its tax base. Since the capture of Carthage took place on 19 October 439, and sailing in the Mediterranean in winter was dangerous, it is possible that news of the event did not reach Ravenna, where the emperor was living, until much later – possibly February 440, a possibility reinforced by the fact that a *novel* (new law) issued by Valentinian concerning the employment of *decurions* (city officials) in January 440 makes no mention of the loss of Africa.[27] If so, the treaty with the Goths was signed before the news arrived.

Panic – even if only at the loss of their food source – swept Rome when news of the Vandal success arrived. Aetius and Valentinian now had to secure alternative sources of grain for the Imperial city. The likelihood is that in the first instance, Aetius followed the example set by Stilicho during the 'Revolt of Gildo' in Africa by arranging for emergency supplies of grain to be transported to Rome from Gaul and Spain.[28]

Clearly demonstrating the difficulties facing the West, a *novel* dated to 2 March 440 ordered a conscription of troops to meet the emergency. A simultaneous *novel* was issued announcing that all landowners should furnish the correct number of recruits for the army, and declaring the punishment for those who did not do so and instead harboured these deserters.[29] In addition, a *novel* from 24 June 440 made arrangement for the protection of the Calabrian coast from upcoming attacks.[30] It is also possible that a lost *novel* calling for a new conscription of troops, which is referred to in a *novel* of 444, also dates to this period.[31]

Thanks to the loss of African grain, a further *novel* was issued allowing Greek merchants to trade in Italy, and at the same time ordered that the walls of Rome were to be repaired to defend against any attack by the Vandals.[32] It would appear that attempts were also made to repair and upgrade the fortifications of Naples.[33]

War

In Hispania, the Vandals had captured a small fleet and used it to raid the Balearic Islands and Mauretania before crossing to Africa. By seizing Carthage, the Vandals had captured the Roman fleet that was permanently stationed there.[34] Although this was most likely mainly transport vessels rather than warships, their capture made the Vandals a naval force to be reckoned with as it allowed Gaiseric to transport a large force anywhere in the Mediterranean.

With the Romans caught off-balance, and wanting to press his advantage in the hope of convincing Rome to accept his conquest as permanent, Gaiseric was determined to use his newly won fleet. As soon as the weather permitted, he struck:

> Genseric [Gaiseric], the enemy of Our Empire, is reported to have led forth from the port of Carthage a large fleet, whose sudden excursion and fortuitous depredation must be feared by all shores. Although the solicitude of Our Clemency is stationing garrisons throughout various places and the army of the most invincible Emperor Theodosius, Our Father, will soon approach, and although We trust that the Most Excellent Patrician, Our Aetius, will soon be here with a large band and the Most illustrious Master of Soldiers, Sigisvuldus, does not cease to organize guards of soldiers and federated allies for the cities and shores,

nevertheless, because it is not sufficiently certain, under summertime opportunities for navigation, to what shore the ships of the enemy can come, We admonish each and all by this edict that, with confidence in Roman strength and the courage with which they ought to defend their own, with their own men against the enemy, if the occasion should so demand, they shall use those arms which they can, but they shall preserve the public discipline and the moderation of free birth unimpaired. Thus shall they guard the provinces and their own fortunes with faithful harmony and with joined shields.

Nov. Val. 9.1 (24 June, 440)

The *novel* clearly demonstrates that the importance of Africa and the threat from Gaiseric was widely acknowledged. Aetius was recalled with his army from Gaul, and the *magister militum* Sigisvult was deploying those troops stationed in Italy to defend against the impending attack. More significantly, by June 440, envoys had already been sent to the East and Theodosius II had agreed to send troops. Part of the reason for Theodosius' quick decision was that the court at Constantinople itself feared attack: although the nature and the dating of defensive building works on the Sea of Marmara has been questioned, the fact that the author of the *Chronicon Paschale* associates the work with the Vandal threat clearly demonstrates the alarm which was caused in the East by the Vandal seizure of Africa.[35]

In the meantime, Gaiseric was intent on retaining the initiative, and, determined to force the West to come to terms, he set sail for Sicily.[36] It may be that his choice was determined by an invitation, and possibly on information received, from Maximin, a bishop serving the Arian communities in Sicily.[37] He began by laying siege to Panormus, the island's main naval base.[38] Taking the city would have a three-fold purpose. First, it would increase the pressure on the emperor to accede to Gaiseric's seizure of Carthage. Second, the capture of ships in the port would hopefully increase the size of Gaiseric's fleet, whilst simultaneously lessening that of his opponent. Third, it would make a campaign by the Empire against Africa more difficult by removing the obvious logistical base for an attack.

It would appear that Syracuse, Aetna (unknown), Lilybaeum (Marsala), Thermae (Sciacca), Solus (Soluntum) and other places were also attacked and ravaged, as a *novel* issued in Italy after June 440 states that they were to be treated differently from other places by only paying one-seventh of the taxes levied prior to the Vandal attack.[39] Sadly, the text after the word 'Solus' has been lost and so any specific details concerning the reason for the *novel* are unknown. Although the fact that ports were attacked may simply be that they were adjacent to the sea and therefore easy to access for the sea-going Vandals, it is possible that one of the reasons for the choice of targets was an attempt to devastate Sicily's ports in order to damage the island as a logistical base for operations against Carthage.[40] In addition, there was a major raid on Sardinia, and at least one group of Vandals crossed the Straits of Messina to attack Bruttium.[41]

Yet the East was not to escape attention: there are suggestions, although nothing definitely attested, that Gaiseric ordered raids on the East in 440.[42] Many reasons can be given for such raids, but the most obvious would be the gaining of intelligence and the desire to interrupt Eastern preparations; it was known from the *novel* of Valentinian that Theodosius was sending help, and attacks on the East would inform Gaiseric whether these claims were true and also of the state of readiness in the East.

But there are also other possible reasons for the attacks on both East and West. One of these is economic. Although Africa was the main granary for the West, Sicily and Sardinia – the two main objects of Gaiseric's attention – were the 'supplementary granaries' for Italy, so much so that Salvian called them the 'storehouses of the imperial treasury'.[43] In addition, in the East, the island of Rhodes was a major port 'athwart the route' between Alexandria, the source of grain for Constantinople, and the Imperial city.[44] It is possible that Gaiseric was doing his utmost to disrupt the flow of supplies to both Rome and Constantinople, to put pressure on the Imperial governments to come to terms, as well as disrupting any attempt to gather supplies to feed an army preparing to attack Africa.

A further reason has been suggested: 'Attacks on southwest Italy, Sardinia and Rhodes were added warnings to Valentinian III and Theodosius II against intervention.'[45] Although a possibility, the assertion is open to doubt. The attacks were more likely to stir rather than deter a response. It is more likely that Gaiseric was attempting to retain the initiative and, possibly more importantly, it would force the two empires to divert troops to defend against attack rather than allowing them to be gathered together to form an invasion force.

Whatever the reasons, Gaiseric's campaigns in both East and West were to end without permanent gain. By the end of 440, Vandal forces had been recalled to Africa, at least from Sicily but probably from all other areas.[46] It is possible that Gaiseric retained control of Lilybaeum, although this is uncertain. The main reason for the recall was probably the news from his eastern forces that the East had actually begun to prepare for a campaign in Africa. However, Gaiseric's position in Africa had also come under threat from an unexpected source.

Sebastianus

In 432, following the death of Bonifacius, his son-in-law Sebastianus had briefly occupied the position of *magister militum* before being driven out upon the return of

Aetius. Sebastianus had fled to Constantinople, but once established, he had allowed his followers to engage in 'piratical' activities in the Hellespont and Propontis.[47] With his position threatened, Sebastianus had fled from Constantinople, attempting to take refuge with Theoderic and the Goths in Aquitaine.[48] Rebuffed, he went to Barcelona, but being declared a public enemy had left there and travelled to Africa.[49]

Informed that Sebastianus had landed in Africa, Gaiseric almost certainly became worried by the possibility that Sebastianus would be able to use his father-in-law's reputation to rouse the inhabitants and retake Africa: Bonifacius had controlled the region for a long time. In addition, and possibly to Gaiseric's surprise, he became aware that Theodosius had promised to send aid to the West.[50]

Facing the double threat of a Roman commander in Africa and an invasion from Constantinople, Gaiseric left Sicily either late in 440 or early in 441. The actual date is unknown, but a letter from Paschasinus, Bishop of Lilybaeum, to Pope Leo I implies that the date may have been early in 441.[51] Gaiseric quickly learned that his fears concerning Sebastianus were unfounded, as Sebastianus was merely seeking asylum from his Roman enemies.[52] Gaiseric took no chances and showed his ruthless streak: fearing Sebastianus' military abilities, Gaiseric had him executed a short time after his arrival.[53]

The Imperial Campaign

Early in 441, Gaiseric learned that the East was actually fulfilling its promise to the West by sending an army to help in the reconquest of Africa.[54] Unfortunately, the sources for the African expedition are few and brief. A hypothetical reconstruction must be made, so it is necessary to remember that other interpretations are possible.

At some point, possibly late spring 441, an armada was dispatched from Constantinople bound for Sicily.[55] As expected, Sicily was to be the main staging point for the combined expedition. It would now be seen how effective Gaiseric's campaigns of the previous year had been. An individual named Pentadius was allocated the task of ensuring that the Roman army was supplied after its arrival in Sicily.[56] Both Prosper and Theophanes give a few details concerning the expedition:

> Theodosius opened hostilities with the Vandals by sending the generals Ariobindus, Ansila, and Germanus with a large fleet. They deferred the business with long delays and proved to be more of a burden to Sicily than a help to Africa.
>
> Prosper, s.a. 441

> Theodosius sent out 1,100 cargo ships with a Roman army commanded by
> the generals Areobindus, Ansilas, Inobindos, Arintheos, and Germanus.
> Gizerich [Gaiseric] was struck with fear when this force moored in Italy
> and he sent an embassy to Theodosius to discuss a treaty.
>
> Theophanes. 5941

The number of generals included in the campaign demonstrate that Theodosius
was intent on regaining Africa. It also implies that, although not necessarily a large
expedition, the army was still a force to be reckoned with. Ariobindus was *magister militum praesentalis*, and probably the senior officer.[57] Germanus was almost
certainly the *magister militum vacans* mentioned in the *Code of Justinian*.[58] Ansila,
Inobindos and Arintheos are unknown apart from these references.[59] The list of
commanders and sheer number of vessels carrying troops suggests that this was a
significant military expedition, probably comprising a large part of the *praesental*
army stationed in Constantinople, as well as elements of the field army of Thrace.
The commanders would expect to receive further reinforcements from the West.
In theory, the combination of a medium-sized army plus the *praesental* army from
the West – recently freed for action by the peace treaty with the Goths – should
easily have been enough to win.[60]

There is no direct evidence that Gaiseric's attacks on Sicily had any detrimental
effect on the Roman expedition. However, analysis suggests that, if he had retained
control of the city, his conquest of Lilybaeum may have caused an interruption in
the planned crossing to Africa. Firstly, the port was the obvious launching point for
the attack, and with it in Vandal hands there may have been debate as to what course
of action to take: besiege and retake the city or simply go on to Africa. The latter
would be affected by the second factor. Unless neutralized, Vandal ships in the
city's harbour could easily attack the rear of the expedition as it crossed to Africa.
Caution was needed. In addition, should the city be left in Vandal hands, troops
would need to be left in other Sicilian cities to defend against possible Vandal raids
from Lilybaeum. These factors may have caused a delay as debate raged, which
allowed issues in the East to further hamper the progress of the expedition.

Surprisingly, Aspar, the *magister militum* who had campaigned in Africa against
Gaiseric between 430 and 434 and so had first-hand knowledge of the region,
remained in Constantinople. The most likely reason behind his retention is that
tensions had begun to rise between Constantinople and both the Persians and
Huns, demanding the attention of Theodosius' most trusted general.[61] Given the
circumstances, both the Persians and Huns could be expected to make the most of
the temporary absence of an Eastern *praesental* army in Sicily.

Yet it is also possible that his remaining in Constantinople had a political reason.
It has been suggested that the reason for the delay is that the generals in Sicily were

members of Aspar's clique. In a strong political position, it is feasible that Aspar didn't want to risk defeat in Africa as it would lose him power and prestige. Just as importantly, Aspar didn't want a victory in Africa as it could lead to an increase in the prestige of the victorious commander, so leaving his own position vulnerable.[62]

With these aspects in mind, it is unsurprising that the expedition reached Sicily and then stopped. Once ashore, according to Prosper, they 'deferred the business with long delays and proved to be more of a burden to Sicily than a help to Africa'.[63] This may be supported by a papyrus from Ravenna dated to 445/446. In this, a tax paid into the *fiscus barbaricus* ('money for barbarians': specifically, a tax paid for the upkeep of *foederati*) is to revert to the owner. The dating of the tax, rather than the papyrus, suggests that the loss to the *fiscus barbaricus* was during the period when the Imperial armies were in Sicily prior to the projected invasion of Africa. If so, it implies that a large part of the produce of Sicily was appropriated for the supply of the troops as they waited for the commanders to give orders to cross to Africa, and supports the claim by Prosper that the campaign placed a major strain on the resources of Sicily.[64]

Alongside the aforementioned difficulties, and especially those concerning possible damage to port facilities, there was the need to coordinate the forces of East and West, and to decide upon the command structure of the invasion force: for example, whether an Eastern or Western commander would be in overall charge of the army.[65]

The delays proved costly for the West. It is almost certain that orders from Constantinople swiftly arrived to stop the attack. The Persians and Huns were threatening war, so the East was now faced with a war on three fronts: Africa, Persia and the Danube. The threat from Persia would always be a major concern for the East. The Huns across the Danube were also a formidable foe, threatening to invade and threaten the Imperial city of Constantinople. In the light of these observations, and although Theophanes claims that in the face of a major attack 'fear overcame Gaiseric and he sent an embassy to Theodosius II', it is possible that Gaiseric's envoys were welcomed in Constantinople, as Theodosius would have seen Gaiseric as the least threatening of his personal worries.[66]

Accordingly, negotiations were entered into with Gaiseric's envoys.[67] Throughout these events, Gaiseric would have maintained contact with both Imperial courts in the hope of avoiding a major confrontation: with his army being, in effect, the 'nation in arms', a defeat would be catastrophic and almost certainly destroy the Vandals as a separate entity. Although Gaiseric had been able to defeat the allied armies in Africa, he knew that he could not defeat the combined *praesental* armies of East and West. However, he would have known that, since the reign of Arcadius, the East had preferred to husband its armies, instead using diplomacy and money to pacify potential attackers. Although in this case the Vandals were occupying a vitally important province, Gaiseric may have hoped that the Eastern traditions would help to convince the East to follow their traditional policy, especially when combined with the threat of an external assault.

Gaiseric's hopes were to be more than fulfilled. Shortly after the expedition had set sail, the Persians attacked. It is almost certain that Aspar was sent to deal with the invasion.[68] Although the war was to be of short duration, ending in June 441, it was clear that a continued attempt to evict the Vandals from Africa would tempt the Persians into invading the East.[69]

To make matters worse, with the majority of the *praesental* and Thracian armies in Sicily, the Huns attacked Thrace, capturing several cities, before going on to 'devastate' Illyricum (see Map 1).[70] At the same time, internal rivalries within the Eastern command system also appear to have raised their head. John, a Vandal who was *magister militum per Thracias*, was 'treacherously killed by Arnegisclus', one of his subordinates.[71] The war effort against the Huns was to be hampered by internal politics.

In these circumstances, Theodosius could not afford to fight a war on many fronts, and accordingly he was willing to agree terms with Gaiseric that would otherwise have been unacceptable. This was to be a severe blow to the West: unable to muster enough forces to reconquer Africa on their own due to the ongoing wars in other theatres, the West would be forced to accept any treaty agreed by Theodosius.

In late 441, the East began to gather forces to face the Huns.[72] Unexpectedly, and for an unknown reason, Attila and Bleda, joint kings of the Huns, accepted a one-year truce and withdrew from Illyricum.[73] They may have heard of the postponement of the campaign against Gaiseric and withdrawn with their loot while they had chance.

The Treaty of 442

Over the winter of 441–442, the treaty was hammered out. Finally, peace was negotiated and Theodosius recalled his forces from Sicily.[74] For the East, the treaty was just in time: the truce with the Huns had expired and they had renewed their attacks on Illyricum. For the West, the treaty was a disaster. At a stroke, they lost their richest province and the source of the grain supply needed to maintain Italy free from famine. Within a short time, the loss of tax revenues would bankrupt the Empire. For Gaiseric, the settlement was the culmination of a dream.

Given its importance, it is unfortunate that no comprehensive account of the terms still exist. Instead, it is necessary to analyze the fragments that remain in the hope that they will shed light on the treaty. Two examples, from the works of Prosper and Procopius, illustrate the difficulty faced by modern historians.

The statement in Prosper's chronicle is very brief:

> The Augustus Valentinian made peace with Gaiseric and Africa was divided between the two into distinct territories.
>
> Prosper, s.a. 442

The report in Procopius is slightly more detailed, but unfortunately is also slightly confused. It would appear that he has conflated the treaties of 435 and 442, which, given the timescale between the treaties and Procopius' writing, is understandable:

> [Gaiseric] made a treaty with the Emperor Valentinian providing that each year he should pay to the emperor tribute from Libya, and he delivered over one of his sons, Honoric [sic], as a hostage to make this agreement binding.
>
> Procopius, 3.4.13

The use of the term 'Libya' is clearly from the earlier treaty of 435: there is no mention of the Vandals taking Africa Proconsularis and Carthage. However, the paying of 'tribute' and the sending of Huneric (Honoric) as 'hostage' both appear to refer to the treaty of 442.

The specific nature of the 'tribute' is open to debate, but a simple solution exists. When Gaiseric had first captured Carthage, he had cut the supplies of grain to Italy, so it is almost certain that the term 'tribute' refers to the restoration and continuation of the grain supply from Africa. Since the provinces in Africa produced a very large excess of grain, this was a small price for Gaiseric to pay in return for being accepted as the ruler of Africa.[75]

Victor of Vita gives a little more information:

> Byzacena, Abaritana and Gaetula, and part of Numidia he kept for himself; Zeugitana and the Proconsular province he divided up as 'an allotted portion for his people'.[76]
>
> Victor of Vita, 1.13

Although this list should clarify matters, there are problems interpreting Victor's list of provinces.[77] Byzacena and Proconsularis are straightforward. His identification of 'part of Numidia' is problematic. It may be meant to represent 'Numidia Proconsularis', the north-eastern corner of Numidia, which included Hippo Regius. Given that this was the Vandals' 'capital' prior to 439 and they would have spent time and money renovating the city for their own use, this is very likely. Gaetulia is even harder to identify. The likelihood is that Gaetulia included southern Byzacena and perhaps south-eastern Numidia. If true, this may have given the Vandals a frontier beginning to the west of Hippo and running almost directly south to the salt lake known as Chott Melrhir. In which case, the border may have run from the coast to Guelma and then followed the Roman road south before passing between Thamugadi and Theveste to the lake. Although there is no indication that the Romans regularly used such artificial features as roads to create borders in Africa, given the confused and fraught nature of the negotiations, this feature may have acted as a simple method of defining territory.

The region called Abaritana is also unknown by that name at this date.[78] However, since the western and southern boundaries of the Vandal settlement may already have been identified, it is probable that Abaritana refers to the eastern boundary, which means that the region is the western part of Tripolitana.

In some respects, the information above is supported by other sources on Roman Africa. For example, there is good evidence that between 442 and 455 Rome retained control of Mauretania Caesariensis, Mauretania Sitifiensis and the region known as Numidia Cirtensis, which was the western part of Numidia with its centre at Cirta.[79] However, all of the above is supposition based on the few remaining sources, and it should be noted that other conclusions can be drawn.

There is one caveat to the above hypothesis. Although it is sometimes assumed that all of 'Roman Africa' was under the direct control of the Vandals, this was not the case: 'more than half a dozen Berber princes were able to set themselves up in the western provinces'.[80] During the years that followed, Gaiseric would have to come to some agreement with these princes in order to secure his borders.

To help cement the treaty, Gaiseric's son, Huneric, was sent as a hostage to Ravenna. Merobaudes describes his time in the capital as a success, especially since it resulted in Huneric becoming attached to the Imperial family.[81] After less than two years, and prior to the reading of Merobaudes' poems – which occurred sometime around 443 – Huneric had become engaged to Eudocia, daughter of the Emperor Valentinian.[82] Although the proposal is usually accepted simply at face value, it is possible that the betrothal was not a serious proposition by the West, but merely aimed at ensuring that Gaiseric continued to adhere to the terms of the treaty. Whatever the cause of the betrothal, not everybody in the West was happy: Merobaudes, in the panegyric celebrating Aetius' third consulship in January 446, appears dismayed that the 'invader of Africa' had dared to enter into 'close connections' with Rome.[83]

It is also possible that Gaiseric initially expected a daughter of the emperor to serve as a counter-hostage to Huneric. However, the Imperial family did not exchange hostages from its members. If this is true, the betrothal may have been proposed as an alternative to giving a hostage, and so can be seen as a counter-balance to Huneric becoming a hostage.

It has been suggested that Gaiseric's reason for accepting the betrothal was simple: 'Barbarians of late antiquity were generally unable to resist the prospect of a connection with the imperial family.'[84] It has also been proposed that for the Imperial family, the betrothal was 'equally comprehensible' as 'Gaiseric's Vandals furnished the possible means of offsetting the influence of ... Aetius'.[85] Although this is possible, and may form part of the reasons for the proposal, a simpler theory presents itself: the proposed acceptance of Gaiseric and his family into the Imperial family was simply a cheap means of ensuring the continuation of the treaty. Despite their apparent strength, the West was desperate to remove any possibility of the Vandals breaking the treaty and again halting the grain supply to Rome.

Whatever the case, with the remote possibility of the marriage going ahead, Huneric could theoretically be in line for the throne. To avoid any possible confusion, Eudocia's claim to inheritance was declared ineligible to avoid a barbarian being Valentinian's heir. Pulcheria thus became the heir apparent in the West.[86]

There can be little doubt that the treaty removed the obligation of the Vandals as *foederati*.[87] It is even possible that in one entry, Prosper may imply that the Vandals were now *de facto* independent, although it is questionable whether Rome recognized their independence *de jure*: 'the edicts of Valentinian III during the period 442–455 show that the Empire still regarded the provinces of Africa Proconsularis and Byzacene as legal entities, and interpreted the Vandal presence in those provinces as a temporary situation'.[88]

Merobaudes may also give a further detail on the nature of the agreement, although this is slightly more conjectural. In the second panegyric he 'uses the adjective *socius* [which] with other tenuous evidence suggests that the Empire bestowed on Gaiseric the ancient status of *socius et amicus cum foedere*' (ally and friend by treaty).[89] This would help explain both the fact that the Empire could accept the Vandals' occupation of Africa and that for a long period Gaiseric continued to honour the treaty, since he was being acknowledged as virtually the equal of the emperor. The impression that Gaiseric was now an important player within the Empire would have been reinforced by the prospective marriage between Huneric and Eudocia.

Alongside these factors, Gaiseric knew that war was not the best use of his newly conquered territory. Although there is no doubt that some trade continued despite the war, as brave traders took the risk of passing through the war zone in the knowledge that scarcity would have made their goods more valuable, the conflict was a major dislocation in the economic life of Africa. To reap the full benefits of his conquest, Gaiseric needed Carthage to return to being the focus of trade in order to tax the commerce passing through the city.

Chapter 9

Consolidation and Expansion

The Vandal Settlement

Vandal culture ... had been moulded by a full generation of military activity (and inactivity) with the Western Empire, and their political systems similarly were created from the immediate needs of this peripatetic mercenary lifestyle.

Merrills and Miles, *The Vandals*, p.56

For Gaiseric, it was obvious that Vandal security would rely on three major factors: the cooperation of the conquered Roman subjects, possible alliances with other barbarian leaders and the 'good will of Romans abroad', the latter including, above all, Roman emperors.[1] With the Vandals numbering possibly as few as the 'low tens of thousands', ruling a Roman population estimated as high as '1–3 million', Gaiseric knew that should the population be roused to rebel by one of the emperors, his forces would be very heavily outnumbered.[2] The fact that for a long time the Vandals were at peace with the Empire suggests that Gaiseric was able to ease relations with the two emperors, even if only because they had far greater threats to their survival than the Vandals. In addition, the sources for events are all Roman, and as such rarely describe the exchange of envoys outside those arriving at the Imperial court. As a result, it is likely that envoys between the barbarian kings was more common than revealed in the written evidence.[3]

In the short term, however, Gaiseric was secure in the knowledge that he was safe from attack by the Empire, so was now able to distribute lands and positions of power as he thought fit.

Byzacena, Abaritana and Gaetulia, and part of Numidia he kept for himself; Zeugitana and the Proconsular Province he divided up as an allotted portion for his people; and he allowed Valentinian ... to take for himself the remaining, and now devastated provinces.[4]

Victor of Vita, 1.13

The most productive parts of the African territory – Africa Proconsularis, Byzacena, Tripolitania and parts of Numidia – were now ruled by the Vandals (see Map 9). Most of the conquered lands were kept under Gaiseric's direct control, but he 'gave the best and richest land [Africa Proconsularis] to his sons and the Vandal people', although Carthage itself remained in his own hands, and he established his royal palace on Byrsa, the Acropolis of Carthage.[5]

The 'best and richest land' was later known as the *sortes Vandalorum* ('lot/ allotment of the Vandals'), a phrase used by Victor of Vita simply to mean 'land of the Vandals'. The nature of these divisions is confused and open to interpretation, with some historians believing that the land of the dispossessed Roman senators was given to the troops, whilst others claim that it was the income from the land, not the land itself, which was distributed.[6]

Apart from the biased and apocalyptic diatribes of Christians such as Victor of Vita, there is little evidence that Gaiseric immediately uprooted large numbers of Romans in order to satisfy the requirements of his troops. Nor is it likely that he instituted a purge of Roman farmers in order to settle his people: throughout his life, Gaiseric appears to have understood the limits of his power and to have worked within those boundaries to the greatest possible benefit for himself and his people.

As a result, it would make more sense if he used methods traditional to the Empire in order to lessen the disruption of the takeover and ensure a quick return to profitability for Africa. It is probable that at this early stage only the income from the land was given to Gaiseric's troops, following the Roman tradition of *honesta missio* (literally 'honorable mission'), which in return brought hereditary service in the army, a fact of which Gaiseric would have approved.[7] The net result was that the Vandals simply replaced the Empire. The Vandal warriors took the place of the Roman Army, whilst Gaiseric and the Vandal nobility replaced the emperor and the aristocratic landowners. In other words, the Vandal nobles 'effectively stepped into the shoes of the Roman authorities that had ruled Africa previously and took over the existing administrative regime, including the tax system', whilst the warriors received the traditional stipends of regular Roman troops whilst remaining billeted in towns – mainly Carthage.[8]

However, many troops would have been at retirement age, and consequently soon after the settlement they would have been given land out of the *fisc* (imperial exchequer) and *agri deserti* (uninhabited lands). It is probably the resulting use of both the traditional financial system for the serving warriors plus land being given to troops on retirement that may explain the confusion surrounding the term *sortes Vandalorum* in both the ancient sources and modern interpretations: obviously, however, this is speculation rather than attested fact.

The remaining Romans paid their usual taxes, but to the king, not the emperor. The only difference in these cases appears to have been that the leases issued by the Vandals were dated by the regnal year of the Vandal king, rather than using the

Roman dating system.[9] The down-to-earth change of 'landlord' doubtless eased the transformation from Roman to Vandal Africa, as well as proving simple for the new Vandal rulers and settlers to understand and keep track of. However, the maintenance of Roman institutions can easily result in the suffering and dislocation caused by the Vandal takeover being minimized.

The hypothesis that barbarian occupations of Roman territory were peaceful has doubtless been augmented by the nature of the kingdoms created. Rather than being completely new entities with 'barbarian' methods of rule being imposed upon a defeated population, the new rulers simply inserted themselves into the existing hierarchy and used the existing Roman institutions for their own purposes. For example, the Roman dignities of *illustris*, *spectabilis* and *clarrisimus* remained in use amongst the Romano-African nobility, and the survival of the posts of *flamines perpetui* and *sacerdotalis provinciae Africae* implies a continuation of the provincial council, doubtless now being used to advise the king about his new kingdom. In addition, the *cursus publicus* ('postal service'; 'imperial messengers') also remained in existence.[10]

Indirect evidence for a continuation of Roman posts can also be found after the Byzantine reconquest of AD 533. Following the collapse of the Vandal kingdom, the Eastern Emperor Justinian I is attested as having appointed *commerciarii*, *apo eparchontes* and a *diocetes provinciarum* in Africa to control trade and tolls, supervise state workshops and gather taxes from the province.[11] Although only attested at this time, it is hard to believe that these posts were a creation of Justinian, and that no equivalent posts had existed prior to the Vandal conquest. The clear implication, therefore, is that they had been in place prior to the Vandal invasion and that the Vandals had continued to use them, before Justinian finally appointed his own men to the posts vacated by the destruction of the Vandal court.

It has also been suggested that the change in use of some buildings in post-conquest Africa was imposed by the Vandals, and was thus evidence of the changes made by Gaiseric and his successors as they exercised their rule in the region. However, it has recently been noted that, in reality, these changes were simply following a trend that was already in evidence in the archaeology of the fourth century. As a consequence, these should actually be interpreted as being a sign of continuation of Roman trends rather than of Vandal changes.[12]

The fact that the Vandals, and other 'successor kingdoms', continued to use late-Roman methods, titles and functionaries to run their kingdoms can easily lead to the impression that the takeover was gentle and disruption was minimal. To some degree, this has to be acknowledged: Gaiseric appears to have been a pragmatic individual and there is little doubt that he knew that the Roman method of running Africa was the most efficient. The notion is reinforced by the fact that the Vandals appear to have quickly assumed Roman tastes after the conquest, although in reality this should probably be amended to 'Romano-African' tastes: there remained distinct regional differences between the majority of the Africans and Romans in Italy, with possibly only the highest echelons of African society attempting to emulate the Roman model as practised in Italy.[13]

On the other hand, it should be accepted that along with the continuity there was heavy disruption as the local aristocracy was ousted and the incoming Vandals were put in their place. The new landowners would need time to adapt to their new roles as much as the Romano-Africans would need time to adjust to their new masters. It is probable that much of the vitriol poured upon the Vandals by Victor of Vita and other Nicene writers is founded upon friction between the new Vandal landlords and their Romano-African subjects over legal jurisdiction and appropriate behaviour.[14]

The signing of the treaty also helped Gaiseric in one other way; to make a further major change to Vandal culture. At this time, before Gaiseric could fully impose himself on his kingdom, the Vandal government was 'an uneasy coalition ... [of] ... the ruling clan of the Hasdingi ... [supported by a] ... polyglot elite of Vandals, Alans, Goths, Suevi and Hispano-Romans'.[15] This coalition was in the process of absorbing the local African aristocracy, who would provide them with a functioning Roman bureaucracy with which to run the new kingdom. Yet overall, Gaiseric was working within the milieu of a Germanic system in which it was the norm that the eldest male relative would secure the throne after the death of the king. Obviously, Gaiseric's half-brother and predecessor Gunderic had children who would inherit the kingdom before Huneric, Gaiseric's eldest son. One of the major factors in the Treaty of 442 was the betrothal of Huneric and Eudocia, daughter of Valentinian III. A major contributing factor to the betrothal was that it ensured widespread support for Gaiseric's attempt to change the rules: it would take a strong personality to argue that the son of the previous king who was also a member of the Imperial family should not be allowed to rule. Interestingly, one of the justifications for the later invasion of the Vandal kingdom by the Eastern (Byzantine) Empire was that Gelimer, the last king, was a usurper and the Empire was invading to remove him.

It is possible that at the same time as the apportionment of land, Gaiseric acted to organize his people, both socially and militarily. Over the decades of the Asding Vandal migration following the crossing of the Rhine in 406, they had absorbed Siling Vandals, Alans, Goths, tribesmen of other tribes, plus Roman slaves and malcontents. The distribution of land and political positions now allowed Gaiseric to implement social reforms aimed at establishing the 'political stratigraphy' of his new kingdom.[16] One of his main aims was doubtless to establish his own family as the dominant force within the Vandals at the expense of many Vandal nobles, who would be unhappy with the lessening of their influence.[17]

Gaiseric also appointed Germanic individuals to help run the kingdom. For example, alongside Roman bureaucrats, he chose a man named Heldica to be the *praepositus regni* ('Governor of the King'). He may also have organized the equivalent of the Roman *concilium* (council), a group of powerful individuals who would advise him on events and decisions both inside and outside the kingdom.[18] Although necessary, the reforms certainly resulted in unhappiness amongst previously powerful members of the aristocracy who felt they had been unfairly omitted from the new hierarchy – as will be seen shortly.

At the same time, he would have been able to establish a military hierarchy within which the different groups would either be merged into one cohesive force or have their speciality acknowledged. For example, despite modern assertions, it is likely that the Alans in the army retained their speciality as horsemen armed with bows and ancillary weapons rather than conforming to the Vandal norm. Yet the one thing that is certain is that throughout these reforms, Gaiseric ensured his power at the top of the pyramid.[19]

Romano-Africans

With respect to the Romano-Africans, Gaiseric's treaty in 442 'proved his power and importance by securing and maintaining the diplomatic friendship of the Roman Emperor'. In addition, the new connection with the royal house by the betrothal of Huneric to Eudocia gave the Vandals a kind of legitimacy. To emphasize the continuity of the regime, Gaiseric made the political and cultural choice to maintain many Roman institutions, partly to reassure multiple audiences throughout the Mediterranean that under the Vandals, 'Romanness in Africa' would be safe.[20]

Politically, the Vandal conquest was obviously a major change in the fortunes of previously powerful Romano-Africans. Some large villas were seized by the Vandal aristocracy, but this was mainly in urban districts rather than in the countryside.[21] The low number of Vandal aristocrats, as opposed to the native inhabitants, may be surmised from the fact that many villas vacated by fleeing Romano-Africans were left empty by the new regime – unlikely had there been enough Vandal aristocrats to fill all of the empty villas.

Although the evidence is tenuous, it is also possible that Gaiseric determined to promote a new generation of Romano-African aristocrats from those families who had not been amongst the leaders prior to the Vandal conquest. For example, his sons Huneric and Theoderic each employed a *procurator domus* ('local steward', 'Superintendent of the Household'), named Saturus and Felix respectively, who appear to have been drawn from non-aristocratic families.[22] If true, the episodes imply that Gaiseric was intent upon replacing the absent aristocrats with *parvenus* whose loyalty was likely to be to Gaiseric, the man who had promoted them, rather than to the Empire. However, should they prove to be troublesome, they could easily be removed: Saturus, the superintendent of Theoderic's household mentioned above, apparently continued to oppose the Arianism of the Vandals, and his continuous criticisms finally resulted in him losing his position and property.[23]

Gaiseric was to adopt one further novel approach, which was with the dating system in Africa. He selected the capture of Carthage as the first year of his reign, dating his kingship to this year.[24] There are several possible reasons for this decision. Possibly the most important is that he may have been attempting to eliminate the fact that he was actually the king of an invading people. By dating his reign to the capture of Carthage, he may have been linking his reign specifically with Africa, in the hope that his Roman subjects would accept that they were important to him, as it implied that prior to their inclusion in his kingdom, his rule was not worthy of mention. If successful, the novel approach would be a major feat of propaganda.

The strategy may have worked, at least in part, as evidenced by the discovery of forty-five written tablets dating to the end of the fifth century which affirm the use of the new dating system.[25] In addition, there is the evidence of epigraphy. Sadly, the analysis of surviving inscriptions is biased due to the wealthy nature of the individuals or families who erected them. Nevertheless, the use of the new dating system in the epigraphic record implies that at least a section of Romano–African aristocracy accepted the right of Gaiseric to rule in Africa, rather than constantly opposing the Vandals. Three known inscriptions can probably be dated to the reign of Gaiseric, all of them dated using the years of his reign.[26] This would not have happened if the families involved were opposed to Gaiseric's rule.

The same may also be true of the written record, where the anonymous *Libellus de computo paschali* of 455 makes reference to the tenth and sixteenth years of Gaiseric's reign.[27] However, it should be noted that the author may simply have been using the date as employed by his masters at Carthage, and as such it does not necessarily mean that the author supported the regime. Yet it does suggest that by at least 455, many Romano-Africans had finally been persuaded that Vandal rule was permanent and that, accordingly, they had little choice but to join with the regime or accept that they were not going to advance socially.[28]

Although the majority of the sources are Nicene, and so opposed to the Vandals, reaction to the settlement was not always specifically antagonistic. The 'primitive but pure barbarian' was a long-standing theme with Roman writers and was always compared to the 'degenerate, pleasure-loving Romans' by moralistic authors attempting to demonstrate the error of Roman ways. According to Salvian in his *De gubernatione* (On the Government of God – published before 451 and possibly soon after 442):

Let us compare the actual devastators of Africa with the people whom they conquered. ... They had, as it is written in the Scriptures, entered 'a land flowing with milk and honey,' ... Who would doubt that the Vandals, upon entering such a country, would plunge into all manner of filthy and unclean vice? Or, to speak more moderately, that they would at least copy the constant behaviour of the people of Africa, into whose province they had come? ... In such great abundance of wealth and luxury, however, not one of them was rendered effeminate. ... Who can help admiring the Vandals? They entered the wealthiest cities, where ... vices were common, and took over the riches of dissolute men in such a way that they rejected their corrupting customs and now possess and use those things that are good, and avoid the degrading influence of those that are evil ... Sexual vice has been completely abolished by them. ... I said that the cities of Africa were full of monstrous vices, and especially the queen and mistress of them all, but that the Vandals were not polluted. ... They have removed from every part of Africa the vice of effeminacy, they have even abhorred intercourse with harlots, and have not only shunned or done away with it for the time being, but have made it absolutely cease to exist.

Salvian, *De gubernatione Dei*, 20–22

This was obviously a moralistic composition, and doubtless the purity of the Vandals has been greatly exaggerated by Salvian, but it is interesting to note that Malchus claims that soon after Gaiseric's death, the Vandals 'lapsed into every kind of weakness'.[29] Although doubtless all of these works were to some degree a rhetorical exercise, the impression remains of Gaiseric being a strong king who kept his subjects' worst natures under control, whereas the Romano-Africans – and especially the aristocracy – had lost the confidence of Nicene Christian writers.

The Empire

Gaiseric's actions in annexing the lands of powerful, rich absentee landlords and in forcing the resident Roman landowners to flee resulted in a large pressure-group in Ravenna and Constantinople agitating for the recovery of Africa.[30] Although Gaiseric may have felt that he could defeat a Western invasion, he knew that a joint East-West attack would probably result in the revolt of the indigenous people. Even though such a campaign could possibly be defeated, the losses and disruption caused by a war and internal unrest would seriously damage Gaiseric's financial position. Under the constant threat of invasion, Gaiseric doubtless retained a large proportion of his troops in Carthage rather than allowing them to disperse in order to farm personally.

It should be noted, however, that once the immediate threat of invasion had passed, the attitude of Gaiseric to the dispossessed Romans did in some respects relent. Some of them later returned to Africa and at least some of their property was returned.[31] It is only after a treaty had been agreed that some of the Vandal troops may have been released from immediate service, especially those who had been involved in the fighting since before 429 and so have been close to retirement age, to begin their new lives as farmers and landholders.

The emergence of a Vandal land-owning peasant class can lead to confusion concerning the division between Vandals and Romano-Africans after the first disruption of the invasion. Yet in part this is due to an unspoken division between regions of the Roman Empire – especially between East and West. The hypothesis is emphasized by an episode that damages the illusion of an Empire that remained united against barbarian attacks. During the flight of the aristocracy, an aristocrat named Eudaemon fled to Italy, where he rose to a position of some importance. His daughter Maria did not escape with him. She was taken captive and sold into slavery. Although it is nowhere stated that the Vandals were responsible, it is difficult to assign the event to any other group, given Maria's high rank in Africa.

What makes this episode important to a study of the period is that Maria was sold into slavery in Syria, a part of the Eastern Empire. The concept that a daughter of a Western Roman aristocrat could be sold into slavery in the Eastern Empire is usually overlooked by historians. Furthermore, despite her acknowledged status, her new owner demanded payment before he would release her, and it was only the actions of local people, who gathered the money and secured her release, that allowed her to rejoin her father in the West. Even more remarkable is the fact that Theoderet, our source for this event, leaves the reader with the impression that Maria was released only because of her noble birth, and that as a consequence the enslaving of Western citizens in the East was not unusual.[32] The question remains as to how many more Africans were sold into slavery in the Roman East and why there was no sense of unity between the citizens of East and West, despite modern expectations.

Alongside the inherent divisions between East and West, the attitudes of the Romano-Africans themselves may in some ways help to explain the fact that they were ready to cooperate with the Vandals. Although seen by many as being simply 'Roman', and therefore obviously opposed to the Vandal conquest on Imperialistic grounds, by the fifth century the Romano-Africans 'had managed to become Roman while remaining African'.[33] This duality may have helped them adapt to the new regime, as they would remain 'African' and their 'Roman' nature could be satisfied by the continuing trade and contact with the Empire. The change from Imperial to Vandal rule would therefore not have involved a major change in outlook. This may explain why many local men slowly aligned themselves with the Vandal regime, rather than remaining loyal to the Imperial legacy.[34]

Religion

The incoming Vandals may have been Christians, but they followed a different form of Christianity to the Western Empire.[35] In the West, Nicene (Catholic) Christianity had become dominant, although several other forms of Christianity had continued to be followed: in Africa there was allegedly a small Arian section in Hippo Regius – the home of Saint Augustine – on the eve of the Vandal invasion. Yet it should be remembered that even amongst Arians there were differences in either the form of worship or the specific belief in the nature of Christ. Although the Vandals were Arians, they followed a form that was closer to Nicene Christianity than other, more strict, variations of Arianism.[36]

As seen in the passage from Salvian quoted above, some Nicene chroniclers adopted the stance that the Vandals were God's punishment for an Africa that had become degenerate and had abandoned God's teachings. From a slightly different perspective, and if Procopius is to be believed, Gaiseric saw himself as an agent of God, from whom he had received the kingdom of Africa. Evidence of this can be found in a later episode. When he was about to depart on a seaborne raid against the Empire, he was asked where the ships needed to go. He replied: 'Obviously against those with whom God is angry.'[37] If Gaiseric did see himself as God's agent, it would have been important to Gaiseric to retain God's favour, and doubtless this included the continuation of Arianism as the Vandal's religion. The necessary outcome of this attitude would be an attempt to convert the whole of Africa, towards which ideal Gaiseric of necessity supported the Arian Church and possibly passed laws on 'public decorum'.[38] The complete conversion of Africa would in turn have 'erected a permanent barrier to imperial reconquest'.[39]

Consequently, many of the Catholic churches were given to the new Arian clergy, who also received some of the land confiscated from the Roman aristocracy, no doubt in order to make them self-sufficient and a powerful force to support the king. When Gaiseric later allowed some of the Roman aristocracy to return, the land 'donated' to the Church was not restored to the returning Romans.[40]

The limited information available suggests that early in his reign, Gaiseric focused upon the suppression of the Nicene church in Africa Proconsularis, the location of the majority of the *sortes Vandalorum*.[41] In Carthage, Gaiseric seized the cathedral, along with the Basilica Maiorum (which housed the relics of St Perpetua and St Felicitas) and two churches important to the cult of St Cyprian.[42] Although eventually some of the clerics who had fled would be allowed to return, these buildings remained in Vandal hands until the Byzantine reconquest in 533.

In the majority of cases, though, the Nicene incumbent was left in control of their church until their death by natural causes. At this point, Gaiseric's order forbidding the ordination of Nicene bishops resulted in the vacancy of that position until external factors changed the situation. For example, after Gaiseric had banished bishop Quodvultdeus in the mid-440s, his metropolis was deprived of a bishop until the ordination of bishop Deogratias in October 454 after negotiations with Valentinian III.[43] After Deogratias' death, the bishop's see was to remain vacant for a further twenty-four years, with Gaiseric again forbidding the ordination of bishops to the vacant see.[44] Obviously, the situation was the same for sees outside the capital.[45]

It is customary to see the 'genius' of Gaiseric in his dealings with the Nicene hierarchy, but it is possible that in this case he was listening to advice from his Patriarch, Jucundus – if, in fact, Jucundus was Patriarch at the start of Gaiseric's reign, as the paucity of the sources mean that Jucundus' involvement must remain a possibility rather than a fact.[46] Jucundus, more than the secular ruler, may have seen the importance to Vandal rule of not creating any Nicene martyrs who would act as a focus of anti-Vandal sentiment when he advised Gaiseric's son Theoderic not to execute a man named Armogas.[47]

Of even more importance, however, was the fact that the majority of the Nicene clergy were also members of high-ranking families in Africa. To execute bishops who were their fathers, sons or brothers would, of necessity, ensure that the African elite were hostile to Gaiseric.[48]

Yet contrary to the constant portrayal of dealings between Vandals and Romans being hostile, and despite the ancient portrayal of a rigid demarcation between the Vandal conquerors and native Romans, close analysis of the sources suggests that there was a 'much more porous border between Arian and Nicene and much more traffic across it than our sources are willing to disclose'.[49] It should be remembered that our sources are Nicene Christians hostile to the Arian Vandals, but that many of the Vandals' new subjects were either not Nicenes or were not as strict in their observance of Nicene strictures about dealing with heretics. Although there was always a divide between the Arian Vandals and their Nicene subjects, laws enforcing a separation between Arians and – especially – the Nicenes explain why later kings ordered persecutions of Catholics: the law may have been needed in order to maintain Vandal identity and stop them being absorbed into the majority population.[50]

There remains the question of how the Vandals treated the Donatists, the group decried as heretics by the Nicenes for their refusal to accept the appointment of ecclesiastical office either by or to individuals who had earlier renounced their beliefs during the persecution of Diocletian. It is likely that they too were put under pressure to become Arians, and were disadvantaged by the laws passed by Gaiseric and his successors. Sadly, there is little information concerning the Donatists contained within the Nicene works of Victor of Vita and others.

It is interesting to note that although Gaiseric did begin to put pressure on the natives to convert to Arianism, his successors – especially Huneric – were to go to further extremes. It is possible that Gaiseric was taking care not to antagonize the Roman emperors, whereas later rulers believed that they were secure from Imperial reprisals. Yet throughout Vandal rule, the 'techniques of religious coercion ... were closely modelled on imperial methods for the suppression of heresy': the Nicenes in Africa were to become the victims of the conversion methods that had previously been used against their adversaries.[51] The methods may have been brutal, but, despite the rhetoric in the sources, there does not appear to have been a bloodbath.[52]

Instead, Gaiseric used internal exile, redistribution of church property and the elimination of bishoprics through attrition rather than using terminal means to promote Arianism. Yet the first of these methods appears slightly strange until it is recognized that an internal exile to a territory within the bounds of the Vandal kingdom, or sometimes to territory belonging to associated Moors, meant that there was no great influx of dispossessed clerics arriving in Rome and/or Constantinople clamouring for the emperors to take direct action by invading Africa in order to restore Nicene rule to the region. This was to remain a constant worry for Gaiseric, as evidenced by the fact that even the mere threat of a subversive act was enough to have Gaiseric exile bishop Felix of Hadrumetum, when the latter simply received a foreign monk named John.[53]

Despite opposition to Vandal rule, at least in the late 440s and into the 450s the Nicene clergy became aware that Arianism was a threat as many Romano-Africans began to convert, if only to be able to gain positions of prestige within the Vandal hierarchy – as demonstrated by the sheer volume of anti-Arian literature being produced.[54]

Economy

In one major way, however, Gaiseric was able to change the nature of African society. The vast majority of the production of Africa was geared towards supplying Italy with necessities via the system of *annona* (supplying goods instead of tax). After the Vandal conquest, Africa was to a large degree freed from this burden, and although the Vandals themselves must have appropriated some of the *annona* for themselves, as well as supplying Rome according to the accords of the treaty, these demands were doubtless less than the combined earlier requirements of Rome and Italy.

Despite the fact that the 'tribute' would have continued to siphon goods, especially grain, for the Empire, African traders were now allowed to trade a significant proportion of the surplus produce in other markets, including southern Gaul, Spain, north-western Italy and Sicily.[55] Alongside these, trade continued with Rome and southern Italy, although now the customers were expected to pay for the goods they received, rather than relying upon government 'donations' due to the *annona*.[56] In addition, the archaeological survival of African red slip ware in the East demonstrates that trade continued with the Eastern Empire, although possibly to a lesser degree than prior to the Vandal invasion – perhaps due to either anti-Vandal sentiment or the rise in production of local wares, or a combination of the two factors.[57]

Although the evidence is sparse and open to distortion due to the nature of the archaeological record, it would appear that it was not only the East where trade from Africa went into decline: trade with southern Gaul also appears to have dropped – possibly in part due to the antagonism between the Vandals and Goths. On the other hand, trade with Hispania appears to have grown, possibly due to the continuing contacts between the Vandals and the peoples of Hispania.[58] Taxes from all of these activities would have helped to finance the embryonic Vandal kingdom.

Despite the loss of some markets, it would appear that under Vandal rule, agricultural prosperity in Africa grew, as well as African red slip ware production.[59] In addition, texts show that slaves, grain, clothes textiles, sponges, figs, cumin, salt, wild animals and wood were also exported from Africa, and Carthage was reported to have a 'remarkable silver-working district', but obviously the trade in these items has left no trace in the archaeological record.[60]

The increased output was doubtless partly due to the observation of Gaiseric and his successors that the greater the produce, the greater the tax that could be levied upon it. Although the precise dating of these changes is impossible, it is tempting to assume that Gaiseric, probably the most perceptive of the Vandal kings, had recognized this factor from an early date and had implemented changes from early in his reign, most likely shortly after the conclusion of the treaty of 442. Whatever the case, the continued movement of individuals away from Africa to both the East and West implies a continuation of trade patterns.[61]

Alongside the change in the nature of exports, Gaiseric began to introduce his own coinage, which appears to have begun early in his reign.[62] Minted following Imperial examples, the production stated, more than any other method, that the Vandals were now independent and a force to be reckoned with. Few examples of early coinage have been found, but if these are attributed correctly, and if they are reproductions from life, they may represent the only likeness of Gaiseric that has come down from antiquity.

The Moors

During the Early and Middle Imperial periods, the Moorish rulers had been attached to the Empire, although usually still seen as outsiders by many. The majority learned neither Greek nor Latin, instead retaining their own language. In addition, they remained for the most part pagan, as evidenced by the attempt after the Byzantine reconquest of 533 to convert the Moors to Christianity.[63] Their refusal to accept the Imperial religion or language attests to their desire to remain a people free, wherever possible, of Imperial domination. By the fifth century, and especially during periods of unrest and civil war in Italy, such as that between Bonifacius and Valentinian III, the Moors were liable to throw off their allegiance to the Empire and make raids into Imperial territory:

> But what shall I say of the devastation of Africa at this hour by hordes of African barbarians, to whom no resistance is offered, while you are engrossed with such embarrassments in your own circumstances, and are taking no measures for averting this calamity? Who would ever have believed ... Africa ... should now have suffered the barbarians to be so bold, to encroach so far, to destroy and plunder so much, and to turn into deserts such vast regions once densely peopled?
>
> Augustine, *Epistle* 220.7 (AD 427) to
> Boniface: c.f. *Epistle* 185 (AD 416).

When the Empire had been strong, the Moors had remained loyal. The Vandals were seen as being strong, and as a result, after the Vandal conquest, Moorish leaders 'sought and received the symbols of rule from the new Germanic monarchs just as they had done earlier from the Roman proconsuls'.[64] However, over time – and possibly beginning in Gaiseric's reign – the borders of both the Mauretanian and Numidian provinces became dominated by Moors, doubtless with the acceptance of the Vandals, who were apparently content to retain firm control over the more prosperous coastal regions.[65]

Yet the Numidian provinces were, by and large, part of Imperial territory, and in 445, Valentinian III legitimated 'private armies' in the province of Numidia Cirtensis and ordered them to calm 'Numidian unrest' and defend the province from 'external barbarians'.[66] It has been suggested that this was an order aimed at preventing Vandal raids on the province, and possibly allowing the private armies to raid Vandal territory in return.[67] Although a possibility, given that there is no other evidence for conflict between Gaiseric and the West it is more likely that the order was given because the region was suffering from the encroachments of Moors rather than Vandals, taking advantage of Roman weakness and in the knowledge that the Vandals would not take action against them.

In fact, the episode probably highlights a major factor that is often ignored when discussing Roman Africa and the Vandal conquest. The earlier conflicts fought by Bonifacius against the Vandals are evidence that Roman power was slowly fading and being replaced in the pre-Saharan frontier zone by 'dual states'; Moorish chieftains nominally federated to Rome exercising rule over a mixed population of Romano-Africans and Moors, sometimes opposed by Romano-African notables fielding small armies for local defence.[68]

For his part, Gaiseric was to use the fact that the Moors had not been wholly part of the Empire as a place to exile Nicene opponents, where they would be unable to use their influence to stir opposition to Vandal rule in Africa: for example, the Moorish king Capsur, who not only accepted Nicene opponents as exiles but also sent a report to Gaiseric concerning the exiles' behaviour. Furthermore, when Gaiseric ordered that the exiles be executed, the sentence was carried out.[69] The alliance between the Moors and Vandals would be an important piece of Gaiseric's success between the conquest of Africa and his death.

The Vandal Peace, 442–454

The treaty of 442 was a landmark in Roman affairs. Although Valentinian and Aetius saved face by claiming that the Vandals had settled in Africa under Roman rule, the reality was that the government in Ravenna had agreed to the permanent loss of territory to a barbarian king, and acknowledged that they did not have the troops to retake it without help from the East.[70] Yet, surprisingly, Gaiseric did not attempt to take advantage of Roman weakness to further enlarge his realm.

This was in part due to the fact that the Vandals, and especially Gaiseric, realized that they would provoke a further invasion from the East if they attempted to attack the West. After all, it was a matter of luck that the Eastern expedition had been halted by the attacks of both the Persians and Huns. There is no evidence, as suggested by some historians, that there was a political and military agreement between Gaiseric, Attila and the Sasanian Persian Yezdigerd II.[71] Furthermore, Gaiseric may have been following the standard barbarian policy of attacking the West when it was weak or divided, and coming to terms with the emperor when the West was stronger and more able to defend itself.[72] After 442, Aetius firmly established himself in power in Italy and his military ability helped to delay further erosion of Roman power.

Yet there was a further factor in the protracted period of peace following the treaty of 442: Gaiseric was not yet totally secure in his kingdom. Prosper notes that following the treaty:

> Some of Gaiseric's magnates conspired against him because he was proud even among his own people, due to the successful outcome of events. But when the undertaking was discovered, they were subjected to many tortures and killed by him. Whenever others seemed to venture the same thing, the king's mistrust served to destroy so many that he lost more men by this anxiety of his than if he had been overthrown in war.
>
> Prosper, s.a. 442.

As with the Goths, the modern perception that the Vandals were a unified kingdom under the rule of Gaiseric conceals the reality of many different nobles and groups being unhappy with the rule of one man. Furthermore, it is possible, though unprovable, that Aetius and Theodosius had been able to send agents to Africa who had managed to provoke the conspiracy.[73] As a consequence, it would have been very risky of Gaiseric to provoke another war with the West, since it was possible that many of his own followers would change allegiance, so weakening his forces and giving a greater chance of victory to the Romans.

There is one further factor that needs to be explored. Victor of Vita records that at an unknown date, Gaiseric had his predecessor and half-brother Gunderic's wife and children killed, possibly at Cirta (Constantine).[74] Victor gives no context with which to help date the affair, and many dates are plausible and have been proposed. However, the signing of the treaty may be the most obvious occasion. It is probable that the magnates' rebellion of *c.* 442 had hoped to remove Gaiseric and replace him with Gunderic's unnamed son(s). The rebellion most probably occurred whilst Huneric was a hostage in Italy, and so would be unable to take counteraction should his father be killed. Having a viable and 'legal' candidate would have encouraged the magnates in the belief that they could succeed. However, the fact that no corroborating evidence is forthcoming from other sources means that this must remain conjecture rather than attested fact.

If having Huneric as a hostage in Italy was a factor, the conspiracy can date from any time between 442 and 450, when Huneric was definitely back in Carthage.[75] It may even be that part of the reason for Huneric's return was the overthrow of the plot and Valentinian III's realization that although Gaiseric was at peace, his successor may be more aggressive and cause great problems for the Empire. The Empire obviously saw Gaiseric as the most trustworthy of the Vandals, otherwise Huneric would not have been released at all.

Although specific evidence only dates to a later period, contacts between the Romano–African elite and the Empire may have resumed soon after the treaty of 442.[76] Whilst this may have been a concern to a ruler worried about the loyalty of his new subjects, it would suit Gaiseric's long-term strategy, ensuring a quick return to a normality that would allow trade to resume, in turn allowing Gaiseric to begin taxing the trade in order to maintain his (apparently) slightly precarious position at the head of the Vandal kingdom.

Yet there was one major difference in the nature of the contacts between the Romano–Africans and the elite in Rome. Previously, exchanges had been an internal matter between citizens of the Empire, but now such contacts could be interpreted as being at the level of international diplomacy.[77] Yet whilst this is a tempting hypothesis, it must be discarded. Although in some respects the theory is correct, in that Vandal Africa was no longer paying taxes or politically directly connected to Rome, Gaiseric had ensured that the Vandals were now seen as a legitimate component of the Empire. As such, African-Roman contacts were still to a large degree internal communications – as long as they did not hint at rebellion against Vandal rule.

In addition, during Gaiseric's reign some Romano-Africans were allowed to return. These tended to be secular individuals, who were able in many cases to reclaim at least some parts of their estates, but only where these were not seen as being vital to Gaiseric's security, or only parts of their estates where the rest had been taken by Gaiseric's supporters.[78] Gaiseric appears to have been determined to fulfil the terms of the treaty he had signed with Valentinian III and Aetius and remain at peace with Rome. This was in part likely due to the stability and wealth of the Vandal kingdom: he would not wish to risk the threat of war with a commander of Aetius' ability, especially as the regime was accepted by the East and as such would be supported in case of war.

It is possible that shortly after the conquest, the intellectual culture that had thrived during Roman rule reappeared and continued throughout the period of Vandal rule. This is a sign that Gaiseric valued Roman traditions, the main difference being that he now wanted these traditions to support Vandal rule rather than Imperial ideology.

Similarly, once affairs had settled down after the treaty and Gaiseric had secured the land and wealth to reward his followers and 'establish his own royal magnificence', it would appear that Gaiseric guaranteed the 'rights of all [his] subjects – Vandal and Romano-African alike – to own and manage property'.[79] This was especially the case in marginal properties which remained in the possession of Romano-African owners.[80] The concept is reinforced by the attestation that Romano-Africans still had the right to give, bequeath and inherit property after the Vandal conquest.[81] In fact, it would appear that soon after the conquest, 'something resembling the late Roman legal system, continued to function in Vandal Africa', yet although Roman legal terms and methods were applied, there can be little doubt that Gaiseric retained the right to override Roman law should he desire, especially if a Romano-African was involved in a legal debate with a Vandal.[82]

A single notice in Hydatius suggests that during the extended peace the Vandals did not remain idle in Africa, but instead continued to maintain their warlike outlook. In 445, only three years after the signing of the treaty, the Vandals conducted a raid on the region known as *litus Turonium* – probably Turoqua – in Gallaecia (see Map 9).[83] Although sometimes interpreted as an attack on the Empire, the reality would seem to be that *litus Turonium* was probably in a region ruled by the Sueves, who in the early 440s had begun expanding their territories into Baetica and Carthaginiensis, regions largely vacated by the Vandal emigration in 429.[84] It is even possible that Gaiseric had maintained a claim to rule a few Vandals who had remained in Baetica, and since they had been attacked by the Sueves, he had mounted a reprisal in the hope of discouraging further assaults.[85] If true, and this seems likely, the attack was not a breach of the treaty of 442, as the Romans were also fighting the Sueves during this period and may instead be evidence for the continuation of the treaty.[86]

However, all of the evidence for the period 442–454 is slight and therefore open to interpretation. It is possible that the time was one in which political alliances shifted, and one historian has suggested that the period up to the Hunnic invasion of Gaul in 451 was a balance of a Gothic-Sueve alliance against a Roman-Vandal alliance.[87] However, this doesn't take into account the continuing wars between the Sueves and Goths, and it should be noted that the historian in question was writing soon after the Second World War and during the Cold War, when major political blocs were a fact of life. Consequently, the approach may reflect more on the events of the mid-twentieth century rather than the mid-fifth century.[88]

Of the few references in the sources, even fewer contain concrete information that is not open to interpretation. For example, in early 450, food supplies ran low in Italy and Valentinian III issued an edict commanding that 'delinquent shipmasters' bring their services up to 'traditional standards' in order to relieve the famine.[89] It is possible that the Vandals were not supplying the same quantity of grain to Italy as had been the norm prior to 442, and that, as a consequence, when crops in Italy failed, famine was the result. This is possible, but without a secure context remains hypothesis.

More significant is the suggestion by historians that the Empire did little to aid the exiles in the recovery of their lands, as the edicts issued in the West 'exhibit his [Valentinian's] inclination to accept the state of affairs established by the Treaty of 442', although the 'expectation of the eventual recovery of Proconsularis and Byzacene is strong'.[90] In fact, it would seem that by 451, Valentinian had given up any hope he had for a swift return of the lands conquered by the Vandals. On 13 July 451, he decreed that 'some emphyteutic and imperial land in Mauretania Caesariensis and Sitifiensis should be given to nobles who had lost estates in Africa'.[91] The treaty with Gaiseric was holding and the exiled aristocrats were now being forced to accept that Valentinian was in no position to force him to relinquish Africa.

Attila

As noted above, there is no evidence of an alliance between Gaiseric and Attila when the latter invaded Gaul in 451, apart from a single notice in contemporary sources, where Priscus claimed that Attila attacked the West partly because he was 'laying up a store of favour with Gaiseric'.[92] The source is probably referring to a single part of Attila's massive diplomatic assault prior to the physical invasion. It is known that Attila sent messages to Theoderic the Goth telling him to break his alliance with Rome, and to Rome claiming that he was attacking the Goths on Rome's behalf, so it is likely that simultaneously he sent envoys to Gaiseric claiming that he was doing the Vandals a favour by attacking their hereditary enemies, in the belief that this could dissuade the Vandals from supporting Rome militarily.[93] Priscus, aware of the embassy, has interpreted the incident to his own tastes.

Obviously, and despite Attila's reservations, there was little chance of Gaiseric supporting Rome in the upcoming war: not only was this a 'European' war, but the outcome would dictate Gaiseric's decisions in the near future. A Roman victory would ensure that Gaiseric adhered to the treaty, as Rome would be perceived as remaining relatively strong. A Hunnic victory, however, would mean that Gaiseric could take advantage of Roman weakness to expand his kingdom. In addition, the exchange of envoys and ongoing discussions probably meant that there was not enough time for Gaiseric to gather a force together and transport it to Gaul before the Battle of the Catalaunian Plains.

It has also been noted, possibly as evidence that Gaiseric was supporting Attila in the war, that Nestorius relates that:

> The cities of Africa and of Spain and of Muzicanus and great and glorious islands – I mean Sicily and Rhodes and many other great ones – and Rome itself have been delivered over for spoil unto the barbarian Vandal.
> Nestorius, *Bazaar of Heracleides*, 2.2.379

The work is sometimes attested, due to the contents, as having been written around 451.[94] If this was to be true, it would mean that at some point between 442 and 455, there was an otherwise unattested war between Gaiseric and the East. However, the fact that Nestorius includes the Sack of Rome (455) in his list suggests that at least the later parts of the work were written post-455.

There is a further reason for Gaiseric not to join Attila in any attacks upon the Empire. In either 451 or 452, Eudocia became of an age where marriage was possible between her and Huneric. Gaiseric is unlikely to have committed any acts to endanger the marriage. As it turned out, the victory went to Rome and Gaiseric continued to maintain the peace.

Yet the marriage did not happen. Certainty is impossible, but it may have been due to intervention by Aetius. Although Aetius had been in control of the West for nearly two decades, his family had no guarantees of continuing importance after his death. Given the context, it is obvious that Aetius had designs of his own to marry his son Gaudentius to one of Valentinian's daughters.

The refusal of the Imperial family to allow the marriage may have been the cause of some problems faced by Valentinian, who on 29 June 452, issued a decree regarding the 'uncertainties of navigation' surrounding Sardinia.[95] However, despite some recent claims, there is no reason to believe that this was caused by Vandal activities around the island.[96] Instead, the decree may be seen as a continuation of the problems facing the supply of Italy, similar to the way in which in 450, Valentinian had ordered 'delinquent shipmasters' to bring their services up to 'traditional standards'.[97] In fact, it may be more likely that the problems around Sardinia were either the result of locals realizing that the Roman fleet was ineffective, and so deciding to revert to piracy to enrich themselves, or the actions of the Goths in Gaul attempting to strengthen their political position with Rome. Sadly, certainty is impossible.

Taking these events into account, it is probable that throughout the years of peace following the treaty of 442, Gaiseric appears to have focused solely upon ensuring the peace and prosperity of his new kingdom. The Empire was treated with respect and the treaty adhered to faultlessly in the desire to avert war. The Moors were included in the new regime and used as a place to exile recalcitrant ecclesiasts. In return, Gaiseric turned a blind eye to the Moors' incursions into Imperial territory. Finally, so long as nothing disturbed the peace or incited unhappiness amongst his people, Gaiseric ensured that Roman institutions and methods of rule, including legal precedents, were maintained throughout his realm. In this manner he guaranteed peace and prosperity for his people. It was only events outside the kingdom that were to result in the outbreak of fresh hostilities.

The Rhine at Mainz. Somewhere along this part of the river, the Vandals made their first crossing into Imperial territory.

Eastern Gallaecia. Although characterized by many historians as a wild and uncultivated territory, it is clear that the Asdings would have no trouble surviving in the region.

Siliqua of the Usurper Maximus from Hispania. His survival amongst the barbarian coalition would cause continued friction with the Empire.

The Consular diptych of Constantius III, dated to c. 417, possibly celebrating the victory of the Goths over the Vandals.

Valentinian III. He was emperor of the West during the majority of Gaiseric's reign.

Leo I. The main threat to Gaiseric came from the Eastern Empire, especially during the reign of Leo I.

Qasr al–Seghir. This bay on the coast of North Africa may be the place where the Vandals landed after crossing from Hispania.

Roman ruins at Hippo Regius. The home of Saint Augustine, Hippo was besieged by the Vandals before being captured and used as the Vandals' first capital in Africa.

Coin of Bonifacius. Gaiseric twice defeated Bonifacius in battle, before Bonifacius left Africa to overthrow Aetius in Italy.

The Missorium of Aspar. Possibly made in 434 after Aspar's return from his campaign against Gaiseric in Africa.

The Byrsa at Carthage. This area was the centre of Vandal power in Africa.

A coin possibly depicting Gaiseric. Although usually highly stylized, coins may be the only depiction of Gaiseric to come down from antiquity

Solidus of Petronius Maximus. Maximus' seizure of the throne was one of the pretexts for Gaiseric's attack on the city of Rome.

Mosaic pavement from Carthage. Dating from the late fifth or early sixth century, the mosaic may depict a Vandal cavalryman, although this is not certain.

'Genseric sacking Rome'. The painting by the Russian artist Karl Pavlovich Briullov (painted between 1833 and 1836) is a highly romanticized depiction, with Gaiseric on horseback, Pope Leo I to the right, the Imperial women in the centre and the menorah of the Temple of Jerusalem in the background.

The beach at Elche. These holidaymakers are almost certainly unaware that a major sea battle took place along this coastline.

Cap Bon. The defeat of the Roman armada at Cap Bon was Gaiseric's greatest military victory and ensured the continuation of his kingdom into the next century.

Roman ruins at Lilybaeum. The city may be the only one in Sicily which the Vandals attempted to conquer on a permanent basis.

Romulus Augustulus and Odovacer. A nineteenth–century illustration of the 'barbarian' *magister militum* removing the last Western Roman Emperor from the throne. The later peace treaty between Gaiseric and Odovacer was made in Gaiseric's declining years.

Vandals and Romans in battle, in another nineteenth–century illustration. The battles between the Vandals and the Romans would ensure that the Western Empire was unable to survive.

Chapter 10

The Sack of Rome

Deteriorating Relations

Following the defeat of Attila in Gaul in 451 and the retreat of the Huns from Italy in 452, Aetius' position in Italy seemed assured. Yet ironically, the death of Attila in 453 removed the greatest threat to the Empire and resulted in some in the Roman court seeing Aetius as no longer necessary.[1] The ensuing civil war amongst the Huns would have been greeted with even greater relief, but tempered with the news of a Gothic attack in Gaul, first in the north and then against the city of Arles.[2] In addition, after agreeing a new peace treaty with the Goths, unrest broke out again the following year in Hispania and a joint Gothic-Roman force commanded by Frederic, brother of the Gothic king, slaughtered large numbers of the *bacaudae* of Tarraconensis 'under orders from the Roman government'.[3] The Empire was still under extreme pressure.

Aetius

In Italy, at some point prior to 454, Eudoxia, the wife of Valentinian, had proposed that a man named Majorian, a member of Aetius' staff, be married to Valentinian's daughter Placidia, the heir to the throne since their eldest daughter Eudocia was betrothed to Huneric, Gaiseric's son, and so ineligible to rule.[4] Politically, Aetius could not allow the promotion of such a rival and Majorian was forced to retire from active service.[5] Instead, Valentinian was induced to accept the betrothal of Placidia to Aetius' son Gaudentius.[6]

The betrothal was the last straw for some members of the court. Two major political figures at court began to intrigue against Aetius. One was Petronius Maximus, a major political force in the West who had been consul in 433 and 443, and was created *patricius* some time before 445.[7] The other was Heraclius, a eunuch and the *primicerius sacri cubiculi* (officer of the imperial bedchamber). The two men began a conspiracy to overthrow Aetius.[8] Using his close contact with Valentinian, Heraclius was able to convince the emperor that Aetius was using the betrothal as a means of overthrowing Valentinian himself.[9]

On either 21 or 22 September 454, Aetius was in a planning meeting with Valentinian to discuss proposals to raise money, when:[10]

With a shout Valentinian suddenly leaped up from his throne and cried
out that he would no longer endure to be abused by such treacheries,
before stabbing Aetius with his sword: Heraclius, who was nearby, withdrew a concealed cleaver and the two men, raining blows upon Aetius'
head, killed him.

Priscus (fragment) 30. 1 = John of Antioch (fragment) 201

Many other supporters of Aetius' regime were also killed.[11]

Valentinian recalled Majorian from his 'retirement' and made him *comes domesticorum* (Count of the Household).[12] Believing that Valentinian would now allow
him to marry Placidia, Majorian would have been happy to oblige the emperor. At
the same time, and knowing that Aetius' death would also precipitate actions in the
wider world, Valentinian sent envoys to the Goths, Sueves, Alans and Vandals.[13]

The fact that the barbarian rulers now failed to act has resulted in some historians making the 'reasonable deduction that Valentinian succeeded in reassur-
ing these peoples of his good intentions'.[14] On the other hand, it is just as likely
that the whole affair came as a massive shock to everybody, since nobody would
have expected Aetius to be killed by his own emperor. Along with the other rulers,
Gaiseric would have been surprised, but the envoys from Valentinian to Gaiseric
may have carried further information and requests from Valentinian. Sadly, these
are nowhere recorded in the sources so it is necessary to revert to deduction in
order to arrive at a reasonable conclusion.

One of the few facts known about the embassy is that the Arian Gaiseric was persuaded by Valentinian to reinstate the Nicene bishop's seat in Carthage, after a gap
of fifteen years. As a result, on Sunday, 24 October 454, a man named Deogratias
was ordained as the Nicene Bishop of Carthage.[15] Of greater surprise is that before
his death on 5 January 457, Deogratias was also allowed to ordinate a number of
bishops in Africa Proconsularis.[16] The reasons for Gaiseric's religious U-turn are
unknown. It has been suggested that his concessions were probably in response to
Valentinian confirming that the marriage of Eudocia and Huneric would now go
ahead.[17] This seems a reasonable deduction, especially when it is taken into account
that, as a Nicene, Eudocia would need a senior bishop to tend to her religious
needs, and in Africa this would of necessity be the Bishop of Carthage.

However, this conclusion should not also be taken as evidence that Gaiseric was
oblivious to the fact that Aetius had many supporters in Rome and there was the
possibility of a backlash against Valentinian's action. From later events, it appears
possible that Gaiseric ordered his army to muster at Carthage early in the campaign season of the following year to take advantage of whatever happened within
the Empire. Also suggestive of Gaiseric's early decision to prepare for hostilities
is the fact that a contingent of Moors would also be included in the campaign he

was to lead the following year.[18] As Aetius was killed late in September, by the time the news reached Gaiseric the sailing season in the Mediterranean was over so whatever happened there was nothing that Gaiseric would be able to do in the remainder of 454. Negotiations with the Moors over how many men and what rewards they would gain doubtless took place over the winter of 454–455, as the distances involved and time needed for both travel and talks could otherwise not have taken place in the narrow window of time between the death of Valentinian and Gaiseric's arrival in Italy.

It quickly became clear that there would indeed be a backlash following the fall of Aetius. Marcellinus, the military commander of Illyricum – or, more specifically, Dalmatia – immediately renounced his loyalty to the emperor.[19] In response, Valentinian appears to have deployed the majority of the Italian forces in the Po valley to defend the passes into Italy. Simultaneously, the deployment would remove them as a threat to his own person. The fact that Rome was being denuded of defenders would doubtless be of interest to Gaiseric.

Death of Valentinian III and the Appeal from Eudoxia[20]

Gaiseric's preparations – if they were made – were timely. Whilst attending training sessions on the Campus Martius on 16 March 455, Valentinian was assassinated. He had been training with the troops in the hope of gaining their loyalty:

> Valentinian rode in the Field of Ares (the *Campus Martius*) with a few bodyguards and the followers of Optila and Thraustila. When he had dismounted from his horse and proceeded to archery, Optila and his friends attacked him. Optila struck Valentinian on his temple and when he turned around to see the striker he dealt him a second blow on the face and felled him, and Thraustila slew Heraclius. Taking the emperor's diadem and horse, they hastened to Maximus.
> John of Antioch (fragment) 201.4–5 (trans. Gordon, pp.52–53)[21]

So died the last male of the Theodosian dynasty.

With the assassination of the emperor accomplished, Maximus needed to move quickly as there were other possible successors to the throne, the two most prominent being Maximianus – previously a *domesticus* (bodyguard) to Aetius – and Majorian. In the context of the times, securing the loyalty of the army was paramount. Maximus acted fast:

> The military forces were divided among themselves, some wishing Maximus to assume the royal power and some eager to give the throne

to Maximianus ... In addition, Eudoxia, the wife of Valentinian, strongly favoured Majorian. But Maximus gained control of the palace by distributing money and forced Eudoxia to marry him by threatening her with death, thinking that his position would be more secure. So Maximus came to the leadership of the Roman Empire.

John of Antioch (fragment) 201.6

On 17 March, the day after Valentinian's death, Maximus was proclaimed emperor in Rome.[22] Not content with one marriage to the previous dynasty, Maximus further ordered that Eudoxia's daughter Eudocia marry his son, the newly proclaimed *Caesar* Palladius, despite the fact that she was betrothed to Huneric, son of Gaiseric.[23] In addition, Maximus may have deployed troops who were loyal to his opponent away from the capital in order to minimize the danger they posed to his own person. This news would be of great interest to Gaiseric.

Eudoxia was, understandably, furious at her treatment.[24] Pondering her options, she allegedly reached a decision which could be interpreted as a betrayal of Rome. It is so odd that it is now ignored by many historians, probably being seen as mere rumour and scandal rather than fact.[25] Eudoxia could not appeal to the East for help, since Eastern Emperor Marcian would most likely not be willing to intervene on her behalf.[26] The Western court was also either unable or unwilling to take her part against the new emperor, so the most obvious course of action – and the one she purportedly took – was to appeal to Gaiseric, her potential son-in-law, for help.[27]

Although at first surprising, when the move is analyzed it is clear that Eudoxia would not have been betraying Rome: Gaiseric was settled in Africa as *socius et amicus cum foedere*.[28] As an ally of her deceased husband, Gaiseric was the obvious person for her to appeal to. Moreover, Maximus' decision to force Eudocia to marry Palladius would be an added incentive to Gaiseric to evict Maximus from the throne. Eudoxia may have been hoping that Gaiseric, as her ally, would enter Italy, remove Maximus, and then join with her to elevate Majorian, her choice as the next emperor of Rome.

If the account is accurate, sadly for Eudoxia she made one grave error in her assumptions. Ancient political entities did not regard treaties the same as modern politicians, where policies are generally transferred intact from one government to the next and only change slowly. In the ancient world, the enthronement of a new emperor resulted in the imposition of the new emperor's policies, whether these accorded with the old policies or not. The net result was that treaties were not with political entities, but with the individual rulers. Consequently, it was usual when an emperor (or barbarian king) died that envoys were sent to all of the other rulers in order to confirm that the existing treaties were to continue or to attempt a revision of agreements.

Gaiseric's alliance and treaty was with Aetius and Valentinian, the individuals who had concluded the negotiations with him.[29] As a result, upon their deaths the treaty was perceived by Gaiseric as being ended. With his alliance now void, with the death of his 'ally' Valentinian, and no doubt hoping to create further disorder, Gaiseric instantly cut the supply of grain to Rome. In addition, without the military threat of Aetius, Italy was now a valid target. The alleged message from Eudoxia, if it arrived, would have reinforced Gaiseric's belief that internal disorder in the Empire would result in minimal opposition to a military strike.[30] Deciding upon a swift attack, Gaiseric set sail, not just for Italy, but directly for Rome.

The Sack of Rome

Even now, with powered ships, sailing across the Tyrrhenian Sea takes about 24 hours. Ancient ships depended upon the wind direction for power. It has been calculated that the journey between Carthage and Rome usually took between two and four days.[31] However, this was with a following wind (the Scirocco). The journey from Rome to Carthage, sailing against the Scirocco, would have taken longer – possibly a week or more. Assuming that it took some days after 17 March for Maximus to establish his regime and appoint trustworthy ambassadors, the envoys sent to Carthage would probably not have arrived much before the end of March, if not in April. Presumably, any messages from Eudoxia would have arrived a day or two earlier, depending on whether they could take an assigned ship or had to wait for a merchant vessel making the trip.

Given the loyalty of many Romans to Aetius, the news of Valentinian's assassination may not have come as a big surprise to Gaiseric. However, he may have found it interesting that the army in Rome had been split between supporting two men for the vacant throne, and that Maximus may have sent disloyal troops away from the capital. If true, the latter may have given Gaiseric the idea that Rome was not properly defended. Rome itself was now the target.

There remains the question of why Gaiseric actually landed in Italy so soon after Valentinian's death. Several options have been proposed. For example, it has been suggested that a major factor was that he was unhappy with an alliance that had recently been signed between Rome, the Goths in Gaul and Sueves in Hispania.[32] This remains a possibility, but should probably be seen as unlikely. Past history would have demonstrated to all parties that the only treaty that had stood the test of time was that between the Vandals and the Empire. On the contrary, the agreements between Rome and either the Goths or Sueves had rarely lasted more than a year or two, so although Gaiseric may have felt a small qualm about the treaties, he would have known that before long they would break down.

It is tempting to believe, although impossible to prove, that Eudoxia's reported request for help is true and that only when the letter arrived did Gaiseric realize both that Maximus was extremely unpopular and that Rome itself was a viable target. Without the letter, Gaiseric would be relying on the reports of merchants and spies, which would have been of varying reliability. On the other hand, throughout his life, it is obvious that Gaiseric was willing to take risks, so there is no guarantee that he reacted only when the presumed letter arrived.

Knowing that the end result would be the sack of the capital, most historians have taken it for granted that Gaiseric's main aim was always the capture of the city. This is unrealistic. As just noted, Gaiseric was reliant upon information from spies, envoys and merchants for information. Given the time lapse between events in Italy and news reaching Carthage, when Gaiseric set sail he would have been unsure of what he would find when he landed in Italy. At this point, Gaiseric would have been keeping his options open and hoping for further, reliable news. Nevertheless, even with limited information, Gaiseric was prepared to take the initiative.

The question then remains of why Gaiseric, after thirteen years of peace, decided not just to attack the Empire, but to launch an assault on the city of Rome itself. The ancient sources themselves note that with the death of Valentinian, the treaty was now void.[33] In theory, Gaiseric was now morally free to act. In addition, there is no evidence that Maximus sent an embassy to Gaiseric to either resume the old treaty or sign a new one.[34] In essence, Gaiseric may have felt threatened by Maximus and was worried in case of the outbreak of war, possibly with the West supported by the Goths.

A further reason may have been the request of Eudoxia – if indeed it was sent, which may be unlikely. However, it should not be assumed that Gaiseric was intent upon rescuing Eudoxia from Maximus: the most likely outcome of the request was that Gaiseric was informed of the chaos in Rome following the assassination of Valentinian and the realization that Rome was vulnerable.

A third possible reason was sheer greed: although the city had been sacked by Alaric and the Goths in 410, it would have been known that Alaric's sack had been almost gentlemanly, and that the majority of the city's wealth remained intact. The downside to this theory is that Gaiseric was risking a counter-attack from the joint-forces of both East and West. As a result, although sheer greed may have been a factor in the decision to attack, it may not have been the most important one.

A fourth was the need to ensure that Eudocia would marry Huneric. A major factor in Gaiseric's plan to change the inheritance laws of the Vandals was the fact that Huneric would be a member of the Imperial family, and so his rule would receive a massive political boost. Above all else, Gaiseric needed to guarantee that the marriage went ahead.

It has been suggested that Gaiseric's motive was 'because Avitus was proclaimed emperor in Gaul'.[35] Obviously, Avitus was only proclaimed emperor on 9 July, after

Maximus' death and the sack of Rome, so this cannot be accurate.[36] Instead, it has been alleged that Gaiseric was aware of the possibility of a Gothic alliance with the Roman forces in Gaul to take Rome. In that case, Gaiseric would fear an attack by a Romano-Gothic alliance.[37] This is an interesting proposal, and, as noted above, the fear of attack was doubtless a motive, but the hypothesis does not seem likely. The major flaw in the argument appears to be that no allowance is made for the time needed for all of the necessary information to pass across the Mediterranean, for Gaiseric to then muster the troops and ships, and then sail to Rome. The theory may therefore be dismissed as extremely unlikely.

A final reason may have been financial, but the opposite to that possibility already proposed. By this date, it was clear to all concerned that the West was financially crippled. The loss of Africa had earlier resulted in Valentinian declaring the Empire bankrupt. With this in mind, Gaiseric may have seen the attack as a means of making sure that it was economically impossible for the next emperor – whoever he was – to mount a campaign against Africa.[38]

On reflection, there is another possibility. It is impossible to know Gaiseric's motives, since no source relates the sack from the point of view of the Vandals. Yet it is hard to believe that Gaiseric was expecting to capture the city without a fight. It may be – though this is conjecture – that when he advanced to the city walls, Gaiseric was following the example set by Alaric in both 408 and 409. On those occasions, Alaric had not been intent on capturing Rome, but rather on forcing the Emperor Honorius to come to terms.

It is possible that in like manner Gaiseric landed in Italy and advanced on the capital in order to extract major concessions from Maximus, perhaps including a revision of the tribute of grain to Italy and the ceding of territory in Africa and/or Sicily. Only when he discovered that Maximus had been killed and that the city was defenceless did Gaiseric begin to believe he could take it, even though he knew that the act was likely to cause the Eastern Empire, with its greater military resources, to intervene. This is possibly a more reasonable conjecture than those which believe that Gaiseric expected to capture the capital from the start of the campaign.

With his campaign planned, Gaiseric would have taken with him a large enough force to threaten the city and, if needed, mount an apparent assault with at least some prospect of success. To prepare the fleet, organize the troops and gather the supplies necessary for the journey would have taken quite some time – hence the belief that he had begun preparations over the winter of 454–455.

Landing near Rome, Gaiseric advanced to 'Azestus', a place near Rome.[39] Maximus heard the news on 31 May, so the landing took place either on 30 or 31 May.[40] Maximus immediately panicked and fled.[41] As he was leaving the city, either a member of his bodyguard or a bystander threw a rock that hit him on the temple and killed him, and the crowd then tore his body to pieces.[42]

Sadly for the citizens of Rome, prior to his death, Petronius Maximus seems to have failed to send orders to the *praesental* army in Italy requesting that they assemble and march to the aid of Rome as the Vandals approached the city. In Rome, left with only the guardsmen and possibly a few small contingents of troops to man the walls, the citizens panicked.[43]

They allegedly turned to the most important individual remaining in the city for help. In 452, Leo, the bishop of Rome, had been sent as an envoy in order to secure the release of prisoners held by the Huns (the claim that he convinced Attila to leave Italy is mistaken).[44] Leo agreed to meet Gaiseric, who advanced towards Rome on 2 June.[45] Contrary to the hopes of Eudoxia, he did not come as a liberator:

> Holy Bishop Leo (*sancto Leone Episcopo*) met [Gaiseric] outside the gates and his supplication mollified him through the power of God to such an extent that, when everything was given into his hands, he was held back nevertheless from burning, killing, and torture.
>
> Prosp., a. 455

Interestingly, Leo's sermon of 6 July 455, shortly after the Vandals had left the city, makes no mention of Leo's intervention and lays the securing of the city's safety in the hands of God.[46] It should be noted that throughout his life, Leo appears to have avoided self-promotion: '[T]his silence is only characteristic of the man, in whom there is no trace of vain-boasting, and who consistently sank the personality of himself as well as of others in the principles and causes which absorbed him.'[47]

If the reasons for Gaiseric's decision to invade Italy as noted above are correct, then it must be assumed that he was not expecting to be given entry to the city. However, the temptation to follow in Alaric's footsteps and put the Imperial capital to the sack was too tempting to resist.

Gaiseric acceded to Leo's request. Taking temporary residence in the Imperial palace, Gaiseric ensured that there was little in the way of the rape or killing common during the sack of a city.[48] Nevertheless, the sack of Rome by the Vandals was a far more thorough affair than that of 410 by the Goths under Alaric. Several accounts of the sack survive – for example:

> On the third day after Maximus was killed, Gaiseric, king of the Vandals, entered Rome and during fourteen whole days denuded the city of all its riches and took with him the daughters and wife of Valentinian and many thousands of captives. The intercession of Pope Leo restrained him from arson, torture, and murder.
>
> Victor of Tonnena, s.a.455

[Gaiseric] .. captured the city, and … took everything from the palace, even the bronze statues. He even led away as captives surviving senators, accompanied by their wives; along with them he also carried off to Carthage in Africa the empress Eudoxia, who had summoned him; her daughter Placidia, the wife of the patrician Olybrius,[49] who then was staying at Constantinople; and even the maiden Eudocia. After he had returned, Gaiseric gave the younger Eudocia, a maiden, the daughter of the empress Eudoxia, to his son Huneric in marriage, and he held them both, the mother and the daughter, in great honour.

Malchus, *Chron.*, 366

From Hydatius we gain confirmation that Gaiseric took 'Valentinian's widow, his two daughters, and Gaudentius, son of Aetius' to Africa.[50]

Although Gaiseric had agreed not to kill or torture the inhabitants of Rome, the Vandals now ransacked the city for a period of fourteen days (2–15 June).[51] The Vandals and their allies the Moors emptied the treasury and the temples of their valuables, including the spoils taken from the sack of Jerusalem by Titus, son of the Emperor Vespasian, in the first century. Also taken was Gaudentius, Aetius' son.[52] On 16 June, the Vandals, having laden all of their ships with booty and captives, left Rome and sailed back to Carthage. The only damage recorded to the city during the sack was that part of the roof of the temple of Jupiter Capitolinus was stripped before the looters realized that it was simply gold-plated copper and not solid gold.[53]

The sack was a far more thorough affair than that of Alaric in 410. There are three main reasons for the difference. One is that Alaric was still attempting to come to terms with the Empire, and his sack was more a demonstration of his loss of patience than any desire to alienate the emperor. The second is that Alaric and his men were a land-based force with a limited amount of transport available, so there was a limit to the amount of booty they could handle. Finally, Alaric would not have wanted to compromise the mobility of his army too much by having vast amounts of booty to transport and defend.

Gaiseric, on the other hand, was taking advantage of Roman weakness rather than negotiating with Valentinian. But of even more significance is that Gaiseric was leading a seaborne assault. The ships which had carried his men, augmented by those captured during the landing at Ostia, the port of Rome, were capable of carrying far more plunder than Alaric's land-based army.

Yet there still remained a limit to the amount of goods that could be carried, along with the Vandals and Moors who had undertaken the sack. As a result, it is almost certain that the claim by Roman writers that Rome was 'emptied of all its wealth, and many thousands of captives, all that were satisfactory as to age or occupation, along with the Queen and her children, were taken away to Carthage' is an exaggeration.[54]

Many captives were no doubt taken into slavery, but the concept that the Vandal fleet could carry the army, plus the vast amounts of booty described, along with 'many thousands of captives', is hard to believe, especially as the number of sailors and guards needed to ensure the compliance of the captives would need to be large. The number of captives taken given in the sources thus appears to be highly exaggerated.

The sack of Rome was a disaster for the Empire. At a stroke, Gaiseric had reduced the West from a position of bankruptcy to one of penury: in 456, Avitus, the successor to Maximus, was unable even to pay his Gothic mercenaries and was forced to strip the bronze from public works and sell the scrap metal to merchants in return for the necessary money.[55] Any attempt to attack Gaiseric in Africa was going to need special measures.

Once back in Africa, 'the throng of captives [were] divided … into groups'. Before they could be sold into slavery, Deogratias, the newly appointed bishop of Carthage, 'sold all the gold and silver vessels used in worship and freed the free-born people'.[56] It would appear that either during the capture of Carthage some of the Nicene church paraphernalia had been left intact, or that Deogratias had brought the necessary vessels with him from Rome after his appointment.

Eudocia was kept in safety prior to her marriage to Huneric, following the earlier betrothal and agreement of 442. As Placidia was betrothed to Olybrius, she was not married to anybody by Gaiseric. Instead, both she and her mother Eudoxia were simply held by Gaiseric in Carthage.[57] The reason for taking Eudoxia and Placidia – as well as Gaudentius – to Carthage is not usually investigated, it simply being seen as the obvious move for Gaiseric. Accuracy is impossible, but there remains one major factor: Eudoxia, Eudocia and Placidia were the last members of the Imperial house. Gaiseric specifically wanted Huneric to marry Eudocia and become a member of that house. Yet the political upheavals in Rome following the sack would probably make the city unsafe for the Imperial women. In this context, it is possible that Gaiseric took the women, especially Eudoxia, to Carthage for their own safety, a possibility reinforced by the fact that when he did release them, they were released to the relative safety of the Eastern court.[58]

A state of war obviously now existed between the Vandals and the Empire. Modern historians have sometimes called this the Fourth Punic War (the first three being fought between 264–241 BC, 218–201 BC and 149–146 BC), and it may have been seen as such by contemporaries – especially the Vandals, who attempted to insinuate themselves into Punic traditions, but this is a mistake.[59] The only common factor is the relative location of the combatants. The first wars were a fight for control of the Western Mediterranean by two rising powers: in the latter, it was the rising power of the Vandals against the declining power of Rome. In the former it was the Romans who usually had the initiative, in the latter it was the Vandals. As will be seen, in the following years, Gaiseric did everything in his power to maintain that initiative.

Chapter 11

War

After the sack of Rome in AD 455, the sources become confused and confusing. The works of writers such as Priscus, who wrote 'histories', have been lost, with only either fragments or excerpts written in later histories surviving. Consequently, it is necessary to rely on the various 'chronicles'. Although all of these sources are in themselves interesting, the difficulty lies in the fact that the majority are very fragmentary, do not contain enough information to establish a context and so are difficult – if not impossible – to date accurately.

The outcome for the study of Vandal history is that after 455, most references to Vandal attacks, whether general records of unspecified attacks or of attacks on specific places, cannot be dated accurately, so it is impossible to establish a secure chronology. It is therefore necessary to establish dates at which events are most likely to have happened. In addition, actions are only interpreted from a Roman point of view, so it is necessary to resort to speculation concerning Gaiseric's strategy and motives. Readers are advised that the dating and outline of events, plus the analysis of Gaiseric's personal intentions that are contained from here onwards, are, except where otherwise stated, open to interpretation and revision.

Eudocia

Although certainty is impossible, as the very few sources concerning Eudocia's exile in Africa are undated, it is probable that it was either late in 455 or in 456 that Huneric was finally married to Eudocia, as agreed in the treaty of 442.[1] Their son Hilderic appears to have been born in the mid-late 450s, most likely in 456 or 457.[2] Gaiseric was doubtless happy with the marriage on all levels, especially politically: theoretically, any sons of Huneric and Eudocia would have a claim to the throne of the West, although there was no chance of the Senate in Rome acquiescing to the rule of a *'semi-barbarus'*. Of more importance, Gaiseric's successors for at least two generations would have links to the Imperial family, a major propaganda coup. However, thanks to events surrounding the marriage, neither the East nor the West accepted Eudocia's marriage as valid.

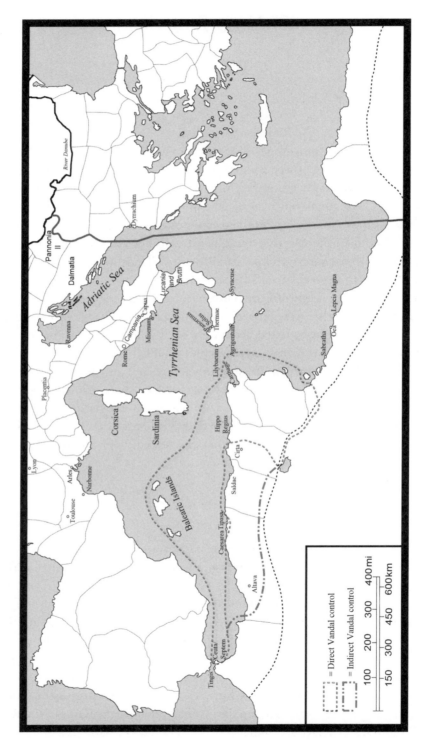

Map 10: The Romano–Vandal War.

456

After the death of Maximus, in July 455 the Imperial throne passed to a man named Avitus, who retained Majorian as *comes domesticorum*, and Ricimer, an individual of mixed barbarian descent, was appointed *comes* ('Count', 'military commander'). Ricimer was destined to be Gaiseric's main opponent in the coming years.

Over the winter of 455–456, a flurry of envoys was sent from Italy. Probably before any others, Avitus sent ambassadors to Marcian, the Eastern emperor, asking to be accepted as Emperor of the West and requesting support against the Vandals.[3] He also sent envoys to the Vandals, instructing them to stop their attacks and to return their hostages, probably including the claim that the women would be safe during his rule. After receiving Avitus' envoys, Marcian sent embassies to Gaiseric demanding that the Vandals cease from attacking the West and release their royal captives.[4]

Secure in Africa, and with a large fleet at hand, Gaiseric refused to treat with the Empire.[5] In this decision, Gaiseric was almost certainly acting in the knowledge that although Avitus had an alliance with the Goths, the other barbarians both within and on the borders of the Western Empire would almost certainly react to the sack of Rome and the swift turnover of emperors by going on the offensive. In addition, he would have learnt early in 456 that the East had rejected Avitus' claim to rule.[6] The sack of Rome meant that the West did not have the financial ability to launch a campaign of reconquest on its own. A divided Empire was all the incentive Gaiseric needed to continue the war.

Over the winter of 455 to 456, Gaiseric arranged a new treaty with the Moors aimed at attacking the Empire, almost certainly using the enticement of the vast amount of predicted booty as a lure.[7] The alliance was beneficial to both sides. Not only would it allow Gaiseric to dispatch more men on the sorties to Sicily, Italy and other islands in the Mediterranean, but he could now use a mixed force of Vandal and Moorish troops to assume control of those areas of Africa that were still under Roman rule. For the Moors, the amount of booty they could seize in joint attacks on the Empire with the Vandals would be far greater than anything they could hope to accomplish on their own in Africa.

On a personal level, a successful war would be of inestimable value to Gaiseric. Expansion would increase the Vandals' tax base, give him extra lands with which to reward his followers, keep the Vandal troops and Moors occupied, and maintain and even enhance Gaiseric's claim to be a successful warlord. In addition, and possibly of greater importance, the capture of African ports would eliminate any bases in Africa from which the Empire could launch a counter-attack on his kingdom.

Gaiseric rebuffed the ambassadors sent over the winter of 455–456, and also dismissed an embassy including an Arian bishop named Bleda which was sent in 456 by Marcian from the East.[8] This was a mistake. Gaiseric was probably relying on the fact that Marcian had refused to recognize Avitus to deter Marcian from supporting the West. Possibly unexpectedly, Gaiseric's refusal to comply with his ambassadors resulted in Marcian becoming so angry that Avitus' 'usurpation' became secondary: Marcian began making preparations for war.[9]

Yet after the embassy had left empty-handed, Gaiseric would not have known of Marcian's response, so in the meantime a large Vandal army was sent west along the coast to conquer ports along the seaboard of Roman North Africa.[10] It may be at this early date that the cities of Tipasa, Caesarea and Septem were taken by the Vandals.[11] At the same time, once the sailing season arrived in March, a large raiding force of sixty ships was sent to harass the coasts of Italy, Sicily and other islands in the region.[12]

The Battle of Agrigentum[13]

Facing the Vandals was the newly appointed *comes* Ricimer. With Rome sacked, it would not be hard for Avitus to guess that the next attack would fall on Sicily. The city of Lilybaeum, in the extreme west of the island, was an obvious target and it is likely that the garrison was reinforced. Ricimer, however, based himself at Agrigentum and awaited the expected invasion. It would seem that Gaiseric made the sensible assumption that Lilybaeum would be heavily defended, and so attacked further along the coast. Whether Ricimer was acting on information, was simply lucky or accurately read Gaiseric's strategy is unknown, but the attackers landed at Agrigentum. As the Vandals left their boats and began their attempt to ravage the territory around the city, Ricimer attacked them and 'with a ruse' – in all likelihood an ambush – defeated them. The survivors fled.[14] Ricimer's victory in Sicily probably made the Vandals wary of attacking the island. However, other raids had been launched against mainland Italy and the islands to the north of Sicily.

Despite the defeat, Gaiseric remained in a strong position. The citizens of Rome were demonstrating against Avitus due to the lack of grain from Africa, which was needed to feed the city. Avitus was forced to rely on local supplies during the emergency, yet not only were these insufficient, but the transport network was in disarray thanks to the Vandals' attacks: neither the land nor sea route was free from threat.[15] This was especially the case in southern Italy, which the Vandals ravaged unopposed. They may even have sacked the city of Capua.[16] It is sometimes claimed that either in 455 or 456 the Vandals sacked the city of Nola, as recorded by Gregory of Rome in his *Dialogues*, but it should be noted that the Paulinus referred to by Gregory died in 431, so this attack relates to that of the Goths under Alaric in 410.[17]

Although Sicily was now free from attack for at least one campaign season, the Vandals were also harassing the other islands around Italy. It would appear that

Majorian was given command of troops and sent to Corsica: 'In Corsica there was a slaughter of a multitude of Vandals.'[18] Although neither Majorian nor Ricimer is named in the sources, it is most likely that it was Majorian who was commanding this army.[19] Although usually attested as a naval battle, this is open to doubt. The passage in question can be translated in a variety of ways, and, given the context, it is more likely that the Vandals landed and were defeated than they were beaten in a pitched battle at sea. The status of the Roman navy in the Tyrrhenian Sea in this period is unknown, and the loss of ships during the Vandal attack of 455 may have made Avitus unwilling to risk a sea battle.[20] What ships were available were almost certainly mainly transports, and these were used to ferry troops to threatened areas.

It is unknown how Gaiseric reacted to the defeats in two small-scale battles. All imaginable outcomes are possible, ranging from the recall of his men and the end of attacks for the year to him gathering his forces and organizing larger-scale raids that were less vulnerable to counter-attack. The former is probably more likely. The attacks were probably staged over a period of at least a month, so by the time he learned of the defeats the end of the sailing season was approaching. The raiders may have been under instruction to return to Africa whether the defeats had occurred or not.

The Death of Avitus

Over the winter of 456–457, events in Italy helped Gaiseric's expansion policy. He may have expected a reaction to his attacks, and probably did not expect the West to dissolve in turmoil. Ricimer and Majorian rebelled against Avitus, who fled but was caught and defeated at the Battle of Placentia (Piacenza). Avitus and a small group of survivors took sanctuary in a nearby shrine, where they were besieged.[21] Captured, he was consecrated as bishop of Piacenza.[22] However, Avitus may have attempted to escape to his power base in Gaul, and he was killed somewhere between late October 456 and early February 457.[23]

The death of Avitus resulted in parts of the south of Gaul revolting. The citizens of Lyon flatly refused to acknowledge the validity of any new emperor appointed in Italy to take Avitus' place, as demonstrated by an inscription set up in June 458.[24] Furthermore, and with complete disregard for the Western court, the citizens sent a delegation in the form of an archdeacon of the city to the new Eastern Emperor Leo, asking that their taxes be remitted.[25] Alongside the evidence from Lyon, Sidonius relates a few snippets concerning the *coniuratio Marcelliniana*, an attempt to revolt instigated in southern Gaul, centred on Narbonne.[26] Although details are limited, the city appears to have raised the standard of revolt.[27] Of more importance, the death of Avitus, sponsored by the Goths, would result in the Goths declaring war. The next emperor would have to deal with a Gothic war and a Gallic revolt alongside any resumption of Vandal attacks.

Majorian

Although the Roman populace and Senate were happy with the removal of Avitus, the feeling was not shared throughout the West. Alongside the unhappy Goths and cities in southern Gaul, the 'Ripuarian' Franks seized the opportunity to extend their dominion by invading Imperial territory. At an unknown date in 457, they captured the cities of Cologne and Trier.[28] The increased chaos would only act as a spur to Gaiseric's expansionist ambitions.

As was usual, envoys were sent to Marcian in the East.[29] But on 26 January 457, the Emperor Marcian died and it was not until 7 February that Leo became the new Eastern emperor. Leo sent messengers to Rome, who arrived on 27 February 457 and appointed Ricimer as *patricius* and Majorian as *magister equitum*, with Ricimer retaining the senior post of *magister peditum*. Of far more significance to Gaiseric, Leo cancelled Marcian's proposed campaign against the Vandals.[30]

Possibly in reaction to the disappointment, on 1 April 457, Majorian was acclaimed emperor by the army.[31] The news would have come as no surprise to Gaiseric, who would have been more concerned about the prospective Eastern attack. The cancellation of Marcian's African campaign was doubtless a relief to Gaiseric. In effect, he was given a free hand to ravage the West whilst the East stood by and watched. Nevertheless, it is likely that he maintained guarded diplomatic relations with the East, keeping peace with the East whilst continuing to attack the West.[32] By the fifth century, the strategy of *divide et impera* (divide and rule/conquer) was a well-tested one, allegedly being first attributed to Philip II of Macedon in the fourth century BC and used by Julius Caesar in the first century BC when conquering Gaul. Gaiseric's use of the strategy should therefore come as no great surprise: his mastery of the strategy would become apparent in the following years.

Vandal Attacks Resume

Majorian sent Ricimer to the south of Italy to face any renewed Vandal attacks. With war impending in Gaul, and the Roman navy almost completely ineffective, Gaiseric was aware of a further advantage. Although the cities of northern Italy were defended by walls, since they had regularly faced attacks from across the Alps, those of the south were not so well protected because they had previously been safe from barbarian attacks. Consequently, they were vulnerable to attack by fast-moving marauders, despite the fact that the raider had no access to siege engines.[33] Gaiseric dispatched a strike force from Carthage, this time under the leadership of the (unnamed) husband of Gaiseric's half-sister.[34] The ensuing events are described in some detail by Sidonius:

A savage foe was roaming at his ease over the unguarded sea. Under south-erly breezes he invaded the Campanian soil and with his Moorish soldiery attacked the husbandmen when they dreamed not of danger; the fleshy Vandal sat on the thwarts waiting for the spoil, which he had bidden his captives to capture and bring thither. But, of a sudden thy bands had thrown themselves between the two enemy hosts into the plains which sunder the sea from the hills and fashion a harbour where the river makes a backward curve. First the multitude of plunderers flees in terror towards the mountains, and so, cut off from the ships they had left, they become the prey of their prey; then the pirates are aroused and mass their whole forces for the battle. Some land their well-trained steeds in hollow skiffs, some don the meshed mail of like hue to themselves, so get ready their shapely bows and the arrows made to carry poison on the iron point and to wound doubly with a single shot. Now the broidered Dragon speeds hither and thither in both armies, his throat swelling as the zephyrs dash against it ... From everywhere a shower of steel comes down, but from our side it comes down on the throats of the foe ... Soon as the Vandal began to turn and flee, carnage took the place of battle ... In their panic flight the horsemen plunged pallid into the water and passed beyond the ships, then swam back in disgrace to their boats from the open sea.

Sidonius Apollinaris, *Carmina*, 5.385f.

The date of the attack is unknown, but the inference from Sidonius is that it was at some point early in the summer, as it is described as happening shortly after Majorian was acclaimed as emperor. It would appear that the Moors were sent out to scout and ravage the countryside whilst the main Vandal contingent waited at their ships for news. The events of the previous year, when raids on both Sicily and Corsica had been heavily defeated, appear to have instilled a level of caution in Gaiseric's son-in-law. Sadly for the Vandals, it was not enough: Ricimer managed to insert his army between the Moors and the Vandals, forcing the Moors to flee to the mountains, where they were killed by the local inhab-itants. Re-forming their troops, the Romans under Ricimer faced the Vandals in pitched battle. After a brief period of contact, the Vandals turned to flight, boarding their vessels and fleeing the scene of their defeat. Gaiseric's son-in-law was one of those killed in the attack. Ricimer's ability to ambush the enemy had again ensured a victory.

Analysis of the battle can give some indications as to the methods used by the Vandals. One aspect clearly demonstrated is that due to the defeats of the previous year, the Vandals were now more cautious in their attacks, never knowing where the Roman forces were going to be stationed. The result was that they used a scouting force to determine whether a landing was going to be opposed. A second fact is that they used the Moors – who still retained their reputation as excellent light cavalrymen – to do the scouting. The implication here is that the Vandals may have transported at least the horses of their Moorish allies on their joint expeditions, although the Moors were also famed for the skirmishing infantry and so it is possible that no horses were carried. If the Moors' horses were transported, some of the Vandals' own horses may also have been carried, but if so, numbers would have been kept to a minimum in order to increase the ships' capacity to transport raiders to their targets and ship the booty home afterwards.

As usual, certainty is impossible, but a third defeat in two years, and this time including the death of his son-in-law, probably persuaded Gaiseric that further attacks on Italy would be unprofitable. He appears to have changed strategy. Sadly, very little information survives regarding Vandal activity throughout these years, so no precise dates can be given to any of these events. However, the defeat in Corsica, combined with the determined resistance in Italy, suggests that the Italian peninsula and the nearby islands were deemed to be too dangerous for attack. As a result, it is likely that Gaiseric focused his main attacks upon annexing the whole African coast to the west of Carthage, perhaps including the Balearic Islands.[35] These may have been captured around 457–460, if not a little later, with the islands taking second place to the mainland of Africa. However, the Balearics were almost certainly the first non-African territory annexed, as implied by events in 460.

The Empire Resurgent

Gaiseric's expansion was aided by the fact that Majorian had major problems to solve before he could think about the Vandal menace. Financially and politically, Rome was in turmoil. Majorian could only pacify the West by restoring some sort of stability, based around his personal rule. He began by raising taxes, as implied by *Novellae 2, 5* and *7*.[36] His laws targeted the rich and powerful who had previously both refused to pay taxes and kept to their estates to avoid legal action.[37]

Alongside raising taxes, Majorian needed to appoint new functionaries. The most important of the new men was named Aegidius, a native of Gaul who had a strong political base in the north of Gaul, who was appointed *magister militum per Gallias*.[38] Aegidius' task was to help pacify Gaul, especially the fractious Goths.

Majorian also sent envoys to Marcellinus, who was still in control of Dalmatia. Marcellinus came to terms with Majorian, with the result that the eastern flank of the Western Empire was now secure. Possibly at the same time, Majorian promoted a man named Nepotianus to the post of *magister equitum*, which he had himself vacated upon becoming emperor. The decision may have helped Marcellinus to settle on supporting Majorian, as Nepotianus was married to his unnamed sister and the couple had a son, Julius Nepos. The latter would be a main player in the story of the last years of the West.[39] Ricimer remained the *magister peditum*, and the plan appears to have been for him to remain in Italy to defend against any further Vandal assaults, whilst Majorian, Nepotianus and Aegidius conducted campaigns in Gaul.

The tax measures appear to have worked to great effect. Majorian used the money raised to hire mercenaries from the barbarian tribes 'living in the Danube basin':[40]

> Bastarnian, Suebian, Pannonian, Neuran, Hun, Getan, Dacian, Alan, Bellonotan, Rugian, Burgundian, Visigoth, Alites, Bisaltan, Ostrogoth, Procrustian, Sarmatian, Maschan have ranged themselves behind thine eagles; in thy service are the whole Caucasus and the drinker of the Don's Scythian waters.
>
> *Sidonius Apollinaris, Carmina,* 5.474–479

Majorian was intent upon regaining control of the West.

With a large army being gathered, and recognizing the importance of sea power if the Vandals were ever to be defeated, he used at least some of the new taxes to finance the construction of a large navy, intent on retaking Africa:

> Meanwhile you built on the two shores fleets for the upper and lower sea. Down into the water falls every forest of the Apennines; for many a long day there is hewing on both slopes of those mountains so rich in ships' timber.
>
> Sidonius Apollinaris, *Carmina,* 5.441–442

The new fleets consisted of 300 ships, a massive investment of time, money and material.[41] The two fleets were perhaps those stationed traditionally at Misenum and Ravenna on the Tyrrhenian and Adriatic Seas respectively.[42] The fleet at Misenum was doubtless to help defeat the Vandals. That at Ravenna would have two main duties. Their major task was to help in the reconquest of Africa, while also facilitating Majorian's contacts with Marcellinus in Illyricum.

Gaiseric quickly became aware of the proposed invasion. Majorian doubtless gave the projected campaign as the reason for the intense taxation being levied. It was no secret, as it was referenced extensively by Sidonius in a panegyric given to the emperor in December 458.[43]

At the same time, Majorian would have declared his intention of bringing the Burgundians, Goths and Sueves to heel. Despite being worried by the threatened invasion, Gaiseric now knew that there were prospective allies in Western Europe. At some time in 458, a Vandal embassy arrived in Toulouse to negotiate with the Goths, and a joint embassy then went to Hispania to talk with the Sueves.[44] Sadly for Gaiseric, the Sueves refused to join the alliance, but there is a good chance that the Vandals and Goths put aside their traditional enmity in the face of the common enemy.[45]

At some point in the summer, Aegidius subdued both the city of Lyon and the Burgundians.[46] He then moved to Narbonne, the centre of the *coniuratio Marcelliniana*, before returning to Arles.[47] Theoderic had earlier attacked Arles and now returned to trap Aegidius in the city – possibly reinforced in his commitment by the new treaty with the Vandals.[48] Marching across the Alps, Majorian ordered Nepotianus to head south with a large detachment of troops to relieve the siege.[49] Nepotianus and Aegidius fought a battle against Theoderic, defeating the Goths.[50] Theoderic quickly came to terms and peace was restored in southern Gaul. Any treaty with the Vandals was short-lived.

The resurgence of the West, plus the building of a fleet, would have caused concern in Carthage, but it is probable that Gaiseric learned from informants that Majorian was intent upon restoring Roman rule in Gaul and Hispania before attempting an assault on Africa. It may also be now that Gaiseric became aware that Majorian's plan was to avoid the usual route of attack via Sicily, but concentrate his forces in southern Hispania before crossing at the Straits of Gibraltar, mirroring the earlier Vandal action. Such a move would be logical, since Majorian's campaign would first move against the Burgundians, then the Goths, then the Sueves. Rather than taking the army back to Italy, then to Sicily and across to Africa, it made sense to simply make the short crossing from the south of Hispania. It also meant that the crossing would be a long way from Vandal-dominated waters.

If the hypothesis that Majorian's plans were well-known is true, it would explain some otherwise confusing aspects of Gaiseric's apparent strategy. The most likely route for an attack on Africa would see the Roman army transported first to Sicily and then across to somewhere in the region of Carthage: in fact, this was to happen twice in later years. Yet there is no evidence that Gaiseric attacked Sicily in 457–460, which would have been an obvious strategy to disrupt the impending assault. Either controlling or severely damaging cities and installations in Sicily could have limited the ability of the West to mount and supply a successful crossing. As Gaiseric did not attack Sicily, it can be assumed that he knew of Majorian's plans and reacted accordingly.

459

Over the winter of 458–459, Majorian remained in Gaul. It is possible that he had been hoping to transfer the army from Hispania to Africa in 459, but events thwarted any such plan. He probably expected that the Vandals would concentrate their attention on Sicily, leaving him with a free crossing to Africa in the far west.

Yet Sicily would still need to be defended and the majority of the West's forces needed to be retained for the assault. Of even greater utility, if a large force was deployed to Sicily, it could cross to Africa in a separate campaign to that from Hispania – or at least threaten such a crossing and so pin Vandal troops in Carthage.

Majorian therefore opened negotiations with Marcellinus in Illyricum, hoping that Marcellinus would send troops to garrison Sicily. Any such plan was thwarted by external events. In 458, Leo had stopped payments to barbarian settlers in Pannonia, most notably the Amal Goths (Ostrogoths) under their ruler Valamir.[51] In response, Valamir invaded the territory of Marcellinus in 459, reaching the Adriatic and the city of Dyrrachium.[52] Under barbarian attack, there would be no possibility of Marcellinus helping Majorian in 459. Majorian would have to wait an extra year before bringing Gaiseric to heel.

It can be suggested that Gaiseric used the time well. He sent repeated envoys to Majorian in an attempt to negotiate a peace, but these were all rebuffed.[53] These are usually described as 'insincere', but this almost certainly represents the adherence of the Roman sources to the *topos* of barbarian perfidy rather than Gaiseric being so confident of victory that he could afford to toy with Majorian.[54] Gaiseric would have wanted a treaty, hopefully recognizing at least some of his new acquisitions and perhaps including a clause that Eudocia's marriage to Huneric be recognized as legitimate. Otherwise, he would have to risk an all–out war.

If all of the above hypotheses are accurate, Gaiseric would have known that he needed to take proactive action. Consequently, it was likely in 459 that he annexed the Balearic Islands. The financial benefits of owning the islands may have been less than the cost of maintaining garrisons there, so there needed to be an overriding reason for Gaiseric's decision to permanently occupy the islands rather than simply ravage them. The likelihood is that he was aware of Majorian's plans and was determined to hinder them wherever possible. It would be difficult to attack the Roman fleet along the coast without a base, and the Mediterranean cities of Hispania were, as far as is known, still under Roman control.

The obvious course of action was to annexe the Balearics and use them as a base, in the hope that an opportunity would arise when the Vandals could take the Roman fleet by surprise as it travelled along the Hispanic coast. If true, an expedition was sent and a fleet stationed on the islands with orders to maintain a watch upon the predicted route of the Roman invasion.

Possibly at the same time, but maybe at the start of 460, Gaiseric is alleged to have torn down the walls of all of the cities in Africa except Carthage in order to stop them being captured and used as secure bases by Majorian.[55] It has been suggested that the measure was taken prior to the later campaign in 468, but this seems unlikely: that campaign was coming from Italy via Sicily, so Carthage can be assumed to have been the main target.[56] Gaiseric also appears to have poisoned the wells in the Mauretanias that would be used by Majorian as he advanced across the north of Africa.[57] He was obviously not confident of success in the Western Mediterranean.

Africa

Although the main threat to the Vandal kingdom was external, internally, Gaiseric was aware that Nicene dissidents could easily rise up and support the upcoming Roman invasion. As a result, he became determined to promote Arianism, doubtless as a symbol of loyalty to the Vandal regime, rather than the Empire. As a result, in the late 450s into the 460s, Gaiseric decreed that only Arians were to hold 'offices at the Vandal court'.[58] His aim may have been to create a theologically pure kingdom, although this is open to question. He appears to have been a realist and would have recognized that there was little chance of gaining total conversion to Arianism.[59] He may instead have been attempting to ensure that anyone in a position of power who could either betray him personally or the kingdom as a whole by giving away information was an Arian, and therefore almost certainly unwilling to betray him to the Nicene Empire.

Having used all of these schemes in an effort to protect his kingdom, Gaiseric awaited the campaign season of 460 secure in the knowledge that he would have to face the might of the Western Roman Empire.

Chapter 12

Majorian's African Campaign

After having been forced to pause in Gaul for a year, Majorian's main objective for 460 was the obliteration of the Vandal kingdom in Africa. First, he needed to pacify Hispania in order to secure his lines of communication. Fortunately for Majorian, the Sueves, the main opposition in Hispania, chose this moment to engage in a series of political upheavals. Majorian was to take advantage and push the Sueves back into Gallaecia, at least for the duration of his campaign.

Gaiseric

Gaiseric would take full advantage of the delay in Majorian's projected campaign. As Roman forces built up and the campaigns in Gaul and Hispania developed, Gaiseric continued to send envoys to Majorian attempting to secure peace, but these were all rebuffed. With the failure of the embassies, Gaiseric had several possible responses.

One was to launch a major assault against either Sicily or the Italian mainland, or both, in order to distract at least some of Majorian's forces. However, Italy was being defended by Ricimer, who had already defeated two Vandal raids, so it was not a viable option – no attacks on Italy are recorded. This left Sicily. It is possible that Gaiseric dispatched an army to Sicily in the hope of forcing Majorian to abandon his plans in order to defend the island. Unfortunately for Gaiseric, Majorian's agreement with Marcellinus to station troops in Sicily now bore fruit. Either late in 459 or early in 460, Marcellinus crossed to Sicily.[1] He soon showed that he was a capable commander: 'Marcellinus slaughtered the Vandals in Sicily and put them to flight from the island.'[2] The distraction – if such it was – had failed.

All that was left for Gaiseric was to defeat Majorian himself, hopefully before he had crossed with his army to Africa. The naval forces presumably stationed in the Balearic Islands would now have to deliver a knockout blow. They did not have long to wait. Some time after 28 March 460, Majorian left Arles heading for Hispania, accompanied by his own army and a large force of Goths supplied according to the Romano-Gothic treaty of 458.[3] In May, he crossed the Pyrenees and began the march to Carthaginiensis.[4] It would seem likely that part of the combined Romano-Gothic force moved to Gallaecia to attack the Sueves.[5] Under attack, the Sueves would be unable to interfere with Majorian's great campaign. With Marcellinus in Sicily, Ricimer in Italy, the Goths and Burgundians under control and the Sueves preoccupied in Hispania, Majorian prepared for the defining campaign of his career.

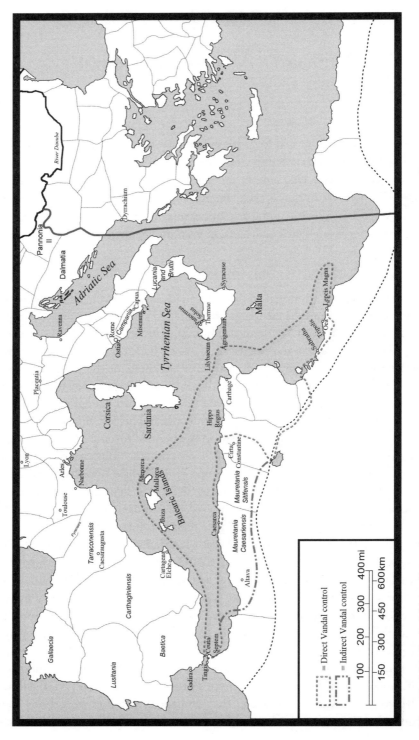

Map 11: Majorian's African Campaign.

The Navies[6]

Few historians have analyzed the course of events from a naval perspective, evaluating the reasons for Majorian's decision to travel via Hispania from a logistical viewpoint.[7] In order to fully understand the dilemmas faced by both Gaiseric and Majorian, it is necessary to look at the composition of the respective navies on the eve of the invasion.

Gaiseric: the Vandal Navy

The nature of any ships captured by the Vandals in their annexation of Carthage in 439 is unclear. Although no naval force is attested as being stationed in the city, Carthage's main trade was the export of grain to Rome: the insignia for the *Proconsul Africae* in the *Notitia Dignitatum* has in the lower panel an image of ships carrying grain. Given the need to maintain ships and build new ones to replace any lost due to the weather or simple accidents, the port of Carthage would have stored large amounts of timber in the shipyards ready for use when the need arrived. Although the same is true, but possibly to a lesser extent, in Ostia, the port of Rome, and possibly in Misenum, it is more likely that the majority of repairs to ships navigating to and from Africa, along with the expense, were done in Carthage when at all possible: the province could easily afford the cost. As a result, Gaiseric would have had access to shipbuilding materials and the expertise to use them for nearly two decades before war again broke out with Rome. Furthermore, the wood used would have been properly seasoned prior to use. It is likely that the majority of vessels built under Gaiseric's orders were transports to allow his men to conduct raids, possibly with a few warships to protect the transports from attack by Romans or pirates.

However, from 439–442, the Vandals had been concerned with the threat of the Empire uniting to crush their newly won kingdom. Although the treaty of 442 would to some degree have lessened their worry, Gaiseric was a wily commander and would have been continuously preparing for a forthcoming war with the Empire. In addition, once Gaiseric had sacked Rome, he would have been extremely wary of a Roman backlash, especially if the new Western rulers could organize a joint campaign with the East.

His decision to maintain vessels for the use of the Vandal army, rather than trade, may be implied by the speed at which he crossed to Italy and sacked Rome upon hearing of the death of Valentinian III, as well as by Victor of Vita's mentioning of the cutting of trees in Corsica 'for the King's ships'.[8] Although the latter is ascribed to the later reign of Huneric (477–484), the peaceful reign of Huneric stands in contrast to the military expansion under Gaiseric, suggesting that Huneric followed his father's example. The evidence all implies that Gaiseric was building warships to defend his transport fleet as well as new transports.

In this context, it is almost certain that Gaiseric would have ordered a large number of *dromons* to be built, aimed at deterring an attack from the Empire, defeating an Imperial fleet en route to Africa or attacking the Romans as they disembarked troops in Africa itself, when they would be most vulnerable. These *dromons* were small, agile ships with a single bank of oars, at this date the most common warship in the Mediterranean. Sadly, there is no evidence whatsoever of the composition or numbers of the Vandal fleet. The only clue that survives is Gaiseric's response to Majorian's building of a large fleet – as will be seen. On the other hand, Gaiseric had one major advantage: the years of sea-borne raiding meant that he had experienced crews with which to fight any sea battles.

Majorian: The Roman Navy

The Vandals had previously been defeated on Mediterranean islands by Majorian and Ricimer. In order for the Romans to transport troops to Sicily and Corsica, it was necessary to have a fleet in the Tyrrhenian Sea capable of moving substantial numbers of men. In the narrow seas between Italy and the adjoining islands, the fleet was almost certainly composed of transports and conscripted merchant vessels, with few, if any, warships. The latter had simply not been needed and the Empire did not have the monetary surplus to allow the building and maintaining of a war fleet prior to the attack on Rome in 455: such a measure would have been seen simply as an unnecessary luxury.

In this context, the information given by Sidonius, that Majorian had built two fleets (quoted above),[9] needs to be assessed. Although the existence of at least one small fleet in the Mediterranean prior to Majorian's reign is obvious, the lack of warships was a major failing. It is certain that at least a considerable proportion of the new ships being built were *dromons*, constructed to face Gaiseric's warships in battle. Unfortunately, such ships needed skilled crews and Majorian did not have access to a ready supply of such men. Most of the peoples with a long tradition serving in ships were either under barbarian control (e.g. Carthage) or in the East (e.g. Rhodes or the Phoenician ports). In part this helps explain Majorian's strategy of travelling via Hispania. With raw crews, it is likely that Majorian was unwilling to risk losing both the new *dromons* and the accompanying fleet of transports in a single sea encounter off the coast of Africa.

Furthermore, a major landing on the coast near to Carthage would be an extremely hazardous undertaking. A large army would take a long time to disembark and be exceptionally vulnerable to an attack by a mobile army that could move fast and catch them when they were disorganized. At the same time, the fleet itself would be exposed to a naval assault from the Vandal fleet. Even with a large number of *dromons*, to attempt such a landing with untrained crews was an exceptional risk and one that Majorian did not wish to try, especially when faced with Gaiseric's experienced crews.

In fact, given the size of the invading army, the majority of the ships being built were undoubtedly transport vessels aimed at moving as many men as possible as quickly as possible from one continent to the other. Such vessels would be easy targets for the Vandals' warships, and it was due to this that Majorian decided to use his fleet to transport his troops across the Straits of Gibraltar, a long way from Carthage and where he hoped to avoid armed resistance. In this context, the modern hypothesis that the decision not to attack direct from Sicily to Africa was either a mistake or seems odd appears to be mistaken.[10]

One other factor demands attention. Majorian was planning to lead an army into territory that was at least nominally hostile. It would, therefore, be necessary for him to arrange for the gathering of large supplies of food and equipment along the route he planned to use. The unconquered areas of Hispania would be asked to provide supplies for the army, but whether these would suffice for the whole campaign is doubtful. Consequently, it is likely that large quantities of provisions were stockpiled in the southern Gallic ports. It would be easier to transport these by sea to the Straits of Gibraltar, and Majorian may have been planning to use his fleet as a mobile supply base, following his route as he marched across North Africa. Sadly, no sources comment upon how Majorian planned to keep his men fed, so these conclusions must remain hypothesis.

The Campaign

Gaiseric was obviously not convinced that he could defeat the upcoming invasion. The evidence for his lack of conviction lies in the fact that he laid waste to those areas of Mauritania that Majorian would traverse and allegedly poisoned the wells that the Roman army would have to use.[11] These are not the actions of a ruler convinced that he would win, and demonstrate that Majorian's forces were large enough to cause at least serious damage to the Vandal presence in Africa, if not to wipe it out completely. Gaiseric's panic also implies that the newly made Roman fleet was far larger than his own: even though the majority were only transport vessels, crammed with soldiers, these could still put up a stout defence against a *dromon*.

Gaiseric did, however, have one advantage. Majorian had made a major strategic mistake: he had broadcast his intention to invade and it was obvious that the plan was for the major assault to come from Hispania. In addition, it was clear that the main body of the army was marching through Hispania and would not be boarding the vessels until Majorian was ready to make the actual crossing. Gaiseric knew that although Marcellinus, now in occupation of Sicily, could theoretically mount an invasion via Malta, this was unlikely given that the vast majority of the Empire's newly raised resources were focused upon Hispania.

The question remained as to what Gaiseric could do with the information to defeat Majorian. Although impossible to prove, as no sources describing events from the Vandals' viewpoint survive, what follows is based upon existent Roman sources coupled with analysis of the distances involved, and is hence the most likely course of events.

The distance between Carthage and Cartagena is about 600 nautical miles – longer if following the shoreline. In good weather, this could be expected to take at least four days.[12] This would have been one of the main factors in Majorian's decision to attack from Hispania. The campaign through Gaul and Hispania would solve the majority of the problems faced by the Empire in Europe, and to simply continue the move across the Straits of Gibraltar would both save time and remove the operation from the regions dominated by the Vandals. With any luck, the crossing would be completely unopposed.

If Gaiseric was a competent commander – and everything about his career implies that he was – then he would have known that the invasion was at its most vulnerable immediately prior to or during the crossing. The distances involved meant that Gaiseric could not base his fleet in Carthage and expect to take the Roman fleet unawares: it would simply take too long.

The implication is that either in 459 or very early in 460, when it became obvious that the invasion was bound for the Straits, Gaiseric led his forces out of Carthage and established at least one base in the Balearic Islands, probably on Ibiza, the nearest island to the Hispanic coast. The distance from Ibiza to the mainland is around 100 nautical miles, which in good conditions could be sailed in one day.

Having made his decision, Gaiseric waited in the hope that an opportunity would arise for an attack that would destroy, or at least weaken, the invasion force as it sailed down the coastline. Although certainty is impossible, it is likely that Gaiseric remained in Carthage. Hydatius only states that the fleet was composed of Vandals, not led by Gaiseric in person.[13] It is almost certain that it was whilst Gaiseric – or his designated commander – was in Ibiza that they were on the receiving end of a massive stroke of luck.

The Battle of Elche

Having rejected Gaiseric's negotiations, Majorian had carried on with his invasion plans. The fleet had been given orders to meet at *Portus Illicitanus*, near Elche, on the Bay of Alicante, 40 miles from Cartagena. Marching separately with his army, Majorian moved slowly south and reached the city of Caesaraugusta.[14] He did not wait long in the city, choosing to leave soon after his entry to travel towards the embarkation point.

Following orders, the Roman fleet had moved to Elche and awaited the arrival of Majorian with the army. What happened next is shrouded in mystery. The Vandals may have had scouts out who saw the advancing Roman fleet as it sailed towards Elche and returned to inform the main fleet. They may have received the information when they accosted local fishermen, or been told by traitors of the Roman fleet's presence.[15] Although Roman writers commonly used the *topos* (reworking of traditional concepts) of 'traitors' to explain otherwise-inexplicable Roman defeats, betrayal remains a possibility. The unanswerable question remains as to how the 'traitors' knew where to find the Vandal fleet.

The most likely explanation, using the few sources that remain, is that the Vandal ships accosted local fishermen – Hydatius' 'traitors' – who told them that the fleet was at Elche. If this is true, it would explain several uncertain factors that are otherwise hard to understand. The first of these is that the Romans were totally unaware of the Vandal presence, which would not have been such a surprise if they had seen the Vandal ships observing them.

The second would answer why the Vandals took the decision to attack so quickly. The Empire's near bankruptcy and the fact that Majorian had recruited a large number of land forces probably meant that he didn't have the money to recruit large numbers of trained sailors to man the fleet, so the ships would have inexperienced crews. In addition, the lack of finance probably resulted in the Roman ships being manned by skeleton crews: enough men to manoeuvre the ships, but not many more. In theory, this would be all that was needed for an unopposed landing in Tingitana. Even if the landing itself was opposed, at that point the army would be available to help fight a sea battle by manning the ships. What Majorian had not expected was that Gaiseric was fully aware of all of these factors and would attempt to stop the invasion before the fleet reached the Straits of Gibraltar.

Whatever the course of events prior to the Vandals learning of the Roman fleet being at Elche, what happened after is not open to doubt. The Vandals attacked. No details have survived of the course of the battle. Several sources claim that the Roman fleet was captured, but the chances are that the majority, if not all, of the transport ships were destroyed, whereas wherever possible the Roman *dromons* would have been captured and taken for use by the Vandals.[16] The Vandals had enough ships to transport their raiding parties, but additional combat vessels to face further threats would be welcomed.

The question remains as to how a Vandal fleet was able to defeat a Roman fleet with such consummate ease. The factors outlined above of the Roman ships having only skeleton crews of poorly trained men would not have helped the Roman cause. If the Roman army had been present, the outcome may have been different. Yet there was one further advantage with the Vandals. Their attack took place in the harbour, leaving little room for even a well-trained navy to outmanoeuvre their less-numerous opponents. Taken by surprise, and probably with their untrained crews ashore, there was little doubt about the outcome of the attack: the fully equipped, manned and experienced Vandal fleet had little difficulty in defeating the Roman armada, even though heavily outnumbered.[17]

Aftermath

Majorian was still marching south with his troops when he received the devastating news that the fleet had been destroyed.[18] Unsurprisingly, he was dismayed by the news. With the loss of his fleet, his dream of conquering Africa was at an end.[19] All of the surviving sources demonstrate that Majorian now suffered a complete loss of confidence.[20] Possibly after spending a little time organizing affairs in Hispania – the exact timescale is unknown – he withdrew to Arles.[21]

On the other hand, Gaiseric would have been elated at the success. Throughout the remainder of the year, it would appear that envoys were passing between Majorian in Hispania and Gaiseric in Africa. From his position of new-found strength, 'King Gaiseric sought peace from the emperor Majorian through envoys'.[22] The first of these envoys doubtless found Majorian in Hispania, but they would later have needed to travel to Arles.[23] An agreement was eventually reached and a peace treaty signed 'on shameful terms'.[24]

What these terms were is nowhere described by the sources. The most likely conditions included the West's acceptance of the Vandal dominion of the whole of the North African coastline west of Carthage, including those provinces retained by Rome in the treaty of 442, as well as any islands in the Mediterranean that Gaiseric had occupied.[25] These might have included Sardinia and/or Corsica, as well as the Balearic Islands.

The question of the Vandal conquest of Africa has often caused confusion. Victor of Vita states:

> After Valentinian [III] died he [Gaiseric] gained control of the coastline of all Africa, and with his customary arrogance he also took the large islands of Sardinia, Sicily, Corsica, Ibiza, Mallorca and Menorca, as well as many others.
>
> Victor of Vita, *History of the Vandal Persecutions*, 1.13

The passage has caused confusion amongst historians, not least because Victor was writing during the persecution of Catholics by Huneric, son of Gaiseric. As a result, his claims are open to debate due to his overt antagonism to the Vandals, his exaggerations in order to prove his points, plus the confusion caused by the problematic dating of many of the events he details. There is no guarantee that the Vandals occupied all of these territories from 460 onwards.

In addition, Procopius describes the campaigns launched by Belisarius in 533 to retake the cities lost to the Vandals:

> First he sent Cyril to Sardinia ... and ordered Cyril to send a portion of the army to Corsica. ... And to Caesarea in Mauretania [he sent] ... John with an infantry company ... Another John ... he sent to Gadira on the Strait ... and the fort there which they call 'Septem'. ... And to ... Ebusa and Majorca and Minorca. ... He also sent some men to Sicily in order to take the fortress in Lilybaeum, as belonging to the Vandals' kingdom.
>
> Procopius, *History of the Wars*, 4.5

This is probably an accurate description of Belisarius' actions. Procopius was an eyewitness to many of these orders, so his account is accepted as being trustworthy. Sadly, though, his account belongs to the following century and therefore does not include the dates at which these regions were taken by the Vandals; it only notes that by 533, these regions were under Vandal control – although in the case of Lilybaeum, it was the Goths of Italy who exerted actual authority.

Following the descriptions above, many historians accept that Gaiseric extended his hold along the whole coastline, but this has been questioned. Studies of epigraphy have clearly demonstrated that inscriptions found to the west of the city of Constantine are dated using the 'Mauretanian Provincial Era', which began in AD 40. East of Constantine, the dates on inscriptions follow the 'Vandal Era', which began in 439. This implies that the Vandals never extended their empire along North Africa further than Constantine.[26]

Yet these apparently contradictory facts can be reconciled. Prior to the war of 460, Gaiseric learned that Majorian was planning a campaign via Hispania. In order to deny the Roman fleet access to harbours, probably in 459 – if not before – Gaiseric had campaigned along the north coast of Africa, securing the ports listed in order to deny them to the Romans. With the defeat of Majorian's expedition, to ensure the continued security of his kingdom, it is likely that Gaiseric maintained garrisons in these cities to deter any further attack from the West. This would explain both the claim that these cities needed to be retaken from the Vandals in 533 and the lack of Vandal epigraphy in the region: it was only the cities/fortresses on the coast which were in the hands of the Vandals. The hinterland, probably whilst accepting Vandal suzerainty due to the lack of an army with which to defend itself, was allowed to govern itself and so retained its own dating conventions on inscriptions.

In the case of the Mediterranean islands, it is probable that at this stage the Vandals claimed control of both the Balearics and Corsica, but their possession of Sardinia had been disputed earlier by Majorian, so it is likely that it remained outside their control.[27] On the other hand, and despite later claims, it is likely that Sicily remained a Roman possession. Majorian would have known that the Senate would never accept the loss of the island, a major source of grain. The concept that the two largest islands remained under Roman control is implied by Victor of Vita when he lists them alongside territories that were ravaged by Vandal attacks rather than being captured and part of the Vandal regnum.[28] Gaiseric now had a small empire to rule, a major achievement for a man who had at one point led only a small group of disaffected barbarians in Hispania.

Also included may have been the acceptance that Eudocia's marriage to Gaiseric's son Huneric, as per the treaty of 442, was legitimate. Majorian may even have been forced to pay a dowry to Eudocia. This would not damage Majorian's reputation, as it may have been agreed as part of the treaty of 442, and so may have been demanded by Gaiseric.

Yet Gaiseric would have known that Majorian was now in a precarious position politically. He needed Majorian to remain as emperor in order to give himself the time to cement his position in his newly won territories. Consequently, Gaiseric would certainly have consented to the restoration of the grain supply from Africa to Rome, and agreed to halt all of the attacks on the West, especially on Sicily and Italy.[29]

It is possible that also included in the treaty, and perhaps an attempt to allow Majorian to save face and present the campaign as at least a marginal success, was an agreement by Gaiseric to return Eudoxia and Placidia, the wife and daughter of Valentinian III, taken as captives by the Vandals in 455.[30] In 454, the Empress Eudoxia had attempted to arrange a marriage between Placidia and Majorian.[31] It is possible that Majorian saw Placidia's release as a chance to marry her, which would give him a legitimate claim to continuity from the dynasty of Theodosius and so protect him from the fallout from the humiliating defeat. On Gaiseric's part, such a marriage would ensure the safety of the Imperial women, as well as his own family's continued connection to the Imperial family. It should be noted, however, that including the return of the Imperial women to Rome as part of the agreement is speculation, although possibly reinforced by the circumstances surrounding the actual return of the captives in 462.

There remains the question of why Majorian agreed to the signing of a treaty that was seen, even in the East, as 'shameful'.[32] There are two factors which may be deemed the most likely. One is that in gathering the invasion fleet, he had used all of the available ships and so had none left to even manage a staged crossing of the Straits of Gibraltar. The second is that in destroying the fleet, the Vandals also destroyed the supplies that were to be used by the army in Africa. With the loss of the supply ships, the invasion was no longer practical. In these circumstances, a peace treaty would be a good thing for the Empire, as it would allow it time to recover and rebuild its forces.

Yet there is one further factor which is never discussed. At the time of the treaty, Gaiseric was about 70 years old. It is possible that Majorian believed that if he waited only a short time, the elderly and brilliant Gaiseric would die and be replaced by his son Huneric, whose reputation may have suggested that he would be a far weaker adversary than his wily father.

Whatever the reasons, given the distances between Hispania and Carthage, and the complex negotiations involved in the discussions, it is probable that the peace treaty was only concluded either late in 460 or, more likely, early in 461. Once the negotiations with Gaiseric were complete, if not before, Majorian returned to Arles.[33] If he had been based in Ibiza, Gaiseric would have returned to Carthage – probably to a hero's welcome.

Chapter 13

The Renewal of War

461

M ajorian had based his rule and his tax laws on the subjugation of the barbarian peoples settled within the Empire. The campaign had failed, and it is certain that a large part of the Senate and people of Rome, not just Ricimer, would have been very unhappy with Majorian's rule. Retaining only his personal *bucellarii*, Majorian headed for Rome, where he appears to have been planning to continue with his political reforms.[1] On 3 August, as he neared Dertona (Tortona) in northern Italy, he was met by Ricimer and a strong military force:[2]

> While returning to Rome from Gaul ... Majorian was treacherously ensnared and murdered by Ricimer, who was driven by spite and supported by the counsel of jealous men.
>
> Hydatius, 205 [210], s.a. 461[3]

Hydatius does not name any of the 'jealous men', but it is likely that the Senate had lost patience with their young, inexperienced and they believed incompetent emperor. The defeat at Elche and Majorian's instant negotiations with Gaiseric had ensured his own untimely death.

The death of Majorian marked a key point in the decline of the West. Aegidius, the *magister militum per Gallias* (Master of the Troops in Gaul), Marcellinus in Dalmatia and Nepotianus, the *magister militum* who at this point was in Hispania, had all supported Majorian's regime. All three of these refused to accept the domination of Ricimer, effectively removing Hispania, northern Gaul and Dalmatia from the Empire. In the case of Marcellinus, Ricimer had exacerbated the rivalry: whilst Marcellinus was still in Sicily, Ricimer bribed the Huns who formed the majority of Marcellinus' forces.[4] Furious, and with the backbone of his army gone, Marcellinus returned to Dalmatia.

Knowing that the West was vulnerable, Ricimer doubtless sent envoys to Gaiseric. None of the extant sources record any embassies between Gaiseric and Rome, yet it is certain that envoys were exchanged and negotiations pursued between Gaiseric and both halves of the Empire. It is usually accepted that immediately after the death of Majorian in AD 461, Gaiseric renewed his attacks on the West. Given the context of the negotiations (and soon-to-be-signed treaty) with the East, this must be seen as unlikely. Instead, he would have opened simultaneous negotiations with the West. It is almost certain that had war been ongoing, the treaty with the East would have included terms which would halt the attacks. It is more likely that during 461 and 462, Gaiseric withheld his forces and focused upon exchanging envoys with both halves of the Empire. In the following year, one of these would come to fruition.

In the meantime, Ricimer and the Senate made a fateful choice. It had been traditional to allow the senior emperor, now obviously Leo I, to nominate an emperor for the other half of the Empire. Ricimer decided not to ask the Eastern Emperor Leo for a nominee for the vacant throne. Instead, the choice fell on a senator named Libius Severus, a native of Lucania.[5]

The decision was unacceptable in the East. Leo refused to acknowledge Severus as legitimate, further widening the rift caused by his later treaty with the Vandals.[6] It is likely only after Leo had refused to acknowledge Severus that Gaiseric conceived of the idea of asking that Olybrius be married to Placidia, a factor he could then use to his advantage should the West not agree to his demands.

462

With regards to the West, Gaiseric may have hoped that Ricimer or the new emperor would ratify the treaty signed with Majorian in 461, yet in reality he would have known that this was unlikely. At least part of the reason behind Majorian's assassination was that the Senate in Rome was unhappy with his capitulation in the face of Vandal pressure. There was little chance of the West confirming a treaty which they abhorred. From the Roman viewpoint, envoys from Ricimer (either sent in 462 or dispatched after the death of Majorian in the previous year) maintained pressure on Gaiseric to refrain from attacks upon the West.

Given the context, Gaiseric would have focused upon coming to an agreement with the East. 'Divide and rule' was a longstanding strategy used in the ancient world, and a study of Gaiseric's policies reveal that he was a master of the technique. Envoys were sent to Constantinople, and although the absolute accuracy of the text is uncertain, it is possible that Priscus gives some idea of the nature of the talks.[7]

Ambassadors from the East echoed the sentiments of the West that Gaiseric should not attack, but also stressed the need for him to release the Imperial women he had kept in Africa since the sack of Rome in 455.[8] Gaiseric appears to have presented his terms for the cessation of attacks and the return of the women. From the East he demanded that the 'patrimony of Valentinian III' – a part of the property of the deceased emperor – be given to him for Eudocia, possibly as part of a dowry, plus

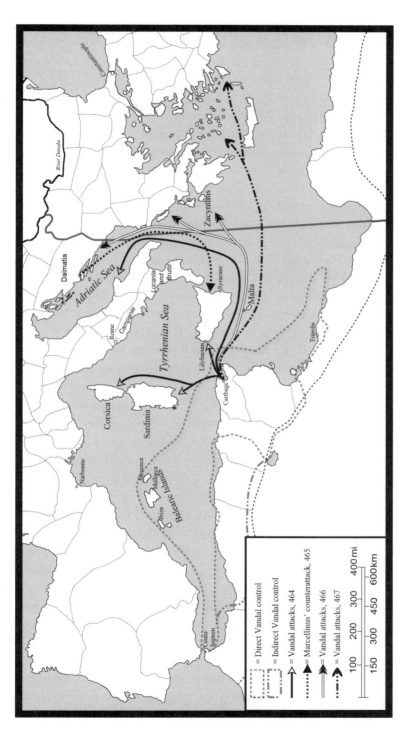

Map 12: The Vandals at War. Note that the dates are conjectural and the specific direction of the attacks has been drawn for reasons of clarity.

an acknowledgement of the validity of Eudocia's marriage to Huneric.[9] Likewise, from the West he demanded property for Eudocia, plus that the property previously owned by Aetius be given to Aetius' son Gaudentius, who was also in Africa.[10]

The Treaty of 462

After protracted negotiations, Gaiseric manoeuvred Leo into a position advantageous to the Vandals. In 462, a treaty was duly signed.[11] Leo, under pressure from Aspar not to become involved in Western affairs, acceded to Gaiseric's demands and the ownership of part of the lands previously owned by Valentinian were allotted to Gaiseric on behalf of Eudocia.[12] Determined to prevent the two halves of the Empire uniting against him, Gaiseric agreed not to attack the East and, possibly in return for the East's acknowledgement of Huneric's marriage to Eudocia, arranged for the transportation of Eudoxia and Pulcheria to Constantinople.[13] Their long captivity in Carthage was over. In many respects, they had served their purpose. Eudocia's marriage to Huneric had now been recognized by legitimate emperors in both the East and West, and there was no value in keeping the other women hostage. Furthermore, the two women would probably be kept free from harm in the East, as they were little threat to Leo. It is also possible that a small payment was made to ensure the release of Eudoxia, although this is not supported by all of the sources.[14] Nevertheless, Gaiseric had secured peace with the East.

Some historians have suggested that Olybrius had also been captured during the sack of Rome and that Gaiseric arranged for him to marry Pulcheria whilst the two individuals were captives in Africa.[15] Due to the poor quality of the sources, this remains only a possibility, but it is more likely that Olybrius had been sent to the East prior to the sack, so it was only after the return of the women to Constantinople that Olybrius married Pulcheria. It is also likely that Gaiseric insisted on the marriage as part of the treaty of 462: it is possible that Gaiseric, as Pulcheria's oldest male relative, used his position to choose a suitable suitor from the Western Empire.[16] Although speculation, it is tempting to see the marriage as part of a long-term strategy on the part of Gaiseric to manipulate the succession in the West to ensure that Huneric remained related to the Western Emperor.

One thing is certain: Gaiseric had already gained Majorian's acceptance of the marriage between Huneric and Eudocia, and had now secured Leo's recognition of Huneric as a member of the Theodosian House, although with the caveat that he was not eligible to be emperor. Gaiseric, probably the most politically astute of the barbarian kings, could now use the newly accepted family relationships to his advantage. Of more immediate importance, peace with the East meant that the weaker West was now isolated.

In the East, the treaty was probably accepted with relief. Leo had ensured that the Empire would not come under Vandal attack. Yet this had come at a cost. The East had agreed not to interfere in the West, possibly expecting the ongoing negotiations between Carthage and Rome to come to a successful conclusion.[17] This clause in the treaty can be seen as a major piece of cunning on Gaiseric's part. He would have known that Severus and Ricimer would refuse to sign a new treaty, and now Leo had refused to acknowledge Severus as Western emperor but had also agreed not to support the West should the war resume.

Although this can be seen as a short-sighted decision by Leo, he was in an awkward position when signing the treaty: he needed to bear in mind the mood of the Eastern populace, but more importantly, that of the army and army commanders, especially Aspar.[18] These men did not want a war with the Vandals, especially not when it was to support a Western usurper. Leo needed to free himself from Aspar's influence before he could take definitive action in the West. Whatever the case, even contemporaries now acknowledged that Gaiseric had succeeded in dividing the Empire.[19] More worrying for the West, Gaiseric may now have been able to use the Eastern treaty as a means of putting pressure on the West to accede to his demands.

The West

This was because the attempt to (re)negotiate a treaty with the new Emperor Severus in the West failed. Although the need for a renegotiation is sometimes questioned, it should be remembered that political and military direction in the ancient world was dependent solely upon the whim or desire of the incumbent rulers. None of the ancient nations had an administrative structure that allowed political policy to be carried over from one ruler to the next. The most obvious example of this is the transfer of power from Trajan (98–117) – the epitome of Roman military aggression – to Hadrian (117–138). The latter immediately abandoned many of Trajan's conquests and reverted to a more defensive stance for the Empire. Roman policy could be a very personal matter.

With this in mind, it is clear that with the death of Majorian, the treaty signed in 460/461 needed reaffirmation from the new regime.[20] The West, crippled by military defeat, loss of taxes and the need to maintain a large army to face the threat of Aegidius, Marcellinus and the Vandal raids, could not afford to agree the terms. In addition, Ricimer, the power behind the army, was anti-Vandal and so predisposed to rejecting the treaty.[21]

It is probable that news of the Vandal treaty with the East arrived during the negotiations. Although a relief for the East, the signing would have caused alarm and anger in the West. Without Eastern support, Ricimer and Severus knew that come the new year, the attacks on Sicily and Italy would almost certainly resume unless a new agreement was reached with Gaiseric, but they simply could not allow the signing of a new agreement acknowledging the humiliating terms that had caused the downfall of Majorian. There was little chance of Gaiseric accepting anything less.

Gaiseric now had two major factors in his favour. One was that he had signed a treaty with Leo I in the East, so it would take a major change of policy for the East to declare war on him. The other was that the Western Empire was unstable and the chances of a military defence rested solely on Ricimer's shoulders – and Ricimer could not be everywhere at once.[22] Aegidius in Gaul, Marcellinus in Dalmatia and Nepotianus in Hispania had all refused to acknowledge the new regime. Not only had this effectively removed Hispania, northern Gaul and Dalmatia from the Empire, but it meant that Italy was facing threats from the north, east and west. Under extreme pressure, Ricimer did not have enough troops to also defend extensive coasts in Italy and Sicily from Vandal attack.

The War Resumes

Given the prolonged negotiations and the presumed attempts by Gaiseric to arrange treaties with both East and West, with the opening of the campaign season of 463, when weather permitted sailing, Gaiseric resumed the war with the West. As noted earlier, it is assumed in this narrative that the Vandals only resumed their attacks in 463 after securing a peace treaty with the East, despite the claim by some historians that Gaiseric began the attacks immediately after the death of Majorian.

Gaiseric could now claim that the war was legitimate due to the West's failure to adhere to the treaty signed with Majorian, and to Severus' refusal to give Gaudentius his inheritance from Aetius. Now that Leo had refused to acknowledge Severus, Gaiseric could also announce that he thought that he was fighting on behalf of Olybrius, a member of the Imperial family who in Gaiseric's opinion should be emperor.[23] The latter claim would be an embarrassment to Leo, who would find it difficult to justify war with the Vandals when they claimed to be supporting a legitimate alternative against a usurper whom Leo himself refused to acknowledge.

Where exactly the Vandal attacks took place, and in which year, is unknown, as the sources are vague and dates non-existent. For example, Victor of Vita lists Hispania, Italy, Dalmatia, Campania, Calabria, Apulia, Sicily, Sardinia, Bruttium, Lucania, Old Epirus and Greece amongst the places attacked, without giving details or dates with which to outline Gaiseric's strategy.[24] Moreover, it should be acknowledged that as Roman sea power faded, natives even of 'Roman' regions could find it easier to resort to piracy in order to gain greater rewards than was usually found during 'normal' years. Therefore, it is also conceivable that these piratical attacks would then be attributed to the Vandals, despite this being incorrect.[25] What follows is an attempt to link all of the information into a coherent chronological narrative, but it should be acknowledged that viable alternatives are plausible.

With the resumption of the war, Gaiseric obviously stopped the flow of African grain to Rome. Almost immediately, pressure upon Severus would have risen as the city would have been threatened with famine. Alongside the blockade, Gaiseric ordered raids, probably this year along the Tyrrhenian coast and on Sicily, and possibly on Sardinia. The raiders had instructions to avoid defended places, as Gaiseric did not want to reduce his fighting ability by losing men in these raids.[26] Nor did he want to cause heavy casualties amongst the Roman defenders, as this would damage the legitimacy of his claim to be fighting on behalf of Olybrius.

Yet the raids seem to have increased in intensity from the previous war. Although certainty is impossible, several factors could have united to ensure that the Vandals' offensives were at their severest for a long time. The first of these is that, following the signing of a treaty with Leo, Gaiseric no longer feared an attack from the East and so was willing to allow more men than previously to go on raids rather than stay in Carthage to defend the homeland. In addition, they could stay away for longer and ravage over greater areas.

Although the citizens of Rome were now threatened with famine, of more importance politically was the fact that senators who had financial investments in Sicily and Sardinia would have seen their interests damaged. In response, they demanded that Severus secure peace with Gaiseric. Severus – or Ricimer – acceded to the demands and again sent envoys to propose peace with Gaiseric, who unsurprisingly rejected the terms.[27]

Also unsurprising was that, with Aegidius in Gaul and Marcellinus in Dalmatia also threatening war, the West could not cope with the Vandals' hit-and-run tactics. The West had suffered a major defeat in 460 and had now lost control of the majority of Gaul, Hispania and Dalmatia. It was probably only with the onset of the raids in 463 that Gaiseric realized just how weak the West had become. As a consequence, it is possible to speculate that it was only at this point that he determined on further expanding his dominions.

This was because, although nowhere explicitly stated, the vast majority of the Roman Army was probably retained in northern Italy to face Aegidius to the north and Marcellinus to the east. As a result, those Mediterranean islands which may not have been seen as vital by the Romans – who were almost certainly intent on defending the arable areas in Italy and Sicily to feed the capital and surrounding regions following the grain embargo – were undoubtedly left unguarded. In addition, and as already noted, Priscus states that only 'defended' areas were avoided by the Vandals.[28] As they were undefended, it is most likely either late in 463, or more likely in 464, that Gaiseric sent troops to annexe Corsica and Sardinia. He may also have attacked Sicily with the intention of gaining a foothold in the west of the island to pre-empt any counter-attack. Officially, he would have claimed that he was reconquering these areas on behalf of Olybrius.

In dire straits, envoys were sent to the East to appeal for help – the first of three such embassies.[29] Sadly for the West, the East had only recently signed the treaty and so the request for aid was rebuffed.[30] However, Leo did take non-military action. In late 463, Phylarchus, who had already been used as an envoy by the East, was sent to Marcellinus in Dalmatia to ensure that he did not attack Italy.[31] From the lack of any attack, it would seem that the embassy was a success, so at least one potential threat had been nullified. As an added bonus, war had broken out between Aegidius and the Goths in Gaul. Another potential invader had thus been neutralized, at least for a short time.

After this, Phylarchus travelled on to Africa. He would probably have informed Gaiseric that, far from ensuring that Olybrius became next emperor, he was damaging the West and so weakening the chances of Olybrius being successful. Unsurprisingly, this mission did not go well and Gaiseric refused to stop the attacks.[32]

464

Not long after the opening of the campaign season, in May 464, Gaiseric received an embassy from an unexpected quarter. Envoys arrived in Carthage from Aegidius, having sailed past Gallaecia and so come to the notice of Hydatius.[33] The embassy is usually dated to 463, but since it is suggested that the Vandals did not begin their attacks until 463, then maybe the embassy would arrive in 464 after the resumption of hostilities was well-known.

The nature and consequence of this embassy are unknown. It is possible that Aegidius wanted help removing Severus from the throne in Italy, by military and/or political pressure on Ricimer and the Senate. Possibly more likely, given the ongoing war with the Goths, Aegidius may have been hoping to persuade Gaiseric to declare war on Theoderic. Vandal attacks in the region of Narbonne, in alliance with Aegidius, could easily persuade Theoderic to make peace. Sadly, the reason for the mission is nowhere outlined in the sources, so the only safe assumption is that Aegidius wanted help 'of some sort'.[34] Whether it was successful or not is also unknown. All that is known is that the embassy returned to Aegidius in September. Before joint action could be taken, Aegidius died – according to Hydatius in the same year as the embassy, but certain dating is impossible.[35] Rather than acknowledging Severus, the Roman army in Gaul chose Aegidius' son Syagrius to be the new leader of the Gallic field army in the north.[36] Syagrius was to have a long and distinguished career.

Whatever the date and aims of the embassy from Gaul, it is probable that at the opening of the sailing season, the Vandals launched raids on the Adriatic coasts of Italy in an attempt to divert attention away from their campaigns to conquer Sardinia, Corsica and western Sicily. The gradual erosion of its territory meant that the Vandal attacks were now becoming a serious threat to the existence of the Empire. Desperate, Severus sent envoys to the East begging for the use of a fleet with which to defeat the Vandals. Leo refused the request, citing the existing treaty he had with Gaiseric, but did agree to send a second embassy to Africa in an attempt to secure peace.

A man named Tatianus was dispatched to intercede with Gaiseric on behalf of the West. It is possible that the use of Tatianus as envoy may have been a sign that Leo was beginning to regret the signing of the treaty in 462. Tatianus was a member of the opposition to Aspar, and it may have been Aspar who was the moving force behind the earlier peace treaty. If true, the appointment could signal a 'hardening of Leo's policy' regarding Gaiseric and the West.[37] Whether true or not, it was to no avail: Gaiseric refused to stop the attacks.[38]

Despite Marcellinus and Aegidius being neutralized, 464 was a bad year for Rome. With the Vandals attacking in the Mediterranean and Leo refusing to send help, in northern Italy an invasion led by Beorgor, king of the Alans, crossed the Alps and advanced as far as Bergamum (Bergamo).[39] Proving that the Empire still had some life, an army led by Ricimer in person defeated the Alans in battle at Bergamum.[40] This was the only good news for the Empire. Attacked on all sides, Severus and Ricimer could do little to stop the marauding Vandals but continue to send delegations to Leo hoping for military help.

465

With the Empire seemingly disintegrating, the West desperately needed help from the East and it is likely that an unrecorded series of envoys were in continuous motion between the two emperors. It should be emphasized that what follows is nowhere described in detail in any of the primary sources and is simply an attempt to link together disparate information to make sense of a confusing series of events. Although internally logical, it should not be taken as definitive.

Over the winter of 464–465, a major political change took place in the East. Up until this time, the leading military commander in the East had been Aspar. During his period controlling the army, Aspar had maintained that the East should not become involved militarily in Western affairs. In late 464, Leo appears to have begun to take more personal control and, despite the fact that the army was loyal to Aspar, Leo started to assert his power. In this context, Gaiseric's refusal to stop the attacks on the West can be seen as a mistake, as the continued refusals appear to have become too much for Leo. Yet without the approval of Aspar, supplying military aid was difficult. On the other hand, although he could not send the main army, Leo could order help to go from other quarters. The evidence is fragmentary and open to different interpretations, yet it would appear that in 465, following orders from Leo, 'Marcellinus slaughtered the Vandals in Sicily and put them to flight from the island'.[41]

The theory that Marcellinus acted either on his own initiative or at the request of Ricimer can be discounted. It is unlikely that he had the ships needed to transport the troops and supplies to the island on his own. Even more telling, when last in Sicily, his troops had been bribed by Ricimer, and unless under instruction from and assisted by Leo, he would almost certainly have been unwilling and unable to risk a repeat of the episode.[42] Surprised, the Vandals were easily defeated and evicted from the island. In the meantime, Leo continued political manoeuvres to reduce Aspar's power.[43]

As usual, in the new year the Vandals had launched their annual raids, almost certainly on Italy as well as Sicily, but this year also on Hispania – possibly on the north Mediterranean coast, and maybe on Cadiz (see Chapter 12).[44] The reason for an attack on Hispania is unclear, but it may have been in order to divert Gothic attention away from Gaul and so lessen the pressure on Aegidius, if the embassy sent from Aegidius to Gaiseric noted above was asking for help against the Goths. As Aegidius had died in the same year as the embassy, Gaiseric probably had little political profit from the venture.[45]

Death of Severus

Although Marcellinus' arrival in Sicily would have annoyed Gaiseric, who may have known that the move was ordered by Leo, it was too late in the year to mount a reprisal against Marcellinus or the East. Circumstances would alter Gaeseric's plans. On 14 November 465, Severus died in Rome.[46] Although Ricimer is usually suspected of having a hand in the death, Sidonius Apollinaris states outright that it was due to natural causes.[47]

At approximately the same time, the Gothic King Theoderic was assassinated by his brother Euric, who quickly assumed the throne.[48] Euric was unlike his brother. Whilst Theoderic appears to have been willing to work with the Roman authorities, it soon became clear that Euric was intent upon increasing the power of his own kingdom at the Empire's expense. The pressure on the West was increasing to ever higher levels.

466

Over the winter of 465–466, Ricimer bowed to pressure and sent envoys to Leo requesting that Leo nominate an emperor. The West could no longer afford to have an emperor unrecognized in the East, nor cope with the demands of the Vandalic War.[49]

There was an obvious successor in the form of Olybrius – the husband of Placidia, daughter of Valentinian III – yet at this stage there may have been little chance of him being crowned. Gaiseric was campaigning ostensibly on his behalf,[50] so for Leo to nominate Olybrius could be interpreted as bowing to political pressure from a barbarian. As if to ensure that Olybrius would not be chosen, Gaiseric continued his attacks on Italy into 466.

Unfortunately for the West, the request for an emperor coincided with a period of political turmoil in the East. Aspar had remained the dominant military commander for many years, but Leo was now determined to either raise up a rival to balance Aspar's influence or eliminate him once and for all.

The flashpoint was a war that erupted between the Goths and the Sciri on the East's northern frontier. Both sides sent envoys to Leo asking for help.[51] Aspar, who was either a Goth or an Alan, advised the emperor not to become involved, but was overruled and Leo supported the Sciri against the Goths.[52] Presumably shortly afterwards, Aspar's son Ardabur, who was serving in the East as *magister militum per Orientem*, was accused of treachery and removed from his post.[53]

Although the pressure against Aspar was mounting, he was still recognized as an outstanding military commander and in either late 466 or 467, he was sent to Thrace to deal with an invasion by Goths and Huns.[54] Aspar quickly defeated the barbarians. Although his power was waning, Aspar was still a force to be reckoned with.

Sadly for the West, these events in Constantinople absorbed Leo's attentions and by the end of 466 he had yet to make a decision about who to nominate as the new Western emperor.

Gaiseric

In the meantime, following Marcellinus' arrival in Sicily, Gaiseric changed his tactics. Gaiseric may have been unwilling to attack the East. Although Leo may have prompted Marcellinus, the East had not declared war. One of Gaiseric's main preoccupations in the past had been to prevent the two halves of the Empire uniting against him, so attacking the East was out of the question.

Instead, knowing that Marcellinus was defending Sicily, Gaiseric probably ordered attacks on Marcellinus' territories in Dalmatia in an attempt to force him to return to defend his homeland.[55] In some respects this would make sense: forcing Marcellinus back to Dalmatia would seriously weaken the West's defences in the rest of the Mediterranean. Accounts of events in the following year suggest that either Gaiseric's strategy was successful and Marcellinus was forced to evacuate

Sicily, or political developments in the East made it necessary for Marcellinus and his army to return. Whatever the case, Marcellinus' presence in Sicily left Dalmatia short of defenders, and the Vandals made the most of the opportunity and 'plundered Illyricum'.[56]

Yet whatever strategy Gaiseric followed in 466 was irrelevant in one major respect: the most important decision would be that made by Leo. He was expected to nominate an emperor for the West, and the main question would be concerning the actions he would then take regarding the ongoing war with Gaiseric.

467

Over the winter of 466–467, Leo and the Eastern court debated their options. Obviously, they could not choose Olybrius, as Leo was now opposed to Gaiseric and his policies.[57] Finally, Leo nominated an emperor for the West: the *magister militum* and *patricius* Anthemius. In the previous decade, over the winter of 456–457, the Emperor Marcian may have planned to make Anthemius the Western Emperor, but Marcian had died before this could take effect.[58] Majorian had eventually been made emperor. Anthemius would now get his chance.

Anthemius appears to have been a capable military commander. He was born in Constantinople around 420.[59] Following his father in a military career, Anthemius appears to have been made *comes rei militaris per Thracias* (Count of the Military in Thrace) in 454 and sent to re-establish the Roman frontier on the Danube after the death of Attila the Hun. Shortly after, he had been promoted to the rank of *magister utriusque militiae*, nominated as consul for 455 and given the title *patricius*.[60] At some point between 459 and 462, he had defeated an Ostrogothic force in battle before triumphing over an army of Huns that had captured Serdica, possibly in the winter of 466–467.[61]

In spring 467, Leo ordered Anthemius to travel to Italy, according to Procopius with the 'explicit task' of making war on the Vandals.[62] To ensure his acceptance by Ricimer and the Senate in Rome, negotiations took place to allow Ricimer to marry Anthemius' daughter, Alypia.[63] Sadly for Ricimer, it soon became apparent that Alypia did not like her new husband.[64]

Possibly as a counter-balance to Ricimer, Anthemius was accompanied by an army led by Marcellinus, who was made *magister militum* and *patricius*.[65] At this point, the military power of the East when compared to the impoverished West was clearly demonstrated to all, as Anthemius arrived in Italy with a 'well-equipped army of vast proportions'.[66] Marching towards Rome, on 12 April 467 – possibly at Brontotas, 3 miles from Rome – Anthemius was proclaimed emperor.[67]

When Anthemius entered Rome, the city was suffering badly from famine, probably due to the shortage of food brought about by Gaiseric's embargo, and a raging pestilence was devastating the people.[68] At roughly the same time, there was a pestilence in Italy focused on Campania, strange celestial phenomena and an outbreak of cattle disease – the last two specifically dated to 467.[69] In addition, at an unknown date in 467, there was an earthquake in Ravenna.[70] The omens concerning Anthemius' reign were not good.

Despite the problems, Anthemius disposed of his troops and commanders in preparation for the upcoming campaign against the Vandals. He may have been planning to appoint Ricimer to the command of the troops defending the north of Italy, or it is possible that his plans were disrupted slightly when a section of the Ostrogoths invaded Noricum early in his reign.[71] Whatever the case, Anthemius ordered Ricimer to repel the invaders. The Ostrogoths were defeated whilst they were still in Noricum, and preparations for the invasion of Africa continued.[72] Ricimer appears to have remained in the north, whereas Marcellinus was sent once again to secure Sicily for the West.[73]

Gaiseric

As Anthemius was entering Italy in early 467, Leo sent Phylarchus to Gaiseric, the third such embassy:

> The emperor Leo sent Phylarchus to Gaiseric to inform him about the sovereignty of Anthemius and to threaten war unless he left Italy and Sicily. He returned and announced that Gaiseric was unwilling to submit to the commands of the emperor but was preparing for war because the treaty of 462 had been broken by the Eastern Romans.
>
> Priscus, fragment 40 (trans. *Gordon*, 1960)

If Procopius is accurate when he states that Anthemius had been sent by Leo with instructions to wage war against Gaiseric, the warning by Philarchus that the East would declare war if Gaiseric did not accept Anthemius as Western emperor would seem to be disingenuous.[74] Yet Leo would have known what Gaiseric's reaction would be. Gaiseric could not accept Anthemius as emperor, as in the previous years he had conquered Mediterranean islands, almost certainly 'in the name of Olybrius'. If he accepted Anthemius as emperor, he would be compelled to return control of all these territories to the West. In addition, he would have to accept that Huneric was no longer a member of the Imperial family, a cornerstone of his succession policy in Africa.

Unsurprisingly, Gaiseric refused the demand that he accept Anthemius as emperor and halt the attacks on the West. In effect, Gaiseric had declared war on the East, removing any objections from Eastern generals that the East should not interfere in the war with the Vandals. As the Empire and the Vandals lurched towards war, African merchants had their goods confiscated.[75]

Euric

Yet Phylarchus may not have been the only envoy to land in Africa in 467. Hydatius notes several envoys passing between Euric, king of the Goths, the Sueves in Hispania and Gaiseric.[76] The purpose of these missions is nowhere given, but the fact that throughout his reign Euric was determined to expand his kingdom at the expense of the Empire, suggests that either Euric or Gaiseric was attempting to form an anti-Roman coalition intent upon exploiting Roman weakness to their own advantage. The fact that the Sueves confined their attention to Hispania throughout this period implies that they were not the prime movers in the attempt to form an alliance. The embassies were not a success: hearing of the East's intention to send a large army, the Sueves and Goths quickly recalled their envoys and awaited developments.[77]

Gaiseric's attacks

In response, Gaiseric diverted the majority of the spring raids away from Italy and the surrounding islands to the eastern Mediterranean – although raids on the West continued.[78] Not expecting Gaiseric to take the initiative, the East was taken by surprise. There is only one piece of evidence for an attack by Gaiseric on the East prior to 468. Procopius claims that an attack by Gaiseric was the reason for Leo sending an expedition in 468,[79] but fails to give a specific location for the attack.

It is certain that the Vandals did attack the East in 467. This is implied by the claim in the *Life of Saint Daniel the Stylite* that there was anxiety in Alexandria in Egypt due to a rumour that Gaiseric was going to attack the city.[80] From internal evidence within the source, it is clear that the story was rife in 467.[81] The citizens of the East were correct in their assumption that Gaiseric would attack, as later that same year, probably as soon as the sailing season began in early-mid spring, the raids on the East began.

On the other hand, doubts have been cast on the claim that all of the attacks listed in the sources as being by the Vandals are correctly attested. It has been noted that some of the Roman citizens – especially in the East – were prone to resort to piracy at times when the Empire was seen as being vulnerable, or when local conditions meant that piratical raids would be beneficial. This was especially the case with the Isaurians of Cilicia (see Map 1), who appear to have been working against the Empire in the 440s.[82]

Yet the greatest difficulty in describing Vandal activities during the war with the East is that the sources do not describe the course of the conflict, instead simply giving a list of areas attacked by the Vandals. This list of areas raided includes: Epirus Vetus and Nicopolis;[83] Achaea and the adjacent islands;[84] Hellas, Achaea including Caenopolis and possibly Olympia and Zacynthus;[85] and Caenopolis and Zacynthus (again).[86] As a consequence, it is impossible to outline a convincing strategy followed by Gaiseric during the conflict. Alongside these attacks on the East, the sources note the continuous attacks along the Tyrrhenian coast and on Sicily in the West. It is even possible that some extra forces were sent to Sardinia, perhaps to pose as a threat to Rome itself.[87]

Yet there may be one datable attack on the East. Usually dated to 468, an attack on Rhodes and the surrounding areas should probably be dated to the year before.[88] In 468, Gaiseric would have recalled all of his forces to face the upcoming invasion, so raids in that year are extremely unlikely. In this case, it is also possible that en route to Rhodes and during the return journey, the Vandal forces paused to raid Achaea and the adjacent islands.[89] If true, it may be that Gaiseric was attempting to force the East to dilute its strength by deploying some of its troops to defend important bases in the East. It is also possible that he was hoping that the threat of further attacks on the transport lanes around Rhodes would disrupt the supply of grain travelling from Egypt to Constantinople, thereby producing an economic reason for the East to negotiate for a new peace. When combined with the reported threat to Alexandria, the main embarkation point for the grain, the theory gains at least a little weight.[90]

Marcellinus

Similar to the East, events in Italy are complicated by the meagre nature of the sources and the subsequent confusion in dating events, especially with regards to the information stated by Hydatius.[91] As noted above, Hydatius says that Marcellinus had evicted the Vandals from Sicily in 465.[92] However, later, in an entry dated to 467, Hydatius writes that 'An expedition to Africa organized against the Vandals was recalled because of "a change of weather" and the unsuitability of sailing.'[93] Sadly, Hydatius gives no context for his claim. Interestingly, the *Consularia Constantinopolitana* also suggests that Marcellinus led a campaign against the Vandals in the first year of Anthemius' reign, but as Hydatius appears to have used this source, the support is not conclusive.[94] As a result, it is necessary to resort to speculation.

It is feasible that Hydatius, living in Hispania, had heard two stories in different years relating to the same event, and consequently misreported that Marcellinus was in Sicily on two separate occasions: once in 465, the other in 467. Hydatius had simply not realized that the two stories were of the same event. On the other hand, it is possible that Hydatius was correct in describing two separate campaigns. If this is the case, it is possible to theorize that Marcellinus was sent by Leo in 465 to relieve the pressure on Sicily. After Gaiseric had attacked his homeland, Marcellinus may have returned home in 466, before returning to Sicily in 467 under orders from Anthemius.

The hypothesis makes sense. The West needed at least three commanders in 467: Anthemius to defend the mainland in person, Ricimer in Noricum repelling invaders and dissuading attacks on northern Italy, and now Marcellinus in Sicily to complete the defence of what was left of the Western Empire.

In addition, it is possible – though impossible to prove – that on this occasion Marcellinus was given further orders. With Euric quiescent due to his need to cement his rule and a large group of invading Ostrogoths defeated, Anthemius did not need a large army to garrison Italy. It is possible that troops were available and were placed under the command of Marcellinus.

Since Gaiseric was now at war with the East, it may have been expected that the majority of his troops would be away from Africa raiding the eastern Mediterranean. Should this be the case, it was possible that a lightning attack on Africa from Sicily using the few forces available would destroy the Vandal kingdom.

Such a victory would have been a major political coup for Anthemius. In addition, the Vandals had amassed vast amounts of booty from their raids over the years, so the reconquest could have made the West financially viable for the vital first years of Anthemius' reign, possibly even financing the reconquest of further regions of the West. Unfortunately for Anthemius and Marcellinus, the chance was ruined by bad weather.[95] The invasion of Africa would have to wait until the following year.

Chapter 14

The Roman Invasion*

The most detailed description we have of what happened comes from Procopius' *War Against the Vandals*.[1] As is usual, care needs to be taken when analyzing such texts. For example, it derives from other sources and Procopius may have edited events described in the originals to fit into his own narrative, which aimed to promote the military achievements of his hero, Belisarius, who conquered the Vandals in a swift campaign in AD 533–534. Further, it is uncertain how the original sources gained their knowledge, so their accuracy is also indeterminate. However, as it is the source with the greatest level of detail, it must be used in order to attempt an analysis of the campaign. When utilized in conjunction with other sources, an even more detailed picture of events can be reached.

Gaiseric would have known that a joint East-West campaign was being planned for 468. The campaign was no secret: on 1 January 468, Sidonius Apollinaris delivered a panegyric to Anthemius full of hope for the unity of East and West and victory over the Vandals.[2] The start of the sailing season was usually the cue for attacks on the West, but on this occasion there can be little doubt that the only ships that left Africa were scouts and messengers determined on finding out where the campaign was to be launched from and to. It is also likely that Gaiseric, at this time nearly 80 years old, knew that defeat would mean the destruction of everything he had achieved. Apart from skeleton garrisons, it is probable that he recalled all of the Vandal troops to help in the defence of the homeland.

In the meantime, Anthemius sent envoys in the hope of establishing good relations with the Goths, Sueves, Salian Franks and *Brittones* (Bretons). In a perfect world, Anthemius would want peace treaties to be signed, as the vast majority of the army would be sailing for Africa, leaving Italy exposed to attack. It would be of little comfort to Anthemius if the conquest of Africa was accomplished but the army left in Italy was decimated in defeat to the barbarians and the city of Rome sacked once again. Although the missions to the Goths, Sueves and Franks ended

---

* Much of the following information was first outlined in Patricians and Empires (Pen & Sword, 2016), but here an attempt has been made to analyse the situation from a Vandal perspective.

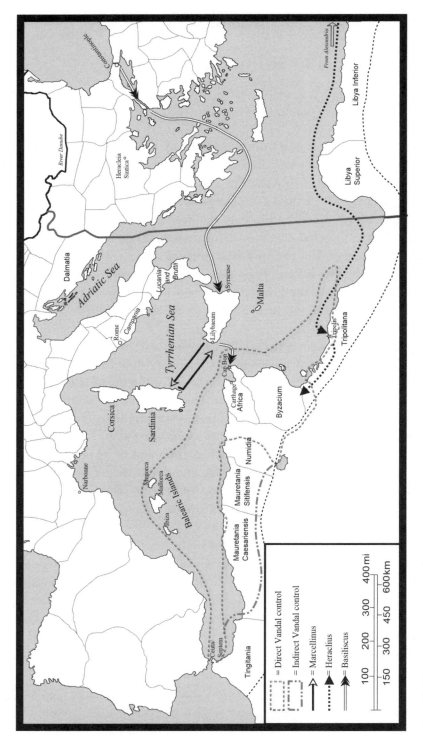

Map 13: The Roman Invasion of 468.

in failure, Anthemius needed Eastern support and there was no assurance that the East would be in a position to help in the following year, so despite the political setback, the invasion would go ahead.[3]

The Roman Campaign

It is likely that Anthemius, Marcellinus and Ricimer had little input when planning the campaign against the Vandals, as it was masterminded by Leo in Constantinople, who supplied most of the men, ships and resources for the operation.[4] Yet although Leo was the instigator behind the campaign in Africa, it is probable that Anthemius had a greater degree of control of operations in Italy and the surrounding islands due to his proximity to the area and access to up-to-date intelligence.

Despite some caveats concerning the attribution of troops to specific areas of the campaign, a study of all of the sources outlines Leo's grand strategy. The invasion was to be based upon three different strikes. A small army would attack Vandal possessions in the western Mediterranean, to pin down and defeat Vandal forces outside Africa and act as a diversion. A second, larger force would invade via Egypt, travelling along the north coast of Africa to capture Tripolitana before moving on to Carthage itself. The third and main attack would be a direct assault on the Vandals' African territories, carried out by a large fleet and supporting army.

Command of the first task force was given to Marcellinus, now *magister militum* in Italy, who was sent with a mixed army of Eastern and Western troops to seize Sardinia, the Vandals' major conquest outside Africa.[5] Despite the fact that Marcellinus' army is sometimes seen as being composed only of Eastern troops, the fact that Hydatius describes it as an 'Allied' force implies that the army was a mix of Eastern and Western troops, doubtless being based around a core formed of Marcellinus' rebuilt *comitatus* (retinue of warriors).[6] Doubtless the intention was to reconquer Sardinia, distracting the Vandal garrison and either destroying it or at least ensuring that it could not be removed to protect Africa until after it had been heavily defeated and demoralized. Yet the decision may have had more than just strategic concerns: it may have been swayed by the urgings of Pope Hilarius, himself a native of Sardinia.[7]

The second attack was to be led by a man named Heraclius.[8] Previously probably a *comes rei militaris*, Heraclius had gained experience fighting the Iberians (in the Caucasus) and the Persians, so he was an experienced soldier.[9] As with the campaign in Sardinia, the plan appears to have been to attack peripheral areas where the Vandals had key garrisons, pinning them before defeating them. In this way, any men who escaped would be demoralized and return to Carthage telling of the superiority of the Roman troops. Further, it would limit the options available to Gaiseric, as he would not be able to mount a diversionary attack on Egypt from Tripolitana. However, the main purpose of the secondary two attacks was doubtless to divide Vandal forces, allowing the main thrust to easily conquer Africa itself.

To command the main invasion fleet, Leo chose a man named Basiliscus, the brother of Leo's wife Verina.[10] Apart from his Imperial connections, Basiliscus appears to have been *magister militum per Thracias* between 464 and 467–468, having 'many successes against the [Ostro-]Goths and Huns'. He was awarded the consulship in 465, possibly as a reward for his service in Thrace.[11] For the upcoming campaign, he was recalled from Thrace and almost certainly given the post of *magister militum praesentalis*.[12] There may have been more qualified generals available for the command, but there was little chance of any other commander being chosen. This was a large expeditionary force that could easily be used in an attempt to overthrow Leo. As a family member, Basiliscus was probably the safest choice. Priscus describes him as 'a successful soldier but slow-witted and easily taken in by deceivers', but this description is given only after the campaign – at the time of his appointment, there would have been few who doubted his ability.[13]

For the campaign, Leo emptied the Eastern treasury, possibly spending four years' worth of revenue:[14]

> And the Emperor Leo ... was gathering an army against them [the Vandals]; and they say that this army amounted to about one hundred thousand men. And he collected a fleet of ships from the whole of the eastern Mediterranean ... [and] ... they say, thirteen hundred *centenaria* were expended by him.
>
> Procopius, 3.6.1–2

> Whereupon the emperor, aroused to anger, collected from all the eastern sea 1,100 ships, filled them with soldiers and arms and sent them against Gaiseric. They say that he spent 1,300 *centenaria* of gold on this expedition.
>
> Priscus, fragment 42 (trans. Gordon, pp.120–21)

According to the original text, the number given by Priscus was 100,000 ships. This has been emended by Gordon, the translator, to 1,100, as the original number is obviously far too large and the latter corresponds to the 1,113 vessels claimed by Cedrenus.[15]

> Joannes Lydas [Lydus – John the Lydian] ... says that 65,000 pounds of gold and 700,000 pounds of silver were collected. [and] ... those that administered these things reveal, 47,000 pounds of gold were raised

through the prefects, 17,000 pounds of gold through the count of the treasury, and 700,0000 pounds of silver, apart from adequate amounts raised from the public funds and from the Emperor Anthemius.

Candidus, fragment 2 (trans. Gordon, p.121)

The large number of ships in these sources is almost certainly an exaggeration, as can be adduced from Theodorus Lector, who gives a figure of 7,000 sailors (*nauta*) to man the fleet.[16] Although this lower figure may be more realistic, there remains a major difficulty. If the Latin word *nauta* used by Theodorus is translated as the usual 'sailor', and the number of ships is accepted as 1,100, this gives an average of only six sailors per vessel. Obviously, the figures cannot be made to agree with each other.

Assuming that Theodorus is correct, and that it may take as few as twenty sailors to man a vessel, this would give a fleet of 350 ships. This may be more likely than the 1,100 vessels assumed by Cedrenus, yet some modern historians prefer the latter, in which case the 7,000 men attested by Theodorus needs correction. This has led to at least one modern historian translating *nauta* as 'marines', bypassing the need to lower the number of ships.[17] Obviously, certainty is impossible but it is feasible that the lower number of ships is more reasonable: amongst other things, this would account for the speed and decisiveness of later events.

Yet it should be remembered that the fleet was not purpose-built for the upcoming campaign. Although it is probable that some warships were specially made and intended for the defence of the fleet, the majority of the ships were transport vessels for carrying troops, animals and supplies. To increase the number of vessels available, Leo relied on the requisitioning of merchant ships, ironically including large numbers of ships originating from Carthage, so in effect, part of the Vandals' merchant fleet was to be used to invade Vandal Africa.[18]

The logistical problems of supplying the extremely large force over long distances also needs to be assessed before the number of troops given by Procopius can be accepted at face value. Unfortunately, there is no other information concerning the origins or numbers of men used, so the details are unknown. As a result, any attempt to estimate them is merely guesswork. All that can be said with certainty is that this was the largest military force assembled to campaign in the West in the last days of the Western Empire.

A further complication in assessing troop strength is that Leo had planned a three-pronged attack. None of the sources state whether the troops used by Marcellinus and Heraclius were included in the total. If the numbers are given for the entire war, as seems likely, then the main invasion fleet led by Basiliscus would have been smaller than usually accepted. Marcellinus would need a fleet to carry his troops and ensure that they could land safely in Sardinia, and it is clear from later evidence that Heraclius was accompanied by a fleet as he traversed the North African coast.[19]

Despite modern estimates, no numbers are given for the men assigned to either Marcellinus or Heraclius, and all of the numbers suggested are based upon figures proposed for other armies, which are themselves often conjecture, usually based upon the *Notitia Dignitatum*, a document seventy years out of date. As a result, and despite temptation, no numbers will be given for any of the armies used by Marcellinus, Heraclius and Basiliscus. Yet one thing is certain: the diversion of ships and men away from the main projected invasion of Africa meant that Basiliscus probably would not have the overwhelming superiority in men and ships usually accorded in the sources and accepted by some more modern accounts.

Vandal numbers are completely unknown. Earlier, it was noted that upon their entry to Africa the Vandals probably had a population of less than 80,000 people.[20] This would mean an army of between 20,000 and 30,000 men. Yet in one way the army had changed from earlier. Access to the horse herds of Africa meant that the army was composed 'largely (it would seem) of mounted warriors'.[21] This is a possibility, but after only eighteen years in Africa there is no guarantee that the horse herds were sufficient to mount the entire army, although later this became a possibility. What is most likely is that a high proportion of the army at this time was mounted, but the majority may have remained infantry armed with spear, sword and shield, alongside a few skirmishers armed with javelins and bows. On this subject, certainty is once again impossible. What is certain is that despite the recall of forces, large numbers of men were tied down as garrisons for the main coastal cities in Africa, as well as in Sardinia and, possibly, Corsica.

Sardinia and Tripolitana

As the campaign season opened, Marcellinus landed in Sardinia and 'drove out the Vandals and gained possession of it with no great difficulty'.[22] This adds credence to the hypothesis that Gaiseric had recalled his forces to Africa, leaving behind only a small garrison to ensure that the island did not spontaneously rebel.

At the other end of the Mediterranean, Heraclius travelled first to Egypt to collect 'an army drawn from Egypt, the Thebaid and the desert'.[23] As noted above, it is impossible to calculate the number of troops Heraclius had under his command, as although the *Notitia Dignitatum* lists over seventy units in the regions of Egypt and the Thebaid, the document is out-of-date, and even if accurate, a garrison would need to be left to ensure the safety of Egypt. The only clue given by Theophanes is that he includes 'the desert' in his description, which implies that Heraclius may have had a contingent of Saracen (Arab) allies.

Travelling west, they caught the Vandals by surprise.[24] However, unlike Marcellinus, Heraclius had to defeat the enemy in a pitched battle:

And Heraclius was sent from Byzantium to Tripolis in Libya, and after conquering the Vandals of that district in battle, he easily captured the cities, and leaving his ships there, led his army on foot toward Carthage. Such, then, was the sequence of events which formed the prelude of the war.

Procopius, 3.6.9

The description suggests that Heraclius was first transported by a fleet from Egypt to near Tripolis, where he landed and fought the Vandals. After this, wary of the threat of the Vandal fleet nearer to Carthage, he left the ships in Tripolis. As already noted, when combined with the seaborne campaign against Sardinia, the strategy of attacking on three fronts was to seriously weaken the fleet available for Basiliscus.

Africa

As the secondary attacks completed the first part of the campaign, Basiliscus seized the initiative in the Mediterranean. Not waiting for the invasion fleet to be amassed, he used part of his newly-acquired navy to attack Vandal shipping: 'When no small force from the East had been collected, he engaged frequently in sea fights with Gaiseric and sent a large number of ships to the bottom.'[25] No source describes the strength of this fleet, nor the battles fought. It is most likely that Basiliscus was attacking the small number of Vandal ships being sent out to gather vital intelligence for Gaiseric.

Once the fleet had gathered, Basiliscus finally set sail for Africa, doubtless using the recently subdued Sicily as a staging point for the landings (Belisarius was to later use the same route in his assault on Africa). Coming from Constantinople, it would be impractical for Basiliscus to copy Majorian and attempt the subtle approach of a landing via Hispania. Instead, the decision was taken to mount a direct frontal assault on Carthage with the main force:

> But Basiliscus with his whole fleet put in at a town distant from Carthage no less than two hundred and eighty *stades* [a *stadion* was 185 metres in length: therefore the landing was around 52 kilometres or 32 miles from Carthage] ...[at a place] named Mercurium [Cap Bon].

Procopius, 3.6.10

The fact that Basiliscus landed so near to Carthage was obviously seen by Procopius as a mistake, reinforcing his depiction of Basiliscus as a poor commander. This is unfair and reflects Procopius' bias more than contemporary accepted military practice. In an era where major naval expeditions were extremely rare – the only other example is Majorian's failed venture – Basiliscus was breaking new ground.

Doubtless his idea was to land near Carthage, cow the Vandals into submission simply by a display of force, capture the city and end Vandal rule in Africa. However, by opting to land very near to Carthage, he left himself open to rapid counter-attacks, a problem exacerbated by later events. Using the benefit of hindsight, Procopius is comparing Basiliscus, whose expedition ended in failure, with his hero Belisarius, the epitome of how Procopius thought a general should act, but who had Basiliscus' campaign to use as a guide.

Gaiseric

Basiliscus finally landed in Africa with the troops.[26] Procopius notes Gaiseric's (alleged) reaction to the invasion:

> So overcome was Gaiseric with awe of Leo as an invincible emperor, when the report was brought to him that Sardinia and Tripolis had been captured, and he saw the fleet of Basiliscus to be such as the Romans were said never to have had before.
>
> Procopius, 3.6.12

Gaiseric, whose army was based upon a small Vandal population, was understandably stunned by the size of the fleet and the number of troops being landed. In 467, Anthemius had arrived in Italy with a 'well-equipped army of vast proportions'.[27] Yet this force had not drained the East's resources. Gaiseric was now faced with an invasion that had cost the East 'four years' worth of revenue'.[28] There can be little doubt that Gaiseric was not expecting such a massive reaction from the East.

Although Gaiseric knew of the upcoming attack and was ready to face the invasion, he would not have known the exact landing place targeted by Basiliscus, which explains why Basiliscus appears to have landed unopposed. Yet although the fact that Basiliscus landed so close to Carthage is sometimes seen as a mistake by historians, the proximity to Carthage was also dangerous for Gaiseric. A single defeat could easily lead to the loss of his kingdom, with the victorious Romans entering Carthage and capturing the Vandals' treasury. Without money and with a major defeat, Gaiseric may have lost support amongst his people, and the Moors of the interior may have reneged on their alliance and attacked him from the rear. Gaiseric was now in a perilous position.

Given the Romans' overwhelming force, Gaiseric had little option but to send envoys to Basiliscus:

> And Gaiseric, profiting by the negligence of Basiliscus, did as follows. Arming all his subjects in the best way he could, he filled his ships, but

not all, for some he kept in readiness empty, and they were the ships which sailed most swiftly. And sending envoys to Basiliscus, he begged him to defer the war for the space of five days, in order that in the meantime he might take counsel and do those things which were especially desired by the emperor.

Procopius, 3.6.12f.

It is often accepted, following Procopius and others, that the envoys were false and that Gaiseric was simply stalling for time. Although a possibility, the difficulty lies in the necessary assumption that Gaiseric was completely convinced of his ability to win the upcoming battle(s). Gaiseric may indeed have had such self-confidence that he assumed victory would be assured and the envoys were merely a ploy.

On the other hand, it is just as likely that the elderly Gaiseric was hoping that the East would accept peace on terms which, whilst possibly damaging to the Vandals' military reputation, would leave them in possession of Africa. It is only when he realized that Leo was determined to destroy the Vandal kingdom that he continued the fight.[29]

Procopius' claim concerning the 'perfidious' nature of Gaiseric's negotiations, stating that he only asked for an armistice in order to amass his forces, also has a precedence in Roman historiography. For example, Ammianus states that the Gothic leader Fritigern had fraudulently opened negotiations with Valens prior to the Battle of Adrianople in 378.[30] As such, the claim may be part of the Roman literary tradition rather than a statement of fact.

Given the context outlined above, the fact that Basiliscus accepted the envoys at face value is understandable. He was at the head of (probably) the largest army assembled by the Empire for many years, and, in conjunction with his overwhelming fleet, it was only natural for him to believe that Gaiseric would want to come to terms with the Empire before his kingdom was annihilated.

Yet there were two factors overlooked by Basiliscus. One was that Gaiseric had previously achieved such a level of independence and security that he was unwilling to relinquish it without a fight. If the above account is accepted, then the request for five days in which to consider the matter makes sense. Leo had used a large amount of the East's wealth to mount the expedition, so would not have accepted the continuation of the Vandal kingdom in any form – especially if the result would be the resumption of Vandal attacks in the future. Consequently, Gaiseric would doubtless have found the terms proposed by Basiliscus to be unacceptable. His most likely reaction would be to stall for time in which to generate ideas as to how the invasion could be defeated.

The second – and most important – factor is that Gaiseric was one of the greatest commanders the barbarian kingdoms would ever produce. A study of

Gaiseric's history clearly shows that he was a superb military and political leader. He had taken control of Africa in two campaigns, the first ending in 435 and the second in 442. In both of these he had succeeded in his aims.[31] Furthermore, he had easily defeated Majorian's attempt at reconquest and had then been able to politically isolate the West from the East, although he appears to have badly misjudged Leo's willingness to ignore his own attacks on the West. Possibly due to the latter, Basiliscus appears to have underestimated his opponent.

Either by himself or in discussion with his council, Gaiseric quickly realized that the expedition's main weakness was its reliance on the fleet. Without the fleet, the Roman army would struggle to feed itself in a hostile environment, especially if Gaiseric retained control of Carthage, as the Romans would be unable to mount or support a siege of the city. He needed to destroy the 'mobile supply base' that was the Roman fleet. If this hypothesis is correct, after recognizing his opponents' weak spot, Gaiseric used the negotiations as a way of buying the time necessary to come up with an appropriate strategy, as well as making his own preparations for the clash.

Procopius sees the delay as the defining moment of the campaign:

> If he [Basiliscus] had not purposely played the coward and hesitated, but had undertaken to go straight for Carthage, he would have captured it at the first onset, and he would have reduced the Vandals to subjection without their even thinking of resistance; so overcome was Gaiseric with awe of Leo as an invincible emperor, when the report was brought to him that Sardinia and Tripolis had been captured, and he saw the fleet of Basiliscus to be such as the Romans were said never to have had before. But, as it was, the general's hesitation, whether caused by cowardice or treachery, prevented this success.
>
> Procopius, 3.6.11–12

The Battle of Cap Bon

The reason for Procopius' scathing comments is easy to understand. Using the delay for negotiations to his advantage, Gaiseric decided to utilize a tactic that had been used in the fifth-century BCE, but on a previously unknown scale.[32] Whether suggested by Romano-Africans educated in the Classical tradition or by one of his council, or whether it was Gaiseric's own idea, is unknown. What is known is the following:

> [Gaiseric arranged for the truce], thinking, as actually did happen, that a favouring wind would rise for him during this time … The Vandals, as

soon as the wind had arisen for them which they had been expecting ... raised their sails and, taking in tow the boats which, as has been stated above, they had made ready with no men in them, they sailed against the enemy. And when they came near, they set fire to the boats which they were towing, when their sails were bellied by the wind, and let them go against the Roman fleet. And since there were a great number of ships there, these boats easily spread fire wherever they struck, and were themselves readily destroyed together with those with which they came in contact. And as the fire advanced in this way the Roman fleet was filled with tumult, as was natural, and with a great din that rivalled the noise caused by the wind and the roaring of the flames, as the soldiers together with the sailors shouted orders to one another and pushed off with their poles the fire-boats and their own ships as well, which were being destroyed by one another in complete disorder.

Procopius, 3.6.17–21[33]

Gaiseric was not content to simply let the fireships complete his victory. Intent on destroying as many Roman vessels as possible, even as the fires were spreading amongst the Roman fleet:

Already the Vandals too were at hand ramming and sinking the ships, and making booty of such of the soldiers as attempted to escape, and of their arms as well. But there were also some of the Romans who proved themselves brave men in this struggle, and most of all John, who was a general under Basiliscus ... For a great throng having surrounded his ship, he stood on the deck, and turning from side to side kept killing very great numbers of the enemy from there, and when he perceived that the ship was being captured, he leaped with his whole equipment of arms from the deck into the sea. And though Genzon, the son of Gaiseric, entreated him earnestly not to do this, offering pledges and holding out promises of safety, he nevertheless threw himself into the sea, uttering this one word, that John would never come under the hands of dogs.

Procopius, 3.6.22–24

The description of John's refusal to submit stands in stark contrast to Basiliscus' reaction to the defeat.

Given later events, it would appear that Gaiseric targeted the ships carrying provisions for the invasion: without food, the large Roman army would be in a perilous position. Basiliscus was now cut off from supplies, except for what he could forage in Africa. In addition, not only could the Vandals harass any Roman troops gathering food, but they had almost certainly continued the Roman practice of storing food in cities in order to deny access to potential enemies in Africa.

The only way to secure a victory would be to defeat the Vandals in battle or lay siege to Carthage. The Vandals would be unwilling to face the massive Roman army, and without a fleet, Basiliscus had no way of effectively laying siege to Carthage: the Vandal fleet could not only keep the city supplied with food, but could transport reinforcements into the city. In addition, the Vandal fleet could take troops out of the city and land them to the rear of the Roman siege lines, possibly with devastating results. There was now little chance of the campaign successfully taking Carthage. Using his remaining ships, Basiliscus embarked the army and sailed to Sicily, where he was joined by Marcellinus.[34]

Analysis

Ancient historians believed that individuals were responsible for victories and defeats. An energetic and capable commander won, whilst an ineffective and incapable commander lost. Roman sources rarely accept that the ability of enemy commanders could account for a defeat. The traditional method of assigning blame for such defeats, especially in the Late Empire, was 'treachery'. Where exactly the blame was to lie depended upon the popularity of the military commander. In 460, the cause of the failure of Majorian's campaign against the Vandals was given as 'treachery' on behalf of unknown individuals. Majorian was popular and the failure could not be ascribed to him by the sources.[35]

Basiliscus was not popular. The fact that he had lost a campaign that seemingly could not be lost meant that, although Gaiseric was castigated for his 'treachery', Basiliscus was the scapegoat for some contemporary historians. As a result, the majority of the sources blame Basiliscus. In part, this was due to the sheer scale of the defeat. It would be difficult for contemporaries to understand how such a massive invasion could be so simply defeated. In fact, the defeat was so traumatic that, over time, Basiliscus' failure was transformed.

Procopius' claimed that:

> They say, too, that he [Gaiseric] sent also a great amount of gold without the knowledge of the army of Basiliscus and thus purchased this armistice.
>
> Procopius, 3.6.12f.

Procopius goes on to add that 'Basiliscus, either as doing a favour to Aspar in accordance with what he had promised, or selling the moment of opportunity for money, or perhaps thinking it the better course', waited blindly for Gaiseric to strike, and so a large part of the fleet was either destroyed or captured.[36] By the early sixth century, the story that Basiliscus had been bribed by Gaiseric was common, since it is also included in the history of Theodorus Lector.[37] Yet there is no independent contemporary evidence for such a claim.

Later, the tale took a more sinister twist. For example, according to Malalas, Basiliscus 'accepted bribes from Gaiseric and betrayed the ships and all the men in them. Basiliscus was in the only ship to escape, all the rest being sunk.'[38] Possibly the only deviation from the theme is that of Theophanes, who claims that Leo was willing to accept the defeat as he was more concerned about the primacy of Aspar, 'needing Basiliscus and Heraclius for his plot against Aspar'.[39] In this narrative, although Basiliscus is still at fault, the defeat was in some ways a blessing for Leo, as he could from then on focus upon internal affairs and the removal of Aspar from his position of power.

Whether caused by incompetence, treachery or simply due to the underestimation of an opponent, the defeat was a catastrophe for the West. On his return to Constantinople, Basiliscus sought sanctuary in the Church of St Sophia, but fortunately for him his sister Verina interceded with her husband and his life was saved, although he was exiled to Heraclea Sintica in Thrace. [40]

Heraclius and Marcellinus

When he received news of Basiliscus' defeat, Heraclius was still on his way towards Carthage. Realizing the futility of continuing the advance, Heraclius withdrew – probably to Tripolitana – before taking ship to Constantinople, where, in 471, he aided Leo in the final overthrow of Aspar.[41]

The fate of Marcellinus was to be completely different. After the reconquest of Sardinia, it seems that he returned to Sicily, possibly in preparation to join the campaign in Africa. Shortly after Basiliscus' return, in August 468, he was 'destroyed treacherously by one of his fellow officers'.[42] One historian has noted that although the quote 'you have chopped off your left hand with your right' is usually ascribed to Valentinian III's execution of Aetius, it maybe should be ascribed to Gaiseric and the killing of Marcellinus.[43] Although the attribution is far from secure, what is certain is that internal politics had removed one of the West's most effective commanders.

Chapter 15

End Game

The victory was unexpected and decisive. At one stroke, Gaiseric had deprived the East of four years' revenue and crippled the Eastern navy. Just as important, Gaiseric had firmly established himself as the leading figure in Mediterranean affairs, although obviously this could not be acknowledged in either Rome or Constantinople.

There remains the question of who was actually responsible for the victory. After all, Gaiseric was now aged about 79 and it is possible that he was reliant upon younger military commanders for both ideas and leadership during campaigns. The only method which is useful in this context is to analyze the military efficiency of his immediate successors and judge whether they, or their commanders, were as successful as Gaiseric. The answer to this is a definite 'no', although with caveats. Huneric and the following kings were in no way as successful as Gaiseric, but – as will be seen – there was no need for them to embark on the major military campaigns common in Gaiseric's reign, so it was not necessary for them to display any military capability which they might have. Yet the few hints of political ability they show clearly demonstrates that they were not of the same calibre as Gaiseric, so alongside the clear description in the sources of Gaiseric being the driving force behind the Vandals, the implication is that the elderly Gaiseric really was the man who devised the victorious strategy.

As for personal leadership, this remains a possibility, but again it must be accepted that there are doubts about his personal involvement. His advanced age, plus his alleged infirmity – Jordanes writes that Gaiseric was 'lame in consequence of a fall from his horse' – mean that it is unlikely that he took a personal part in the naval campaign. Unlike when riding a horse, on board a ship his medical condition would have been a distinct disadvantage in hand-to-hand fighting.[1] As a consequence, it is safe to assume that he took no personal part in the actual battle, except perhaps by attempting to direct the operation from a nearby command vessel.

Yet in reality, whether he took a personal part is irrelevant. He gained the credit and his reputation soared to new heights. Following the victory, the remainder of AD 468 was doubtless spent repairing damaged ships, healing the wounded and worrying about whether the East would make a second attempt at invasion. Although defeated, the Empire's greater resources meant that the East still retained the initiative. Gaiseric would not take any action until he knew what the East's next move would be. This would be his only worry, as affairs in Europe would soon reduce the West's ability to make independent war.

Internally, the victory was of immense importance. Prior to 468, many Romano-Africans may have been hoping for a reconquest by the Empire, the removal of the Vandals and the return of 'normality'. Following Gaiseric's unequivocal victory, however, Romano-Africans realized that the chances of a Roman reconquest were extremely slim. At this point, they may have decided to throw their lot in with the Vandals, adopting barbarian dress and causing confusion in Africa over who was or was not a Vandal.[2] As the hopes of reconquest receded, even the majority of Roman-Africans who did not want to be Vandal may have become resigned to their status as subordinates in a Vandal-led kingdom.

Euric and Gaul

Despite the focus of both ancient and modern historians being on the African campaign, many other events unfolded whilst the West was concentrating its attention upon Africa. The most important of these included the increased activity of the Gothic King Euric, but mainly the breakdown of the relationship between Anthemius and Ricimer.

With the West focused upon Africa, and the Sueves in Hispania refusing to come to terms with him, Euric launched a 'massive and devastating' attack on Lusitania in 468, after which he attacked Pamplona and Zaragoza, before subjecting all of northern Hispania to his rule.[3] Before the end of the year, Euric had established a large protectorate in the north of Hispania. He then took his troops further south, where he quickly 'overthrew Tarraconensis'.[4]

Alongside their problems in Hispania, the West also lost the north of Gaul to the Frankish King Childeric, possibly in alliance with Syagrius, son of Aegidius.[5] It was obvious that at some point the Franks in the north would come into conflict with the Goths in the south. Whatever the outcome, the victor would doubtless be in opposition to the Western Empire.

Italy

If events outside Italy demanded that the West retain a united front, inside Italy the opposite happened. There is no evidence that Ricimer was involved in the death of Marcellinus at the end of the disastrous African campaign, but following Marcellinus' assassination, relations between Ricimer and Anthemius began to deteriorate. Anthemius started calling Ricimer '*Pellitus Geta*' ('A skin-clad Goth'), whereas Ricimer referred to Anthemius as '*Galata concitatus*' ('Excitable [Temperamental?] Galatian').[6] At a time when the West needed to be united, attention in the capital was focused upon internal tensions.

469

Throughout 469, attention in Italy remained divided between affairs in the capital, where Anthemius and Ricimer remained at odds, and events in Gaul, where the Franks and Goths began to expand their influence. It is certain that, once it became clear that no invasion was imminent, Gaiseric took the opportunity given by his dominance in the Mediterranean to launch raids against both East and West – although it should be noted that the evidence is weak and secure dating non-existent.[7] The net result is that it is again necessary to resort to hypothesis.

The attacks on the East may have focused upon Rhodes and possibly the Greek islands and mainland. Although certainty is impossible, it is viable to speculate that in the year following the failed invasion, Gaiseric was intent upon damaging the infrastructure that had allowed the East to send troops west. If so, then the obvious targets were staging posts along the invasion route, especially along the Greek coasts. In addition, an attack on Rhodes would again threaten the grain supply to Constantinople from Egypt, thus allowing Gaiseric to put pressure on the East to come to an agreement rather than continue the war.[8]

With the West in turmoil, Gaiseric almost certainly dispatched troops to secure control of the African coastline, and possibly also to Tripolis to test the possibility for reconquest. Whether he also launched assaults on Sardinia – taken by Marcellinus in 468 – and Sicily in the hope of securing the islands whilst the Empire was weak and demoralized is unknown, but from later events it is probable that, at some point, the Vandals regained control of Sardinia and at least the region around Lilybaeum in Sicily.

470

Despite their disagreements, both Anthemius and Ricimer acknowledged that Italy needed defending against the Vandals, as otherwise their hold on power would be weakened, possibly terminally. Leaving Anthemius in Rome, Ricimer, as sole *magister militum* in the West, assumed responsibility for the defence of Italy.[9]

His attention was soon diverted back to Rome:[10]

> Anthemius, the emperor of the West, fell into a serious sickness by sorcery and punished many men involved in this crime, especially Romanus, who held the post of Master of the Offices [*magister officiorum*] and was enrolled among the patricians, being a very close friend of Ricimer.
>
> John of Antioch, fragment 207

Frightened by the death of his close friend, Ricimer decided to remove Anthemius from the throne and established his headquarters at Milan with 6,000 men.[11] Civil war now broke out in Italy. At this crucial time, events in the East also descended into chaos. Either late in 470 or early in 471, Leo had his *magister militum* Aspar executed.[12] Faced with political and military turmoil, and needing to keep a firm control of events, Leo was in no position to send military aid to Anthemius.[13]

In Gaul, Euric took full advantage of Rome's civil war by expanding into the Auvergne, capturing much territory.[14] At the same time, he may have led a campaign further south against Roman territory to the west of the Rhone. Internal events in Italy had given the barbarian kings the chance to expand, and unfortunately for Rome, Gaiseric in Africa and Euric in Gaul were both capable military and political leaders who took full advantage of Rome's weakness.

The 'Second Invasion'

It is sometimes suggested by modern historians, using information contained in Theophanes and John of Antioch, that Leo attempted another invasion of Africa in 470.[15] The entry in Theophanes is dated by internal textual evidence to 470–471.[16] This states that in 470, Leo ordered Heraclius to lead his men towards Carthage. The entry is seen as being reinforced by John of Antioch, who claims that the West had gathered a force of 6,000 men in Sicily for war in Africa – ostensibly to support the East's Tripolis campaign – but that they had been recalled due to the outbreak of the civil war between Anthemius and Ricimer.[17]

The episode must remain a possibility: the dating of nearly all events in the fifth century is questionable. However, Theophanes then has the African troops being recalled to Constantinople after a treaty was agreed with Gaiseric. Heraclius and his men were doubtless recalled during the confusion surrounding the execution of Aspar, so at the latest this would have occurred in early 471. Taking into account the amount of time needed for the campaign, for the ensuing envoys and then for the recall of the troops, plus the fact that with the rapidly increasing tension between Leo and Aspar it is unlikely that Leo would have risked a second attack, the claim is rejected here. In addition, the description by John of Antioch is fragmentary, and it is unclear whether he has mistakenly assumed that the 6,000 men taken to Milan by Ricimer had been in Sicily rather than in southern Italy preparing to defend against Vandal attacks. Instead, the basic outline as described by Procopius is used and the attack described by Theophanes is placed in the events of 468.[18]

On the other hand, it is possible that Theophanes' account includes one factor that is correct, that Gaiseric was concerned about attacks being launched from Tripolitana and that he sent envoys to Leo requesting a truce. As a consequence, when Gaiseric proposed the treaty, Leo 'agreed … [as] at that time [Leo] needed Basiliscus,

Herakleios and Marsos for a plot against Aspar'.[19] To ensure peace, Leo appears to have ceded Tripolitana to the Vandals, secure in the knowledge that should he need to, he could easily retake the area: after all, Heraclius' invasion had been one of the few successes of the African campaign of 468. On the other hand, Gaiseric was now secure from attack from the East, and, of far more importance, Leo had accepted the status quo and the East was once more an inactive partner with the West against the Vandals.

471

In fact, due to internal political difficulties the only aid Leo could send to his Western associate was political, arranging a marriage between Anthemius' son Marcian and Leo's daughter Leontia.[20] Leo was giving his full backing to Anthemius, and Ricimer now knew that ousting Anthemius would lead to the East withdrawing all support from the West. In addition, pressure in Gaul was mounting. In 471, the Goths laid siege to Clermont, although the siege was unsuccessful.[21] Under extreme pressure, the 'nobles of Liguria' begged Ricimer to come to terms with Anthemius, and Epiphanius, Bishop of Pavia, acted as an emissary.[22] In March 471, the two parties came to an agreement and civil war was averted.[23]

Shortly after, a large part of Anthemius' Italian army was placed under the command of his son Anthemiolus and advanced to Arles to counter Euric's aggressive moves.[24] At an unknown place a battle took place and the Goths were victorious, killing all of the Roman commanders and many of their troops before laying waste to local Roman territory.[25]

Africa

Little is known of affairs in Africa at this time, but it is likely that in 471 Gaiseric received some sad news. Eudocia, daughter of Valentinian III, wife of Huneric and mother of Hilderic, had lived in Africa for sixteen years, ever since her abduction during the sack of Rome in 455.[26] As Gaiseric's main link with the Theodosian family, she had been a valuable political pawn. In 471, Eudocia was allowed to leave Carthage and travel to Jerusalem, where after only a few days' stay she died.[27] Interestingly, this is anecdotal evidence that Gaiseric and Leo had indeed signed a peace treaty in 470: it would be unlikely that Gaiseric would allow Eudocia to leave and enter the Eastern Empire if he was still at war with Leo.

There must have been compelling reasons for her being allowed to leave Africa, although none are given. This is especially the case due to her political value to both Gaiseric and the Empire. However, the fact that she died shortly after reaching Jerusalem suggests that just before being allowed to leave it was discovered that she was suffering from a terminal illness – she was only in her early 40s when

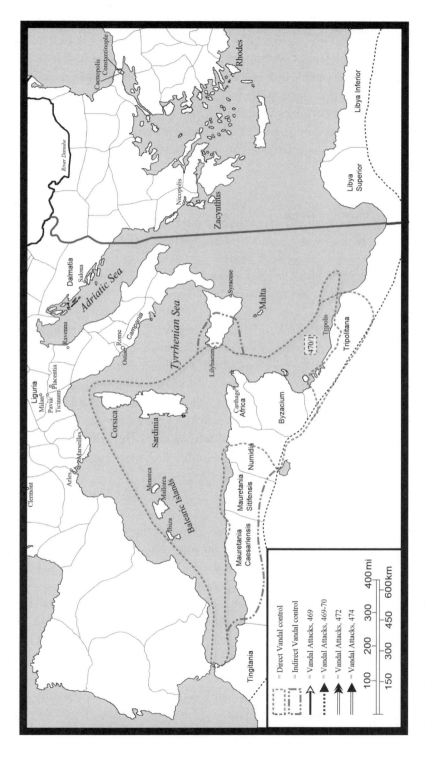

Map 14: Gaiseric's Last Campaigns.

she died. In this context, her travelling to Jerusalem is understandable. Gaiseric was allowing her to go on pilgrimage to the Holy Land before her death, imitating the example of Helena, Constantine I's mother, and he knew that her short life expectancy would ensure that she was not used politically against him by the East. Whatever the case, once she was known to be 'safe', Leo took the unexpected opportunity of declaring that the *Patrimony* previously allocated to her in the treaty of 462 had been confiscated.[28] Although the Vandals and the East may have been at peace, there was still a great deal of tension between the two.

472

The chronology of events in 472 is extremely confused. All that can be confidently assumed is that the civil war resumed in Italy. Ricimer left Milan and marched his troops south. Coming near to Rome, he set up his camp at the *pons Anicionis* and laid siege to the city.[29] Whilst the siege was ongoing, an envoy was dispatched from the East who would decisively affect events in the West.[30]

> Meanwhile ... Leo ... sent to Rome Olybrius, a Roman patrician, after he and Rusticus had served in the consulate, so that, as a representative of the Roman senate, he might quell the hostilities that existed between Anthemius and his son-in-law Ricimer. In addition, Leo enjoined upon him in his directive that, after he had reconciled Anthemius and Ricimer, he should depart from Rome and go to the king of Africa, the Vandal Gaiseric, with whom Leo did not doubt that he had great influence because the sister of Olybrius' wife Placidia had married his son, and persuade him to reconcile himself with him [Leo].
>
> Malalas, 373–74

There are several additional sources who comment upon Olybrius being sent to Italy, and Malalas later suggests that Leo was hoping that Olybrius, who as a member of the Western dynasty by marriage could claim the Western throne, and possibly even the Eastern, would be killed in the West, so removing a political embarrassment.[31] Yet taking Malalas at face value suggests that Leo was hoping for two major benefits from the embassy. One would be the cessation of the West's civil war. The second, and possibly of even greater importance, was that Gaiseric was using his relationship with Olybrius as an excuse for war. Gaiseric continued his raids in the early 470s, ostensibly demanding that Olybrius be made Western emperor. On a political level, Gaiseric would find it hard to continue his attacks on Italy, supposedly in support of Olybrius, if Olybrius himself asked that they be stopped. The move could clearly be seen as a political master-stroke by Leo.

When Olybrius arrived in Italy, events took an unexpected turn. Either in April or at the latest in early May, Ricimer proclaimed Olybrius as the new emperor.[32] His reasons for this are unknown, but they most likely focused upon two major factors. The most important was that Olybrius had a claim to the throne via his wife Placidia. Olybrius would almost certainly be accepted in the West. The other is that throughout this period, Gaiseric had been free to attack the West at will. By fulfilling Gaiseric's ambition to have his son's father-in-law on the Western throne, it is possible that Ricimer was hoping to halt Gaiseric's attacks as it would satisfy the latter's desire to be related to the Western emperor.[33]

It should be noted, however, that Ricimer had been hostile towards Gaiseric throughout his recorded life, so it is unlikely that an alliance was signed with Gaiseric. The two men appear to have harboured a 'mortal enmity'. Ricimer believed himself to have royal blood, whereas Gaiseric was illegitimate, and Gaiseric simply saw Ricimer as a major obstacle to his own ambitions in the West.[34] In addition, such an alliance may have been totally unacceptable to the citizens of Italy, who had borne the brunt of Vandal attacks over the preceding decades.[35] Nor is there any evidence that Olybrius would ever have been willing to accept Gaiseric as a political ally, despite their familial relationship – although he may have taken it for granted that after his elevation, Gaiseric would stop the attacks on the West.[36] Given the evidence, it is more likely that the situation was simply a happy coincidence rather than Ricimer attempting to secure Gaiseric's support.[37]

Death of Anthemius

Having found a suitable replacement, Ricimer's troops finally forced their way into the capital and, on 11 July 472, Anthemius was beheaded.[38] Although the troops directly under Ricimer's command were kept under control, other sections of the victorious army proceeded to sack the defenceless city.[39] Pope Gelasius (Pope 492–496) lists the sack of 472 alongside those of the Gauls in the fourth century BC and of Alaric in AD 410.[40] Interestingly, the sack by the Vandals in 455 is omitted from this list. Having lost troops and finance in the civil war and sack of Rome, the evident weakness of the West was now visible to all and helps explain many of the events that were to happen later.

Olybrius and Ricimer

After the victory, Ricimer quickly 'established Olybrius as emperor at Rome, with the approval of the Senate'.[41] Sadly for Olybrius, Leo maintained his dynastic connection to Anthemius and refused to accept Olybrius' rule as legitimate. This was not to cause Ricimer much difficulty, as only thirty-forty days after the victory he died.[42] According to the *Fasti vindobonenses priores*, he died on 18 August 472.[43]

Olybrius chose Ricimer's nephew Gundobad as the new *magister militum*.[44] Shortly after, in the seventh month of his reign, Olybrius too died, allegedly of dropsy (oedema).[45] Upon his death, the new *magister militum* Gundobad appears to have sent envoys to Constantinople asking Leo to nominate yet another candidate, so there was now an *interregnum*. In the new year, Gundobad would lose patience and nominate his own emperor.

Gaiseric

It is completely unknown what Gaiseric and the Vandals did over the summer of 472 prior to the elevation of Olybrius to the throne. The likelihood is that the Vandals continued their attacks on the West, focusing upon areas which had previously been untouched and were undefended. Gaiseric would have given his men orders to avoid battle wherever possible, as he would not have wanted to weaken his military power unnecessarily.

Once Olybrius had been declared emperor and the news had spread to Africa, it is almost certain that these attacks stopped. Towards the end of 472, Gaiseric would have been awaiting envoys from his family member in Italy, and it is possible that envoys did indeed arrive and that Gaiseric formalized his relationship to the new emperor and halted all attacks on the West without going as far as forming an alliance. What happened after Leo refused to acknowledge Olybrius is completely unknown. It is possible that Gaiseric would have resumed his attacks on the East, announcing that these would only end when Olybrius was acknowledged as emperor by Leo. Before this could happen, towards the end of 472, Olybrius died of natural causes.

473

In late February 473, Gundobad named a man named Glycerius, the *comes domesticorum* (Count of the 'Domestics'; an elite unit of the Imperial Guard), as the new emperor, and on 3 March 473, Glycerius was crowned in Ravenna 'with the support of the army'.[46] The reasons behind Glycerius being crowned at Ravenna rather than Rome are unknown. However, throughout the early part of his reign he was to remain in northern Italy, possibly so that he could be near to the frontier and so react to events in the East.[47]

Unsurprisingly, Leo refused to acknowledge Glycerius as the new Western emperor. Glycerius and Gundobad were on their own, which was bad news, as the Gothic King Euric sent one of his commanders to invade Italy.[48] At the same time,

Euric led his troops into southern Gaul. In 473, the Goths finally captured Arles and Marseilles.[49]

As if to add insult to injury, probably after the Gothic attack, the Empire was soon faced with yet another major invasion, this time from the Ostrogoths:

'The [Ostro-]Goths began to lack food and clothing … so … approached their king Thiudimer and … begged him to lead forth his army. He summoned his brother [Vidimer] and, after casting lots, bade him go into the country of Italy … saying that he himself as the mightier would go to the east.

Jordanes, Getica, 283

Vidimer died shortly after entering Italy and was succeeded by his son, also confusingly named Vidimer.[50] Rather than fighting another battle, Glycerius determined to use money and politics to remove the new threat from Italy:

The emperor Glycerius, after bestowing gifts and saying that Vidimer's relatives, the Visigoths, ruled there, transferred him from Italy to Gaul, which then was assailed on all sides by various peoples.

Jordanes, Getica, 284

Although it is possible that Glycerius was hoping that Vidimer and his people would act as a disruptive influence within the Gothic kingdom, it soon became apparent that this would not happen, and instead his actions had merely added to the strength of the Gothic realm.

Julius Nepos

As was to be expected, Glycerius' elevation to the throne did not meet with the approval of Leo in the East: 'When Leo, the emperor of the East, learned of the election of Glycerius, he appointed Nepos as general of an expedition against him.'[51]

Little is known of Julius Nepos prior to his nomination by Leo. Nepos was the son of the sister of Marcellinus, 'ruler' of Dalmatia, who had been assassinated during the campaign of 468.[52] It is possible that his father was Nepotianus, *magister militum* in Hispania under Majorian, who had earlier thrown off his allegiance to the court in Rome following Majorian's assassination by Ricimer in 461. He also appears to have married a niece *(neptis)* of the Emperor Leo – hence the epithet 'Nepos'.[53] Nepos is first mentioned in an entry in the *Codex Justinianus* dated to 473, when he is called *magister militum Dalmatiae*. However, it should be noted that he may have been given the title much earlier, possibly as early as 468 or 469, shortly after Marcellinus' death.[54]

Unfortunately for Nepos, Leo had waited too long to make his decision – possibly due to his own declining health – and by the time he had decided, winter had arrived and so Nepos was forced to wait until 474 before making his bid for the throne.

Gaiseric

What action Gaiseric was taking at this time is completely unknown. As noted earlier, it is possible that he would have attacked the East in support of Olybrius, but with Olybrius dead it is far more likely that at this point Gaiseric finally acknowledged that he needed to make a lasting peace with the Empire, as he no longer had major political cards to play. This may have been due in part to the fact that he had become 'disillusioned at the meaningless gyrations of imperial politics'.[55] The rapid turnover of emperors meant that attempting to reach a political solution to the never-ending war with the West was becoming ever more difficult. As a consequence, Gaiseric may have focused most of his attention upon the consolidation of the overseas territories wrested from the West.

In addition, Gaiseric was now in his mid-eighties, an advanced age for a man who had been continuously involved in high level politics for the previous forty to fifty years. Although unattested in the sources, the likelihood is that Gaiseric now entered into negotiations with Leo in the East in the hope of securing a permanent peace treaty. However, it should also be accepted that Gaiseric was determined to take advantage of Roman weakness, so it is possible that at this point he resumed his attacks on both East and West in order to ensure the greatest possible concessions from the Empire when the time came to sign a treaty. However, the surviving sources do not clarify his actions.

474

It is quite likely that Leo, now in his mid-seventies, refused to agree to a long-term treaty with Gaiseric, as, rather than letting go of the past and thinking solely of the future, he may have held a grudge concerning the long-lasting raids and the defeat of Basiliscus' invasion. If so, Gaiseric was soon to be rewarded. On 18 January 474, the old emperor died of dysentery.[56] His grandson Leo II, son of Leo's daughter Ariadne and Zeno the Isaurian, became emperor, aged just 7.

Three weeks later, Leo II 'nominated' his father Zeno as joint emperor.[57] Unfortunately for Glycerius in Italy, Zeno decided to follow his predecessor and confirmed the nomination of Julius Nepos.[58] In early spring 474, Nepos crossed to Italy. According to Marcellinus:[59]

The Caesar Glycerius, who held the imperial power at Rome, was deposed from power at the port of the city of Rome by Nepos, son of the sister of the former patrician Marcellinus. From Caesar he [Glycerius] was ordained a bishop, and he died ... Nepos, who had expelled Glycerius from the emperorship, was acclaimed as emperor at Rome.

Marcellinus comes, Chronicle, s.a.474–475

Nepos was crowned emperor in June 474 and installed a new regime in Italy.[60] This left no room for Gundobad, who returned to Gaul and later became King of the Burgundians. In theory, the West now returned to a more viable regime, as the addition of Illyricum to Italy and the remnants of Gaul gave the West added revenues and manpower, and being Zeno's nominee could result in Eastern military support if required.

Gaul

Unsurprisingly, Nepos' first action was to face Euric in Gaul. Following the capture of Arles and Marseilles in 473, Euric appears to have continued to campaign in Provence in 474, intent upon annexing the whole of the region. Later events suggest that Euric succeeded in extending his conquests in this area.

Further north, in the Auvergne, in 473, Euric had been repulsed from the walls of Clermont by a defence led by Sidonius Apollinaris.[61] In 474, Euric appears to have made another concerted attempt to capture the city. The attempt again failed, possibly due to the actions of Gundobad, who throughout this period appears to have retained his position as one of the joint kings of the Burgundians and who may have been campaigning in the same region with Burgundian forces.[62]

The Vandals

With the death of Leo, the peace treaty of 470 between the Vandals and the East had lapsed, and Zeno was anxious to remove the threat posed by the Vandals to Eastern security.[63] Accordingly, he appointed a senator named Severus to act as an ambassador and, after making him a patrician, sent him to Africa.[64]

Unfortunately for the East, Gaiseric learned of the proposed embassy and before it could arrive he launched a swift attack, capturing the town of Nicopolis on the coast of Epirus and possibly raiding the regions of Caenopolis and Zacynthus.[65] Gaiseric was intent upon making the most of his raiding prowess before political events forced them to halt, but mainly wanted to put pressure on the East in order to obtain the best possible terms to any peace treaty signed.

It may be in this context that an entry in Jordanes' account needs to be viewed. Jordanes claims that Gaiseric sent an embassy to Theoderic Strabo, one of the two major non-Roman players in Eastern politics after the death of Aspar.[66] Strabo had previously fought against the East after the death of Aspar, and it may be possible that Gaiseric was attempting to form an alliance with Strabo that would increase the pressure on Zeno to come to terms. Later evidence implies that the embassy was a success, as when Zeno agreed terms with Strabo (after the death of Gaiseric), one of the conditions was that Strabo would not be asked to fight against the Vandals.[67]

It is also possible that Gaiseric finally arranged a treaty with the Goths in Gaul at the same time. Obviously, Jordanes' main focus in the *Getica* (History of the Goths) was the kingdom in Gaul, and although it is nowhere explicitly stated, it is possible that he is alluding to a treaty with Euric. It should be noted that Jordanes' antipathy towards the Vandals precludes a definitive statement.[68]

After prolonged discussions in either late 474 or early 475, Severus finally managed to negotiate an 'eternal alliance' with Gaiseric on behalf of Zeno:[69]

> But at that time Gizeric [sic] was plundering the whole Roman domain just as much as before, if not more, circumventing his enemy by craft and driving them out of their possessions by force, as has been previously said, and he continued to do so until the emperor Zeno came to an agreement with him and an endless peace was established between them, by which it was provided that the Vandals should never in all time perform any hostile act against the Romans nor suffer such a thing at their hands. And this peace was preserved by Zeno himself and also by his successor in the empire, Anastasius. And it remained in force until the time of the emperor Justin.
>
> Procopius, 3.7.26

It would appear that Gaiseric had resumed his attacks in order to extract the maximum possible concessions from the Empire. His strategy was to reap massive rewards. Although in many ways a standard treaty, there was a major difference in the new agreement. It was the first 'non-personal' treaty signed by Gaiseric.[70] In effect, the treaty was not simply between Zeno and Gaiseric, but was extended to the period after the deaths of both of the signatories and thus can be seen as a treaty between states rather than individuals.[71] This may be the first sign that Gaiseric was beginning to think of the long-term future, rather than simply extorting the best deal for himself.

As part of the deal, Carthaginian priests and deacons who had been exiled were finally allowed to return to their posts in Africa, although the bishopric of Carthage remained vacant.[72] The relaxing of Gaiseric's prescription of Catholic clergymen is usually taken as a major concession by the Arian Gaiseric, but there is a caveat:

Emperor Zeno was an acknowledged Monophysite whereas the majority of Romano-Africans were Nicene Catholics. As a result, the Catholics in Africa were unlikely to respond positively to any Monophysite clergymen who were appointed by Zeno.[73]

In return, it is likely that Gaiseric agreed to restore any remaining hostages and other captives to the East. It is possible, though not mentioned, that Gaudentius, the son of Aetius, may have returned to the Empire after his long stay in Africa.[74] Obviously, the treaty would have also recognized the authority of the Vandals in the territories they had conquered – possibly including the permanent return of Tripolitana to Vandal rule after its annexation by the East in the campaign of 468.

For Zeno, the treaty allowed the East to remove garrisons from coastal towns for other purposes. It may also have had a clause that Gaiseric recognize Nepos as the legitimate emperor and refrain from attacking the West.[75] Whether included or not, the clause was to be made immaterial by events in the near future.

Gaul

Whilst these political manoeuvres had been ongoing in the East, in the West, Nepos' forces in Gaul had been defeated:

> Euric ... seized the city of Arverna [Clermont], where the Roman general Ecdicius was at that time in command. He was a senator of most renowned family and the son of Avitus ... Ecdicius strove for a long time with the Visigoths, but had not the power to prevail. So he left the country and (what was more important) the city of Arverna to the enemy and betook himself to safer regions.
>
> Jordanes, *Getica*, 240–41 (translation Merow)

It was probably at around this time that Nepos acknowledged that the West did not have the ability to survive without Eastern support. The Goths now controlled most of Provence and the Vandals most of the Mediterranean islands. Italy was under severe threat and did not have the men or finances to oppose the enemy.

474–475

Nepos doubtless sent envoys to the East, but Zeno was unable to help. In November 474, the young Leo II had died of an illness and time was needed for Zeno to mourn and bury his son. Of far more import for the East, in January 475, a coup led by Basliscus, the commander of the failed African expedition, forced Zeno to abandon Constantinople and flee to Isauria. The hostility against Zeno may have been caused to some degree by the treaty with the Vandals.

Realizing that he was on his own, at least in the short term, Nepos sent Epiphanius, the man who had brokered the truce between Anthemius and Ricimer, to Euric in late 474 to discuss peace and appointed a Pannonian named Orestes as *magister militum*. Orestes, who had had a long service in the Imperial army and had been a follower of Aetius in his earlier years, now found himself *magister militum praesentalis* and *patricius* in command of the army in Italy at a time of political and military crisis.[76] Nepos, an Eastern nominee, may have hoped that Orestes would act as an intermediary between himself and the Senate, helping to secure senatorial support for his new regime.[77]

475

In Gaul, Epiphanius was successful in his mission, the 'bonds of peace having been undertaken', but at this stage it was only a truce.[78] In the new year, a further embassy of four bishops was sent to discuss the terms of a full treaty. This was the only good news for Nepos. Early in the year, news arrived from the East of Zeno's overthrow and he now had no option but to come to terms with the Goths and Vandals, whatever the cost.

The Gothic Peace Treaty

Early in the new year, although the exact date is unknown, Nepos agreed terms with Euric and the long war against the Goths was over. The terms were harsh and would severely damage Nepos' standing as emperor. Under pressure from the Senate in Italy, and especially those members who had land holdings in southern Gaul, he was forced to request the return of Provence, captured by Euric in the previous year's fighting. Euric agreed, but demanded a major concession: that the region of the Auvergne be handed to him. Despite the knowledge that such a treaty would severely undermine his position, Nepos had little choice but to accept.

It is sometimes claimed that Euric also demanded that the Goths now be accepted as totally independent from the Empire. This appears to be a misinterpretation of the terms of the treaty. Ennodius claims that as part of the treaty, Nepos 'at least is willing to be called friend [*amicus*], who ought to be called master [*dominus*]'.[79] As a consequence, it is clear that the 'sovereignty of the Visigothic kingdom was not recognised de jure in 475':[80] only de facto – which explains why Euric was now able to begin the process of consolidating his regime.

There remained the ever-present raids from Africa to be dealt with. As with Euric, Nepos was forced to the conclusion that victory was impossible and that the only means of saving the West was to reach an accommodation with Gaiseric similar to that made with Euric. Prolonged negotiations may have begun, but it is unlikely that these came to a satisfactory conclusion before internal events intervened.[81]

The tacit acceptance of the Goths as a separate political entity was against Roman tradition and would have caused great anger in the West, especially in Gaul. Although not specifically mentioned in the sources, it is clear that Euric was now the king of an autonomous kingdom, as he immediately began a 'persecution' of Christian bishops and for a short period many churches became vacant as bishops were executed, evicted or died and were not replaced.[82]

The Senate refused to accept Nepos' decision. It would appear that in their dismay, the Senate were supported by Orestes, the new *magister militum praesentalis*. What follows is extremely confused, largely because the sources fail to include the details needed for a full description of events, but it would appear that, following the 'disgraceful' treaty and with the overthrow of Zeno in the East, which removed Nepos' Eastern support, Orestes agreed to lead the army in revolt against the new emperor:

> While Nepos was in the city, the Patrician Orestes was sent against him [Nepos] with the main force of the army. But because Nepos dared not undertake the business of resisting in such desperate conditions, he fled.
> *Auctuarii Hauniensis ordo prior,* s.a.475[83]

Realizing that he had no hope of resisting Orestes and the Italian army, Nepos fled to Salona in Dalmatia on 28 August 475 and Orestes entered Ravenna.[84] Nepos' brief direct reign of just fourteen months was over. However, once back in the safety of Dalmatia, he was to continue to claim the throne for the rest of his life.

Orestes

Orestes is most likely the same man that had served as '*notarius*' ('secretary', 'senior civil servant') to Attila and had been Attila's envoy to Constantinople in 449 and 452.[85] After the death of Attila, Orestes had returned to the Empire. It has been claimed that his 'career' amongst the barbarians may have resulted in his being distrusted in Rome, but, given that for the previous twenty years the *magistri* had been full-blooded barbarians, the fact that Orestes was actually a Roman almost certainly outweighed any possible distrust.[86]

Sadly, the lack of information regarding Orestes' origin is mirrored by the lack of source material concerning his time in control of the Western Empire. On 28 August 475, he found himself the new controller of the West. Not one of his actions from this point until the end of October is known, but it is probable that he sent messengers to Basiliscus in the East – Zeno was still in exile – informing him of events and asking for feedback, possibly in the form of recognition for a Western nominee for emperor.

The two-month *interregnum* whilst the messengers returned from Constantinople would have been used to arrange for envoys to go to the Goths and Vandals, for appointments by the new regime, and for the consolidation of Orestes' power. Throughout this time, he appears to have remained in Ravenna, as this was the best place to send and receive messengers from the East.

The New Emperor

What response Orestes received from Basiliscus is unknown, but, with or without the blessing of the *in situ* Eastern emperor, on 31 October 475, Orestes crowned his teenage son Romulus as the new Roman emperor.[87] Needless to say, Orestes retained real power in his own hands.[88] On his accession, Romulus took the traditional title of *Augustus*,[89] but his contemporaries soon began to refer to him as *Augustulus* ('little Augustus') and it is by a combination of these names that he is known to posterity – Romulus Augustulus.[90]

476

The removal of Nepos acted as a spur to Euric in Gaul. In 476, Euric attacked again. As in 473 and 475, his target was Provence, and once again he took the cities of Arles and Marseille.[91] The Empire was now obviously almost completely defenceless.

Gaiseric

The fact that Euric again resumed the offensive immediately put pressure on Orestes. Knowing that he would get no help from the East, and aware that he needed to gather all of his available troops into one major force in order to repel the Goths, Orestes was forced to send envoys to Gaiseric in the hope of arranging a peace treaty.[92] If accomplished, the troops garrisoning strategic towns on the coast of Italy could travel north to reinforce Orestes' army. It was also possible that Gaiseric would use the overthrow of Nepos as an excuse to attack Italy on behalf of Zeno, which would be damaging and embarrassing to both East and West and cause a further rift in relations between the two.[93]

Surprisingly, given the weakness of the West, at some point in 476 – allowing time for events to unfold, probably between mid-summer and autumn – a treaty was concluded between Orestes and Gaiseric.[94] The details are nowhere outlined, but the majority opinion – based on both contemporary and later events – is that Orestes recognized Gaiseric as being in full control of Africa, Sardinia, Corsica and the Balearic Islands. In Sardinia at least, the island was later run by a governor appointed by the king: in the 530s, the governor was Godas, who rebelled against the Vandals and invited the Eastern Empire to intervene.[95] It is likely that the institution was begun by Gaiseric, who needed the territories he ruled to be run smoothly by *in situ* governors rather than from distant Carthage. In addition, the garrison of the island contained at least one group of Moors, as these are referred to in the *Code of Justinian*, but whether the same applied to other territories and islands is not certain.[96]

In addition, Gaiseric had managed to regain a foothold in Sicily during the previous decade. Later events are confused and some historians have suggested that he was attempting to lay claim to the whole of the island. However, it should be acknowledged that the slim archaeological evidence from sites excavated in Sicily and dated to the period of the mid-fifth century suggests that the island was the scene of raids, not occupation.[97] What appears clear, however, is that the Vandals had managed to capture Lilybaeum and its environs.[98] It is also likely that they had made major inroads into the rest of Sicily, but there is no indication of where their control ended. It is possible that these conquests were also recognized by Orestes.

There only remains the question of why Gaiseric was willing to come to terms with Orestes when he was in such a position of strength. As usual, certainty is impossible, but it is likely that at this time he was attempting to reach terms with all major military powers in the Mediterranean. Born *c.* 390, Gaiseric was now in his mid-late 80s, and later events suggest he may have been suffering from poor health.[99] Knowing that his end was near, he may have been determined to bequeath to his son Huneric a rich and viable realm free from war with any external powers. Given the pacific nature of Huneric's later rule, it is likely that Gaiseric knew that his son did not have his own political or military ability, and decided that over-riding peace was the only way the Vandal state could survive.

The treaty would soon need to be renewed. At some point in 476, the barbarian troops in the Roman Army asked for lands in Italy on which they could settle.[100] Orestes refused the request outright.[101] The most obvious reason for the refusal is that Orestes was attempting to establish a new dynasty. Giving land to the barbarian troops would doubtless have alienated a large section of the Senate and aristocracy, which would not have been an acceptable legacy for his son after his own death. The refusal to deal with the barbarians had immediate repercussions.

Balked in their attempt at acceptance, the mercenaries turned to one of their number in the hope of getting satisfaction. The man's name was Odovacer.[102] Of uncertain origin, by 472, Odovacer was part of the Roman military establishment, helping Ricimer in his war against Anthemius – possibly after becoming one of the emperor's bodyguards.[103] He was placed in command of the 'Torcilingi, Sciri, and Heruls', who appear to have been the barbarian warriors who formed the backbone of the *praesental* army in Italy.[104] Approached by the troops, Odovacer promised to grant their request for land if they made him king. Accordingly, on 23 August 476, Odovacer was proclaimed *rex*, after which he mustered his forces before advancing against Orestes.

Unaware of Odovacer's decision, Orestes agreed to meet him at Ticinum.[105] Travelling north with his *bucellarii* ('mercenary bodyguard'), Orestes entered the city and his bodyguard, taken by surprise, clashed with the main army. In the resulting conflict, the city was severely damaged.[106]

Losing the battle, Orestes withdrew and rallied his few remaining loyal troops. On 28 August 476, Odovacer led his troops against the *patricius* and, near to Placentia (Piacenza), defeated him in battle.[107] The majority of Orestes' forces were killed, captured or driven off, while Orestes himself was captured and executed.[108] After regrouping his forces, Odovacer marched towards Ravenna.

The East

The confusion prevalent in the West was being mirrored in the East. Also in August 476, Zeno led an army to Constantinople and laid siege to the city. Shortly afterwards, he entered the city and regained the throne, after which Basiliscus and his family were exiled to a fortress in Cappadocia, where they were incarcerated in a cistern and allowed to die from exposure.

Having defeated and killed Orestes, Odovacer marched his troops across the north of Italy towards Ravenna. Quickly entering the city, Odovacer authorised the deposition of the young Emperor Romulus. Fortunately for Romulus, according to the majority of the sources, the young man was granted his life due to his 'youth and beauty', allowed to retire to live with relatives on an estate called Lucullanum in Campania and granted a pension of 6,000 *solidi* per annum.[109] With the removal of Romulus, Julius Nepos was once more the undisputed claimant to the Western throne. Yet his previous rule in Italy had alienated the Senate, and it was clear to everybody that he would not be able to recover his throne without Eastern help.

Odovacer and Zeno

Envoys were sent to the East, and after long deliberation Zeno sent a reply to Odovacer. Although theoretically supporting Nepos, Zeno effectively announced that Nepos would not be receiving any military support from the East. Zeno needed his forces to ensure acceptance of his return to power.[110] In return, and aware of Zeno's weak position, Odovacer adopted a policy of appeasement. He sent the Imperial regalia to Constantinople, yet minted coins in the name of Nepos and outwardly accepted Nepos as the emperor – secure in the knowledge that after his previous escape from Rome, Nepos would never dare to actually set foot in Italy without an Eastern army to protect him.[111]

In the meantime, Odovacer allowed his men to settle – presumably in the Po valley in northern Italy – in the traditional Roman manner as *foederati* ('allies'), although whether they took land from Roman citizens or occupied vacant land owned by the Roman state is unclear. However, the fact that there is no mention of any problems arising from the settlement implies that the latter may have been the method in at least the majority of cases.[112]

Euric

In Gaul, Euric had again extended his dominion. Without Eastern support, Odovacer had no option but to enter negotiations with the Goths from a position of extreme weakness. Unable to counter Euric, Odovacer was forced to cede Provence.[113] In no position to intervene, Zeno had little option but to give Imperial sanction to the treaty.

Gaiseric

Alongside the treaty with Euric, Odovacer most desired a treaty with the man who had been the bane of the West since 435: Gaiseric. It would appear that immediately upon his accession, Odovacer sent envoys to Gaiseric in the hope of securing peace for his own regime, as the treaty Gaiseric had made with Orestes was now invalid. Since Odovacer became the ruler of Italy in August 476 and the sailing season ended in November, it is clear that he was an astute politician with a grip on the realities of his situation. Before the end of the year, a deal was struck between Odovacer and Gaiseric.[114]

As usual, the details of the treaty are unknown, the only specific information being the testimony of Victor of Vita:

> Sicily, he [Gaiseric] later conceded to Odovacer, the King of Italy, by tributary right. At fixed times Odovacer paid tribute to the Vandals as to his lords; nevertheless, they kept back some part of the island for themselves.
>
> Victor Vitensis, *Historia Persecutionis Africanae*, 1.14

As usual, the ambiguity of the phrasing has confused historians. It is sometimes claimed that prior to the treaty, the Vandals had claimed the whole of the island for themselves, and that in order to regain the lost territory Odovacer was forced to pay tribute. On the other hand, it must be remembered that Victor was writing in the context of Vandal Africa and so it is likely that he is repeating the propaganda as presented by Gaiseric and Huneric. It is far more likely that Gaiseric had earlier captured the city of Lilybaeum. It is possible that the Vandals had then managed to impose a form of protectorate over at least some of the island, demanding tribute in return for not attacking. After the treaty, it was the city of Lilybaeum that was retained by the Vandals, but that part of Sicily dominated by the Vandals was returned to Imperial control.[115] In effect, Odovacer had agreed to pay tribute in order to secure peace with Gaiseric.

In this context, the treaty would fit into the context of fifth-century Romano-barbarian politics, specifically with relation to the political arch-master Gaiseric. He was demanding and receiving recognition of his conquests, and extracting tribute in order to halt his attacks on the West – specifically Italy. This would allow Gaiseric to consolidate his Empire in preparation for his expected death: after all, he was now in his mid-late 80s.[116]

His timing was perfect, as on 24 January 477, Gaiseric, the Vandal who had for so long tormented the Empire, died.

Conclusion

Aftermath

It is easy to overestimate the effect of the passing of Gaiseric. Although he had spent the vast majority of his rule at war with either or both halves of the Roman Empire, just prior to his death he had arranged peace treaties with them both. Even so, it could be expected that with his death the West would attempt to take advantage of the fact that his son Huneric had nowhere near the military and political brilliance of his father. In reality, the West was too far gone in decline to make any such move.

Gaul was now in the hands of barbarians, either the Franks in the north or the Goths in the south. The rump 'Kingdom of Soissons' that had been founded by Aegidius and inherited by his son Syagrius had collapsed and was now part of the Frankish realm. The only region even remotely under Roman control was Brittany, ruled by men who had fled before the Germanic advance in Britain, but even here there was little or no loyalty for the regime in Italy.

In Hispania, the Sueves had expanded their control in the north-west, but the main beneficiary of the Imperial collapse had been the Goths, who under the pretence of working under Roman authority had established a protectorate over the central and eastern parts of the peninsula. Only in the south were there cities who owed nominal allegiance to Rome, but there is no evidence to suggest whether these regions remained loyal to the Empire or were now simply under local authority but nominally accepting their 'citizenship' in order to maintain local loyalties rather than disintegrate into inter-regional conflict.

In Africa, the Vandals had spread their dominion over large parts of the diocese, although many of the internal regions did not come under direct Vandal control, but instead accepted the titular rule of the Vandals whilst maintaining their own regional practices, founded upon Roman models. Only the regions under the rule of the Moorish princes were free from either Vandal or Roman rule, maintaining their independence from either whilst accepting the symbols of their rule from the Vandals. Whilst Gaiseric remained alive, none of these Moorish rulers would attempt to assert their specific independence, but after his death, they slowly began to exert independent authority and later engaged in outright warfare with their Vandal 'rulers'.

In those parts under direct Vandal control, once it was clear that the Empire was unable to reconquer the lost provinces, it would appear that many

Romano-Africans became reconciled to the new regime, helped by the fact that the Vandals quickly assimilated Roman tastes and fashions. In this new milieu, 'after the death of Gaiseric several Roman poets arose, such as Luxorius, Felix and Florentinus, and especially Blassus'.[1] But there was to be no historian who was the equivalent to Jordanes for the Goths or Cassiodorus for the Ostrogoths.

Huneric

As planned long in advance by Gaiseric, Huneric ascended the throne. It quickly became clear that Huneric did not have the political or military ability of his father, and, possibly thanks to his marriage to Eudocia (daughter of Emperor Valentinian III), his reign began with a policy of appeasement with Rome. Soon after his accession, he entered negotiations with the East, and the legacy of Olybrius' ties to the Vandals surfaced when, in AD 478:

> Ambassadors came to Byzantium from Carthage, under the leadership of Alexander, the guardian of Olybrius' wife [Placidia]. He formerly had been sent there by Zeno with the agreement of Placidia herself. The ambassadors said that Huneric had honestly set himself up as a friend of the emperor, and so loved all things Roman that he renounced everything that he had formerly claimed from the public revenues and also the other moneys that Leo had earlier seized from his wife [Eudocia] … He gave thanks that the emperor had honoured the wife of Olybrius.
> Malchus, fragment 13 (trans. Gordon, p.125)

In effect, Huneric withdrew the last Vandal claims over the patrimony of Valentinian III (see Chapter 8) and, despite his Arianism, accepted the appointment of a Catholic archbishop in Carthage.[2] In addition, he allowed some of the property appropriated by Gaiseric to be returned to the original owners.[3] Although the religious policies would soon be reversed, he would become increasingly involved with internal politics rather than attempting to emulate his father in the persecution of the Empire.

In theory Huneric could have taken advantage of Roman weakness, yet he appears not to have done so. It has been claimed that with Gaiseric's death, the treaty between the Vandals and Rome was declared void and the Vandals under Huneric resumed their raids.[4] Yet Victor's statement that 'at fixed times Odovacer paid tribute to the Vandals' implies that Huneric recognized the continuation of the terms agreed with his father and Odovacer also obligingly remained true to the terms.[5]

This was largely due to the fact that Odovacer seems to have recognized that in effect, the West was dead. Rather than putting another puppet emperor on the throne, he sent messengers to Constantinople announcing that he was willing to rule Italy and Sicily under the command of the Eastern emperor, although when Julius Nepos died in 480, he quickly took control of Dalmatia, whether the East was happy about this or not. Before the end of the century, Zeno, emperor of the East, would send Theoderic I (the Great), King of the Ostrogoths, to Italy. Odovacer was defeated and killed.

Sadly for the Vandals, their rulers became weaker over time and Gaiseric's hoped-for system of succession died out. Huneric (ruled 477–484) was succeeded by his nephew Gunthamund (484–496), although Huneric did in fact have a son. Gunthamund was succeeded by his brother Thrasamund (496–523), and he by Hilderic (523–530). Hilderic was Huneric's eldest son, but he was only the third in line after the death of his father.

Relations between the Vandals and the East varied throughout this period, being extremely strained during the persecution of the Catholics in the reigns of Huneric and Gunthamund, but easing when Thrasamund halted all persecutions. Upon his accession, Hilderic was in theory the ideal ruler of the Vandals. He was Gaiseric's grandson, the son of Huneric and Eudocia, daughter of Valentinian III. As such, he had Imperial blood in his veins and could be expected to act as a bridge between the Vandals and the Empire. In addition, Hilderic favoured the Catholicism of his mother, and allowed a Catholic bishop to be consecrated in Carthage. Despite his positive relations with the Empire, the resultant conversion of many Arian Vandals to Catholicism alarmed some of the Vandal nobility, and he was eventually over-thrown by his cousin Gelimer (530–533).

As Hilderic had proved to be a friend to the East, his overthrow was not accepted in Constantinople. Although the Emperor Justinian I sent embassies attempting to restore Hilderic, Gelimer refused to accede to the demand. Justinian's reaction was to send an army under his military commander Belisarius to conquer Africa. Learning of the invasion, Gelimer killed Hilderic, but was himself defeated. In 534, the Vandal kingdom was overthrown and came to a swift and inglorious end.

Gaiseric: The Vandal Who Destroyed Rome

> What ruined everything … was the action of the Vandals in crossing from Spain to Africa … the Vandal chief Gaiseric … was not only a man of genius but one of the most fateful figures in history, for it was he who really brought about the downfall of the Western Empire.
>
> *Saunders, J.J., The Debate on the Fall of Rome', p.15.*

It is possible that the title 'Gaiseric: The Vandal Who Destroyed Rome' could be seen as a little overdramatic. Yet it is hoped that throughout this book it has become apparent that, if any individual has the right to lay claim to being the cause of

Rome's fall, it is Gaiseric. It is simply a matter of chance that the only barbarian leader commonly remembered is Attila, the man who had been 'diverted' from sacking Rome by the alleged action of Leo I, now known as 'Pope Saint Leo I, the Great'. Without this connection, and Attila's paganism and later epithet 'Scourge of God', Attila too may have dwindled in the eyes of history.

The reasons for Gaiseric being promoted above Attila and his peers relies solely on the devastating actions undertaken by Gaiseric and their effect on the West. If, upon his accession, Gaiseric had remained in Hispania with his people and founded a long-lasting kingdom, his actions would make him one of the many causes for the collapse of Imperial authority. Indeed, based upon later events it is possible to say that in all likelihood the Vandals would simply have controlled a kingdom based around their settlement in Baetica, with the Sueves controlling Gallaecia and the Goths the remainder of Hispania. In these circumstances, it is unlikely that the Vandals would have lasted much beyond the end of the fifth century, since the Goths would almost certainly have either wiped them out or absorbed them.

It is not even the decision to cross to Africa that elevates Gaiseric from 'nuisance' to 'destroyer'. If he had simply accepted the status quo following the treaty of 435, the Vandals would again have been one of any number of Germanic tribes that crossed the frontiers and wrested a kingdom from the declining West, albeit one that had travelled further than any other in the hope of securing long-lasting peace. The impact of the Vandals upon Roman history, however, would have been comparatively small.

Ironically, it may not even be the seizure of Africa Proconsularis that was to prove the importance of Gaiseric in the Empire's collapse, although obviously it was a major factor in its demise. It is only when the seizure is coupled with the ensuing policies pursued by Gaiseric that his importance and responsibility become clear. True, the possession of Africa robbed the West of financial viability and ensured that the city of Rome was indebted to a hostile power for its sustenance, but the fact that Majorian was able to convince the Senate of the need for overbearing taxes and that the campaign he used the revenue to finance came close to success suggests that there was still life in the Empire, even without both the revenues of Africa and Eastern assistance.

It is down to both the possession of Africa and the almost-continuous yearly attacks on the West that Gaiseric's importance is to be found. In 454, Aetius was still in control and, although Africa was now lost, he was managing to maintain a slim grip on Gaul and had even been able to rally a coalition to defeat Attila's Huns and confederates at the Battle of the Catalaunian Plains. After his death and the assassination of Valentinian III, however, Gaiseric embarked upon seemingly constant warfare in order to disrupt the West and maintain his standing as an invincible warrior.

It is these attacks which are his historical legacy. The constant need of the West to defend against the Vandals and the political disruption caused by the Imperial failure to deal with these – and other – barbarian attacks resulted in a rapid turnover of emperors who were sacrificed on the altar of their failure to defeat either the Goths in Gaul or the Vandals in Africa. And it was the wide-ranging threat of the latter which was most devastating to Imperial prestige between the sack of Rome in 455 and the coming to power of Euric in Gaul in 466. After this, it was a combination of Euric and Gaiseric that ensured that the West was unable to revive its fortunes.

Yet there is one further way in which Gaiseric's ability outmatched those of any of his Imperial opponents. His skill in ensuring that for the majority of the last two decades of his life, the East and the West were divided and failed to unite against him must rank Gaiseric as one of the most politically astute operators throughout the years of decline of the West. It is too easy to see the West's elevation of emperors unacceptable to the East as the main reason for the East-West division. Yet the fact that even when the two halves were estranged, the East could theoretically come to the aid of the West – as in the preparations being made by Marcian in 456 – means that Gaiseric's political manoeuvres to keep the two halves divided can be interpreted as a major diplomatic success.

Although his political and military ability are at the heart of Gaiseric's success, there is one other feature of his reign that is usually overlooked but which played a major part in his achievements: his longevity. Born around 390, prior to Gaiseric's rise to the kingship in 428, Honorius, Constantine III, Constantius III and John all ruled in the West. After Gaiseric became king, Valentinian III, Petronius Maximus, Avitus, Majorian, Libius Severus, Anthemius, Olybrius, Glycerius, Julius Nepos and Romulus Augustulus – in all, ten emperors – assumed power in the West. The fact that the Vandals were ruled by a single king when at the same time the West was riven by internal disorder and the rule of so many emperors, each with their own agenda, gives another reason why the West was unable to counter Gaiseric.

It is thanks to all of the above factors that Gaiseric deserves his place in the history of the fall of the Western Roman Empire and may be given the epithet 'Destroyer of Rome' – if indeed it can be given to any individual. Yet in reality, the process of decay and division had already begun in the West, and all that Gaiseric's actions did was to speed up the collapse of the Empire by financially bankrupting it and then making certain that political divisions within it meant that only twice in the twenty-one years after the death of Valentinian III was any serious attempt made at the reconquest of Africa.

As a military commander, Gaiseric was never defeated in person, and only on a small number of raids were his forces beaten back by the West. This, coupled with his mastery of the axiom of 'divide and conquer', means that Gaiseric more than any other individual, either within or outside the Empire, was responsible for the collapse of the West, and that he does indeed deserve the title 'The Vandal Who Destroyed Rome'.

The Division of Land, AD 411 and 439

Possibly two of the greatest causes of confusion in the historical record of the Vandals surrounds the manner of their settlements in Spain and Africa. According to the accepted translation of Hydatius 41, in AD 411, the Asding Vandals, Siling Vandals, Alans and Sueves 'apportioned to themselves by lot [*sorte*] areas of the provinces for settlement'.[1] Later, after the annexation of Africa in 439, the Vandals settled on the newly conquered lands. Yet the nature of their settlement remains obscure, with historians debating over the exact meaning of the phrase '*sortes Vandalorum*'.[2]

The Settlement of 412

Despite the fact that the two words under scrutiny are almost exactly the same – '*sorte*' and '*sortes*' – in the past, classicists and historians have assigned meaning to the two words based upon different interpretations. '*Sorte*' is seen as being derived from '*sors*', a Latin word usually translated as '(division) by lot', whereas '*sortes Vandalorum*' is usually translated as 'land allotted to the Vandals', in which case '*sortes*' may be seen as deriving from a different word, '*sortitio*', translated as 'allotment'.[3] In a similar vein, the phrase '*sors hostilitatis*' – 'enemy' or 'alien' – allotment is used by a hagiographer talking of the settlement of the coalition in Hispania.[4]

It is clear from the attitude of more modern historians that, although the translation as 'by lot' is seen as being accurate, problems remain as to how this can be interpreted. How would the weaker of the tribes enforce a decision 'by lot' against the stronger tribes? As if to reinforce the dilemma, one modern historian has declared that although the lands were divided by lot, the Silings and Alans 'had the whip hand, receiving the most important provinces within the partitioned area', whereas others simply note that the largest tribes received the best land.[5] Obviously, this doesn't make sense. If it was by lot, the Silings and Alans couldn't 'have the whip hand': if the Silings and Alans received the best land, then it was either by good fortune or because there was no lottery.

Given the confusion noted above over the translation of '*sorte*' and '*sortes*', it may help to look at the whole of Hydatius' entry for this event:

Subversis memorata plagarum grassatione Hispaniae provinciis, barbari ad pacem ineundam, Domino miserante conversi, sorte ad inhabitandum sibi provinciarum dividunt regiones. Gallaeciam Wandali occupant et Suevi, sitam in extremitate Oceani maris occidua. Alani Lusitaniam et Carthaginiensem provincias, et Wandali cognomine Silingi Baeticam sortiuntur. Hispani per civitates et castella residui a plagis, barbarorum per provincias dominantium se subjiciunt servituti.

Hydatius 41, s.a. 411

The important section of the entry is '*sorte ad inhabitandum sibi provinciarum dividunt regiones*', as noted above usually translated as 'apportioned to themselves by lot areas of the provinces for settlement'.[6] The question then is whether the word '*sorte*' has been translated correctly. Obviously, this remains a possibility and it is feasible that the tribes did indeed divide territory by lot.

However, when looked at in context, this remains doubtful. The difficulty lies with believing that after the events of 406–411, the four tribes were so confident, both in themselves and in the lack of Roman Imperial opposition in Hispania, that they would assume that they could divide Hispania with impunity. As a further point, accepting the translation implies that there was now no opposition from the citizens of Hispania and that the barbarians were free to follow whatever whim they desired. This is difficult to believe. Furthermore, it is also difficult to accept that the stronger tribes would agree to the possibility of receiving the poorest lands simply by chance.

Therefore, the phrase needs to be reassessed to determine the accuracy of the translation. At this point, doubts begin to appear. The most obvious of these is that Hydatius' work was translated in the eighteenth and nineteenth centuries by the individuals best qualified to do so: trained Classicists. Yet there are problems here.

The first of these is that at the time of translation, Classical works were accepted at face value, with none of the textual and contextual analysis that is now applied. Therefore, so long as the translation could be understood and 'made sense', it was thought to be obviously correct. Yet, as already noted, in context, the concept that the four tribes would throw caution to the wind and divide Hispania in any way they chose is extremely doubtful.

The second problem is that in some ways it is possible that the training of the Classicists would work against them. Classicists were – and in some cases still are – trained in Latin using the Classics of the late Republic and early Empire: Caesar, Cicero, Tacitus et al. The assumption of the Classicists was that writers of the third, fourth and fifth centuries followed the example set by their predecessors, both in tone and content.

To some degree the assumption is true. Late antiquity authors whose work attempted to continue that of previous writers do appear to have endeavoured to emulate the earlier works. Yet despite their attempts, some of the words and attitudes of the later period enter their compositions. Nowhere is this more prevalent than in the 'Chronicles' written by Christian writers working far from Italy, the centre of Classical traditions – for example Hydatius in Hispania. There can be little doubt that some of the colloquialisms and changes in use of words are apparent in the later works. In this context, the gap between the Classical writers of the first centuries BC and AD should be remembered: in 300 years many words can change their meaning or emphasis, and it is possible that the Classicists of the eighteenth and nineteenth century did not place enough emphasis on this possibility. This explains the derogatory remarks in pre-twentieth-century authors concerning the poor quality of late Latin literature.

Accepting that the translation may be at fault, it makes sense to look again at Hydatius' wording. At this point, it should be acknowledged that the earlier translations may still be correct, and that reassessment may be unnecessary. On the other hand, a more acceptable rendition may be possible. Interestingly, Latin dictionaries give several variations of the accepted translation based upon less-common usage.

As noted earlier, the word '*sorte*' as used by Hydatius has been seen as deriving from '*sors*', 'a casting or drawing of lots, decision by lot'.[7] Yet a look at the lexicon entry for '*sors*' reveals that other translations are possible. Interestingly, one of the lexicons gives alternatives including 'fate, destiny, chance, fortune, condition, share, part'. This includes the variation used in '*sortes Vandalorum*' – 'shares of the Vandals'.

Having acknowledged that both '*sorte*' and '*sortes*' may have the same root, then it is possible to suggest that they have the same meaning. If true, then the following (rough) translation becomes a possibility:

'A share of lands in the provinces, to divide and settle for [between?] themselves.'

If this – or a similar – translation is accepted, then there was no lottery and the whole event becomes much more easily explained.

One of the reasons for the entry of the four tribes into Spain was the need for Gerontius to increase his manpower prior to his attempt to become emperor. Given that there is no specific mention of these tribes between 409 and 411, it would appear that much of the time was taken by their settling of their peoples in Hispania, with the fighting men serving under Gerontius when he invaded Gaul.

After defeating Gerontius and Constantine III in Gaul, the *magister militum* Constantius may have been surprised at the emergence of yet more usurpers. Facing enemies in Gaul, and recognizing that the barbarian tribes could easily become a source of manpower for his enemies, Constantius, possibly after consultation with Emperor Honorius, decided that a deal needed to be agreed in Hispania. Accordingly, there was an official bequest by the court in Italy granting the Vandals et al a peace treaty plus acceptance of their possession of land in Hispania, though whether this was land given to them earlier by Gerontius or was newly allotted by Honorius/Constantius II is unknown. Whatever the case, this would ensure their service to the emperor in Italy. The hypothesis would also help to clarify why the most powerful tribes received the best land.

This suggestion has been made before, but has been discounted.[8] However, the rebuttal is based upon the translations of both Orosius and Hydatius, where '*sortes*' is given as 'lot'. Furthermore, the rebuttal continues with the observation that neither Hydatius nor Orosius mention any accord between the coalition and either Gerontius or the Imperial government. The claim is accurate.

On the other hand, Hydatius makes no mention of Gerontius' rebellion, whilst Orosius plays down Gerontius' actions and makes no link to Hispania, instead implying that those responsible were Gauls.[9] Consequently, it is possible to suggest that in both cases the writers of these works are operating to their own agendas, which as far as possible meant maintaining Hispania as an innocent party wronged by savage barbarians sent by God. This would not be possible if the barbarians had accepted a treaty with either Gerontius or Constantius/Honorius, as this would damage their claim.

The Settlement of 442: *Sortes Vandalorum*

The difference between '*sorte*' in Hydatius and '*sortes Vandalorum*' is that in the former the translation offers difficulties, whilst in the latter it is the interpretation of the meaning that causes problems. '*Sortes Vandalorum*', meaning 'shares of the Vandals', is the name given to the Vandals' method of dividing the spoils from their conquest of Africa Proconsularis in 439. Possibly originally termed '*funicula hereditatis*' ('heritable plots') by Victor of Vita, '*sortes Vandalorum*' is now the term most in use by Ancient historians.[10]

End Notes

Introduction

1. Merrills and Miles, 2014, 57.
2. Wolf, 1990, 4–5: see also esp. Prop. 1327.
3. Wolf, 1990, 21.
4. It must be calculated backwards from his attested age in records of his death in 477: see below.

Chapter 1: Vandal History and Gaiseric's Early Life

1. It must be calculated backwards from his attested age in records of his death in 477: see below.
2. Illegitimate, Hyd. 89; Proc. *BV*. 1.3.23; Theoph. AM 5931: mother a slave, Sid. Ap. *Carm*. 2.358–60, 5.97.
3. Wolfram, 1997, 163.
4. For example, Bigelow (1918, 1) suggests Potsdam. However, this is linked directly to his thesis linking Gaiseric and Kaiser Wilhelm II, so can be discounted.
5. Goffart, 1980, 14f.
6. Martens, 1989, 59.
7. For an analysis of the reasons surrounding this change of emphasis, see e.g. Martens, 1989, esp. 60.
8. Merrills and Miles, 2014, 29, comparing their importance to that of the Marcomanni or Quadi.
9. Cf Birley, 1966, 232.
10. Cf Clover, PhD Diss. Chicago, 3.
11. On *foedus/foederati*, see Chapter 6.
12. See Merrills and Miles, 2014, 31 and accompanying bibliography for further details.
13. Cf Clover, PhD Diss. Chicago, 3.
14. Zos. 1.48 (Skythians); Dex. *fr*.7; Pet. Patr. *fr*.12M; Hist. Aug. *Aurel*. 18.2 and 33.1.
15. Zos. 1.68; Hist. Aug. *Probus*, 18.1.
16. *PLRE I*, 'Visimar', 969: cf Pet. Patr. *fr*.7: doubts, Merrills & Miles, 2014, 28, 31.
17. Cf Merrills and Miles, 2014, 32.
18. Merrills and Miles, 2014, 33.
19. Merrills and Miles, 2014, 177.

20. Constantius preferred a version which was a compromise between the Arian and Nicene beliefs. Valens was an Arian.
21. Soz. 6.37: Soc. 4.33: Oros. 7.33.19: cf Philost. 2.5. The dating and extent of the Vandal conversion is extremely problematic: see Merrills and Miles, 2014, 178–79 and associated notes.
22. AM 31.2.12f.
23. AM 31.3.3f.
24. 'Now the Vandals and the Alani, as we have said before, had been dwelling in both Pannonias by permission of the Roman Emperors. Yet fearing they would not be safe even here if the Goths should return, they crossed over into Gaul': Jordanes, *Getica*, 31. 161.
25. '*Chuni in Halanos, Halani in Gothos, Gothi in Taifalos et Sarmatas insurrecerunt*'.
26. Lands becoming insufficient, Proc. 3.22–3.
27. Godigisel, Greg. Tur. *HF* 2.9.
28. For a detailed account of Stilicho's life, see Hughes, 2012.
29. AM 31.3.3.
30. 'King of the Goths', for example: Aug., *Civ. Dei*, 5.23; Oros. 7.37.4; Prosp. Tiro. s.a. 400; *Chron. Gall.* 452 no. 50.
31. For example, Williams and Friell, 1995, 155: Wolfram, 1997, 97.
32. Burns, 1994, 198, believes that Radagaisus entered Italy via the Brenner Pass: Kulikowski, 2007, 171, also implies the same when he notes that Radagaisus invaded via Raetia. For the alternative, see e.g. Wolfram, 1997, 97, who believes that Radagaisus entered the Empire via Pannonia.
33. Merrills and Miles, 2014, 34: Wolfram, 1990, 169, giving no contemporary source.
34. *Chron. Gall.* 452. no. 52.
35. Zos. 5.26.4.
36. Williams and Friell, 1995, 155.
37. Claud. *Get.* 419–23: cf Oros. 7.38.3–7; Marc. *com.* a.408. Jordanes, *Getica*, 115, hence blames Stilicho for 'betraying' Gaul; cf Merrills and Miles, 2014, 34.
38. *Cod. Th.* 7.13.16: 7.13.17. Interestingly, Freeman (1886, 54) saw this as a measure to counter the invasion of the Vandals, Alans and Sueves, which didn't happen until later.
39. Oros. 7.37.16: Zos. 5.26.4.
40. Zos. 6.3. Zosimus may have confused events, with the last remnants of Radagaisus' forces that escaped by crossing the Alps turning into Vandals, Sueves and Alans. However, this may actually represent a historical tradition, as discussed during the events of 406 below.
41. O'Flynn, 1983, 41.
42. Goffart, 1980, 17: Maenchen-Helfen, 1973, 72: contra, Courtois, 1955, 40–41, cited in Maenchen-Helfen, 72.
43. Proc. BV 1.22.3–13.

44. Drinkwater, 1998, 273: Gibbon, 1861, II, 249.
45. Possibly adding to the anger of the Gauls and British at the lack of protection from the emperor.

Chapter 2: The Invasion of Gaul

1. Greg. Tur. *HF* 2.9.
2. The claim that a large number of the Siling Vandals remained in situ and gave their name to Silesia is doubtful on etymological grounds: but see Wolfram, 1997, 161.
3. Jer. *Ep*. 123.16.
4. Jer. *Ep*. 123.16.
5. Orosius (7.37) claimed that 'Radagaisus, by far the most savage of all our enemies, past or present, inundated all Italy by a sudden invasion with an army reported to number more than two hundred thousand Goths.' Consequently, it was calculated that the whole people had a population of 400,000, but Gibbon et al estimated that in reality Radagaisus commanded around 60,000 warriors and 130,000 people (Gibbon, 1861, II, 246: cf Freeman, 1904, 19f). Therefore, the invading tribes, being one-third of this force, mustered at least 20,000 warriors and 40,000 dependants.
6. Liebeschuetz, 1990, 13–14.
7. Matthews, 1998, 275f: Kulikowski, 2007, 171f: Williams and Friell, 1994, 84.
8. Drinkwater, 1998, 273f.
9. Muhlberger, 2002, 29–30.
10. Greg. Tur. 2.9.
11. *Chron. Gall. 452* no. 127 (s.a. 442).
12. Oros. 7.40.3.
13. Bury, 1923, 186.
14. Kulikowski, 2000, 326 and n.8: Greg. Tur. 2.9: Oros. 7.40.3.
15. Succession, Greg. Tur. *HE* 2.9: duration of Gunderic's rule, PLRE II 522.
16. Kulikowski prefers to date the invasion to 405 rather than 406, based upon a preference for Zosimus' dating at 6.3.1 rather than Prosper's chronicle at 1230 (2000, 326f). Unfortunately, he weakens his own argument by later labelling Book 6 of Zosimus, upon which he bases the theory, as 'the deeply unreliable Book VI of Zosimus' (2000, 332, n.40, 41).
17. Gibbon, 1861, II, 250: 'The victorious confederates pursued their march, and on the last day of the year, in a season when the waters of the Rhine were most probably frozen, they entered, without opposition, the defenceless provinces of Gaul'; based on, for example, Herodian, 6.7.6–7.
18. Elton, 2004, 40, suggests that the invasion was not coordinated. The events surrounding the nature of the invasion, with the tribes arriving separately, to some degree supports this theory. However, the retreat of that section of the Alans under

Respendial and their participation in the battle with the Franks (see above) implies that a low level of coordination existed.

19. Paul. Bez. *Epig.* 19–31: Mathizen and Shanzer, 2011, 217.

20. This is the standard chronology accepted by many historians, e.g. Bury, 1923, 186–87.

21. For further details and bibliography on the proposed itineraries, see Kulikowski, 2000, 331.

22. Allegedly according to Prosper, but sadly Freeman, 1886, 54 and n.2.

23. Olymp. fr. 12, perhaps giving the date as late 406, cf PLRE II. Marcus 2, 719: Zos. 6.2.1, giving the date as 407; cf Soz. 9.11.2. The claim by Zosimus (6.3.1) that the revolt was due to the barbarian invasion of Gaul and a perceived threat to Britain is extremely unlikely.

24. Dating, Burns, 1994, 210: reason for overthrow, Kulikowski, 2000, 332: cf Oros. 7.40.4.

25. For example, Burns, 1994, suggests 5,500 men, and Drinkwater, 1998, 275, 6,000 men.

26. Drinkwater, 1998, 275, n.42, referencing Hoffmann, 1973, 15–17.

27. Zos. 6.4.

28. This is usually accepted as either a doublet for the Battle of Pollentia (e.g. Ridley, 'Zosimus', 1982, 227, n. 19) or as possibly referring to an attack on the remnant of the third Gothic group that had invaded Italy under Radagaisus (e.g. Ridley, ibid; Freeman, 1886, 57).

29. Freeman, 1886, 54, n.2.

30. Salvian, *de Gub. Dei.* 6.82–4. However, it should be noted that this episode is not clearly dated by Salvian and so could have occurred at any time during the period 406–409.

31. Drinkwater, 1998, 277.

32. Paul. *Euch.* 239.

33. Oros. 7.40.4 and 7. 28.

34. Kulikowski, 2000, 332.

35. See Chapter 4: See also Kulikowski, 2000, 332, footnote 39.

36. Drinkwater, 1998, 276.

37. Elton, 2004, 193: cf Zos. 5.27.2.

38. Halsall, 2007, 213.

39. Oros. 7.40.5.

40. Oros. 7.40.5.

41. Soz. 9.11.4: Oros. 7.40.6.

42. Including his two main representatives, Limenius, the *praefectus praetoriano per Gallia*, and Chariobaudes, the *magister militum per Gallias*: Zos, 5.32.4.

43. He was probably *comes rei militaris*. Drinkwater avoids having to make a decision on Sarus' appointment, leaving it open as to whether Sarus was *comes rei militaris* or

magister militum vacans. For a discussion and further bibliography, see Drinkwater, 1998, 279. n.63.
44. Zos. 6.2.4.
45. Kulikowski, 2000, 334. Zos. 6.2.4; 'Nebiogastes, the surviving magister, made overtures of peace to Sarus and was amicably received by him.'
46. Zos. 6.5.
47. Ausonius, *Ordo Nobilium,* VIII: Zos. 5.27.3, 31.4; 6.1.2, 2.2, 4.1–4: Soz. 9.4.6.
48. This section is reliant on the observations of Drinkwater, 1998, especially 279–80.
49. Zos. 6.4.1–2.
50. Olymp. 13.1.11: Oros. 7.40.7: Both Sozomen (9.11.4) and Zosimus (6.4.1) imply that Constans was promoted specifically for the campaign in Spain. cf Kulikowski, 2005, 335.
51. A man named Apollinaris as *praefectus praetoriano* and Decimius Rusticus as *magister officiorum.* On the appointments, see Greg. Tur. 2.9.
52. It is difficult to reconcile the different accounts given in the sources. This reconstruction is based on Kulikowski, 2000, 335 and n.67, using Soz. 9.11.4–12.1; Oros. 7.40.6–8; and Zos. 6.4.
53. Cf Soz. 9.12.1.
54. Zos. 6.5.1; 6.13.1: Greg. Tur. HF. II.9.
55. This section is heavily reliant on the account given by Zosimus: 5.29.
56. Interpreted as a betrayal, Zos. 5.29: motive for conspiracy, Zos. 5.32–34; cf 5.30.1.
57. Zos. 5.34.4–5. For the date of the execution, *Consularia Italica* p.300, as referenced by Burns, 1994, 216.
58. Zos. 5.37.6.
59. Zos. 5.35.6; 40,000 men, 5.42.3.
60. Zos. 5.37.1: cf Heather, 1994, 215.
61. Zos. 5.38–44.

Chapter 3: Hispania

1. Zos. 6.5.2. This is the only mention of Justus: PLRE 2, *Iustus 1,* 651.
2. Olymp. fr. 17.2.1–5.
3. Cf Zos. 6.5.2. Some historians suggest that the barbarians seized land at this stage and only later was a treaty agreed recognizing their conquests.
4. Bury, 1889, 142: Olymp. fr. 17.1.1–3, where Gerontius makes peace with the barbarians.
5. Jer. *Ep.* 123.1: Dating, Cavallera, 1922, 2:52, referenced in Kulikowski, 2000, 331, n.38.
6. Jerome, *Ep.* 123.16: Kulikowski, 2000, 331.
7. Zos. 6.5.2.
8. Jer. *Ep.* 123.16: cf Olymp. fr. 13.2.28f: Blockley claims that their 'regrouping' noted by Olympiodorus was following a defeat by Constantine, but Olympiodorus'

problems with chronology mean that it is just as likely that they were separated when employed by Constantine and 'regrouped' following their alliance with Gerontius: cf Zos. 5.3.2. On the reliability of the various sources: Kulikowski, 2000, 331, footnote 39; 'Apart from Jerome's letter, Sozomen and three more or less contemporary poems (the *Ad uxorem*, the *Carmen de diuinaprovidentia* and the *Epigramma* of Paulinus …) attest to a barbarian presence in southern Gaul. Soz. 9.12.3 explicitly ties that presence to the rebellion of Gerontius against Constantine III in 409. Oros. 7.40.3 condenses more than three years of events into a single sentence which tells us nothing about chronology.

9. Merrills and Miles, 2014, 41–42 for details and references: it should be noted that not all of the references are appropriate for the claim.
10. Zos. 6.5.2.
11. Cf Gordon, 1960, 35.
12. Defection of Britain and north Gaul due to Constantine's neglect, Zos. 5.6: Timing, Zos. 6.6.
13. Zos. 6.6.1.
14. The 'Rescript of Honorius': 'Honorius, however, wrote letters to the cities in Britain urging them to defend themselves,' Zos. 6.10.
15. Zos. 5.43: Olymp. fr. 12: cf http://www.luc.edu/roman-emperors/westemp5.htm (Western Roman Emperors of the First Quarter of the Fifth Century, Hugh Elton, 1999).
16. Olymp. fr. 13.1.1: Allobichus was later overthrown due to his 'favour' for Constantine, so it is likely that he was putting pressure on Honorius to come to terms with the usurper. Cf http://www.luc.edu/roman-emperors/westemp5.htm (Western Roman Emperors of the First Quarter of the Fifth Century, Hugh Elton, 1999).
17. Zos. 6.12.3.
18. Other examples include the traitors responsible for the defeat of the Roman invasion of Africa in 468 (see below).
19. Cf Mathisen & Shanzer, 2011, 211, n.41.
20. Date, Hyd. 34 [42], s.a. 409: see also, Olymp. fr.16.
21· Barbarians kept near the passes, Burns, 1995, 248.
22. Hyd. 38 [46]; 39 [47], s.a. 410: The four perils of 'sword, famine, pestilence and wild beasts raging everywhere throughout the world' was seen by Hydatius as 'the annunciations foretold by the Lord through his prophets', 40 [48], s.a. 410.
23. Olymp. fr. 30: 'When the Vandals overran Hispania, the Romans fled into walled cities, and so great was the famine that they were reduced to cannibalism.'
24. Zos. 5.38.1, 39.1ff esp. 42.3, 45.4–6, 48.3, 48.4, 5.49.1, 50.2–3, 6.1.1 and 6.6.1: Soz. 9.6.2–7, 9.7.1–4, 9.8.1: Phil. 12.3: Olymp. fr. 3.
25. Hyd. 40 [48], s.a. 410: cf Merrills and Miles, 2014, 42.
26. Oros. *Hist.* 7.41.7

27. Salvian, *De gub. Dei*, 4.21.

28. RIC 10.150–151, 351 with references: see Kulikoswki, 2000, 124.

29. Cf Hyd. 40 [48], s.a. 410.

30. Zos. 6.6–12: Soz. 9.7.

31. Zos. 6.13: Soz. 9.9: cf Hyd. 35 [43], 36 [44], 37 [45] and 39 [47].

32. Hyd. 35 [43], s.a. 410; Theoph. AM 5903; Prosp. A. 410: Placidia, Hyd. 36 [44], s.a. 410.

33. Hyd. 37 [45], s.a. 410.

34. Olymp.fr. 14.

35. Olymp. fr. 14: Soz. 9.12.5.

36. Olymp. fr. 16: cf Soz. 9.12: Zos. 6.13.1.

37. Greg. Tur. 2.9: Soz. 9.13.2: Olymp. *fr.* 17.2.6–7: cf PLRE 2, *Edobichus*, 386.

38. Olymp. fr. 17.1.5–8; fr. 17.2.1–5.

39. Prosp. a. 411: Olymp. fr. 17.1.6–10.

40. Olymp. 7.42.1–3: Oros. 7.42.2.

41. Flight, Olymp. fr. 17.2.10f: Death, Soz. 9.13.

42. Olymp. fr.17.2. See Blockley, 1983, 215 n.42.

43. Olymp. fr. 13.2.30f: cf Soz. 9.12.

44. Defeat and death of Edobichus, Olymp. fr. 17.2.32f. More detailed account of battle, Soz. 9.14.

45. Olymp. fr. 17.2.56f.

46. http://www.luc.edu/roman-emperors/westemp5.htm. Western Roman Emperors of the First Quarter of the Fifth Century, Hugh Elton, 1999. cf Soz. 9.15: Hyd. 42 [50], s.a. 411: Prosp. a. 411: Theoph. AM 5903.

47. Olymp. fr. 18: Hyd. 43 [51], s.a. 411: Renatus Profuturus Frigeridus = Greg. Tur. 1.9.

48. *Chron. Gall.* 452, a. 411.

49. Prosp. a. 412: Olymp. fr. 35.

50. This is deduced from later events: see Hyd. 46 [64], s.a. 412: Prosp. a. 413: Theoph. AM 5904.

51. Hyd. 46 [64], s.a. 413.

52. Hyd. 43 [51], s.a. 411. Unlikely that the revolt dates to 411, as there is the possibility that in 412 Heraclian was nominated for the consulship of 413. Grain, Orosius, 7.42.12: Used revolts in Gaul as exemplars, Philost. 12.4.

53. CTh 9.40.21 (a. 413 Aug 3, MSS 412 July 25): see PLRE 2, *Heraclianus 3*, 539–40.

54. Olymp. fr. 17.2.12f: Prosp. a. 412.

55. Oros. 7.41.7.

56. Clover, 1966, 3: cf Oros. 7.43 and Hyd. 41 [49], s.a. 411: contra, Merrills and Miles, 2014, 44.

57. Olymp. fr. 13.2.30f: cf Soz. 9.12.

58. Thompson, 1982, 154.

59. Hyd. 1.13.
60. Hyd. 41 [49], s.a. 411.
61. Hyd. 41 [49], s.a. 411.

Chapter 4: The Empire Strikes Back

1. Hyd. 46 [64], s.a. 412: Prosp. a. 413: Theoph. AM 5904: Autumn, Hyd. 46 [64], s.a. 412: Prosp. a. 413: Theoph. AM 5904. Bury, 1889, 146.
2. Bury, 1889, 146.
3. Return of Placidia demanded, Olymp. *fr.* 22.
4. Prosp. a. 413.
5. Oros. 7. 42.12–13: Marc. *com. s.a.* 413: Jord. *Rom.* 325.
6. PLRE 2, *Marinus 1*, 724.
7. Hyd. 48 [56], a. 413: Oros. 7.42.14: Olymp. fr. 23: Marc. com. s.a. 413: Cons. Const. s.a. 413: Prosp. s.a. 413: *Chron. Gall.* 452 no. 75: Jord. Rom. 325: Theoph. AM 5904.
8. Oros. 7.42: Olymp. fr. 22.
9. Olymp. fr. 22: cf Bury, 1889, 147.
10. Olymp. fr. 17.
11. Toulouse (Tolosa), Rutil. Namat. 1.496; Bordeaux (Burdigala), Paulinus Pell. *Eucharisticos*, 312: Narbonne (Narbona) Olymp. *fr.* 17.
12. Olymp. fr. 24: Philost. 124: Oros. 7.40.2. 43.2: Prosp. s.a. 416: Hyd [57], s.a. 414: *Chron. Gall.* 452 no. 77: *Chron. Gall.* 511 no. 559: Marc. com. s.a. 410: Jord. *Get.* 159; *Rom.* 323.
13. Cf Bury, 1923, 197–98.
14. Olymp. fr. 24: Narbonne. Hyd. 49 [57] s.a. 414. Jordanes (31) says the marriage took place at Forum Livii, in Italy.
15. For example, Phil. 12.4: Hyd. 57.
16. Prosp. a. 414: cf Gordon, 1960, 41.
17. The Annals of Ravenna give the date as 7 March 413, but this is impossible as the chronology would not allow enough time for Heraclian to sail from Carthage to Italy and return, especially as it would involve sailing in the winter months. Instead, it has been assumed that either the wrong year has been recorded by the annalist, or that a copyist has copied the date correctly but the year incorrectly. Hydatius, 48 [56], is also dated to 413, but in this case it is assumed that the entry for Heraclian's death is simply joined to the entry in a similar manner to many *Chronicles*. See also Phil. 12.6.
18. Olymp. fr. 26.
19. For example, Gordon, 1960, 42: PLRE 2, *Vallia*, 1147–48.
20. Hyd. 52 [60], s.a. 414.
21. Prosp. a. 415: Hyd. 52 [60], s.a. 416: cf Olymp. fr. 26.1.13f.
22. Prosp. a. 417.

23. Olymp. fr. 29.2.

24. Olymp. fr. 26.

25. Olymp. fr. 26.1.

26. This is equivalent to 48 *solidi* per *modius* of grain, whereas the standard rate was 40 *modii* of grain per *solidus*: Blockley, 1983, 218, n. 62.

27. Cf Isid. Sev. *Hist*. 22.

28. Jord, Hist. 163.

29. Jord. Hist. 163: Olymp. fr. 26.1.13f: cf Oros. 7.43.2.8: Philost. 12.4: Prosp. s.a. 415: Hyd. 52 [60], s.a. 414, who merely claims the perpetrator was a Goth.

30. Jordanes (163) cf Oros. 7.9: brother of Sarus, Olymp. fr. 26.1.13f.

31. Olymp. fr. 26.1.22–23.

32. Isid. *Hist. Goths*. 21.

33. Olymp. fr. 31.

34. Placidia restored. Prosp. a. 416 Olymp. fr. 30.

35. Merrills and Miles, 2014, 45.

36. Isid. Sev. *Hist. Goths*. 21: 'After being summoned to Spain by the patrician Constantius, he inflicted great slaughter on the barbarians for the sake of the Roman name.'

37. Cf Merrills and Miles, 2014, 45.

38. Date, Hyd. 55 [63], s.a. 417.

39. Isid. Sev. *Hist. Goths*. 21: Hyd. 59 [67], s.a. 418.

40. Hyd. 55 [63], s.a. 417.

41. Isid. Sev. *Hist. Goths*. 21.

42. Hyd. 55 [63], s.a. 417. Hydatius relates the defeat of the Siling Vandals in a separate entry.

43. Hyd. 49 [57], s.a. 414.

44. Hyd. 59 [67], s.a. 418.

45. Hyd. 59 [67], s.a. 418.

46. Cf Hyd. 60 [68], s.a. 418.

47. Hyd. 61 [69], s.a. 418.

48. Olymp. *fr*. 26.2.5–7: Prosp. a. 419.

49. E.g. Hyd. 62 [70], s.a. 418: Olymp. fr. 34.

50. Kulikowski, 2000.

51. Kulikowski, 2000, 123.

52. Kulikowski, 2000, 126.

53. E.g. Merrills and Miles, 2014, 45–46, where Maximus is captured by Asterius during the raising of the siege of the Erbasian Mountains (see below).

54. Cf *Chron. Gall*. 452 a. 416.

55. Theoph. AM 5911, 5912: Theod. Lect. 317 (93.19–22): Hyd. 64 [72], s.a. 419: cf Soz. 9.16: Prosp. a. 418.

56. Cf Merrills and Miles, 2014, 45.

57. Hyd. 63 [71], s.a. 419.

58. Kulikowski, 2000, 133.

59. Cf Greg. Tur. 2.2.

60. See Kulikowski, 2000, 126, for dissent and bibliography, esp. n. 19.

61. Cf Merrills and Miles, 2014, 45; Asterius inflicted 'a minor defeat on the Vandals'.

62. Cf Aug. *Ep.* 11*, where Asterius is acknowledged as leading a campaign that 'crushed' the revolt of Maximus.

63. Cf *Chron. Gall.* 452, 89.

64. Theoph. AM 5913: Prosp. a. 420: Olymp. fr. 33.2: Philost. 12.12: Hyd. 67 [75], s.a. 420.

65. Philost. 12.12.

66. Seven months, Olymp. fr. 33.1.13f: Prosp. a. 421: Theoph. AM 5913: Hyd. 68 [76], s.a. 421.

67. Prosp. 395.1278: *Chron. Gall.* 511, 571: Hyd. 72.

68. Hyd. 69 [77], s.a. 422.

69. Merrills and Miles, 2014, 46.

70. Hyd. 77, s.a. 422: Salvian, *de Gub. Dei*, 7.11.

71. *Chron. Gall.* 452, s.a. 430, cf Halsall, 2007, 240–41, esp. n. 93.

72. Possid. *Vita S. August.* 28: see Chapter 7.

Chapter 5: Freedom

1. Olymp. fr. 38.

2. Olymp. fr. 39.1: Philost. 1213: Theoph. AM 5915: Hyd. 71 [80] s.a. 424.

3. Prosp. s.a. 423: Philost. 1213: Theoph. AM 5915: Hyd. 74 [83], s.a. 424: date, *Ann. Rav.* s.a. 423. For further references see PLRE 2, Ioannes 6, pp.594–95.

4. Aetius, e.g. Olymp. fr. 43.2: Bonifacius e.g. Olymp. fr. 38.

5. Olymp. fr. 40.

6. Greg. Tur. 2.8.

7. Prosp. s.a. 424: the translation is open to interpretation.

8. Theoph. AM 5915: cf Olymp. fr. 43.1, 43.2: Hyd. 75 [84], s.a.425.

9. Theoph. AM 5915: Hyd. 75 [84], s.a. 425.

10. Prosp. p.65.

11. Olymp. fr. 43.2.

12. Theoph. AM 5915, AM 5916: Hyd. 76 [85], s.a. 425.

13. Hyd. 75 [84], s.a. 425.

14. Proc. BV 1.3.14–15: Joh. Ant. fr. 196: Theoph. AM 591. Although these sources tend to nominate Aetius as the candidate for the scheme, see Hughes, 2012, 78f.

15. Prosp. s.a. 427.

16. For a full analysis of this problem, see Clover, 1966, 18f.

17. For the acceptance of Bonifacius' alliance with the Vandals, see e.g. Bury, 1958, 246f.

18. See Chapter 7.
19. Possidius, *Vita S. Augustini*, 28.
20. Heather, 2005, 267.
21. Mathisen, 1999, 189–91.
22. Merrills and Miles, 2014, 50.
23. For a more detailed analysis, see Hughes, 2012, 66f.
24. For an alternative chronology, see e.g. Merrills and Miles, 2014, 50f: Clover, 1966, 5–8.

Chapter 6: Gaiseric

1. Sidonius Apoll. *Carm.* 5: Procopius, *B.V.* I.3.
2. Bury, 1958, 246.
3. Proc., *BV*, 1.3.22f: cf Bury, 1958, 244.
4. Hyd. 79 [89], s.a. 428.
5. Proc. *BV* 4.12–14: cf *BG* 1(5).3.24.
6. Proc. BG 3(7).1.4.
7. Merrills, 2004, 170.
8. Merrills and Miles, 2014, 51.
9. Wolfram, 1997, 165: Salv. *de Gub. Dei.* 7.27f.
10. Merrills and Miles, 2014, 50–51.
11. Heather, 2005, 267.
12. Cf Proc. BV 1.22.1–12 on earlier divisions.
13. PLRE 2, *Andevotus*, 86, cf Hyd. s.a. 438.
14. PLRE 2, *Andevotus*, 86, cf Cassiodorus, *Variae*, 5.29 for a similar-named individual who was an Ostrogoth.
15. Hyd. s.a. 429.
16. Dating; Prosp. s.a. 427: *Chron. Pasch.* s.a. 428: Hyd. s.a. 429: *Chron. Gall. 452*, s.a. 430.
17. Hyd. s.a. 429 'Gaiseric, king of the Vandals, abandoned the Spanish provinces in the month of May, crossing along with all the Vandals and their families from the coast of the province of Baetica to Mauretania and Africa.' For a more detailed critical analysis of the accuracy of the 'chronicles', see 'Introduction'. But cf, for example, Cass. *Chron.* s.a. 427.
18. Goffart, 1980, App. A, pp 231–34, suggests that the numbers in the ancient sources are actually 'meaningless'.
19. Vict. Vit. 1.1–2.
20. Proc. 3.5.18–19.
21. Pliny, *Natural History*, 3. *Preface.*
22. Ptolemy, *Geography*, 4.1: cf Merrills and Miles, 2014, 53–54.
23. Heather, 2005, 268.
24. Heather, 2005, 269. It should be noted that the province of Mauretania Tingitana was classed as part of Hispania, rather than of Africa, by the Romans.

25. Vict. Vit. 1.2.
26. Bury, 1958, 247: Augustine, *Ep.* 228.
27. Leo, Ep. 12.8 alludes to the status of consecrated virgins raped during the Vandal occupation: cf Merrills and Miles, 2014, 54.
28. Cf Vict. Vit. 1.3–7.
29. Hyd. 77, s.a. 422.
30. Merob. *Carm.* 4 'an offspring of heroes, and a descendant of kings'; Sid. Ap. *Carm* 5, 203f.
31. Schwarcz, 2004, 51.
32. *Inscriptiones Christianae urbis Romae septimo saeculo antiquares, nova serie*, 9370, 9516 and 9517: see Conant, 2015, 68, for a more detailed analysis.
33. Vict. Vit. 1.8. Some of the buildings Victor claims were destroyed by the Vandals had already been 'overthrown' by the Catholics in Africa, whilst others may simply have already been in decline before the advent of the Vandals: cf Moorhead, 1992, 5, n.8.
34. Marcillet-Jaubert, 1968, no. 147.
35. Heather, 2005, 269: Conant, 2015, 276: cf Aug. *Ep.* 220.7.
36. Possidius (Vita S. Augustini, 28) records that Cirta is one of only three churches that the Vandals had not destroyed: 'Of the innumerable churches … only three survive, namely those of Carthage, Hippo and Cirta, which by God's favour were not demolished.'
37. Aug. *Ep.* 230 (AD 429), where Darius, in a reply to Augustine, hopes that the peace with the Vandals will last.
38. Aug. Epp. 229.2; 230.6; 231.7: cf PLRE 2, Verimodus, 1155.
39. *Not. Dig. Oc.* 25; *c.* 15,000 *comitatenses* and 15,000 *limitanei*: Heather, 2005, 268.
40. This is shown by the fact that after he had been reinforced by Eastern troops, Bonifacius lost another battle against Gaiseric: see below.
41. Proc. 3.3.30–31; 3.3.34.
42. Possidius (29) states that Augustine died in the 'third month of the siege'. As Augustine is known to have died on 28 August, this means that the siege began in May or June, depending upon the exact meaning of Possidius' words.
43. Poss. 28. It is probable that the Vandals maintained the ships used in the crossing to Africa and that these followed the main body along the North African coast.
44. Poss. 28.
45. Prosp. s.a. 430.
46. Fourteen-month siege, Vict. Vita, 3.10
47. Proc. 3.3.35: dating the siege, Possidius notes that Augustine died in the third month of the siege; according to Prosper (s.a. 430) the date of his death was 28 August 430, the third month of the siege; the siege lasted for fourteen months, Vict. Vita, 3.10; therefore, the siege was from May–June 430 to July–August 431.

48. A letter of appeal to Theodosius prior to the Council of Ephesus, which convened 7 June 431, mentions the preparations: Clover, 1966, 40.
49. Dating the arrival to 431, PLRE 2, *Fl. Ardabur Aspar*, 166, noting a letter written during the Council of Ephesus in 431; ACOec. 1.4, p.76. Reinforcements from 'both Rome and Byzantium', Proc. 3.3.35.
50. Aetius responsible for arrangements, Heather, 2005, 285.
51. Proc. 3.3.35–36; Evagr. 2.1; Theoph. AM 5931, 5943; Zon. 13.24.12.
52. Evagr. 2.37–38: *domesticus*, Proc. BV. 1.4.7.
53. Theoph. AM 5931; Evagr. 2.1; Proc. 3.4.2f.
54. Cf Merrills and Miles, 2014, 55.
55. Cf Clover, 1966, 41.
56. Clover, 1966, 46–48.
57. Possidius, Vita S. Augustini, 28.

Chapter 7: Settlement

1. Hughes, 2012, 75.
2. Hughes, 2012, 76–8.
3. Hughes, 2012, 78–9.
4. Hyd. s.a. 431.
5. Greg. Tur. 2.9: Clover, 1971, 43.
6. Hyd. s.a. 431. Aquae Flaviae is almost certainly now Chaves, Portugal: http://www.portugal-info.net/transmontana/chaves.htm (May 2010).
7. Hyd. s.a. 432.
8. The order may date to late 431, just after Aetius had left for the campaign in Gaul.
9. Aspar left Africa in 431, Proc. BV. 1.3.36 (autumn 432, left for the East); Niceph. 14.56 (immediately left for Rome): Aspar remained in Africa until at least 434, PLRE 2. *Fl. Ardabur Aspar*, 166; Ps.-Prosp. Lib. Prom. D9; became Western consul in 434, Aspar Missorium.
10. Prosp. s.a. 432; cf *Chron. Gall. 452*, s.a. 432: Marcell. com, s.a. 432; Proc. 3.1.3: cf John Ant. fr. 201.3.
11. Marcell. com. s.a. 432, 435.
12. Cf Stilicho, Constantius (III).
13. Hyd. s.a. 432.
14. *Addit. ad Prosp. Haun.* s.a. 432: '*Pugna facta inter Aetium et Bonifatium in V do Arimino.*'
15. It is possible that Aetius and Bonifacius met in personal combat on the field, with Aetius wounding Bonifacius with a 'long spear': Marcell. com. s.a. 432.
16. Prosp. s.a. 432.
17. Illness, Prosp. s.a. 432, 'Although he fought a battle with Aetius, who was opposing him, and defeated him, he died a few days later of illness': Wounds, *Chron. Gall.*

452, s.a. 432, 'Boniface was wounded in a battle against Aetius but retired from it to die': 'three months later', Marcell. com. s.a. 432.

18. Hyd. s.a. 432; cf Vict. Vit. 1.19
19. Prosp. s.a. 432.
20. The later treaty of 435 was signed in Hippo.
21. *Chron. Gall. 452*, s.a. 432: Prosp. s.a. 432: Maenchen-Helfen, 1973, 86, 90f: cf, for example, Heather, 2005, 262, Aetius returned 'with enough reinforcements to make Sebastian's position untenable'.
22. 'The Goths were summoned by the Romans to bring help', *Chron. Gall. 452*, s.a. 433. Although there is no mention of a battle in the sources, there is a small chance that a battle occurred but that the sources that have survived simply fail to mention it.
23. Hyd. s.a. 433.
24. Visigoth, cf Sid. App. *Carm.* 5.128, 203–04; Merob. *Carm.* 4.17: Pelagia an Arian and daughter baptized as an Arian, Aug. *Ep.* 220.4 (a.427 or 429); PLRE 2, *Pelagia 1*, 856.
25. Although this is nowhere specifically stated, this is the most likely reason for the lack of campaigning represented in the sources. For a similar process undertaken by Stilicho, see Hughes 2010, 30–33.
26. The consul for the East was Areobindus.
27. Aetius fighting Burgundians in 434, Sid. Ap. *Carm.* 7.234: Clover (1966, 53) dates Trygetius' embassy to early 434, as this leaves time for negotiations and for Valentinian to ratify the treaty: *Comes rei privatae, Cod. Th.* 11, 20.42 (19 May 423).
28. Clover, 1966, 53.
29. Prosp. 1321, Proc. *BV* 1.4.12–14; Cassiod. 1225; Isid. *Hist Vand*. 74: Paul. Diac. 13.11: *Additamenta Africana* s.a. 435: *Epitome Carthaginiensis ad Prosper* 1321: *Laterculus Regum Wandalorum et Alanorum* (H) 1.
30. Prosp. s.a. 435: cf *Laterc. Reg. Vand. et Al.* (*Hispani 1*).
31. *Laterc. Wand.* (H) 2: *Epit. Carth. Ad Prosp.* 1339.
32. Edicts dated to 19 May 483 and 25 February 484; cf Wolfram, 1997, 169.
33. Cf Clover, 1966, 58–59.
34. Clover, 1966, 58–59.
35. Cf Clover, 1966, 59–60.
36. See Clover, 1966, 57–58 for a more detailed discussion of this hypothesis.
37. E.g. Schwarcz, 2004, 52.
38. Prosp. s.a. 435. Isidore in his *History of the Vandals* notes only that the Vandals arrived in Mauretania and Africa: *H. Vand*. 74: *Chron. Min. II*, 297.
39. Clover, 1966, 54. Other examples include: Prosp. 1271; Hyd. 49, 69; Oros. 7.40.10, 7.41.7, 7.43.14; Prosp. 1330.
40. Merrills and Miles, 2014, 60–61.
41. For a fuller discussion of the debate surrounding *hospitalitas*, see Halsall, 2007, 422f.

42. CTh. 7.8.5: cf Halsall, 2007, 422.

43. *Annonae*, Clover, 1966, 56: cf Schwarcz, 2001, 266–68: cf Proc. BV. 1.4.12–13.

44. Isid. *Hist. Vand.* 74.

45. Schwarcz, 2004, 57.

46. Eug. *Epistula ad Probam virginem*, ref. and dated in Conant, 2015, 108.

47. Bede, *de temporum ratione*, 66.593.

48. Cf Conant, 2015, 110–111.

49. Schwarcz, 2004, 56–57.

50. Schwarcz, 2004, 53.

51. In his translation and commentary, Moorhead notes that the title *dux* is 'surprising', as Geiseric had 'become king the previous year': Moorhead, 1992, 3, n.2.

52. Halsall, 2007, 243.

53. Heather, 2005, 269, map 10: 286.

54. Bury, 1889, Vol I, 170.

55. PLRE 2, *Geisericus*, 497.

56. Prosp, s.a. 437.

57. Courtois, C, *Les Vandales en Afrique*, Algeria, 1955, 170 and n.2; cited in Schwarcz, 2004, 53.

58. CIL VIII 8634 = CLE 687 = ILCV 1101; *Hic iacet antis/tes s(an)c(tu)sque Nova/tus, ter denos et VII / sedis qui meruit annos. / precessit die X kal(endas) sept(em) b(res), (anno), pro(vinciae) CCCCI*: Aug. Ep. 229.1.

59. Hughes, 2012, 91: cf Courtois, *Les Vandales*, 172–75, cited in Schwarcz, 2004, 54, n.35.

60. *Nov. Val.* 13.1 (Rome, 21 June 445).

61. Dating, Vict. Vit. 1.1.

62. For a more detailed account of Donatism, see Chapter 8.

63. Possid. *V. Aug.* 30.

64. Burgundians rebel, Prosp. s.a. 436; Hyd. s.a. 436.

65. Proc. BV. 1.22.1–12.

66. Prosp, s.a. 437: bishoprics, Courtois, C, *Les Vandales en Afrique*, Algeria, 1955, 170 and n.2; cited in Schwarcz, 2004, 53. Merrills and Miles, 2014, p.266, n. 12, erroneously date the entry to 435.

67. But cf Merrills and Miles, 2014, 61.

68. Goths, Hyd. 98 [107]; Burgundians defeated, Hyd. 99 [108], both s.a. 436.

69. Prosp, s.a. 437: cf Honaratus, *Epistula Consolatoria ad Arcadium actum in exsilium a Genserico rege Vandalorum.*

70. Prosp, s.a. 437: cf Marc. Com. a. 438.

71. Merrills and Miles, 2014, 61.

72. Hughes, 2012, 98–99.

73. Narbonne, Hyd. 101 [110]; Burgundians killed, Hyd. 102 [110], both s.a. 437.

74. Prosp. a. 438.

75. Marc. *com.* a. 438: Vandal name, Merrills and Miles, 2014, 267, n.14.
76. Hyd. 104 [112], sa. 438; cf 'Measures against the Goths went well', Prosp. a. 438.
77. Prosp. a. 439.
78. Cf Merob. *Pan. I*, fr. 2a, 10f.
79. Gothic victory, Hyd. 108 [116], s.a. 439. It is assumed that the victory was early in the campaign season as in the same year Aetius in turn defeated the Goths and this almost certainly followed the Gothic victory and preceded the treaty between Rome and the Goths: see Chapter 8.

Chapter 8: Conquest

1. Mitchell, 2007, 345.
2. For a more detailed examination of these developments, including a more extensive bibliography, see Mitchell. 2007, 346 and associated references: Heather, 2005, 276 f., and associated references.
3. Aug. *Ep.* 93.1.2.
4. Hays, 2004, 103.
5. Cf the description of these events by Gibbon, 1861, II, 334–35.
6. Mitchell, 2007, 312.
7. Heather, 2005, 281.
8. Merob. *Pan. 2*, 153–86.
9. Vict. Vit. 1.7: Prosp. s.a. 437.
10. Arian bishops placed in 'deserted' basilicas, Vict. Vit. 1.9.
11. Heather, 2005, 279f.
12. Prosp. s.a. 439: Marcell. com. *Chron.* s.a. 439; Cass. *Chron.* s.a. 439.
13. Hyd. 107 [115], s.a. 439; *Laterc. Regum Vand. et al.* 2 (439); Marc. *com.* s.a. 439; Cass. *Chron.* s.a. 439. Prosp. 1339: *Add. Afr. ad Prosp.* s.a. 439: *Epit. Carth. ad Prosp.* 1339: Cassiod. *Chron.* 1233: *And. ad Cyclos Dion.* s.a. 439: *Laterc. Reg. Wand.* s.a. 439: *Chron. Pasch.* s.a. 439: *Chron. Gall. 511*, 598: Isid. *Hist. Vand.* 75: Paul Diac. *Hist. Rom.* 13.14: Vict. Vit. 1.12. *Chron Gall. 452* (129) places the event in 440. Although the precise date is sometimes disputed, it was seen as accurate by the Vandals, as it was used by Gaiseric for the dating of at least some of his coins: Steinacher, 2004, 175.
14. E.g. Hyd. 107 [115], s.a. 439: Ps.-Aug. *De acced. ad Gratiam* 2.13.
15. Cf Vict. Vit. 1.14.
16. Schwarcz, 2004, 55.
17. Vict. Vit. 1.12.
18. Prosp. 1339: *Lib. Prom.* 2.50, 72, 76: cf Ps.- Aug. *De temp. barb.* 2.6.
19. Hyd. s.a. 439.
20. Vict. Vit. 1.12.
21. Vict. Vit. 1.14.
22. Heather, 2005, 294.

23. Shanzer, 2004, 286, citing Courtois, *Les Vandales*, 292.

24. Prosp. s.a. 439: Hyd. 109 [117], s.a. 439.

25. For example, Wolfram, 1997, dates this to 442.

26. Jord. *Get*. 36 (184).

27. On the dissemination of news, see Hughes, 2010, 102–03: the law, *Nov. Val.* 4 (24 January 440), dealing with attempts of *decurions* to evade their duties by entering the church.

28. Hughes, 2010, Chapter 8: supplies from Gaul and Spain, e.g. Claudian, *de Cons. Stil. I*, 314f; *de Cons. Stil. II*, 393f.

29. *Nov. Val.* 6.1 (2 March 440).

30. *Nov. Val.* 9.1 (24 June 440); cf Merrills and Miles, 2014, 111.

31. *Nov. Val.* 6.2.1. (14 July 444).

32. *Nov. Val.* 5 (3 March 440).

33. D(ominus) n(oster) Placidus Valentin[ianus providen]/tissimus omnium retr[o principum] / salvo adque concordi [d(omino) n(ostro) Fl(avio) Theo]/dosio Invictissimo Au[g(usto) ad decus no]/minis sui Neapolitana[m civitatem] / ad omnes terra mari[que incursus] / expositam et nulla [securitate] / gaudentem ingenti [labore atque] / sumptu muris turrib[usq(ue) munivit]: CIL X 1485 = ILS 804 = Fiebiger – Schmidt 33.

34. There is much debate about this fleet, with some claiming that as no such fleet is listed in the *Notitia Dignitatum*, no such fleet existed. This does not take into account the realities of having a rich port that would otherwise be undefended and open to raids.

35. *Chron. Pasch.* s.a. 439. On the controversy concerning the walls, Whitby and Whitby, 1989, 72, esp. n.243.

36. For the attacks on Sicily, see: Prosp. 1342: Cassiod. *Chron.* 1235: Hyd. 120: Isid. *Hist. Vand.* 75: Salv. *De gub. Dei* 6.68: cf *And. ad Cyclos Dion.* s.a. 439: *Chron. Pasch.* s.a. 439.

37. Cassiod. *Chron. sub 440*.

38. Gathering of fleet, *Nov. Val.* 9.1. (24 June 440): invasion of Sicily, *Chron. Pasch.* s.a. 439; Cass. *Chron.* 440: Panormus, *Continuatio Chronicorum Hieronymianorum*, 120 (AD 440); Hyd. s.a. 440.

39. *Nov. Val.* 1.2 (after 24 June 440, but the exact date is unknown): Lilybaeum, also Leo EP. 3.

40. Clover, 1966, 76.

41. Sardinia, Salv. *De. gub. Dei*, 6.68; cf Vict. Vit. 1.13: Bruttium, Cass. *Var.* 1.14.14, although the dating is insecure: see Barnish, 1992, 11, n.7. Cf Nestor. *Lib. Her.* Bk2, Pt 2.

42. Prisc. fr. 6: Theoph. AM 5941: cf Nestor. *Lib. Her.* Bk2, Pt 2.

43. Salv. *De gub. Dei*. 6.68.

44. Clover, 1966, 76–77.

45. Clover, 1966, 76.
46. Prosp. 1342.
47. SUID. 145.
48. Hyd. s.a. 444.
49. Hyd. s.a. 445, 449.
50. *Nov. Val.* 9.1. (24 June 440).
51. Pope Leo, *Ep.* 54, 606, 1270–1271: as cited by Maenchen-Helfen, 1973, 108, n.495.
52. Prosp. s.a. 440.
53. Hyd. s.a. 449.
54. An edict addressed to Areobindus shows that he was still in Constantinople in March 441: *Nov. Theod.* 7.4 (6 March 441); cf *Cod. Just.* 12.8.2.4.
55. As with the later expedition of Belisarius, Sicily was the main staging point prior to the planned invasion of Africa itself. Hughes, 2009, 78–79; Proc. 3.13.24f. See also Nic. Call. *HE* 14.57; Cass. *Chron.* s.a. 441.
56. *Cod. Just.* 12.8.2.4.
57. PLRE 2, *Ariobindus 2*, 145.
58. *Cod. Just.* 12.8.2 (440–441). PLRE 2, *Germanus 3*, 505.
59. PLRE 2, *Ansila 1*, 92–93. Prosper allocates the title '*ducibus*' to all three commanders: Prosp. s.a. 441. PLRE 2, *Inobindus*, 592. PLRE 2, *Arintheus*, 142–43, where it is suggested that he is the same individual as '*Agintheus*', although this is open to doubt.
60. But cf Clover, 1966, 81.
61. Maenchen-Helfen, 1973, 110–11.
62. Clover, 1966, pp. 86–87.
63. Prosp. s.a. 441.
64. For a more detailed discussion of the evidence, see Clover, 1966, 93–95, n.2.
65. In a similar manner, Belisarius, in his campaign against the Vandals almost a century later in 533, took advantage of delays in the sea-voyage from Constantinople to Sicily to order his troops and to allocate commands: Hughes, 2010, 78ff.
66. Theoph. AM 5941, 5942; Niceph. 14.57.
67. Cf Rubin, 1986, 682.
68. Marc. Com. s.a. 441.
69. Marc. Com. s.a. 441: attack on Theodosiopolis and Satala, and ending by late June, cf *Nov. Theod.* 5.1 (26 June 441).
70. Thrace: Marc. com. s.a. 441: The war is dated to 442 by Prosper, s.a. 442: Illyricum, *Chron. Pasch.* s.a. 442; Cass. *Chron.* s.a. 442.
71. *Chron. Pasch.* s.a. 441; Marcell. com. 2.80.
72. Marc. com. s.a. 441. The text is ambiguous and implies that Aspar and Anatolius fought against both the Persians and the Huns, which although possible would have entailed long periods of very fast travel.
73. Marcell. com. 441.
74. Prosp. s.a. 442.

75. Schwarz, 2004, 50.
76. Vict. Vit. 1.13; trans. and punctuation Moorhead.
77. This section relies in part on Clover, 1966, 89.
78. It should be noted that the place name 'Abaritana' can also be found in Pliny, *Natural History*, 16.172.
79. Clover, 1966, 89.
80. Wolfram, 1997, 172.
81. Merob. *Carm. 1*, 17–18; *Carm. 2*, 13–14.
82. For a more detailed discussion and bibliography concerning the significance of Huneric's betrothal, see Clover, 1971, 54.
83. Cf Jacobsen, 2012, 138.
84. Clover, 1966, 101.
85. Clover, 1966, 102.
86. Heather, 2005, 371.
87. Clover, 1966, 90.
88. Prosp. 1347: Clover, 1966, 90, n.1: *Nov. Val.* 34.
89. Clover, 1971, 54, esp. n.115.

Chapter 9: Consolidation and Expansion

1. Conant, 2015, 20
2. Cf Merrills and Miles, 2014, 56.
3. Cf Conant, 2015, 37.
4. The Vandal devastation of their previously-held territory is reinforced by the novels of Valentinian, which mention the large reduction in taxes that the regained provinces had to pay in order to allow them to recover – only one-eighth of the pre-Vandal assessment: *Nov. Val.* 13 (21 June 445). The delay was no doubt due to the time taken for requests for remission from the conquered territories to be agreed.
5. Proc. 3.5.11–17: Byrsa, Mitchell, 2007, 347.
6. For a more detailed analysis and bibliography, see e.g. Schwarcz, 2004, 54f.
7. Schwarcz, 2004, 55.
8. *Nobles*, Mitchell, 2007, 347–48: on the warriors, Salvian, *De gub. Dei* 7.89, states that the Vandals were 'city dwellers', suggesting that they remained centred upon the main cities such as Carthage. This would not have been the case if the Vandals had been scattered as farmers throughout Africa.
9. See below.
10. Proc. BV 1.16.12: for a more detailed discussion, Conant, 2015, 46.
11. Conant, 2015, 199.
12. Conant, 2015, 132–33.
13. Cf Conant, 2015, 53–54.
14. On the legal aspects, see below.
15. Clover, 1986, 1.

16. Merrills and Miles, 2014, 69.
17. Merrills and Miles, 2014, 70.
18. Proc. BV 3. 9.8, 21.1, 22.9–11; 4.3.14.
19. Merrills and Miles, 2014, 69.
20. Conant, 2015, 65.
21. Conant, 2015, 48–49.
22. Felix, Vict. Vit. 1.45; Saturas, Vict. Vit. 1.48: cf Conant, 2015, 144.
23. Vict. Vit. 1.48–50.
24. E.g. Conant, 2015, 21.
25. Ward-Perkins, 2006, 201, n.11; referencing C. Courtois et al. Tablettees Albertini:
    Actes privés de l'époque vandale (Paris, 1952).
26. For a full discussion of the epigraphy, see Conant, 2015, 148f.
27. LDCP 1.2, 2.4 and 2.8: LG 428, 429 and 628c.
28. Cf Conant, 2015, 156–58.
29. Malch. FR. 17.
30. Cf Thompson, 1950, 59–60.
31. Fulgentius of Ruspe, Ferrandus, *V. F.* 1.4. Trans. R.B. Eno, *Fathers of the Church*
    95, Washington DC, 1997: referenced in Schwarcz, 2004, 55.
32. Theod. EP. 70.2. For a full discussion of the event, see Conant, 2015, 72f.
33. Conant, 2015, 9.
34. Cf Conant, 2015, 10.
35. Cf Conant, 2015, 160.
36. Conant, 2015, 160.
37. Proc. BV 1.5.24–25: cf Conant, 2015, 183.
38. Suppression of 'heresy', Vict. Vit. 2.1–2: *Lib. Gen.* 616 and 618: Morality, Salvian,
    De gub. Dei, 7.21.89–7.22.100.
39. Conant, 2015, 184.
40. Schwarcz, 2004, 55, citing Duval, N., 'Discussions des communications publiées
    dans le numero 10', *Antiquité Tardive*, 10 (2002), 38.
41. Conant, 2015, 181.
42. For a more detailed analysis of these details, see Conant, 2015, 163–64.
43. Cf Vict. Vit. 1.15f: Lib. Prom. 2.72.
44. Vict. Vit. 1.23.
45. Cf Vict. Vit. 1.23.
46. Jucundus Patriarch, Vict. Vit. 2.13: cf Conant, 2015, 165.
47. Vict. Vit. 1.43–44.
48. Conant, 2015, 165.
49. Shanzer, 2004, 286–87.
50. Examples of laws (all from Victor of Vita): Vandals barred from entering Nicene
    churches, 2.9; Nicenes forbidden to work at court, 1.43; commensality between
    Vandals and Nicenes forbidden, 2.46; two Vandal 'confessors' (near-martyrs), 3.38.

51. Conant, 2015, 161.

52. E.g. Prosp. s.a. 437: Antoninus Honoratus, *Epistola Consolatia ad Arcadium*, PL 50: 567–70: Vict. Vit. 3.41: *Passio septem monachorum* 14 (CSEL Vol. 7).

53. Vict. Vit. 1.23.

54. Quodvult. *Liber Promissorium*, 4.5.7: Conant, 2015, 171–74.

55. Hitchner, in Drinkwater and Elton, 2002, 128: Mitchell, 2007, 348.

56. Mitchell, 2007, 348.

57. Conant, 2015, 92.

58. Conant, 2015, 94.

59. Conant, 2015, 51.

60. Conant, 2015, 90–91: Silver, Aug. *Confess.* 6.9.14.

61. Conant, 2015, 89–90.

62. Cf Clover, 1986, 1, 3.

63. Vict. Vit. 1.35–38: cf Conant, 2015, 262f.

64. Proc. *BV* 1.25.5–6: Conant, 2015, 36.

65. Cf Conant, 2015, 252. On the 'conquests' by the Moors, see CJ 1.27.2.4 (13 April 534).

66. *Nov. Val.* 13.14 (445).

67. Conant, 2015, 275.

68. Cf Conant, 2015, 276–77.

69. Vict. Vit. 1.35.8.

70. On the Vandals being settled under Roman rule, see Merob. *Pan II*, 24f.

71. Cf Rubin, 1986, 682: Clover, 1966, 113–15.

72. Cf Wood, CAH, 537.

73. Halsall, 2007, 247.

74. Vict. Vit. 2.14.

75. Huneric was back in Carthage before the death of Galla Placidia on 27 November 450, Proc. *BV*. 1.4.14–15.

76. Conant, 2015, 104.

77. Conant, 2015, 64.

78. Cf Conant, 2015, 114f.

79. Conant, 2015, 137.

80. Proc. BV. 1.5.15.

81. Dracontius, *Laudes Dei*, 3. 645–47; *Romulea* 5, *subscriptio* 3.160.

82. Cf *Tablettes Albertini*, *passim*: also cf Conant, 2015, 138–39.

83. Hyd. 131: Clover, 1966, 103.

84. Hyd. 114, 119, 123, 134.

85. Clover, 1966, 103–04.

86. Cf Jacobsen, 2012, 137.

87. Clover, 1966, 111–12.

88. Clover, 1966, 112f.

89. *Nov. Val.* 29 and 33: cf Clover, 1966, 125–26.
90. See esp. *Nov. Val.* 12.1–2; 13.14; 34.4: cf Clover, 1966, 125.
91. *Nov. Val.* 34 (13 July 451): Clover, 1966, 123.
92. Prisc. fr. 15, followed by Jord. *Get.* 181.
93. Clover, 1966, 115–16.
94. E.g. 'The book must have been written by Nestorius in the year 451 or 452': Driver and Hodgson, 1925, ix.
95. *Nov. Val.* 36.1
96. Clover, 1966, 127–28.
97. *Nov. Val.* 29 and 33: cf Clover, 1966, 125–26.

Chapter 10: The Sack of Rome

1. Death of Attila, Prisc. frs. 24.1, 24.2; Marcell. com. s.a. 454; Cass. *Chron.* s.a. 453; Vict. Tonn. s.a. 453.2; Theoph. AM 5946.
2. North, *Addit. Ad Prosp. Haun.* s.a. 453: Arles, *Chron. Gall. 511*, no. 621.
3. Hyd. s.a. 453–54.
4. Joh. Ant. fr. 201.6: on Vicus Helena, see Chapter X.
5. Sid. Ap. *Carm.* 5.290–300.
6. Prosp. s.a. 454.
7. PLRE 2, *Maximus 22*, 749–51.
8. Prisc. fr. 30 =Joh. Ant. fr. 201. cf Prosp. s.a. 454.
9. Prosp. s.a. 454. cf Evag. 2.7 (54)
10. 21 Sept = *Addit. ad Prosp. Haun.* s.a. 454: 22 Sept = *Ann. Rav.* s.a. 454.
11. Prisc. fr. 30. 1. = Joh. Ant. fr. 201; Cass. *Chron.* s.a. 454; Marcell. com. s.a. 454; Vict. Tonn. s.a. 454; Prosp. s.a. 454; Theoph. AM 5946: Evag. 2.7 (54): Aetius killed along with a number of *honorati* (distinguished citizens), Hyd. s.a. 454.
12. Sid. Ap. *Carm.* 5.306–08: Joh. Ant. fr. 201, 4–5.
13. Hyd. 161, s.a. 453–54.
14. Clover, 1966, 133: cf Sid. *Carm.* 7. 357–440: Hyd. 170.
15. Prosp. *Cont. Reichen.* 25. s.a. 454.
16. *Kal. Carth. ad Nonas Jan.* (PL, XIII, 1228), cf Clover, 1966, 134.
17. Clover, 1966, 136.
18. Cf Clover, 1966, 139.
19. Proc. 3.6.7.
20. This section can be found in Hughes, 2013. Readers who have that book may wish to skip this analysis.
21. Prosp. 1375: Prosp. *Cont. Reichen.* 27: Prosp. *Auct.* s.a. 455: *Cons. Ital.* s.a. 455: *Add. Ad. Prosp. Haun.* s.a. 455: *Chron. Gall. a. 451*, 623: Hyd. 162: Cassiod. *Chron.* 1262: Marcell. *com.* s.a. 455. 1: Jord. *Rom.* 334, *Get.* 235: Proc. *BV.* 1.4.36: Evag. 2.7: *Chron. Pasch.* s.a. 455: Joh. Ant. fr. 201.5: Theoph. AM 5947: Joh. Mal. 14, 360: Cedren. 605: Niceph. 15.11: Joh. Mal. 360: *Addit. Ad Prosp. Haun.* s.a. 455:

Greg. Tur. 2.8: PLRE 2, *Placidus Valentinianus 4*, 1139: Greg. Tur. 2.8; plot, Vict. Tonn. s.a. 455.

22. Prosp. *Cont. Reichen.* 27, s.a. 455: Prosp. *Auct. Ad ed. A.* 455.2, s.a. 455: *Chron. Gall. a. 451*, 623: Hyd. 162: *Cons. Ital., Fast. Vind. Prior.* s.a. 455: Joh. Ant. fr. 201.5: Marcell. *com.* s.a. 455: *Chron. Pasch.* s.a. 455: Prisc. fr. 30.1 = Joh. Ant. fr. 201: *Addit. ad Prosp. Haun.* s.a. 455: Vict. Tonn. s.a. 455: Joh. Mal. 360, 365: Evag. 2.7.

23. Joh. Ant. fr. 201.6. Hyd. s.a. 455. Whether the betrothal was to Eudocia or Placidia is open to question as there is no definitive identification in the sources, but the former is preferred here.

24. Cf Joh. Ant. fr. 201.6.

25. For example, Halsall, 2007, Heather, 2005, and Mitchell, 2007, ignore Eudoxia's alleged part in Gaiseric's actions, simply noting that Gaiseric was attempting to avenge the insult to his son by Eudocia's betrothal to Palladius. For a detailed analysis, see Clover, 1966, 151f.

26. Theoph. AM 5947.

27. Prisc. fr. 30.1 = Joh. Ant. fr. 201; Evagr. 2.7 (54).

28. Clover, 1971, 54, esp. n.115. See Chapter 11.

29. Cf Halsall, 2007, 255.

30. Dissolution of the peace treaty, Eudoxia's message, and the weakness of the new regime, Prisc. *fr.* 30.1 = Joh. Ant. *fr.* 201.

31. Casson, 1951, 145.

32. Clover, 1966, 119, n.2.

33. Joh. Ant. Fr. 201.6: cf Jord. Get. 235: cf Lib. Gen. 441, 442, who claims that with the death of Valentinian the Empire was at an end.

34. Clover, 1966, 161.

35. Prosp. Auct. ad ed. a. 455 anni 456.

36. Hyd. 163: Mar. Avent. s.a. 455 etc.

37. Clover, 1966, 160.

38. Clover, 1966, 162.

39. Prisc. fr. 30.1 = Joh. Ant. fr. 201.

40. Date, Theoph. AM 5947; cf Prosp. s.a. 455. The *Fasti Vindobonenses Priori* date the event to 12 June, but see Bury, 1923, 205, and n.2, but note that the *Anonymus Cuspiniani* are now referred to as the *Fasti Vindobonenses Priori*.

41. Prisc. fr. 30.1 = Joh. Ant. fr. 201.

42. Prisc. fr. 30.1 = Joh. Ant. fr. 201; Prosp. s.a. 455.

43. Cf Prosp. s. a. 455: 'Gaiseric obtained the city devoid of all protection'.

44. Hughes, 2012, 182–83.

45. All dates are taken from Clover, 1966, 141f., plus associated references.

46. Jacobsen, 2012, 142.

47. Feltoe, 1895, xi.

48. Gaiseric in the palace, Proc. 3.5.1.
49. It should be noted that it was at the time of writing the Chronicle that Placidia was the wife of Olybrius, not at the time of the sack.
50. Hyd. s.a. 455.
51. Prosp. s.a. 455. Vict. Tonn. s.a. 455; Joh. Mal. 14.26 (365–66); Theoph AM 5947, etc.
52. Hyd. s.a. 455.
53. Reynolds, 2011, 178.
54. Prosp. s.a. 455. Vict. Tonn. s.a. 455; Joh. Mal. 14.26 (365–66); Theoph AM 5947, etc.
55. Joh. Ant. fr. 202.
56. Vict. Vit. 1.25.
57. Theoph. AM 5947.
58. Cf Jacobsen, 2012, 143.
59. Merrills and Miles, 2014, 116.

Chapter 11: War

1. Theoph. AM 5947, 5949, 5964: cf Prisc. fr. 29, 30: Hyd. 216: Vict. Tunn. s.a. 464, 523: Isid. Hist. Vand. 77: Paul. Diac. Hist Rom. 14.19: Proc. BV I .5.6, 2.9.13: Joh. Ant. fr. 204: Evag. 2.7: *Chron. Pasch.* s.a. 455: Zon. 13.25, 27: Niceph. 15.11: Niceph. 15.12, mentions in 472 that the marriage had lasted sixteen years at that date.
2. PLRE 2, *Hildericus*, 564–65: according to Procopius (3.9.10) and Corripus (*Ioh.* 3. 263) he was an old man in 530, meaning that his birth dates to some time in the 450s.
3. Avitus' embassy to Vandals, Prisc. fr. 31; Hyd. 166. An embassy to Marcian would be obligatory and is implied by Marcian's repeated envoys to the Vandals; Prisc. fr. 31.
4. Prisc. fr. 24.
5. Prisc. fr. 31.
6. Although Hydatius claims that the two halves of Empire worked together, it would appear that this was by coincidence rather than design: Hyd. 166.
7. Proc. 3.5.22: *Fast. Vind. Prior.* s.a. 455.
8. Prisc. fr. 31.
9. Theod. Lect. 1.7: Clover, 1966, 172–73.
10. Vict. Vit. 1.13.
11. Conant, 2015, 287.
12. Hyd. 456–57 (169 [176]), s.a. 456–457: Prisc. fr. 31.
13. Sid. Ap. *Carm.* 2. 367.
14. Sid. Ap. *Carm.* 2.367. cf Hyd. 169 [176], s.a. 456–457; 'At this time it was announced to king Theoderic [of the Visigoths] that through Avitus a great multitude of

Vandals, which had set out from Carthage for Gaul and Italy with sixty ships, was destroyed after being trapped by Count Ricimer': cf Joh. Ant. fr.202.

15. Cf the famine in Rome during the 'rebellion' of Gildo in Africa in 396: Hughes, 2010, 105.

16. The sack of Capua is mentioned in numerous online articles, most notably by the Encyclopaedia Britannica (http://www.britannica.com/EBchecked/topic/94379/Capua), and in some it is dated to March of that year, but sadly no reference is given to the ancient sources. However, it is mentioned by Landolfus Sagax (15.19f.) as happening 'at the same time' as Gaiseric's sack of Rome. On the widespread nature of the attacks, Prisc. *fr*.24: Vict. Vit. 1.23.

17. 'When as in the time of the cruel Vandals, that part of Italy which is called Campania was overrun and sacked, and many were from thence carried captive into Africa: then the servant of God, Paulinus, bestowed all the wealth of his Bishopric upon prisoners and poor people': Gregory of Rome, *Dialogue* 3.1.

18. Hyd. *Chron.* 176–77.

19. See below: Burgess, 1987, 341: contra, claiming Ricimer, Clover, 1966, 166.

20. For a full discussion, see MacGeorge, 2002, 186 and bibliography.

21. Greg. Tur. 2.11: Joh. Ant. fr. 202.

22. Eusebius of Milan, Vict. Tonn. s.a. 455; cf *Auct. Prosp. Haun.* s.a. 456; *Fast. Vind. Prior.* s.a. 456; Theoph. AM 5948; Jord. Get. 240; Vict. Tonn. s.a. 456; Joh. Ant. fr. 202; Mar. Av. s.a. 456.

23. *Cont. Prosp. ad a 462.* = 'Inpartius Avitus ann. I mens. III./post ipsum mensibus XV reguum vacavit': *Gall. Chron. a. 511*, No. 628 = '*et Avitus occisus est a Maioriano comite domesticorum Placentiae*': cf Greg. Tur. 2.11. Dates: early = Burgess, 1987, 341; late = Mathisen, 1985, 332. The details surrounding Avitus' death are contradictory and have been the subject of extremely different interpretations. For more information on the problems and controversies, see Mathisen, 1985, 327, n.4.

24. CIL XIII 863; Allmer and Dissard, 1892, 27–28: see also e.g. Halsall, 2007, 262.

25. Greg. Tur. *Glory of the Confessors* 62.

26. Sid. Ap. *Ep.* 1.11.6.

27. On the differing interpretation of the *coniuratio*, see Max, 1979, *passim*, and Mathisen, 2007.

28. *Lib. Hist. Franc.* 8: on the dating, Halsall, 2007, 263, and related notes.

29. The fact that messengers were immediately sent East is supported by the speed of response made by Leo; cf MacGeorge, 2002, 196: see below. On Marcian's proposed campaign, see Theod. Lect. 1.7: Clover, 1966, 172–73 and Chapter 4.

30. Ricimer and Majorian appointed by Leo, and date, *Fasti. Vind. Prior.* s.a. 457, but cf MacGeorge, 2002, 197.

31. Date, *Fast. Vind. Prior.* 583: unwilling, Sid. Ap. Carm. 5.9–12: 'at the little columns', Mathisen, 1998. The main difficulty when assessing events at this point is that there are two dates in the ancient sources for Majorian's accession to the

throne. As just noted, the *Fasti Vindobonenses Priores* give the date as 1 April 457: on the other hand, the *Auctarium Prosperi Hauniensis (s.a.* 458) gives the date of his coronation as 28 December 457. Many attempts have been made to reconcile the different dates, some more successful than others. It is now generally accepted that he was first acclaimed by the troops in April but only crowned in Ravenna in December when Leo had agreed.

32. Clover, 1966, 173–74.

33. MacGeorge, 2002, 170.

34. *Sid. Carm. 5*, 388–440: cf Clover, 1966, 174. The Loeb translation claims that the man was his son-in-law, but the original text – *cui regis avari narratur nupsisse soror* – claims the man was married to Gaiseric's (half) sister.

35. Bury, 1923, I, 334.

36. *Nov. Maj.* 2 (11 March 458, Ravenna): *Nov. Maj.* 5 (4 September 458, Ravenna): *Nov. Maj.* 7 (unknown). For further analysis, see Hughes, 2015, 71.

37. *Nov. Maj.* 2.4, (11 March 458, Ravenna).

38. Served alongside Majorian, Prisc. fr. 30: On his support for Majorian, see below: appointment, Greg. Tur. 2.1.

39. Julius Nepos son of Nepotianus, Jord. *Rom.* 338: Julius Nepos nephew of Marcellinus, Marc. *com.* s.a. 474; Jord. *Get.* 239: but see Burgess, 2002, 25 for the opposite view.

40. Cf Thompson, 1963, 235.

41. Sid. Ap. Carm. 5. 441–48: Prisc. fr. 27: Joh. Ant. fr. 203.

42. Mathisen, 2007.

43. Sid. Carm. 5. 62–66, 89–106, 327–49, 352–53, 363–66, 549, 590–96, 600–01. Cf Clover, 1966, 174.

44. Hyd. 192, s.a. 458.

45. Clover, 1966, 175.

46. CIL XIII 863; ET . ME / M OR S / U L P I C / R O S I C / I A E D F: Allmer and Dissard, 1892, 27–28; Mathisen, 2007: see Chapter 4. Cf Mathisen, 1993, 609.

47. See Chapter 4.

48. Paulinus Petricord (Paulinus of Perigueux), *Vita San Martini*, 6.111f: Greg. Tur, de Mir. S. Mart. 1.2.

49. Mathisen, 1979, 620.

50. *Hydatius Chron.* no. 197, 197, s.a. 459: cf Paul. Pet. *Vit. Mart.* 6.111–142; Greg. Tur. *Vit. Mart.* 1.2.

51. Prisc. fr. 28: Thompson, 1963, 235; Heather, 2005, 368.

52. Thompson, 1963, 235: Prisc. fr. 37, 00 Sud. 3.325.23. p.133. See also, Zintzen, Damascii vitae Isidori reliquae, 158.

53. Prisc. fr. 27.

54. Cf Clover, 1966, 177.

55. Proc. BV. 1.5.8–19; De aed. 6.5.2–5: Niceph. 15.27.
56. Clover, 1966, 178, n.1.
57. Prisc. fr. 27.
58. Vict. Vit. 1.43.
59. 'Theologically pure kingdom', Conant, 2015, 170.

Chapter 12: Majorian's African Campaign

1. Marcellinus' crossing, Hyd. 192 [197], s.a. 459: Prisc. fr. 38.
2. Hyd. 223 [227]. Unfortunately this entry in Hydatius is brief and has almost certainly been misplaced by a careless copyist, as otherwise Hydatius dates the episode to either 364 or 365. Historians have assumed that this could not be true, as by the later dates Marcellinus was in opposition to Ricimer and the new Emperor Severus and had placed himself under the command of Leo, who would not have agreed to the attack as it was against the terms of the treaty.
3. Nov. Maj. 11 (28 March 460, Arles).
4. Hyd. 195 [200], s.a. 460.
5. Hyd. 196 [201], s.a. 460.
6. Much of this section is based upon MacGeorge, 2002, 306–11 and was earlier included in *Patricians and Emperors* (Hughes, 2015) so readers who have read that book may wish to skip this.
7. For a major exception, see MacGeorge, 2002, 306–11.
8. Vict. Vit. 3.20.
9. *Sid. Ap. Carm.* 5, 441–442.
10. Cf MacGeorge, 2002, 206.
11. Prisc. fr. 36. 1.
12. Casson, 1951, 139–40.
13. Hyd. 195 [200], s.a. 460.
14. '*His diebus Maioranus imp. Caesaraugustam venit*', *Chron Caes. s.a. 460.*
15. Traitors, Hyd. 195 [200], s.a. 460.
16. *Chron. Gall. a 511*, 634; Mar. Avent. *s.a.* 460; Hyd.195 [200] *s.a.* 460.
17. Hyd. 195 [200] s.a. 460: Isid. *Hist. Vand.* 76: Fred. 2.55: *Chron. Caesaraug.* s.a. 460: Mar. Avent. s.a. 460: *Chron. Gall. a. 451*, 634: Cassiod. *Chron.* 1270: Proc. *BV* 1.7.11–14: Theoph. AM 5964.
18. *Chron.Gall. a 511*, 634; Mar. Avent. *s.a.* 460; Hyd.195 [200] *s.a.* 460.
19. On the Romans not having a fleet after 461, Prisc. fr. 39.1.
20. Mathisen, 1998.
21. Sid. *Ep.* 1.11: *Chron. Gall. a. 451*, 633, 635.
22. Hyd. *Chron.* 204 [209], s.a.460
23. Cf Clover, 1966, 178–79.
24. Prisc. fr. 35.2.
25. Cf Hyd. 209: Joh. Ant. fr. 203: Prisc. fr. 29: Malal. 14.

26. Clover, 1966, 214–15, esp. p.215, n.1.
27. Corsica Hyd. 176, 177: cf Clover, 1966, 215, 222.
28. Vict. Vit. 1.51: cf Clover, 1966, 216–17.
29. Cf Clover, 1966, 179f.
30. Treaty of 442, Hughes, 2012, 122: These women were returned to the East in 462: Hyd. 211 [216], s.a. 462.
31. Hughes, 2012, 188–89: Hyd. s.a. 456; Prisc. fr. 24; Sid. Ap. *Carm.* 2.367.
32. Cf Joh. Ant. fr. 203: Malal. 14.
33. *Chron. Gall. a 511*, 635

Chapter 13: The Renewal of War

1. On his way to Rome, Hyd. 205 [210], s.a. 461; Prisc. fr. 36.2: ' Arranging business essential for the empire and prestige of Rome', Hyd. 205 [210], s.a. 461.
2. Date, *Fast. Vind. Prior.* 588, s.a. 461: cf Marc. *com.* s.a. 461; Theoph. AM 5955.
3. Cf Prisc. fr. 36.2: 'Ricimer's men seized [Majorian], stripped him of his purple and his diadem, beat him, and cut off his head.' According to the *Fasti Vindobonenses Priori*, Majorian was beheaded on the fifth day after the meeting, close to the River Ira: *Fast. Vind. Prior.* 588, s.a. 461.
4. Prisc. fr. 38 (1).
5. Theoph. *Chron.* AM 5955: *Chron. Gall.* s.a. 511, 636.
6. Marc. Com. s.a. 465: Jord. *Rom.* 336.
7. Prisc. fr. 38. 8–10.
8. Prisc. fr. 38. 8–10.
9. The patrimony may have been part of the property in the East from Theodosus I's mother, Galla Placidia: see Blockley, 395, n.154.
10. Prisc. fr. 38. 11f.
11. Hyd, 216, dates the treaty to the first year of Severus' reign. Consequently, it could be dated to 461 but due to the negotiations more likely 462: cf Clover, 1966, 188.
12. Prisc. fr. 38. 15–16.
13. Hyd. 216: Prisc. fr. 29, 30, 40: Proc. BV 1.5.6: Joh. Ant. fr. 204: *Chron. Pasch.* s.a. 455: Zon. 13, 25, 28.
14. Eudoxia ransomed, *Chron. Pasch.* s.a. 455.
15. Cf Clover, 1966, 187, referencing: Prisc. fr. 29: Proc. BV 1.5.6: Vict. Vit. 2.2: Malch. fr. 13: *Chron. Pasch.* s.a. 464: Malal. 14: Theoph. AM 5947, 5949, 5964: Zon. 13.25, 28: Evag. 2.7: Niceph. 15.11: and esp. Hyd. 211 [216], s.a. 462.
16. Prisc. fr. 29: Proc. BV 1.5.6: Vict. Vit. 2.2: Malch. fr. 13: *Chron. Pasch.* s.a. 464: Malal. 14: Theoph. AM 5947, 5949, 5964: Zon. 13.25, 28: Evag. 2.7: Niceph. 15.11: and esp. Hyd. 211 [216], s.a. 462.
17. Cf Prisc. fr. 30.
18. Cf Clover, 1966, 191.
19. Prisc. fr. 30.

20. Prisc. fr. 29–32, but contra, Clover, 1966, 180, 182.
21. Sid. Carm. 2. 346–48.
22. Italy unstable, Sid. Carm. 2. 346–48.
23. Olybrius, Prisc. fr. 38.1: Joh. Ant. fr. 204: Gaudentius, Prisc. fr. 38.2.
24. Vict. Vit. 1.51: cf Proc. BV 1.5.22f; 1.22.16–18: Prisc. fr. 52 (40): Vit. Dan. Styl. 56: Greg. Rom. Dial. 3.1: Nest. Baz. Herac. p.379.
25. Jacobsen, 2012, 137.
26. Cf Clover, 1966, 218.
27. Clover, 1966, 183.
28. Pris. fr. 39. 16f.
29. Cf Clover, 1966, 180, 183.
30. Clover, 1966, 190.
31. Prisc. fr. 39.1.
32. Prisc. fr. 30: cf Clover, 1966, 191.
33. Hyd. 220 [224], 228, s.a. 464–465: Date, Clover, 1966, 182–83, esp. 183, n.1: Muhlberger, 1990, 210–310.
34. Clover, 1966, 184.
35. Hyd. 224, 228.
36. See below: contra, see Drinkwater, 2007, 270.
37. Clover, 1966, 191–92: cf Candid. fr. 1.
38. Prisc. fr. 25, 31, 32, 39.
39. Date e.g. *Anon. Cusp.* s.a. 464: see note 61.
40. *Fast. Vind. Prior.* s.a. 464; Cass. *Chron.* s.a. 464; Mar. *com.* s.a. 464; Paul Diac. *Hist. Rom.* 15.1. Jordanes, *Getica* 236, places the battle in the reign of Anthemius.
41. Hyd. 223 [227] s.a. 465; 227 [231] s.a. 465–466: cf Prisc. fr. 29, 30.
42. Contra, MacGeorge, 2003, 50. Interestingly, MacGeorge later claims (p.54) that Marcellinus will have not had a fleet, discounting her own suggestion that he landed in Sicily on his own initiative.
43. On the interpretation of these events, see Clover, 1966, 192f.
44. Hyd. 131, 200.
45. Hyd. 224, 228.
46. *Pasch. Camp.* s.a. 465; Jord. *Rom.* 336; Jord. *Get.* 236. Given the date of Severus' second *novella*, the date of 15 August given by the *Fasti Vindobonenses Priores* (s.a. 465) is probably a mistake.
47. Sid. Ap. *Carm.* 2. 317–318.
48. Envoys, Hyd. 233 (s.a. 466): Salla, Isid. Sev. 33: Euric's assassination of Theoderic, *Chron. Gall.* 511 10, s.a. 466: Mar. Av. a. 467.
49. Sid. Carm. 2 341–86: Prisc. fr. 30.
50. Prisc. fr. 38. 1–2: see Chapter 8.
51. Goth, Jord. Get. 239, Damascius, Epitome Photiana, 69 = Photius Bbl. 242: Alan, Candidus = Photius Bibl. 79.

52. Prisc. fr. 35.
53. Vit. S. Dan. Styl. 55.
54. Prisc. fr. 39.
55. Proc. BV 1.5.23.
56. Proc. 3.5.22–26.
57. Cf Clover, 1966, 193.
58. Mathisen, 1998, analysing Malalas, *Chron.* 368–369: see Chapter 5.
59. Sid. Ap. Carm. 2. 67.
60. PLRE 2, *Anthemius 3*, 96–98.
61. PLRE 2, *Anthemius 3*, 96–98.
62. Proc. 3.6.5: cf MacGeorge, 2003, 234.
63. Sid. Ep. 1.5.10–11.
64. Sid. Ep. 1.5.10–11.
65. Marc. *com.* s.a. 468: Jord. *Get.* 239.
66. Hyd. 230 [234] s.a. 465–466.
67. Date, *Fast. Vind. Prior.* no.597, s.a.467: cf Marc. *com. Chron.* s.a. 467. Cassiodorus (*Chron.* 1283 s.a. 467) claims this was at a place called Brontotas, 3 miles from the city, whereas Hydatius (231 [235] s.a. 465–466) claims it was 8 miles from Rome. Cf Mar. Avench. A 467.
68. Gillet, 'Rome, Ravenna and the Last Western Emperors', *Papers of the British School at Rome,* Vol. 69, Centenary Volume (2001), 131–67, p.132.
69. Famines, Theoph. AM 5964; Sid. *Ep.* 1.10.2: Pestilence, Gelasius, col. 113; Celestial Phenomena, Hyd. 238 [244] s.a. 467; Cattle disease, Fast. Vind. Prior. s.a. 467.
70. Marc. com. s.a. 467.
71. On context and dating, MacGeorge, 2002, 230.
72. Joh. Ant. fr. 206.
73. See below on Marcellinus in Sicily.
74. Proc. 3.6.5.
75. Malchus fr. 17, p.424: Conant, 2015, 86–88.
76. Hyd. 235, 238, 240, 247: cf Jord. *Get.* 244.
77. Hyd. 236 [240] s.a. 466–467.
78. On the dating of these attacks, see Clover, 1966, 193f; cf Gordon, 1960, 120: attacks on the West are implied by Sidonius (Carm. 2.348–50; cf Theoph. AM 5961). See also, Merrills and Miles, 2014, 281, n.76.
79. Proc. BV 1.5.22–26; cf 1.66.
80. Vit. S. Dan. Styl. 56: poss. Vict. Vit. 1.51.
81. Clover, 1966, 193–94, n.2.
82. Gordon, 1960, 69.
83. Malch. fr. 3.
84. Proc. BV 1.5.22–25.

85. Vict. Vit. 1.51.
86. Proc. BV 1.22.16–18.
87. Second wave of attacks, Proc. BV 1.5.22–25: cf Sid. Carm. 2.348–55: Prisc. fr. 30.
88. Proc. 3.5.22–26: cf Vict. Vit. 1.51: Rhodes, Nest. *Baz. Her.* p.379: Clover, 1966, 193, esp. n.4.
89. Proc. BV 1.5.22–25.
90. Clover, 1966, 222.
91. For more on Hydatius, especially on his dating of events outside Hispania, see the Introduction.
92. Hyd. 223 [227] s.a. 465.
93. Hyd. 232 [236] s.a. 466–467.
94. *Cons. Const.* 468a.
95. Hyd. 232 [236] s.a. 466–467.

Chapter 14: The Roman Invasion

1. Proc. 3.6.8f.
2. Panegyric, *Carm.* 1: Sid. *Eps.* 1.9.6; 9.16.3: cf Greg. Tur. 2.21. Cf MacGeorge, 2002, 236.
3. On the nature of the missions, see O'Flynn, 1983, 118f., and MacGeorge, 2002, 242.
4. Proc. 3.6.1–2.
5. Proc. 3.6.8: '[Leo] bade [Marcellinus] go to the island of Sardinia, which was then subject to the Vandals.'
6. Hyd. 241 (247) s.a. 468; cf MacGeorge, 2002, 57. Marcellinus' *comitatus* of Huns had been bribed by Ricimer in 461.
7. MacGeorge, 2002, 58; *Liber. Pont.* 48.
8. Proc. 3.6.9: Marsus, Theoph. AM 5963.
9. Prisc. fr. 41: PLRE 2, *Heraclius 4*, 541–42.
10. Brother of Verina, Prisc. fr. 53.1; Vit. Dan. Styl. 69; Marc. com. s.a.475; Jord. Rom. 337; Zach. HE 5.1; Proc. 3.6.2 etc. On his competence, see below.
11. Prisc. fr. 53.1: PLRE 2, *Basiliscus 2*, 212–14: *Consulship. CIL V 5685*; Prisc. fr. 53.3.
12. PLRE 2, *Basiliscus 2*, 213.
13. Prisc. fr. 43.
14. Four years, Williams & Friell, 1998, 175.
15. Gordon, 1960, 205, n.11: Cedrenus p.613 (however, this appears to be '1115' in the *Migne Patrologia Graeca*; p.667, see bibliography).
16. Theod. Lect. 1.25.
17. E.g. MacGeorge, 2002, 57, has the translation 'marines'.
18. This is implied by Malchus, fr. 17, where Gaiseric's son and successor Huneric finally renounces the claim to compensation over the loss of Vandal shipping.
19. See below.

20. Procopius (3.5.18–19) noted the claim that there were 80,0000 Vandals, but suggests that the actual number was 50,000.
21. Sid. Ap. Carm. 5. 397–424: Corripus, Ioh. 3. 236–55: Proc. BV 1. 8.20, 1.19.15: CJ. 1.27.1.3.
22. Proc. 3.6.8.
23. Theoph. AM 5963.
24. Theoph. AM 5963.
25. Prisc. fr. 53.1. There is a *lacuna* in the text which is sometimes amended to a specific number.
26. Proc. 3.6.10.
27. Hyd. 230 [234] s.a. 465–466.
28. Williams & Friell, 1998, 175.
29. Cf Proc. 3.6.5.
30. AM 31.12.13f: Hughes, 2013, 191–92.
31. For more details on these campaigns, see Hughes, 2012, esp. 79f. and Chapter 10, 'The Treaty of 442'.
32. Thucydides, *History of the Peloponnesian War*, 7.53.4: '[The rest of the Athenian fleet] the enemy tried to burn by means of an old merchantman which they filled with faggots and pine-wood, set on fire, and let drift down the wind which blew full on the Athenians. The Athenians, however, alarmed for their ships, contrived means for stopping it and putting it out, and checking the flames and the nearer approach of the merchantman, thus escaped the danger.'
33. Cf Theoph. AM 5961.
34. Williams & Friell, 1998, 174–75.
35. Traitors, Hyd. 195 [200], s.a. 460.
36. Proc. 3.6.16.
37. Theod. Lect. 1.25.
38. Joh. Mal. 14.44. Cf Prisc. fr. 53; Phot. Bibl. 79; Theod. Lect. Epit. 399; Zon. 14.1.24–26.
39. Theoph. AM 5963.
40. Proc. 3.6.26; Nic. Call. *HE*. 15.27: cf Bury, 1923, 337.
41. Withdrew, Proc. 3.6.25; Theoph. AM 5963: Helped Leo v. Aspar, Theoph. AM 5963.
42. Date, Fast. Vind. Prior. s.a. 468; Quote, Proc. 3.6.25: cf Pasch. Camp. s.a. 468; Cass. *Chron*. s.a. 468; Marc. com. s.a. 468; Cons. Ital. s.a. 468. But cf Marc. *com*. s.a. 468, who claims that Marcellinus was in Africa.
43. Proc. BV 1.4.28, but cf Damasc. Vit. Isid. 91; Goffart, 1980, 63, n.12.

Chapter 15: End Game

1. Lame, Jordanes, *Get*. 168
2. Vic. Vit. 2. 8–9.

3. Isid. Sev. *Hist*. 34: date, Hyd. 238 [242] s.a. 468.

4. Isid. Sev. *Hist*. 34.

5. Greg. Tur. 2.27. It should be noted that not all authorities accept this tradition.

6. '*Pellitus Geta*', Ennod. *Vit. Epiph*. 67: '*Galata concitatus*', Ennod. *Vit. Epiph*. 53.

7. Joh. Ant. fr. 207, Paul. Diac. 15.2: O'Flynn, 1983, 119; contra, Clover, 1966, 201.

8. Nest. *Baz. Herac*. *2.2.379*: cf Clover, 1966, 76–77.

9. Joh. Ant. fr. 207.

10. See also: Cass. *Chron*. 1289 s.a. 470, where Romanus was killed for a 'capital crime against the State': Paul Diac. 15.2, where he was found guilty of treason: cf Joh. Ant. fr. 207.

11. Joh. Ant. fr. 207. Note that Clover, 1966, 201 n.1, claimed that this is a mistake and that it was Anthemius who went north to Milan.

12. O'Flynn, 1983, 120: Zeno the Isaurian, Jord. Rom. 338.

13. There is no evidence that any military campaign by Leo to support Anthemius would have resulted in an alliance between Ricimer and Gaiseric: see O'Flynn, 1983, 120.

14. The date is secure thanks to Sidonius noting that Gabali was still a Roman city in 469: Sid. Ep. 5.13.2: cf PLRE 2, *Victorius 4*, 1163. These territories were either to the west of, south-west of or within the region of the Auvergne: see Map 17.

15. This is the opinion of, amongst others, Clover, 1966, 199.

16. Theoph. AM 5963 – see Chapter 14 for the full text. Correct dating to 470, e.g. Wolfram, 1997, 173.

17. Joh. Ant. fr. 207.

18. Proc. BV 1.6.9.

19. Theoph. AM 5963: cf Merrills and Miles, 2014, 122.

20. *V. S. Marcelli*, 34; Marc. *com*. s.a. 471; Jord. *Get*. 239; Joh. Mal. fr. 31: PLRE 2, *Leontia 1*, 667.

21. Date, PLRE 2, *Ecidicius 3*, 383–84: cf Sid. *Ep*. 3.3. 3–6: Greg. Tur. 2. 24: PLRE 2, *Ecdicius 3*, 38384.

22. This section relies heavily upon the account given by Ennodius in his 'Life of Epiphanius', especially 51f. As a hagiography, many of the details are suspect but as little other information is available there is little choice but to use it.

23. O'Flynn, 1983, 119: Ennod. *Vit. Epiph*. 51–74.

24. *Chron. Gall*. 511, 13.

25. *Chron. Gall*. 511, 649, s.a. 471.

26. Vict. Vit. 3.19: Vict. Tonn. s.a. 523: 'Sixteen Years', Theoph AM 5964: Zon. 8.25.29.

27. Theoph AM 5964: Zon. 8.25.30: Nic. Call. 15.12.

28. Cf Malch. fr. 13.

29. Paul. Diac. 15.4: MacGeorge, 2002, 254, n.16.

30. Joh. Ant. fr. 209 (1).

31. Cf Mal. 374–75. For a full discussion concerning the arrival of Olybrius and its implications, see Hughes, 2015, 154f.
32. For the dating, see Mathisen, 1998, Olybrius.
33. Merrills and Miles, 2014, 123: cf PLRE 2, *Anicius Olybrius 6*, 796–98.
34. Sid. *Carm.* 2. 357–65: Prisc. 29, 30: cf Joh. Ant. fr. 204: further analysis, O'Flynn, 1983, 124.
35. Clover, 1966, 205–06, n.1.
36. O'Flynn, 1983, 122.
37. Contra, O'Flynn, 1983, 120: PLRE 2, *Anicius Olybrius 6*, 796–98.
38. Joh. Ant. *fr.* 209.1–2, trans. Gordon, 1960, 122f: Malal. 37: Date, *Fast. Vind. Prior.* 606, s.a. 472 – ' *his cons. bellum civile gestum est Romae inter Anthemius imperatorem et Ricimere patricio, et levatus est imp. Olybrius Romae, et occisus est imp. Anthemius V idus Iulias*'.
39. Cass. *Chron.* 1293, s.a. 472: Paul. Diac. 15.4.
40. Gelasius, *Adversus Andromachum*, col. 115: cf MacGeorge, 2002, 255.
41. Malal. 373–75.
42. Thirty days and 'vomiting much blood', Joh. Ant. fr. 209.2, trans. Gordon, 1960, 122–23: forty days, Cass. 1293, s.a. 472.
43. Fast. Vind. Prior. 607.
44. *Fast. vind. prior.*608: Paul. Diac. 15.5.
45. Joh. Ant. fr. 209. 2, trans. Gordon, 1960, 122–23: thirteen days after Ricimer, Joh. Ant. fr. 209. 2: seventh month, Cass. *Chron.* 1293: cf Enn. *Vit. Epiph.* 350: date of 22 October, *Fasti vindobonenses priores (no. 609)*: date of 2 November, *Paschale Campanum*.
46. Date, *Pasch. Camp.* s.a. 473, but cf *Fast. Vind. Prior.* s.a. 473, which gives the date as 5 March. Ravenna and support of the army, Paul. Diac. 15.5. See also: Jord. *Get.* 239; Ennod. *Vit. Epiph.* 79 = pp.350–51; Evag. 2.16; Marc. *com.* s.a. 473; Joh. Ant. fr. 209.2; Mar. Avench. s.a. 473.
47. Mathisen, 1998, *Glycerius*, notes Glycerius' lack of movement but gives no reason.
48. *Gallic Chronicle of 511*, n. 653.
49. *Chron. Caes.(The Chronicle of Saragossa)* s.a. 473: cf Isid. Sev. *Hist.* 34, but see Chapter 15.
50. Jord. *Get.* 284.
51. Joh. Ant. fr. 209.2: Gordon trans., p.122.
52. Jord. Get. 237.
53. Mathisen, 1998.
54. Title, *CJ* 6.61.6a (1 June 473).
55. Proc. BV 4.7.26: cf Merrills and Miles, 2014, 123.
56. *Auct. Haun. ordo. post.* s.a. 474; Theoph. AM 5966; *V. Dan. Styl.* 67: dysentery, Joh. Mal. 376; Cedr. 1. 614–15; Mich. Syr. 9. 4.
57. For details and sources concerning Zeno, see PLRE 2, *Fl. Zenon 7*, 1200–02.

58. At the order of Zeno, not Leo, *Anon. Val.* 7.36, s.a. 474.

59. Cf Joh. Ant. fr. 209.2: *Anon. Val.* 7.36, s.a. 474.

60. Date 19 June, *Auct. Haun. ordo post.* s.a.474: date 24 June, *Fast. vind. prior.* 613–14.

61. See previous chapter.

62. Sid. *Ep.* 3. 7.1: cf MacGeorge, 2002, 273, n.19.

63. Cf Clover, 1966, 208–09.

64. Malchus, fr. 3, trans. Gordon, 1960, 124.

65. Nicopolis, Malchus, fr. 3: Caenopolis and Zacynthus, Proc. BV 1.22.16–18.

66. Jord. *Get.* 244.

67. Malch. fr. 2. On other interpretations of this affair, see Clover, 1966, 202f.: Merrills & Miles, 2014, 123f.: Blockley, 1992, 77.

68. Merrills and Miles, 2014, 123.

69. Cf Malch. fr. 17: Vict. Vit. 4.7.26.

70. Wolfram, 1997, 173.

71. Merrills and Miles, 2014, 123f.

72. Vict. Vit. 1.51–52: Clover, 1966, 210.

73. Clover, 1966, 211.

74. Hostages, Merrills and Miles, 2014, 123f.

75. Cf Malch. fr. 3, 13: Vict. Vit. 1.51: Proc. BV 1.7.26–27. cf Clover, 1966, 210.

76. Jord. *Get.* 241: *Patricius*, e.g. Fast. Vind. Prior. s.a. 475, 476.

77. Mathisen, *Julius Nepos*, 1998.

78. Ennod. *Vit. Epiph.* 91, but cf Sid. *Ep.* 5.12, who refers to a truce, not a treaty.

79. Ennod. *Vit. Epiph.* 79–91, trans. Cook, G.M., in Ferrari, 1952, 324.

80. Wolfram, 1990, 459, n.258: cf 186–87.

81. Mathisen, *Julius Nepos*, 1998, claims that Nepos recognized the Vandals' possession of Africa, Sardinia, Corsica, the Balearics and part of Sicily in a treaty. Unfortunately, he provides no source for the assertion and it is probable that the treaty actually belongs to the reign of Romulus Augustulus – see Chapter 15.

82. Sid. *Ep.* 6.7.6: Greg. Tur. 25.

83. Cf *Auct Haun ordo post.* s.a.475, '*Nepos cum ab Oreste patricio cum exercitu persequeretur, fugiens ad Dalmatias usque navigavit*': Jord. *Get.* 241: *Anon. Vales.* 7.36, s.a. 474.

84. Date, *Fast. Vind. Prior.* 615, s.a. 475: *Salona, Anon. Val.* 7.36, s.a. 474: cf *Auct. Haun. ord. prior.* s.a. 475; Jord. *Get.* 241.

85. Prisc. fr. 7, 8, 11 (2), 12 and 15 (2): *Anon. Val.* 8.38: accepted as same man, e.g. O'Flynn, 1983, 133–34: doubts, see MacGeorge, 2002, 276f.

86. Distrust, MacGeorge, 2002, 276.

87. *Anon. Val.* 8.37; 7.36: *Fast. Vind. Prior.* s.a. 475: *Auct. Haun. ordo prior.* s.a. 475: *Auct. Haun. ordo post.* s.a. 475: *Auct. Haun. ordo post. marg.* s.a. 475: Jord. *Get.* 241; *Rom.* 344: Marc. *com.* s.a. 475: Proc. BG. 1.1.2: Evag. 2.16: Theoph. AM 5965.

88. *Auct. Haun. ordo prior.* s.a. 475: Proc. 1. 1. 2.

89. As shown on coins; PLRE 2, *Romulus 3*, 959–60: Proc. 5.1.2.

90. *Anon. Val.* 8.37; 7.36: *Fast. Vind. Prior.* s.a. 475: *Auct. Haun. ordo prior.* s.a. 475: *Auct. Haun. ordo post.* s.a. 475: *Auct. Haun. ordo post. marg.* s.a. 475: Jord. *Get.* 241; *Rom.* 344: Marc. *com.* s.a. 475: Proc. BG. 1.1.27: Evag. 2.16.

91. *Auct. Haun. ordo. prior.* s.a. 476, 486.

92. It is possible that he simply continued negotiation opened by Nepos prior to his expulsion.

93. Clover, 1966, 212, n.1.

94. Paul Diac. 15.7, stating that it was the year after the accession of Augustulus. See Clover, 1966, for a more detailed analysis of the historiography of the treaty.

95. Proc. BV 3.10.25–27.

96. Cod. Ius. 1.27.1.

97. Merrills and Miles, 2014, 131, 284, n.124.

98. Cf Vict. Vit. 1.14: Merrills & Miles, 2014, 131.

99. See below.

100. Proc. 5.1.5.

101. Proc. 5.1.3–8.

102. On Orestes, see e.g. Eugipp. *Vita S. Sev.* 7: but cf Jord. *Get.* 242.

103. Joh. Ant. fr. 209: bodyguard, Proc. 5.1.6.

104. Jord. *Get.* 242.

105. *Ennod. V. Epiph.* 95–100.

106. Ennod. *V. Epiph.* 358.

107. Ennod. *V. Epiph.* 95–100: *Anon. Val.* 8.37: Eugipp. *Ep. Ad Pasc.* 8: Jord. *Get.* 242: Proc. 1.1.5: *Fast. Vind. Prior.* s.a. 476: *Auct. Haun. ordo prior.* s.a. 476: *Auct. Haun. ordo post.* s.a. 476: *Auct. Haun. ordo post. marg.* s.a. 476: Cass. *Chron.* s.a. 476: Marcell. *com.* s.a. 476.

108. Mathisen, 1997.

109. Anon. Val. 8.38; 10.45: Jord. *Get.* 241–42; *Rom.* 344: Proc. 1.1.7: Theoph. Am 5965: Marc. *com.* s.a. 476: but cf Marc. *com.* s.a.476: Jordanes *Get,* 242.

110. Malch. fr. 10.

111. Coins, Thompson, 1982, 67 and associated bibliography: PLRE 2, Odovacer, Addenda, p. xxxix.

112. Cf Thompson, 1982, 69.

113. Bury, 1923, 343, claims that Zeno acceded to the claim. However, an analysis of his sources suggest this may be an error: Procopius (5.12.20) claims that it was Odovacer who relinquished the claim to Provence, whereas Candidus (fr. 1) notes only that the 'Gauls of the West revolted'.

114. Odovacer takes power in August, *Auct. Haun. ordo post.* and *marg.* s.a. 476: sea closed to navigation, Veg. *Epit. Rei Mil.* 4.39; Clover, 1993, 237.

115. Clover, 1966, 213.

116. Born *c.* 390, died 477.

Conclusion

1. Clover, 1986, 1.
2. Malchus, fr. 17: Vict. Vit. 2.2–6: discussion, Merrill and Miles, 2010, 124.
3. Property returned, Malchus, fr. 13.
4. E.g. Clover, 1993, 239.
5. Vict. Vit, 1.14: see Chapter 15.

Appendix

1. Hyd. 1.13: Burgess, 1993, 83.
2. E.g. Land taken and distributed, Merrills and Miles, 2014, 66: Sarris, 2011, 58, 90: tax revenues, Schwarcz, 2004, referenced in Halsall, 445. n.99.
3. Merrills and Miles, 2014, 67–68.
4. Passio s. Vincentii Aginensis 6, in Allecta Bollandiana 70 (1952): cf Goffart, 1980, 40.
5. Halsall, 2007, 227: cf Kulikowski & Bowes, 2005, 44: Merrills & Miles, 2014, 44.
6. Hyd. 1.13: Burgess, 1993, 83.
7. Lewis and Short, Latin dictionary: http://www.perseus.tufts.edu/hopper/morph?l=sors&la=la&can=sors0#lexicon
8. Thompson, 1992, 154.
9. Oros. 7.42: 'To take up at this point the succession of usurpers as briefly as possible, Constans, the son of Constantine, was killed at Vienne by Gerontius, his count, a worthless rather than an upright man, who replaced Constans by a certain Maximus. Gerontius himself, however, was killed by his own soldiers. Maximus, stripped of the purple and abandoned by the troops of Gaul, which were transferred to Africa and then recalled to Italy, is now a needy exile living among the barbarians in Spain.'
10. Vict. Vita, 1.13.

Outline Chronology

408–409	Britain secedes from Constantine III's rule.
409	Rebellion of Gerontius in Hispania, who proclaims Maximus as emperor: Gerontius offers land to the coalition in return for service. The coalition crosses the Alps. Honorius accepts Constantine III as co-ruler. Second siege of Rome by Alaric, who elects Attalus as emperor.
410	Alaric deposes Attalus but is attacked. On 24 August, Alaric sacks Rome. Placidia, daughter of Theodosius and sister of Honorius, taken captive by Goths. Death of Alaric and succession of Athaulf. Honorius breaks with Constantine III. Gerontius invades Gaul and lays siege to Vienne.
411	Gerontius takes Vienne, lays siege to Constantine in Arles. Constantius, the new Roman *magister militum*, advances on Arles. Gerontius' troops desert and he is eventually killed. Maximus flees to the coalition in Hispania. Constantius takes Arles, Constantine III executed. Revolt of Jovinus in north Gaul.
412	Constantius forces the Goths out of Italy into Gaul. Athaulf agrees to support Jovinus but then turns against and defeats the usurper. In Africa, Heraclian revolts and declares himself emperor. Constantius agree treaty with coalition. The coalition settle in Hispania.
413	Athaulf captures the usurper Jovinus, who is executed. The usurper Heraclian invades Italy from Africa, but is defeated and flees back to Africa. Athaulf is repulsed at Marseilles but captures Bordeaux, Toulouse and Narbonne.
414	Athaulf marries Placidia, sister of the Emperor Honorius. Death of Heraclian. Constantius blockades Goths in Gaul. Birth of Theodosius, son of Athaulf and Placidia.
415	Athaulf leads Goths into Hispania and takes Barcelona. Death of Theodosius. War between the Siling Vandals and Alans against the Goths. Assassination of Athaulf. Short reign of Sigeric. Wallia becomes Gothic leader.
416	Romano-Gothic peace treaty. Placidia returned to Rome.
417	First Gothic campaign: destruction of the Alans.
418	Second Gothic campaign: destruction of the Siling Vandals. Usurper Maximus flees to safety of Gallaecia. Remnants of the Silings and Alans join the Asdings in Gallaecia.
419	Goths settled in Gaul: Kingdom of Toulouse founded. In Gallaecia, Maximus proclaimed emperor. Birth of Valentinian, son of Constantius and Placidia.
420	War between the Sueves and Vandals: Sueves besieged in 'Erbasian Mountains'. Romans under Asterius relieve siege but force under

	Maurocellus advances to Braga, the Suevic capital, and then retreat in disorder: assumed Maximus eliminated.
421	Constantius becomes Emperor Constantius III. Death of Constantius III.
422	Battle between the Vandals and Castinus: defeat of Roman army.
422–443	Placidia and Valentinian move to Constantinople.
423	Death of Honorius. The *magister militum* Castinus elevates a man named John to emperor. Bonifacius in Africa refuses to acknowledge John.
424	Possible campaign to take Africa from Bonifacius by John fails. Eastern Emperor Theodosius II nominates Valentinian as new Western emperor. John sends Aetius to Huns for aid.
421–424	(Precise date unknown) Vandals move from Gallaecia to Baetica.
425	Eastern army invades West: defeats John, who is captured and executed. Aetius arrives with Hunnic army and is given post of *magister militum per Gallias* as inducement to join new regime. Valentinian (III) crowned new Western emperor. Eastern general named Felix the new *magister militum* in West.
426–427	Vandals secure position in Baetica: attack Cartagena, raid Balearic Islands. Small force sent to raid Seville. Goths lay siege to Arles, but attacked by Aetius withdraw and treaty signed.
427	Roman civil war with Bonifacius in Africa. Expedition sent from Italy but defeated. Possible minor campaign by Goths against the Vandals.
428	Second expedition against Bonifacius. Possible alliances between at least some Vandals and Bonifacius. Vandals capture Seville. Death of Gunderic, King of the Vandals: accession of half-bother Gaiseric.
429	May, Vandals begin crossing to Africa. End of Roman civil war. Truce between Vandals and Rome.
430	War resumes. First Battle of Hippo Regius: Gaiseric victorious, Bonifacius retreats into Hippo, which is laid under siege. Death of Felix.
431	Vandals raise siege of Hippo. Arrival of Aspar from the East with reinforcements. Rebellion in Noricum. Franks invade Gaul.
432	Second Battle of Hippo Regius: Gaiseric victorious, Vandals storm Hippo. Bonifacius recalled to Rome. Roman civil war: Bonifacius defeats Aetius at Battle of Rimini. Death of Bonifacius. Attempt to assassinate Aetius, who flees to Huns.
433	Return of Aetius with Hunnic army: Aetius appointed *magister militum*. War with the Burgundians.
434	Trygetius sent to Africa to negotiate with Vandals.

435	Romano–Vandal treaty: Vandals given land in Africa, Gaiseric probably given Imperial post.
436–7	Roman war with Goths, who besiege Narbonne.
437	Gaiseric evicts Catholic bishops from Vandal territory. Barbarian 'pirates' (probably Vandals) attack Empire.
438	'Pirates' plunder parts of Sicily and other Mediterranean islands.
439	Gaiseric takes Carthage by 'a ruse'.
440	Vandal fleets raid Mediterranean.
441	Armada sails from Constantinople intending to attack Vandals, delays in Sicily. Huns attack Eastern Empire.
442	Treaty of 442: Vandals accepted as rulers of Carthage, land previously held by Vandals returned to Empire. Extended peace with Empire. Betrothal of Huneric, Gaiseric's son, and Eudocia, daughter of Valentinian III. Moors come to terms with Gaiseric.
451	Battle of Catalaunian Plains: defeat of Attila.
452	Attila invades Italy, retires without attacking Rome.
453(?)	Proposed marriage of Placidia, daughter of Valentinian III, to Majorian, a member of Aetius' staff. Aetius intervenes: Placidia engaged to Gaudentius, son of Aetius. Majorian retires to estates.
454	Death of Aetius.
455	Assassination of Valentinian III: Petronius Maximus becomes emperor. Vandals sack Rome. Empress Eudoxia and her daughters Eudocia and Placidia taken to Carthage. Accession of Avitus.
456	Envoys sent to Gaiseric from both East and West: rebuffed. Battles of Agrigentum and Corsica: Vandal raiders defeated.
456–7	Roman civil war: Death of Avitus; accession of Majorian. Death of Marcian: Leo new emperor in East.
457	Battle of Campania: Vandals under Gaiseric's half-brother-in-law defeated. Gaiseric changes strategy and moves focus to Mediterranean islands.
457f	Majorian raises troops and builds navy to re-establish Roman control in West.
458	Vandal embassy to Sueves and Goths fails. Rome defeats Goths in Gaul. Vandal raids continue.
459	Vandal raids continue.
460	Majorian leads attempt to conquer Africa: Battle of Elche, defeat of Roman fleet by Vandals.
461	Romano–Vandal Treaty. Assassination of Majorian: accession of Libius Severus. Treaty void. Aegidius in Gaul, Marcellinus in Dalmatia and Nepotianus in Hispania refuse to acknowledge Severus' reign.

462	Treaty between Vandals and East: East agrees not to interfere in West, Eudoxia and Pulcheria released from Carthage.
463	War resumes with West. Vandal raids on Western Empire.
464	Envoys arrive in Carthage from Aegidius. Death of Aegidius.
465	Leo sends Marcellinus to help West. Death of Severus: interregnum. Euric becomes Gothic king.
466	Vandal attacks on Dalmatia (?).
467	Anthemius declared Western emperor. Ricimer defeats Ostrogothic invasion of Noricum. Imperial embassies to Gaiseric rebuffed. Gothic King Euric sends envoys to Gaiseric. Vandal attacks on the East. Possible attempt by Marcellinus in Sicily to invade Africa: foiled by weather.
468	Roman invasion of Vandal kingdom. Marcellinus conquers Sardinia; Heraclius conquers Tripolitana; Basiliscus invades Africa Proconsularis. Battle of Cap Bon: Romans defeated, end of invasion. Death of Marcellinus. Euric extends kingdom into northern Hispania and Tarraconensis.
469	Vandal raids resume against both East and West.
470	Civil war in Italy. Execution of Aspar in East. Euric expands kingdom in Gaul.
471	Truce in civil war. Defeat of Roman forces in Gaul. Death of Eudocia.
472	Resumption of Roman civil war. Elevation of Olybrius. Death of Anthemius. Death of Ricimer. Gundobad made *magister militum*. Death of Olybrius. Gaiseric opens negotiations with both East and West (?).
473	Gundobad makes Glycerius emperor. Euric captures Arles and Marseilles in Gaul. Ostrogothic invasion of Italy, Ostrogoths move on to Gaul and join Euric.
474	Death of Leo I. Julius Nepos nominated as Western emperor by new Eastern Emperor Zeno: invades Italy and crowned emperor. Glycerius deposed. Euric continues Gothic expansion in Gaul.
474–475	Treaty of Zeno and Gaiseric.
475	Truce agreed by Goths and Romans. Roman civil war: Nepos evicted and Romulus Augustulus crowned by *magister militum* Orestes.
476	Treaty of Orestes and Gaiseric. Civil war in Italy: Orestes defeated and killed, Augustulus 'retires'. Odovacer seizes power. Odovacer agrees treaty with Gaiseric. Euric seizes all of southern Gaul.
477	24 January 477, death of Gaiseric.

Select Bibliography

Primary Sources

Ambrose, *Expositio Evangelii Secundum Lucam*
  https://archive.org/details/expositioevange00schegoog
  http://www.ccel.org/ccel/schaff/npnf210
Augustine, St., *Carmen de Providentia Divina*
  http://www.documentacatholicaomnia.eu/02m/039o-0463,_Prosperus_
  Aquitanus,_Carmen_De_Provvidentia_Divina_%5BIncertus%5D,_MLT.pdf
Carmen ad Uxorem (Ad Coniugem Suam), tentatively ascribed to Prosper
  http://unsolicitedtranslations.blogspot.co.uk/2011/05/prosper-of-aquita-
  ine-ad-coniugem-suam.html
Epistles
  http://www.newadvent.org/fathers/1102.htm
  http://www.ccel.org/ccel/schaff/npnf101.i.html
  https://ia601408.us.archive.org/14/items/lettersofstaugus00sparuoft/lettersof-
  staugus00sparuoft.pdf
Cassiodorus, *Chronicle*
  http://www.roger-pearse.com/weblog/2014/12/29/
  cassiodorus-chronicle-now-online-in-english/
Cassius Dio, *Roman History*
  http://penelope.uchicago.edu/Thayer/E/Roman/Texts/Cassius_Dio/72*.html
Constantius of Lyon, *Vita Germani*
Noble, T.F.X. and Head, T., *Soldiers of Christ: Saints and Saints' Lives from Late
  Antiquity and the Early Middle Ages*, 75–106, London, 1995
CSEL
  http://www.earlymedievalmonasticism.org/Corpus-Scriptorum-
  Ecclesiasticorum-Latinorum.html
Eugippius, *Epistula ad Probam Virginem*
  http://archive.org/stream/ExcerptaExOperibusSAugustini/
  Excerpta_ex_operibus_S_Augustini#page/n47/mode/2up
Fulgentius, *Opera*
  https://archive.org/details/operafulg00fulguoft
Gregory the Great, *Letters and Sermons*, Feltoe, C.L., Edinburgh, 1895
  http://www.ccel.org/ccel/schaff/npnf212.i.html
Honoratus, *Epistula Consolatoria ad Arcadium actum in exsilium a Genserico rege
  Vandalorum*
  http://www.documentacatholicaomnia.eu/04z/z_0438-0438__Antoninus_
  Honoratus_Episcopus__Epistola_Consolatoria_Ad_Arcadium__MLT.pdf.html

Hydatius, *Chronicle*, Burgess, R.W., *The Chronicle of Hydatius and the Consularia Constantinopolitana*, Oxford, 1993

Isidore of Seville, *The History of the Goths* Trans. Donini, G., and G.B. Jr., 2nd Edition Leiden, 1970

Jerome, *Epistles*
http://www.newadvent.org/fathers/3001.htm

Leo, *Epistles*
http://www.roger-pearse.com/weblog/patrologia-latina-pl-volumes-available-online/

Mansi, G.D., (1760) *Sacrorum Conciliorum, Nova, et Amplissima Collectio, Tomus Quartus, Ab anno CCCCX. ad annum CCCCXXXI*, Florence
https://play.google.com/store/books/details?id=   OJVAAAAcAAJ&rdid=book OJVAAAAcAAJ&rdot=1

Marcellinus, *comes Chronicle* (Latin)
http://www.documentacatholicaomnia.eu/02m/0474-0534,_Marcellinus_Comes,_Chronicum,_MLT.pdf

Nestorius: The Bazaar of Heracleides, Driver, G.R., and Hodgson, L., (trans.), Ox, 1925
http://www.tertullian.org/fathers/nestorius_bazaar_0_intro.htm

Orosius, *Historiarum Adversum Paganos Libri VII (Seven Books of History Against the Pagans)*
https://sites.google.com/site/demontortoise2000/

Paulinus of Beziers, *Epigramma*
http://archive.org/stream/corpusscriptorum16stuoft#page/502/mode/2up

Pliny the Elder, *Natural History*
https://archive.org/stream/plinysnaturalhis00plinrich#page/n157/mode/2up

Possidius, *Vita S. Augustini*
http://www.tertullian.org/fathers/possidius_life_of_augustine_02_text.htm
https://archive.org/details/sanctiaugustiniv00possrich

Ptolemy, *Geography*
http://penelope.uchicago.edu/Thayer/E/Gazetteer/Periods/Roman/_Texts/Ptolemy/4/1*.html

Salvian, *On the Government of God*
http://www.tertullian.org/fathers/index.htm#On_the_Government_of_God

Sozomen, *Ecclesiastical History*
http://www.newadvent.org/fathers/2602.htm

Thucydides, *History of the Peloponnesian War*
https://en.wikisource.org/wiki/History_of_the_Peloponnesian_War/Book_7

Zosimus, *New History*
http://www.tertullian.org/fathers/

Secondary Sources

Barnish, S.J.B. (Trans.), (1992) *Cassiodorus: Variae*, Liverpool

Bigelow, P., (1918) *Genseric: King of the Vandals and First Prussian Kaiser*, New York

Birley, A., (1966) *Marcus Aurelius*, London

Blockley, R.C., (1983) *The Fragmentary Classicising Historians of the Later Roman Empire*, Vol. 2, Liverpool

Burgess, R.W., (1993) *Hydatius: The Chronicle of Hydatius and the Consularia Constantinopolitana*, Ox

Burgess, R.W., (1987) 'The Third Regnal Year of Eparchius Avitus: A Reply', *Classical Philology*, Vol. 82, No. 4 (Oct., 1987), pp.335–45

Burns, T.S., (1995) *Barbarians Within the Gates of Rome: A Study of Roman Military Policy and the Barbarians, ca. 375–425 A.D*, Indiana University Press
Volume II: https://archive.org/details/historyoflaterro02buryuoft

Bury, J.B., (1958) *History of the Later Roman Empire*, Dover Books
http://penelope.uchicago.edu/Thayer/E/Roman/Texts/secondary/BURLAT/home.html

Bury, J.B., (1923) *A History of the Later Roman Empire*, London, 2 Vols.
http://penelope.uchicago.edu/Thayer/E/Roman/Texts/secondary/BURLAT/

Bury, J.B., (1889) *A History of the Later Roman Empire from Arcadius to Irene*, London
Volume I: https://archive.org/details/historyoflaterro00bury

Cameron, A., and Garnsey, P., (eds), (2004) *The Cambridge Ancient History*, Cambridge

Casson, L., (1951) 'Speed Under Sail of Ancient Ships', *Transactions of the American Philological Association*, Vol. 82 (1951), pp.136–48
http://penelope.uchicago.edu/Thayer/E/Journals/TAPA/82/Speed_under_Sail_of_Ancient_Ships*html

Clover, F.M., (1986) *Felix Karthago*, Dumbarton Oaks

Clover, F.M., (1971) *Flavius Merobaudes: A Translation and Historical Commentary*, The American Philosophical Society

Clover, F.M., (1966) *Geiseric The Statesman: A Study of Vandal Foreign Policy*, PhD Diss, Chicago

Drinkwater, J.F., (2007) *The Alamanni and Rome 213–496: Caracalla to Clovis*, Ox

Drinkwater, J.F., (1998) 'The usurpers Constantine III (407–411) and Jovinus (411–413)', *Britannia* 29 (1998), pp.269–98

Drinkwater, J., and Elton, H., (2002) *Fifth-Century Gaul: A Crisis of Identity?*, Cambridge

Driver, G.R., and Hodgson, L., (1925) *Nestorius: The Bazaar of Heracleides: Newly translated from the Syriac and edited with an Introduction Notes & Appendices*, Ox

Elton, H., (2006) 'Warfare and the Military', in Lenski, N., *The Cambridge Companion to the Age of Constantine*, Cambridge

Elton, H., (1999) *Western Roman Emperors of the First Quarter of the Fifth Century: Constantine III (407–411 A.D.)*
http://www.luc.edu/roman-emperors/westemp5.htm

Evans, A.J., (1887) *Numismatic Chronicle*, 3rd series, Vol. VII.
http://archive.org/stream/thirdnumismatic07royauoft/thirdnumismatic07royauoft_djvu.txt

Feltoe, C.L., (1895) *Gregory the Great, Letters and Sermons*, Edinburgh
http://www.ccel.org/ccel/schaff/npnf212.i.html

Gibbon, E., (1861) *The Decline and Fall of the Roman Empire*, 4 vols, 1861

Goffart, W., (1980) *Barbarians and Romans, A.D. 418–584: The Techniques of Accommodation*, Princeton

Gordon, C.D., (1960) *The Age of Attila*, Michigan

Halsall, G., (2007) *Barbarian Migrations and the Roman West, 376–568*, Cambridge

Heather, P., (2005) *The Fall of the Roman Empire*, MacMillan

Hughes, I., (2013) *Imperial Brothers: Valentinian, Valens and the Disaster at Adrianople*, Barnsley

Hughes, I., (2012) Aetius: Attila's Nemesis, Barnsley

Hughes, I., (2010) *Stilicho: The Vandal Who Saved Rome*, Barnsley

Jacobsen, T.C., (2016) *A History of the Vandals*, Westholme

Jones, A.H.M., and Martindale, J.R., (1971) *The Prosopography of the Later Roman Empire: Volume 2, (A.D. 395–527)*, Cambridge

Kulikowski, M., (2000) 'The Notitia Dignitatum as a Historical Source', *Historia: Zeitschrift für alte Geschichte* 49 (2000), pp.358–77

Kulikowski, M., (2007) *Rome's Gothic Wars: From the Third Century to Alaric*, Cambridge

Kulikowski, M., (2000) 'The Career of the *Comes Hispaniarum* Asterius', *Phoenix* Vol. 54, No. 1/2 (Spring-Summer, 2000), pp.123–41

Kulikowski, M., and Bowes, K., (eds). (2005) *Hispania in Late Antiquity: Current Perspectives*, Boston (Brill)

Lenski, N., (2006) *The Cambridge Companion to the Age of Constantine*, Cambridge

Liebeschuetz, J.H.W.G., (1990) *Barbarians and Bishops: Army, State and Church in the Age of Arcadius and Chrysostom*, Ox

MacGeorge, P., (2002) *Late Roman Warlords*, Ox

Maenchen-Helfen, O., (1973) *The World of the Huns: Studies in Their History and Culture*, University of California Press

Mansi, G.D., *Sacrorum Conciliorum Nova et Amplissima Collectio* http://patristica.net/mansi

Marcillet-Jaubert, M., (ed.), (1968) *Les Inscriptiones d'Altava*, Aix-en-Provence

Martens, J., (1989) 'The Vandals: Myth and Facts About a Germanic Tribe of the First Half of the 1st Millennium AD', in Shennon, S.J., *Archaeological Approaches to Cultural Identity*, London, pp.57–65

Mathisen, R.W., (2006) 'Peregrini, Barbari, and Cives Romani: Concepts of Citizenship and the Legal Identity of Barbarians in the Later Roman Empire', *The American Historical Review*, Vol. 111, No. 4 (October 2006), pp.1011–40

Mathisen, R.W., (1999) *De Imperatoribus Romanis: Julius Nepos* http://www.luc.edu/roman-emperors/nepos.htm

Mathisen, R.W., (1999) *De Imperatoribus Romanis: Valentinian III* http://www.luc.edu/roman-emperors/valenIII.htm

Mathisen, R.W., (1998) *Julius Nepos* http://www.roman-emperors.org/nepos.htm

Mathisen, R.W., (1985) 'The Third Regnal Year of Eparchius Avitus', *Classical Philology*, Vol. 80, No. 4 (Oct., 1985), pp.326–35

Mathisen, R.W., and Shanzer, D., (2011) *Romans, Barbarians, and the Transformation of the Roman World*, Farnham

Matthews, J., (1998) *Western Aristocracies and Imperial Court AD 364–425*, Clarendon

Max, G.E., (1979) 'Political Intrigue during the Reigns of the Western Roman Emperors Avitus and Majorian', *Historia: Zeitschrift für Alte Geschichte*, Bd. 28, H. 2 (2nd Qtr, 1979), pp.225–37

Merrills, A., and Miles, R., (2014) *The Vandals*, Chichester

Mitchell, S., (2007) *A History of the Later Roman Empire, AD 284–641: The Transformation of the Ancient World*, Wiley-Blackwell

Moorhead, J., (1992) *Theoderic in Italy*, Ox

Muhlberger, S., (1990) *The Fifth-century Chroniclers: Prosper, Hydatius, and the Gallic Chronicler of 452*, Arca (Francis Cairns Publications Ltd.)

O'Flynn, J.M., (1983) *Generalissimos of the Western Roman Empire*, University of Alberta

Qasr al-Saghir (Ksar Es-Seghir) http://www.qantara-med.org/qantara4/public/show_document. php?do_id=1011&lang=en

Reynolds, J., (2011) *Defending Rome: The Masters of the Soldiers*, Xlibris

Sarris, P., (2011) *Empires of Faith: The Fall of Rome to the Rise of Islam*, Ox

Saunders, J.J., 'The Debate on the Fall of Rome', *History*, Volume 48, Issue 162 (February 1963) pp.1–17

Schamp, C.H., (2010) 'Difference and Accommodation in Visigothic Gaul and Spain', Master's Theses, Paper 3789 *scholarworks.sjsu.edu/cgi/viewcontent.cgi?article=4785&context*

Schwarz, A., (2004) 'The Settlement of the Vandals in North Africa', in Merrills, A. (ed.), *Vandals, Romans and Berbers: New Perspectives on Late Antique North Africa*, pp.49–58

Shanzer, D., (2004) 'Intentions and Audiences: History, Hagiography, Martyrdom and Confession in Victor of Vita's *Historia Persecutionis*', in Merrills, A. (ed.), *Vandals, Romans and Berbers: New Perspectives on Late Antique North Africa*, pp.271–90

Shennan, S.J., (1989) *Archaeological Approaches to Cultural Identity*, London

Thompson, E.A., (1982) *Romans and Barbarians: The Decline of the Western Empire*, Wisconsin

Thompson, E.A., (1963) 'The Visigoths from Fritigern to Euric', Historia: Zeitschrift für Alte Geschichte, Bd. 12, H.1, (Jan., 1963), pp.105–26

Thompson, E.A., (1950) 'The Foreign Policies of Theodosius II and Marcian', *Hermathena*, No. 76 (November, 1950), pp.58–75

Ward-Perkins, B., (2006) *The Fall of Rome and the End of Civilization*, Ox

Williams, S., and Friell, G., (1994) *Theodosius: The Empire at Bay*, Yale University Press

Wolfram, H., (1997) *The Roman Empire and its Germanic Peoples*, Berkeley

Wolfram, H., (1990) *History of the Goths*, Berkeley

Wood, I.N., (2004), 'The Barbarian Invasions and First Settlements', in Cameron, A., and Garnsey, P., (eds), *The Cambridge Ancient History*, pp.516–37

Index